C000264797

6233
'Duchess of Sutherland'
and the
'Princess Coronation' Class

Brian Radford
and
Brell Ewart

Published by The Princess Royal Class Locomotive Trust, P.O. Box 6203, Ashbourne, Derbyshire DE6 1WW

The Princess Royal Class Locomotive Trust website is at: www.prclt.co.uk

Printed in England by J.T. McLaughlin Ltd., 362 Leach Place, Walton Summit, Preston, Lancashire. PR5 8AS.

Technical Production: Paul Wood, 18 Highgate, Goosnargh, Preston, Lancashire. PR3 2BX.

ISBN number 0-9543969-0-1

©2002 The Princess Royal Class Locomotive Trust. All rights reserved. No part of this publication may be reproduced or transmitted in any form or by any means electronic, mechanical, photocopying, recording or otherwise, without the prior permission of the publisher.

First impression November 2002

Dedication

This book is dedicated to all those people who in the past have made a contribution to the 'Princess Coronation' class of locomotives, from William Stanier and his original design teams of the 1930's, to those who employed their craftsmanship and skills in building and testing them and to those responsible for operating and maintaining of them as one of the world's greatest express passenger locomotives during their years in front line service up to 1964.

To the individuals who, in the preservation era, had the vision to ensure that 6233 was preserved. To those who have had the commitment and dedication to carry on the arduous task of restoration in recent years, enabling an L.M.S. liveried 'DUCHESS OF SUTHERLAND' to be seen again at work on the main line.

If we are to continue to have the privilege of witnessing this locomotive hauling an express passenger train at full speed, then such commitment and dedication will be needed in the future; so finally we also dedicate this book to those who will follow on, in the sincere hope that in future years, by showing the same dedication, it will be possible to keep a 'Princess Coronation' class locomotive in full working order for the benefit of future generations.

Brell Ewart and Brian Radford.

Front end paper: **With a full head of steam and a strong blast of exhaust from the chimney 46233 'Duchess of Sutherland' faces a stiff climb up Camden bank as she sets off from London Euston with the down 'Mid-Day Scot' express for Glasgow on Monday, 21st May, 1956.** (P.H. Groom)

Back end paper: **46233 'Duchess of Sutherland' heads past Strickland Wood on the climb to Shap with the up 'Mid-Day Scot' to London Euston on Tuesday, 6th October, 1959.** (D.M.C. Hepburne-Scott/RAS)

Contents

Appendices

About the Authors

Brian Radford comes from a railway family and started his career as an Engineering Apprentice in the Locomotive Works at Derby in 1952. He moved into the Locomotive Drawing Office in 1956 just in time to make a contribution to the final design work on the British Railways Standard range of steam locomotives. He became a M.I.Mech.E. and a Chartered Engineer, and worked on the design of both the High Speed Train and the Advanced Passenger Train before moving on to become the Senior Project Engineer in charge of the major refurbishment of Inter-City's fleet of Mark 2f, 3 and H.S.T. passenger coaches in the 1980's and early 1990's.

Following his retirement in 1993 he was able to devote more time to his hobbies of music, local history and railways, and he is the author of eight books. He is a Vice President of the Midland Railway Trust, which he played a major role in founding, and is a Trustee of The Princess Royal Class Locomotive Trust.

Brell Ewart is a civil engineer and is Managing Director of his own contracting company in Ashbourne. His interest in railways came from living close to the labyrinth of lines at Staveley Works near Chesterfield as a young boy, and was nurtured at Chesterfield Boys School in the 1960's.

In 1980 he was one of three people who purchased British Railways Standard 2-6-4T 80080 from Barry scrapyard, followed in 1984 by 80098. In 1989 he bought Princess Royal class locomotive 'Princess Margaret Rose' from Butlins. In the mid 1990's Brell was elected Chairman of The Steam Locomotive Operators Association, a post he held for four years before standing down to concentrate on the formation of The Princess Royal Class Locomotive Trust. The trust has since acquired a second Stanier Pacific 'Duchess of Sutherland', the subject of this book.

Both authors played an active role in the Royal Train operation with 'Duchess of Sutherland' on 11th June, 2002 when both were presented to Her Majesty The Queen.

This book is the second co-written by the two authors, who say that they have great fun and satisfaction writing books together on subjects in which both have played major roles.

Introduction

Although this book is essentially about the life and times of just one Stanier 'Princess Coronation' class 4-6-2 express passenger locomotive - No. 6233 'DUCHESS OF SUTHERLAND', drawing together in one volume the story of her design and building, her work for the London, Midland & Scottish Railway from 1938, when she emerged brand new from its Locomotive Works at Crewe and her life from 1948 working for British Railways until withdrawn from service. It inevitably records in parallel the story of all of the other members of the class of 38 locomotives, the most powerful main line express passenger engines ever to run in Britain until their demise in the early 1960's.

Later chapters record of the events in the later life of 6233 which flowed from her being selected for preservation by Butlins for display at their holiday camp at Heads of Ayr in Scotland, and follows on to record her subsequent life at the Bressingham Steam Museum in Norfolk and her return to steam there, and finally her purchase by The Princess Royal Class Locomotive Trust and her recent major overhaul, thanks to a grant from the Heritage Lottery Fund, which resulted in her return to the main line on 4th July, 2001.

The final chapter rehearses the story of how she was subsequently selected to haul the Royal Train carrying Her Majesty Queen Elizabeth II, accompanied by His Royal Highness Prince Philip, Duke of Edinburgh, on her Golden Jubilee tour of north Wales on 11th June, 2002, the first time for 35 years that the train had been steam hauled.

Also included is a large section of appendices giving full historical, technical and other data.

It is an absorbing tale that we have had much pleasure in writing, having spent hundreds of hours drawing it together from many, many sources, and follows on in sequence from our previous book on the life and times the other L.M.S. pacific, No. 6203 'PRINCESS MARGARET ROSE', owned by The Princess Royal Class Locomotive Trust. Thanks to the trust's efforts No. 6233 'DUCHESS OF SUTHERLAND' can now be seen performing brilliantly hauling trains over todays very different railway system in this new millennium, a true icon in her own right representing an age now long gone.

Brian Radford and Brell Ewart.
1st September, 2002.

Chapter One

The Design and Development
of the First 'Princess Coronation' Class Locomotives

Part One - Design

William Arthur Stanier, the designer of the class, was born on 27th May, 1876, the first child of William Henry Stanier, a Great Western Railway employee who worked as Locomotive Superintendent William Dean's chief clerk. He also took an interest in apprentice training, organising technical education classes in the Swindon Mechanics' Institute, and also, with Dean's approval, set up the mechanical and chemical testing of materials being bought in.

The young W.A. Stanier, the eldest of an eventual six children, two of the others also being boys, took up a five year engineering apprenticeship at the Great Western Railway Works at Swindon commencing on his 16th birthday. On completion of his training he had experience in pattern making, worked as a draughtsman, a materials inspector, and then as the technical inspector at the Swindon motive power depot. Promotion to Assistant Divisional Superintendent there came in 1903 before he moved to Paddington in 1904, eventually returning to Swindon as the Divisional Locomotive Superintendent in 1906. In 1913 he became Chief Assistant to the Works Manager at Swindon before becoming Works Manager in January, 1920. He became Principal Assistant to Charles B. Collett, the G.W.R. Chief Mechanical Engineer, in January, 1924, but recognised very quickly that as he was so near to Collett in age, being only five years younger, it would be a case of 'dead man's shoes' if he were ever to gain the top post on the locomotive side. Therefore, when he received an approach from the London, Midland & Scottish Railway to become its Chief Mechanical Engineer he grasped the opportunity and took office on 1st January, 1932 at the age of 55.

Behind the scenes, the approach to Stanier had only come after much in-fighting between those holding key engineering positions as the Chief Mechanical Engineers of the major railway companies. Of these the Midland, London & North Western and Lancashire & Yorkshire Railways were the main English companies, with the Caledonian and Highland Railways in Scotland and a motley selection of other smaller companies. They had all come together at 'grouping' on 1st January, 1923 when the new L.M.S. company had been formed as one of the 'big four.' Sir Josiah Stamp, the L.M.S. Chairman and his Board decided that now was the time to bring in a completely new man with a brief to cut through the old partisan company rivalries which still plagued the locomotive design scene nine years after the event, and William Stanier was the man.

One of his first priorities was to produce designs for much more powerful locomotives to work the main West Coast routes from London Euston to the North-West and Scotland. The first two prototypes of the 'Princess Royal' class 4-6-2's were the result, with No. 6200 'The Princess Royal' emerging from the Company's

A signed cabinet photograph of William Arthur Stanier. (J.B. Radford Collection)

Crewe Locomotive Works on 1st July, 1933, followed on 4th November by the second, No. 6201 'Princess Elizabeth.'

A lot of nonsense has been written about the design of this first class of L.M.S. Pacifics, and the influences that Stanier brought with him from the Great Western. Certainly, and understandably, there were some features that drew on aspects of the G.W.R. 'King' Class of 4-6-0 locomotives that had performed well within the Great Western domestic scene. However, unlike the latter, this new design had four sets of motion and incorporated the carefully assessed best practices and features from the aborted Pacific design of Sir Henry Fowler of the Midland Railway. Low degree superheat, drawn from G.W.R. practice, was at first a feature of the boiler design, but proved to be most unsatisfactory, and costly modifications were found to be necessary to improve the performance of these locomotives and other early Stanier designs.

More locomotives of this type were clearly needed, and a production batch of ten further 'Princess Royal' class 4-6-2 locomotives was built at the Crewe Locomotive Works of the L.M.S., the first locomotive of this batch being No. 6203 'PRINCESS MARGARET ROSE', and the full story of the design and development of this class is covered in our earlier book featuring this particular locomotive and its history. Along with a turbine-driven member of the class, No. 6202, nicknamed 'The Turbomotive,' this gave a total of thirteen available to work the traffic. No. 6203 survives today in preservation and is also owned by The Princess Royal Class Locomotive Trust which owns No. 6233 'DUCHESS OF SUTHERLAND,' and she too is based at the West Shed, adjacent to the Midland Railway Centre's main site at Swanwick Junction.

The possibility of even higher speed traffic had been investigated by the running of test trains on the West Coast main line between London Euston and Glasgow Central on 16th & 17th November, 1936 hauled by the second of the prototype 'Princess Royal' class of 4-6-2 locomotives No. 6201 'PRINCESS ELIZABETH.' With a down train load limited to 225 tons, an average speed of 68.2 m.p.h. was achieved on the outward run, and on the return trip 70.15 m.p.h. achieved with an increased load to 255 tons tare (260 tons gross).

These successful tests proved that more locomotives of this type should be built, but in order to take full advantage of experiences to date, various schemes were got out for a further build of 'Princess Royal' Class locomotives. However, at that time William Stanier was working for the Wedgewood Committee of Enquiry into Indian Railway Finances; a duty that kept him away from his principal job from November, 1936 until March, 1937. Robert A. Riddles, as his Principal Assistant, therefore took on the overall responsibility for the new locomotives, although much of the design approval for them was delegated to T.F. Coleman.

Thomas Francis ('Tommy') Coleman, appointed to the post of Technical Assistant and Chief Draughtsman of the Derby Locomotive Drawing Office from 18th March, 1935 in succession to Herbert Chambers, had served his apprenticeship at Messrs. Kerr Stuart & Company of Stoke-on-Trent from 1900 to 1906. He had come to Derby from the North Staffordshire Railway headquarters in Stoke where he had been taken on as a draughtsman in Locomotive Superintendent J. H. Adams' drawing office on 1st May, 1905. He had later become Chief Draughtsman at Stoke, but when the office closed after grouping, he moved to the former Lancashire & Yorkshire Railway works at Horwich in November, 1926 in the same post, moving on again to the Crewe Works of the L.M.S. as Chief Draughtsman in 1933.

'Tommy', as he was always referred to by the draughtsmen, (but never in his presence!) was a huge man with craggy features and a very blunt manner. He was not happy with the front-end design of the 'Princess Royals,' considering the coupled axle loads to be unsatisfactory. A decision was therefore taken to design and build an improved 'Princess Royal' class 4-6-2 engine, and the 'Princess Coronation' class was the result, although they later came to be colloquially referred to as the 'Duchesses.' The first engines of this new class were initially designed specifically to haul the new and prestigious high-speed luxury 'Coronation Scot' trains introduced by the L.M.S. on 5th July, 1937 during the Coronation year of His Majesty King George VI.

Although officially regarded as being only an improved development of the 'Princess Royal' class of locomotives, Stanier himself had indicated that he was not entirely pleased with either the appearance or the performance of the design used for that class. Therefore significant changes were made to the frames, to the motion (which now had two sets instead of four sets of valve mechanisms), slightly larger diameter cylinders, and also larger, 6ft 9in diameter driving wheels (which incidentally had originally been considered for the 'Princess Royal' class), plus a larger boiler. The last vestiges of Great Western influence were done away with, and, under Coleman's direction, the front end cylinder and valve gear design now owed more to the Hughes rebuilt 4-6-0's of the Lancashire & Yorkshire Railway than to anything else. The tenders, with coal capacity increased to 10 tons, were this time to be fitted with a coal pusher. This followed the experiences gained with the prototype pusher fitted to the tender of Princess Royal Class No 6206 `PRINCESS MARIE LOUISE'. A pusher brought the coal forward nearer to the fireman's shovel as the tender was emptied, since firing the "Princess Royal" engines had proved to be a very arduous task for firemen when they were hauling the long distance express passenger services. Accessing the last few tons of coal remaining at the rear of the tender, despite the self trimming coal plate, was creating problems on the long distance runs, and the engineering details of these coal pushers is described later in this book.

As Eric Cox has rightly observed in his excellent book 'Chronicles of Steam' (Ian Allan, 1967), Coleman, like H.G. Ivatt, had in his own field an "inborn flair for effective and even brilliant engineering. Without anything much by way of academic achievement, and abhorring public speaking and all communal activities such as Institution affairs, he nevertheless, by some hidden

Thomas Francis Coleman, Chief Draughtsman in the Locomotive Drawing Office at Derby and responsible for the design work during Stanier's absence.
(L.M.S. Official/National Railway Museum)

instinct, was able to hit the target of practical and effective design in nearly everything he undertook."

"He reached his greatest heights in partnership with Stanier, who knew what he wanted but was not always able to visualise it in precise terms. Coleman was able to interpret an initial idea and exploit it in a highly individual manner, and Stanier's biggest successes, the 'Duchess' 4-6-2, the class 5 4-6-0, the class 8 2-8-0 and the class 4 2-6-4T, all owed a great deal to Coleman. Indeed the first of these engines could almost be described as a Coleman product, for it was he who proposed most of the modifications to the original 'Princess.' This is no detriment to the general acknowledgment that the 'Duchess' was Stanier's masterpiece, for however much his henchman may have contributed, it was Stanier who carried the full responsibility of the decision to accept or reject each feature."

The main aim of the design improvements was to ensure that the new class of engines could maintain a high continuous speed on the $6^{1}/_{2}$ hour timing for the new prestige train between London Euston and Glasgow Central stations, a distance of $401^{1}/_{2}$ miles. The actual running time, allowing only a five minute stop at Carlisle, was 385 minutes, giving an average speed of 62.6 m.p.h. The high speed running on the more easily graded sections of the route was intended to compensate for the relatively short total distance of only some 30 to 40 miles on really heavily graded sections of the line. The new locomotives had to be master of these requirements.

Eric Arthur Langridge, a senior member of the design team in the Locomotive Drawing Office at Derby at that time, and who lived to be 101, was one of those given major responsibility for producing part of the new design. He had been one of Dugald Drummond's last Engineering Apprentices, having started in the London & South Western Railway's Locomotive Works at Eastleigh in September, 1912, and had come to Derby on 16th April, 1920 to join the staff of the Midland Railway Company's Locomotive Drawing Office. He commented in some detail, in a most informative letter dated 11th November, 1964, written to the late David F. Tee, a noted railway historian, who had enquired about his recollections of the events at that time. Langridge recorded various 'behind the scenes' aspects of the design of the 'Princess Coronation' class as he saw them, some of which first appeared in the authors' previous book on 6203 'PRINCESS MARGARET ROSE' already referred to. Those recorded here are a relevant and integral part of the history of 6233 'DUCHESS OF SUTHERLAND' and of course the class in general. In addition some further relevant sections of that correspondence are here published for the first time.

Langridge wrote:- "You may know what a fluke it was that the 'Coronation' class came about. At various times in a D.O. (Drawing Office) a Chief Draughtsman will say "See what you can do about this 5X or that business." We were ordering up E402 quite in the usual way as another five 'Princesses' with the latest boiler to be 6213-7, when he (Coleman) said "See what you can do to get the biggest boiler and wheels on a 4-6-2." Two schemes were got out within a week - as W. A.S.(Stanier) was off to India on that engine riding enquiry with E.S. (Cox) - both had big boilers - one with a 'Princess' cylinder layout and the other - which I did - based on the L. & Y 4-6-0 four-cylinder arrangement, which seemed to me far superior to the Western way. Mr. Coleman, the C.D. (Chief Draughtsman) hadn't much hope of getting it passed by Stanier....

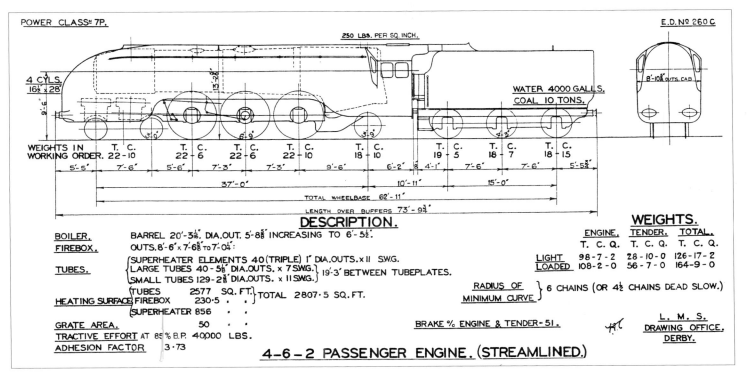

L.M.S. Official Diagram E.D. No. 260C showing the details of the streamlined locomotives Nos. 6220-9. (J.B. Radford Collection)

But the impossible came off and Coleman was told to go ahead 'tout-de-suite.' Stanier was away for six months and Crewe had done the boiler and above platform designs and Derby the rest by the time he (Stanier) saw the drawings."

Surviving Engine Diagrams produced at Derby, as opposed to preliminary sketches, show the variations as the design evolved. Of the three un-streamlined early versions, ED255 is essentially a 'Princess Royal' class engine with 6ft-6in diameter driving wheels and a leading coupled wheel base shortened by nine inches to 7ft 3in and the outside cylinder moved forward by the same distance. ED258 is essentially the same, but with a larger diameter boiler pitched three inches higher and with a shorter, 8ft-0in long firebox. The inside cylinders are inclined and the piston valves are operated by G.W.R. style rocking gear from the outside. Variant ED259 is the same but with a longer 8ft 6in firebox.

The streamlined version, which was produced expressly in response to the edict of the Board responding to pressures from the L.M.S. Publicity De partment which had found itself in competition with the rival L.N.E.R.'s streamlined trains, is shown on ED260. It had the 6ft-9in diameter coupled driving wheels eventually fixed upon, but had a sharper profiled nose and an almost completely hidden chimney. This diagram was later altered to show a more smooth streamlined shape that exposed the top of the chimney. The overall height is shown as 13ft 2⅝in. The evolution of the final shape of the streamlined casing is described later.

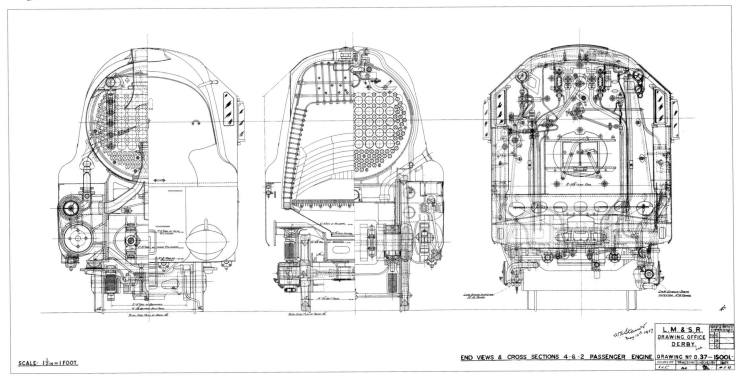

The official L.M.S. drawing No. D37-15001 showing the end views and cross sections for engines Nos. 6220-6224 (J.B. Radford Collection)

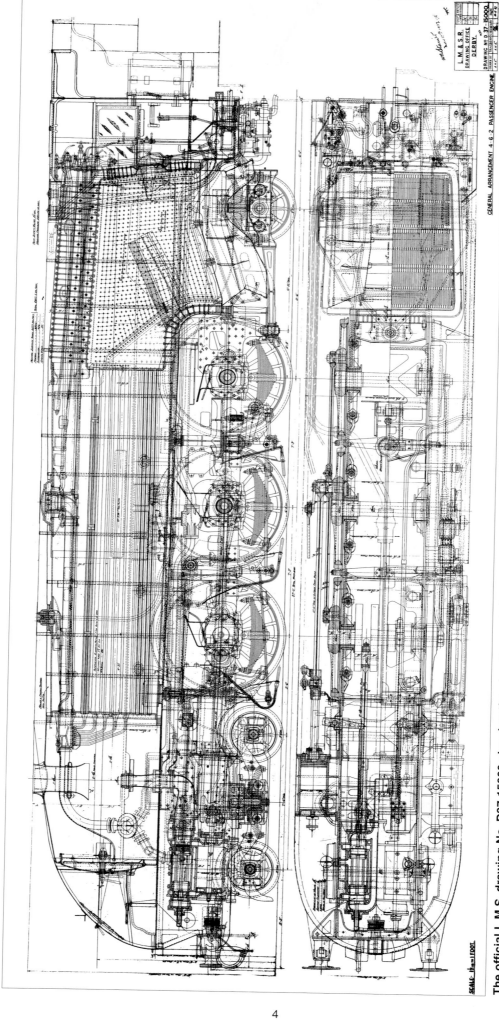

The official L.M.S. drawing No. D37-15000 showing the elevation and plan views for engines Nos. 6220-6224. (J.B. Radford Collection)

Interior view of the Chief Mechanical Engineer's Locomotive Drawing Office on London Road, Derby on 1st May, 1936. All of the draughtsmen seen here were responsible for the majority of the design work for the 'Princess Coronation' class.
(J.B. Radford Collection)

With the design settled to a large extent the drawing offices at Derby and Crewe now set to work to produce the manufacturing drawings. The general arrangement elevation, plan and section drawings and all of the arrangement and detail drawings for the frames, motion, wheels, bogie and pony truck, pipe and rod, lubrication and ashpan drawings and those for the streamlining were produced at Derby whilst the boiler, firebox, smokebox and other details above the running plate were produced at Crewe. Stanier himself signed off and dated the major drawings, the boiler and firebox arrangement drawings for the first five engines being signed off on 20th April, 1937 and the general arrangement drawings for the engine on 10th May, 1937. For the first batch built to Lot No. 402, Nos. 6220-4, these were D37-15000 covering the elevation and plan and D37-15001 showing the end views and cross sections. Some 350 new drawings had been produced for the engine plus the utilisation of other drawings of standard components, etc. which had been used before. The Crewe Drawing Office also produced a further suite of 70 odd drawings for the 4,000 gallon streamlined tender, with the Derby office providing those for the coal pusher.

Langridge concludes his reminiscences as follows:- "We had one of the finest drawing office staffs at that period at Crewe and Derby - the pick of Horwich, Crewe, Stoke and Derby - I think we made a fine job of it. Coleman (subsequently in fact) took all the draughtsmen at Derby engaged on the job to see 6220 (they abandoned the number '6213' as being unlucky) in all its glory in the paint shop. Later we went down to Tamworth one afternoon to see and hear it on the up 'Scot', running like a sewing machine."

MAIN DESIGN FEATURES

The following notes summarise the main design features of the locomotive as built:-

COUPLED WHEEL DIAMETER

On the subject of his choice of 6ft 9in for the diameter of the driving, or more correctly 'coupled' wheels, as recorded in Col. H.C.B. Rogers biography, it was Robert Riddles, then Principal Assistant to Stanier, who "remembered to his shame" that it was he who suggested to Stanier that the diameter might be increased from the 6ft-6in used on the 'Princess Royal' class Pacifics. He went on.... "my reasons were based on a remark by J.E. Anderson, at that time Motive Power Superintendent for the L.M.S. but who had retired in 1932, that beyond a given piston speed the locomotive lost considerably in efficiency, and, as presumably only light loads were to be hauled, longer legs would be able to run faster. This I suppose is true, but I had forgotten that these engines had to start from a stand; and could those big wheels slip!"

CYLINDER AND MOTION DESIGN

In order to keep up a high tractive effort with the larger diameter of driving wheels, the diameter of the four cylinders was increased from 16¼ inches to 16½ inches whilst retaining the 28 inch stroke used in the 'Princess Royal' class.

The pistons themselves were of the hollow box type screwed onto the piston rod, and were provided with three narrow rings, whilst the 9" dia. piston valves, with a stroke of 7¹/₃₂ inches, were fitted with six narrow rings to ensure steam tightness and were designed for lightness. The valve motion was designed to provide

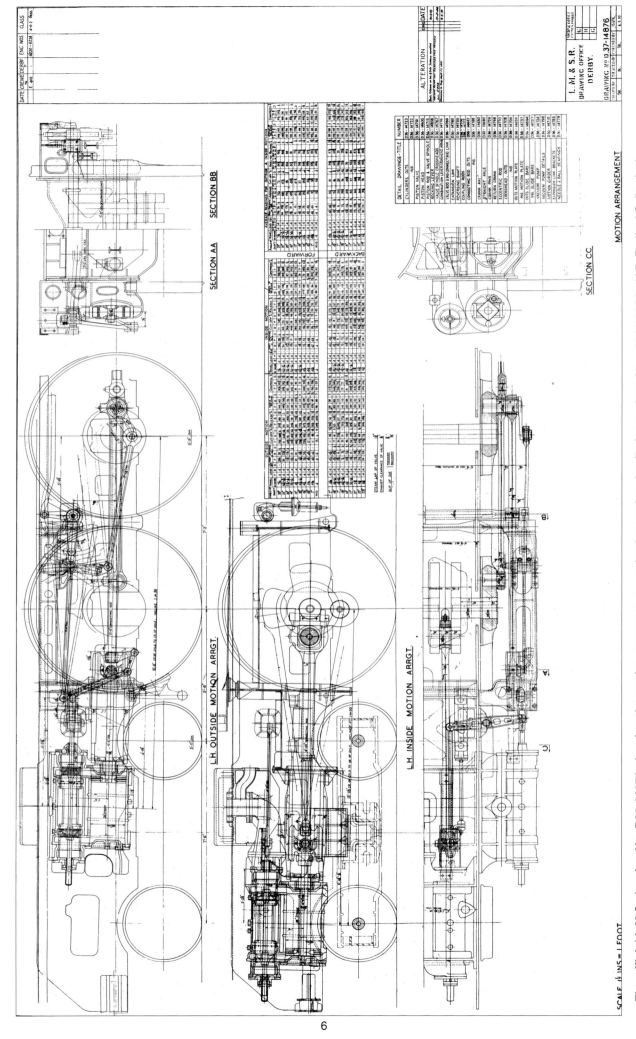

The official L.M.S. drawing No. D.36-14876 showing the motion arrangement and valve setting details for engines Nos. 6220-6224. (J.B. Radford Collection)

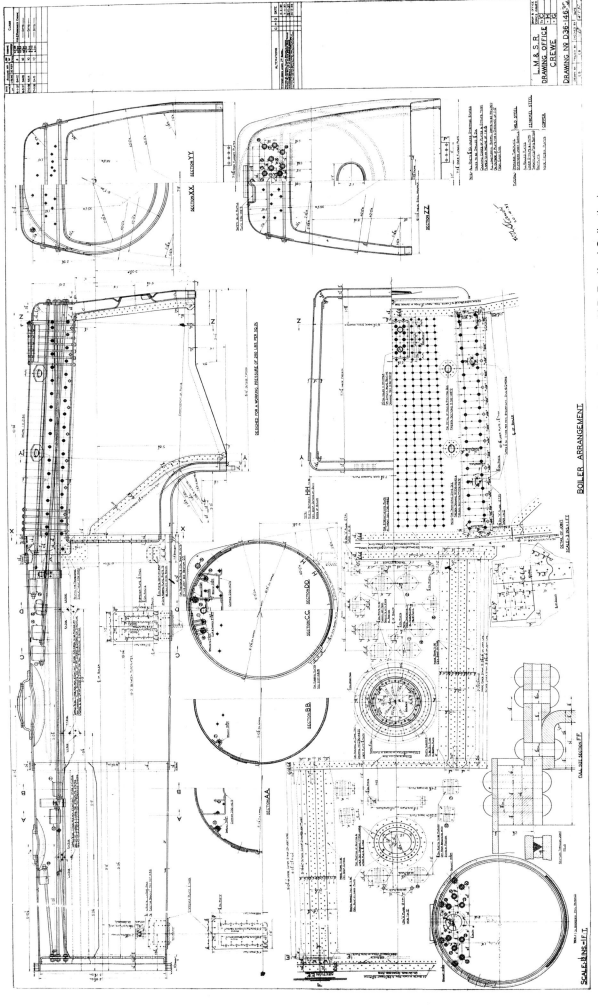

The official L.M.S. drawing No. D36-14639 showing the boiler arrangement for the 'Princess Coronation' class of engines. (J.B. Radford Collection)

7

1³/₄ inches of lap and a maximum ³/₈ of an inch opening of the steam port also of 1³/₄ inches. A clearance of ³/₈ inch was allowed between the piston head and the cylinder cover at each end of the stroke as compared to the minimal figure of ¹/₄ of an inch used on earlier Stanier engines.

Great care was taken with the exhaust passages in the steam chests and cylinders, which were designed with smooth surfaces to give free passage to the steam, whilst at the same time not providing excess volume which would have acted as a reservoir. The exhausts from the inside cylinders and the two outside cylinders were combined in the saddle casting so that the blast pipe could be of the single, straight pipe variety.

Two sets of Walschaerts valve gear were provided, with the valves for the inside cylinders being driven by rocking levers set behind the outside cylinders. They were connected by means of short links to the crossheads of the outside valve spindles. All of the motion pins were fitted with grease gun charged 'Hoffmann' needle bearings to reduce friction, with the exception of the big end bearings for the eccentric rods, which were 'Skefco' self-aligning ball bearings. The complex reversing gear arrangement used on the 'Princess Royal' class was replaced by a rocking lever on the reversing gear bracket, coupled to a straight reversing rod below running platform level.

On this aspect of the design Langridge comments:- "I did the motion arrangement and was interested in trying out the old bent rocking lever: there was nothing in it actually, so we made ours straight. The valve spindle guides were done by a Horwich man, so was the reversing rod - made hollow to increase the diameter and resist twist. Later on I got across an idea - also from Horwich - to put a big lead on the valves - Horwich had it on the Crabs (2-6-0's) - its effect is to increase steam opening when notched up - helps power at high speed. If you make the steam port in the liner wider as well, you can also get a longer opening to exhaust at low cut-offs as well - the valve head always overruns the port on the exhaust side except when highly notched up (that makes the old G.W. (Great Western) habit of giving port sizes on engine diagrams quite useless - they mean nothing, any more than heating surfaces do.)"

"L.M. couldn't get on with G.W. screwed piston heads. You couldn't see flaws in the rods before they broke - so we went back to plain fitting & securing nuts. Regulator lubricator, multi ashpan doors went, drop grate came in & (the) vac(uum) pump went."

The fluted coupling rods and the connecting rods were manufactured from 'Vibrac' high-tensile alloy steel made by the English Steel Corporation at its Vickers' works. These were designed to withstand inertia stresses generated during high-speed running, having a breaking stress of 56 tons per sq. in., within the specified range of 50 to 60, as well as resisting permanent deformation should the engine get into a slip. They could therefore be made of a lighter section than those of the 'Princess Royal' class, saving some 7lb. in weight, even though 2 feet longer at 11ft 0in.

BOILER DESIGN.

The boiler for this new Pacific class was somewhat larger than that used on the "Princess Royal' class locomotives, the barrel having a diameter 2¹/₂ inches larger at the firebox throat plate. The firebox crown was raised by two more inches thus reducing the 2ft. dimension, used up to that time, between it and the firebox wrapper plate. This gave more space on the firebox tubeplate, allowing for 129 small tubes of 2³/₈ inches in diameter x 11 s.w.g wall thickness and 40 superheater flues of 5¹/₈ inches in diameter x 7 s.w.g. These, with the 'Wagner' triple flow superheater elements of 2³/₈ inches outside diameter x 11 s.w.g. thickness and a distance between the tubeplates of 19ft 3in., gave a total heating surface of 2577sq. ft. for the tubes and 856sq. ft. for the superheater (later amended first to 830sq. ft. and then to 822sq. ft.). The larger firebox, which was wider by some 8 inches or so, added a further 5sq. ft. more giving 50sq. ft. in total, thereby adding a further 13.5sq. ft. of heating surface which then totalled 230.5sq. ft. The total heating surface was therefore 3663.5sq. ft. compared

with 2967 sq. ft. for the production batch of the 'Princess Royal' class engines.

The boiler barrel was now 20ft 3¹/₁₆ in. long, increasing from 5ft 8⁵/₈ in. at the front to 6ft 5¹/₂in. at the firebox end. The dome was moved further forward and the top-feed arrangement for feed water was re-designed, using a standard design of caged clack valves set into a manhole casting to save on gauge clearance height. The regulator was of the now standard Stanier horizontal arrangement housed within the dome.

On the subject of boiler design Eric Langridge commented:- 'The tale of the Duchess boilers goes back to that for the 'Turbo.' (the turbine driven 4-6-2 No. 6202.) You know that was the long barrel chap as on 6200 with a few more superheater elements in the first place. Dr. H. L. (Henry) Guy and Struthers of Metro Vickers urged W. A.S. (Stanier) to get a higher superheat and I was given the job of improving the boiler. So I cut out the vertical firebox tubeplate and put a drumhead one in front of a combustion chamber and arranged the firebox plates to lap over each other - no scarfing required. Our suppliers always pressed the copper tubeplates but we did the steel ones and the size of press settled the amount of combustion chamber we could get in.... I also noticed on ordinary combustion chamber boilers you get two humps where the barrel portion fades into the firebox front plate. It was difficult to explain on a drawing as the vertical and horizontal radii are constantly changing, and I had to go to Crewe and stand by while the pattern maker shaved the blocks to the correct shape. Having got over that, the problem was to stay the copper to the steel throat plate, as there was no flat surface: so I had to go and do that on the actual plates. I hadn't the faintest idea how to dimension the thing and was thankful when I actually marked off the first tubeplate from which a template was made. It seems to have been alright as the scheme was perpetuated for the replacement boilers on the 6200's and used on the Coronations."

" I put the tubes up in diameter and, of course, increased the number of large tubes. Originally 6200 had two rows of large tubes with two elements in each - the steam making one pass - in order to keep up the cross section area through (the) superheater and reduce pressure drop. We (later) put on the dome housing (the) regulator and abolished the G.W. organ mouth collectors in the firebox corners. The regulator in the smokebox suffered from distortion - hot gasses, hot and cold steam, all in one casting - and the regulator rod - 2¹/₄ in. dia. G.W. style rod - an appalling affair - was replaced by the usual short rod. By this time the 'Coronation' came along, the barrel was concentric not lying on one side of its cone as in the G.W. - a most expensive boiler shop assembly job and plate development. Also in the 'Coronation' the famous 2ft 0in. figure between the copper and firebox roof plates was abandoned in favour of 1ft 10in., which allowed the biggest barrel diameter in 6ft 9in. wheels. We had pads on the boiler underside just in case the wheels when new at 6ft 9in. took up the full rise in the axlebox gap."

It is worth noting that, after Langridge had schemed out the boiler, the detailed design work was left to J.L. 'Jack' Francis, a senior design draughtsman in the Locomotive Drawing Office at Crewe.

MAIN FRAMES.

These were 1¹/₈ ins. thick and manufactured from a special high tensile acid steel. At each side of the rear end two separate frame plates were spliced to the ends of the main frames and carried through to the rear buffer beam. The outer frames were splayed outwards and the inner frames splayed inwards to take the side bearers for the trailing pony truck.

BOGIE AND TRAILING TRUCK.

The leading bogie had side bolsters to transmit the load from the main frames to the bogie, and the bearing springs were of the inverted laminated type with screw adjustment.

The trailing truck was of the 'Bissell' type, the bogie arm being anchored to the engine cross stretcher immediately in front of the

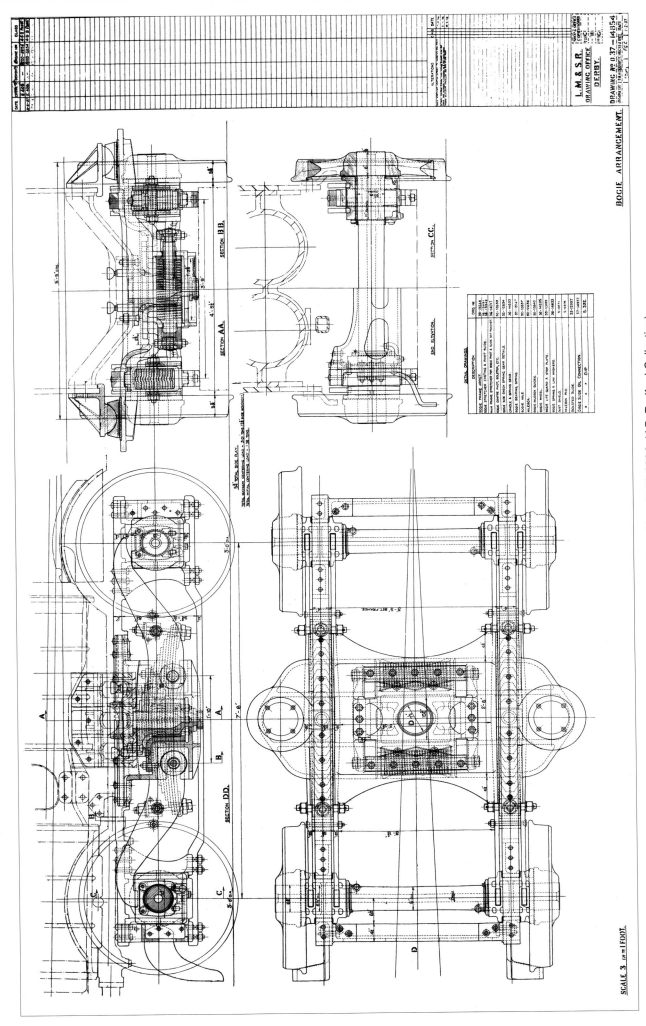

The official L.M.S. drawing No. D37-14854 showing the bogie arrangement for engines Nos. 6220-6224. (J.B. Radford Collection)

9

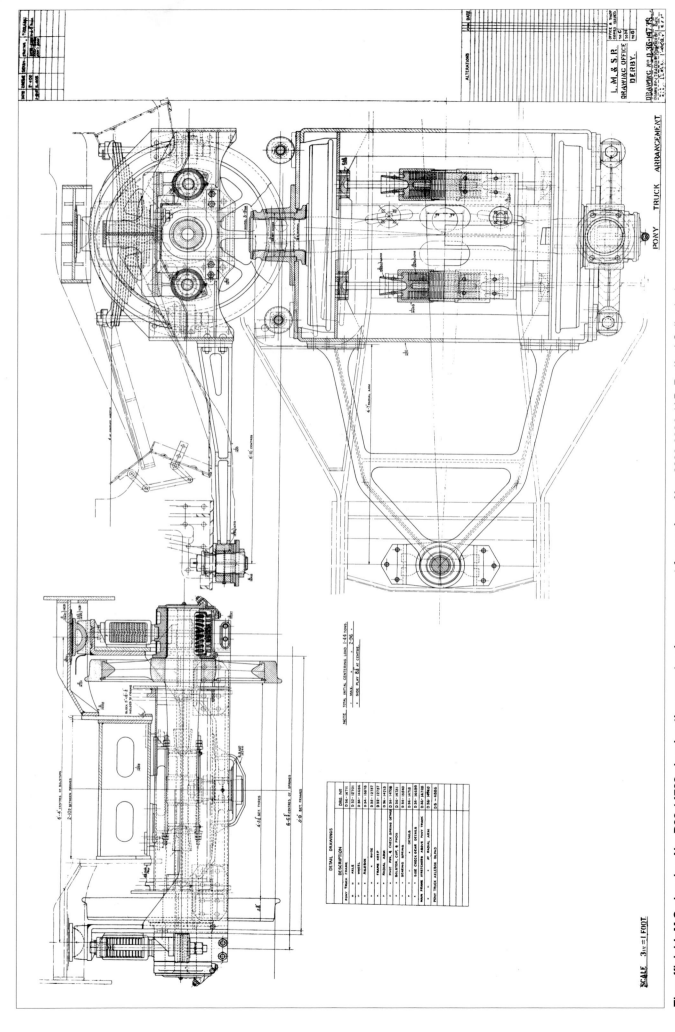

The official L.M.S. drawing No. D36-14738 showing the pony truck arrangement for engines Nos 6220-6224. (J.B. Radford Collection)

firebox throat plate. Side bearing bolsters transferred the loads from the main frame to the bogie.

On this particular aspect of the design Langridge observed:-
"The 'Coronation' bar famed bogie was a queer thing - weight on spitoons pivoted on spheres. So, if the frame got a knock 'cockeyed' it stayed there until another knock put it straight. It could be down on boxes at (the) front and high at (the) back. Crewe weigh bridge had only five tables so no true total weight was available. You weighed half and then pushed the back half on. The Civil Engineers always insisted on designs being able to negotiate 6 chain curves without gauge widening being allowed for. Consequently all L.M. locomotives were sloppy in the boxes, and the 4-6-2's had to have more side play than other lines. Thus the clumsy trailing truck (the last two trucks were neater) came instead of an easy radial axle."

As to general comments on the design, Langridge contentiously observes:- "It's interesting to speculate on what would have happened if no W. A.S. (Stanier) had come and H.P.M. Beames had got the job! I think we should have got somewhere more quickly. But it would have been hard to beat the 'Coronations in the end."

Following the writing of these letters Eric Langridge made a further and significant contribution to our knowledge of the design process which produced the 'Coronations' in a chapter in the book 'The LMS Duchesses' edited by Douglas Doherty and published by Model and Allied Publications Ltd. in 1973. Interested readers are encouraged to obtain a copy of this book and read his contribution for themselves.

PRESENTATION BOOKLET.

A special descriptive booklet was made up by the Chief Mechanical Engineer's department of the L.M.S. describing the design of the first streamlined locomotive No. 6220 'Coronation.' Issued in May 1937. It gave the main technical details and included a photograph and a diagram.

The leading dimensions of the new locomotives as compared to the earlier 'Princess Royal' class are tabulated thus:-

	Earlier Locomotives Nos. 6203-12	New Locomotives Nos. 6220-4
4 cylinders, dia. x stroke	16¼" x 28"	16½" x 28"
Valve gear	4 sets Walschaerts	2 sets Walschaerts
Coupled wheels	6'- 6" dia.	6'- 9" dia.
BOILER:-		
Working pressure, lb./sq. in.	250	250
Firebox heating surface sq. ft.	217	230
Tubes	2097	2577
Total	2314	2807
Superheater sq. ft.	653	856
Grate area sq. ft.	45	50
Tractive effort at 85% boiler pressure	40,300	40,000

The 'Railway Gazette' published an illustrated article entitled 'The Coronation Scot, L.M.& S.R.' giving full technical details of the new locomotives as supplied by the L.M.S. in their issue of 28th May, 1937. This was subsequently reprinted as a separate booklet, and was followed up further with articles in their issues of 18th & 25th February, 1939 entitled 'The Metallurgy of the High Speed Locomotive,' also reprinted as a booklet.

In the introduction the L.M.S. stated:- "The 'Coronation' locomotive, although ranking as the first streamlined express engine on the L.M.& S.R., and being specially intended for high-speed service, is not actually one in which any very great departure has been made from current practice, so far as the material of which it is constructed is concerned. In instituting so important a service as the 'Coronation Scot' train, the first and essential requisite of the locomotive was that already referred to - namely, complete reliability. For this reason, previously untried and experimental materials were not used, and no material has been built into the engine which has not already been incorporated in some form or another on modern locomotives of the L.M.& S.R. from the metallurgical point of view. Therefore, the engine may be said to embody all that is of true worth in the best modern practice."

The official L.M.S. descriptive booklet gives a precise precis of the materials used, and a summary of those not already referred to is given below:-

"Boiler and firebox:- The boiler shell was made of acid nickel steel and the inner firebox and throat plates of copper. The firebox stays were of acid steel with the exception of the outer and top few rows that are subjected to the greatest relative movement due to expansion. These were Monel metal, which contains between 64% and 70% nickel plus traces of manganese and iron, the rest being copper."

"The firebox was extended into the barrel to form a combustion chamber with the object of allowing the hot gases to complete their combustion before entering the tubes. The large flues are screwed into the firebox before being expanded at the other end."

"Firedoor:- The firedoor was of the sliding type, designed to deflect the incoming secondary air down onto the fire."

"Boiler feed:- A Davies & Metcalfe exhaust steam injector with 13 mm cones is fitted on the fireman's side, and on the left hand or driver's side is a live steam injector with 13mm cones, both of these are of the flooded type. Both injectors deliver to the boiler though the top feed clack box which discharges into trays within the steam space wherein any gases contained in the water may become disengaged, the de-aerated water being finally discharged through pipes below water level."

Other features mentioned included the facts that:-

"The boiler was provided with a standard L.M.S. type sand gun to enable the tubes to be cleaned during a run."

"A grid type regulator was fitted inside the dome, with baffles to prevent water entering the steam pipe, and four 2½ in. diameter 'Ross Pop' safety valves were fitted on top of the firebox."

"The cylinder lubrication was from a mechanically driven lubricator, the oil to the piston valve liners being atomised by mixing with saturated steam taken from an independent supply, so that oil was continuously supplied whether the regulator was open or shut. Feeds also supplied the piston packings with a twin supply to each cylinder barrel."

"Hollow axles were fitted and the wheel centres were of acid steel with a specified 50-55 tons per sq. in. breaking strength. 'Gibson' rings secured the tyres to the wheel rims and the balance weights were arranged so as to balance 50% of the reciprocating masses, equally divided between the coupled wheels, whilst the whole of the revolving parts were balanced as far as possible."

"The cast steel axleboxes with pressed-in brasses, were completely lined with white metal on the bearing surfaces, with no oil grooves at the crown of the box to disturb the film of oil. Instead the oil was introduced through a row of holes on the horizontal centre line of the axle. The flow of oil was protected by spring loaded back-pressure valves to keep the pipes full while the engine was standing, so that delivery re-commenced immediately the engine moved."

TENDERS

The 4,000 gallon tenders carried 10 tons of coal, as against the provision of 9 tons on the earlier 'Princess Royal' class tenders. A coal pusher was fitted consisting of a 10½ inch diameter steam cylinder mounted on the sloping floor of the bunker which, when activated, pushed two wedge-shaped rams and two side trailing rams down the slope, thereby moving the remaining coal forwards. The steam supply for this was taken from the steam manifold on the firebox and led through a flexible pipe between engine and tender, with an operating lever just outside the fire iron tunnel. Standard water pick-up gear was provided with deflector plates to channel the water into the scoop and prevent wastage as much as possible. The gear for retracting this and for the tender brake were situated on the tender frontplate.

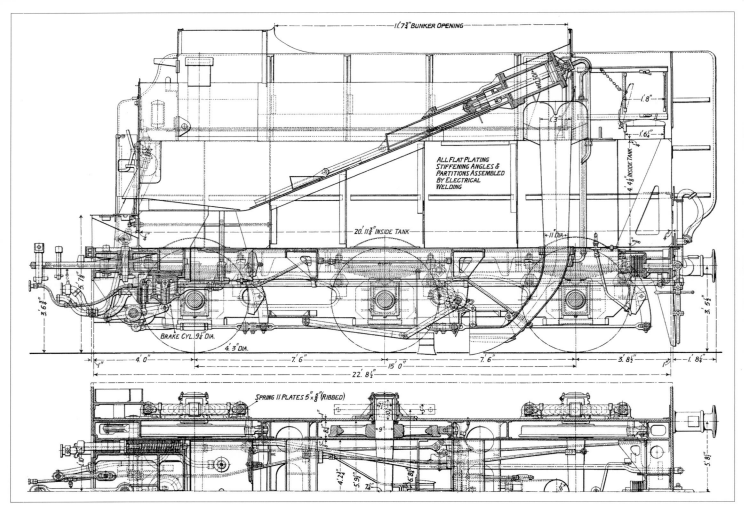

Sectioned view of the tender for the 'Princess Coronation' class of engines with welded tank with end wing plates, coal pusher and water pick-up gear. (L.M.S./ 'The Railway Gazette')

STREAMLINING

The most novel feature of the new locomotives was the introduction of streamlining, a design feature never before used on the L.M.S. Not only was the engine streamlined but also the tender, which had its side plates extended to line up with the rear buffer faces so that the gaps between them and the first coach was partially closed to reduce wind resistance as much as was practicable. An access door had to be provided at the rear at each side of the tender in the top of the side plates to permit water column hoses to be inserted through when filling up the tender tank at one of the filling necks located at each side of the tender.

Coleman sorted out the scheme for the front doors of the engine giving access to the smokebox for maintenance purposes, but it was Robert Riddles who designed the ingenious method of hinging them so that they swung clear.

The shape for the streamlining adopted was only finally decided upon after extensive tests with models in the L.M.S. Research Departments' wind tunnel, then in the paint shop in Derby Locomotive Works, where tests were carried out to represent both head winds and cross winds at various angles. These tests utilised a specially built 1/24th scale model of a 'Princess Royal' class locomotive to which could be attached various shaped front ends. The Derby drawing for this was No. D35-14157 dated 10th September, 1935 and most interestingly titled "1/24th Scale Model of Proposed Streamlined Engine Nos. 6203-6212." Order no. 9245 was issued to cover its manufacture "for wind tunnel tests."

This Derby wind tunnel had been brought into use in 1935, and was of the open circuit (straight through) type 60 m.p.h. design. It was manufactured in the Derby Carriage and Wagon Works to the designs of Dr. F. C. Johansen, the first head of the L.M.S. Research Engineering Section, and was based upon the National

Physical laboratory designs, Johansen having formerly been on the staff there. It utilised a second-hand aircraft propeller and a new motor generator set powered from the works' mains electrical supply.

Clearly, in view of the fact that more of the class were urgently required to handle the traffic on the West Coast main line, the decision was taken to proceed with the production batch of ten

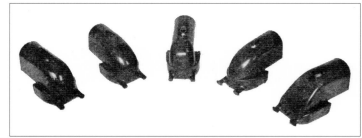

Wind tunnel 1/24th scale test model of the proposed streamlined 'Princess Coronation' locomotive showing removable nose end, and below the various nose-end shapes that were tried before the final design was decided upon. (L.M.S. Official/ Inst. Loco. E.)

more 'Princess Royal' class locomotives whilst the tests proceeded.

A further model to the same scale was produced with the removable sections representing the streamlining which could be modified by adding or paring away the plaster surface to test the effectiveness of combinations of various shapes and combined radii. Various shapes were tried, and one, which incorporated a rather blunt rounded end, which hid the chimney completely, was further refined to give a smoother shape and resulted in the chimney protruding just slightly from the casing, thereby improving the overall appearance. The eventual outcome was that Johansen concluded that this round-nosed streamlined shape, eventually decided upon, had a 20% advantage over a wedge shaped front (as adopted by Gresley of the L.N.E.R. for his A4 class Pacifics), and could well annually be expected to save between £220 and £300 on coal cost per locomotive.

Unfortunately this scientifically based conclusion did not take into account the actual manufacturing costs and, perhaps more importantly, the fitters time consumed by having to deal with the much more difficult access to the working parts during each regular maintenance, which sometimes required parts of the streamlining having to be removed. This latter disadvantage eventually resulted in the complete removal of the streamlined casing from 1946 onwards.

The actual full-sized steel streamlining sections of casing were built up on specially prepared wooden jigs or frameworks, thereby ensuring accuracy of fit when assembled on the light steel framing which was partially carried on the running platforms and resting partially on the boiler clothing. The front casing was formed into twin doors which had vertical hinges allowing the casing to open outwards easily to permit the cleaning of the smokebox, tubes, and other boiler maintenance work in that area. To permit the streamlined nose to fit over the smokebox wrapper and front ring, the top of the smokebox was chamfered down from the chimney leading edge to the face of the smokebox front ring. The front ring outer diameter was elliptical in its top segment but retained the standard L.M.S inner diameter thus enabling the locomotives to utilise the standard smokebox door common to many Stanier locomotives. The running plate in front of the cylinders was separated into two levels with a gap between.

Dr Johansen and Coleman also collaborated on the vee-shaped cab front sheet, which was angled at 45 degrees to eliminate reflections in the cab front windows. Rubber sheeting stretched between the cab roof and the tender front bulkhead, completing the air-smoothed outline in that area.

Stanier himself had rather a jaundiced view about streamlining, referring to it as "something like that blessed word Mesopotamia to the old lady." In his book 'The last Steam Locomotive Engineer: R.A. Riddles, C.B.E.", Col. H.C.B. Rogers writes:- "Most locomotive engineers, certainly those on the L.M.S. heartily disliked this practice of concealing the lines of a beautiful locomotives behind a streamlined casing, and Stanier loathed it. Nevertheless it did appear that, for the sake of publicity and public appeal, it would be necessary to streamline the engines intended to haul the fastest services if the L.M.S. was to draw custom from the L.N.E.R., and the Directors accordingly so decided." Riddles himself recalled being called into Stanier's office one day to be informed that they wanted him to streamline one of his new locomotives, and remembers that Stanier rather caustically observed that "I have decided that it is better to please a fool than tease him. They can have their b****y streamliners if they want them, but we will also build them five proper ones as well!" And so eventually appeared 'DUCHESS OF SUTHERLAND,' now the sole survivor, and her four sisters, the first five of the non-streamlined engines being officially authorised as being built "for comparative purposes!" It seems undoubtedly the case that had Stanier had his way, the "Princess Coronation" class as a whole would have been non-streamlined.

Part Two - Building a 'Princess Coronation' Class Locomotive

The actual building of a locomotive of the 'Princess Coronation' class was a complex business, and a number of essential processes had to be gone through before the final product emerged from the paint shop and entered service.

MATERIAL ORDERING

During the design stages of a new class of locomotive, and also following the placing of the official order for a number of them to be built, advanced material ordering was put in hand for the long lead items, i.e. those that would take the longest period of time to be delivered to the main works, in this case the Crewe Locomotive Works of the L.M.S. Included in these would be such items as special steels for castings and other components, frame and boiler plates, the period of delivery of which could take from weeks to six or seven months. Orders would also be placed for 'bought-in' component parts such as injectors and other boiler fittings, etc. so that these would be ready in stock when required during the erection process.

Delivery of long-lead items took account of the date for laying down the frames of the engine and tender as the first step in the production schedule, and also of the time needed to process the various raw materials through the various workshops to the finished state ready to be installed on the engine and tender on the due date.

FRAMES

The main frame plates of the engine and tender had to be cut from special steel plate, but could be produced from a stack of up to ten at a time. A special investigation had been carried out into the various special steels, particularly from the point of view of welding and cutting by oxy-coal gas or oxy-acetylene processes. With the special steels involved, special controls had to be applied to cutting speeds, the tempering of flame-cut edges and pre-heating before any welding was carried out. Using special steels 1/8 inch thinner than that used previously, a total saving of 17 cwt. per pair of engine frame plates was made.

This work was carried out in the heavy machine shop at Crewe, and, after dressing and post-cutting heat treatments, the various holes drilled and the slotted-out sections machined before a pair of the plates could be set up on stands to form the basic engine chassis, using the cylinder block and the various cross-stretchers as spacers. At this point in the process the splayed rear end frameplates, dragboxes and buffer beams would be attached by rivetting. The frame set would then be mounted on temporary wheels and trundled round the works service lines to arrive in the main erecting shop where the main assembly of the engine would be completed prior to the final painting process.

BOILERS.

The boilers for the whole class were manufactured in the Crewe Works boiler shop, which was at that time set up in the old part of the works complex. Experience in the building and indeed handling of these large boilers had already been gained with the production of those for the 'Princess Royal' class built in 1933-35.

The work involved much special equipment and many skilled hands. Gas and oil-fired furnaces were on hand to heat up the boiler plates. These plates were lifted and carried on giant forks slung from an overhead crane, and in the case of the larger ones, counterbalanced by men seated on the opposite end of them, the plates were swung into position and into the furnace mouth. At this point the men would all leap off, thereby allowing the plate to be lowered into position onto the support blocks in the white heat of the furnace.

After reaching the required temperature, the boiler plates were quickly removed again and fed through a set of giant rollers which were adjusted with each pass, further curving the plates until the required diameter was achieved. The sections of boiler barrel involved the skilled rolling of three separate flat plates into a tapered circular shape so that, rivetted together end to end, they would produce the required item.

Other plates requiring forming would be placed white hot between press blocks in a giant 700 ton capacity hydraulic press, gradually producing the required shape, a process which sometimes took several re-heating and forming exercises. In the case of the throat plates for instance, flanging blocks weighing some 41 tons in all were required to achieve the final shape needed.

Three views of the first engine under construction. Top:- the main frames, below left:- the main frames seen from above, below right:- the complete boiler mounted on the frames from above. (L.M.S./ 'The Railway Gazette')

The front and rear tubeplates, the outer steel firebox wrapper plate and the inner copper firebox, which extended into the boiler barrel to form a combustion chamber, had all to be pressed into shape and then attached to the barrel section. The steel firebox wrapper plates and boiler front plate were then rivetted in position, the roof hangers attached, the inner firebox lining plates were then put into position and the foundation ring round the bottom of the firebox rivetted in place. Finally the firebox crown stays were fitted together with some steel or 'Monel' metal stays, which were screwed into pre-drilled and tapped holes to hold the inner and outer firebox plates at their correct distances apart.

Because of the length of the boiler, and the fact that it had to be held vertically by a crane to permit the rings of rivets to be applied at the barrel joints, etc., modifications to the old boiler shop roof in Crewe Works had already been undertaken. The addition of a new tower section on the roof and a deep pit dug in the floor permitted the required manipulation to be achieved when the 'Princess Royal' class boilers were being constructed some four or so years earlier.

Following this exacting task, the boiler was moved to the boiler mounting shop where the dome casting and top feed rings were attached and the main steam pipe, regulator valve and control rod and lever fitted. After the superheater header casting had been mounted on the front tubeplate, the boiler tubes and superheater flues were fitted. The superheater elements were then slid into place inside the flues and attached to the superheater header. Over 2,700 feet of tubing was necessary to complete this process, and then all of the various firebox end control valves and fittings including the steam manifold were mounted on their relevant face-plates. These fittings, which would of course form part of the main controls and would be in the cab area of the finished engine, were either bought-out standard items or manufactured in the works. In the latter case Crewe Works' own brass foundry had a most important role in the manufacture of the rough castings which were then finished off in the machine and fitting shops.

With all of these fitted or their mounting faces blanked off, the boiler was then tested hydraulically at 30% above working pressure and then in steam up to the set pressure, in this case 10 lb./sq.in above the maximum working pressure of 250 lb./sq. in. and then finally again at the latter. A temporary firegrate arrangement on wheels was used by the works to facilitate testing up to this stage. This allowed quick evacuation of the fire, if ever that became necessary, and also easy disposal of it on completion of the test. Any leaks observed would either be caulked up or the mounting surface re-faced as required.

Finally the cast iron firegrate sections would be fitted, giving a total of 50 sq. ft surface, and the firebrick arch fitted. The normal boiler cladding sheets, carried on crinolines under which went the astbestos boiler lagging, to be followed later by the steel cladding sheets for the streamlined members of the class, and the smokebox itself rivetted onto the leading edge of the boiler barrel. The streamlining panels themselves were fastened to extra-light profiled frames laid over the top of the main cladding sheets on these first locomotives of the class, and these would be fixed in place in the erecting shop once the boiler had been lowered into position on the frames.

WHEELS AND AXLES.

With wheelsets, the wheel centre castings were produced in the steel foundry in Crewe Works, and the process of casting the driving, bogie and trailing truck wheels involved the use of a pattern to make a two part mould, with cores to fill the crankpin and axle holes. After the finest steel scrap had been melted down in the furnaces and pre-heated to some 1,500 degrees Centigrade, it was then poured into the space left by the pattern, and the cast was left to cool for many hours before the black sand mould and loose cores were broken away to reveal the bare metal of the rough casting. This was then fettled (dressed) using pneumatic chisels to remove the flash, where excess metal had flowed into the narrow gaps in the moulds, before it could be sent to the machine shop where the machining was carried out to produce the finished wheel centre.

Here a single machine tool was employed to simultaneously turn the rim profile to take the tyre, and also bore the hole in the centre boss for the axle. The crank pin hole was bored out separately. The pair of wheels were then forced, at a carefully controlled rate, onto the wheelseats on the plain or cranked axle ends at the same time using a 150 ton capacity hydraulic press the whole operation taking about five minutes. These axles had previously been machined from roughly forged steel billets produced by Messrs. Steel, Peach and Tozer of Sheffield, the steel used having a tensile strength of 35-40 tons per square inch. The engine coupled wheel axles for this class were hollow in order to save nearly half a ton in weight in all, and each axle was numbered and registered so that a record could be kept of it during its whole life service.

The coupled wheel tyres, rolled from ingots of high quality steel, were supplied in an un-machined condition by the Steel Company of Scotland Ltd., those for the pony truck axles by the English Steel Corporation and those for the bogie and tender wheelsets by Thomas Firth & John Brown Ltd. Tyres are provided on the wheels because they have to be turned down whilst an engine is in the shops in order to keep their correct profile. Such sizes ensure that the wheel diameter remains within set limits, and the range was kept in the 'Limits and Fits' information books, which could be referred to if a decision to re machine or replace was required. The finished bore is machined to a diameter between $1/16$ in. and $1/8$ in. less than the wheel rim but, when heated up in a ring of gas jets, it expands so the cold wheelset can be lowered into it. As the tyre cools it firmly grips the wheel rim, and a Gibson ring is then rolled into a recess on the inner surface to prevent the tyre from moving away from the recess at the wheels' edge.

A coupled wheelset was then balanced by spinning it on a special rig up to 260 revolutions per minute, equivalent to 60 m.p.h. on the track, and temporary weights were attached to remove any out-of-balance forces so far as was practicable. These weights were then replaced by moulten lead balance weights poured into pockets created by rivetting on side plates covering parts of the spokes at the specific balancing locations. For the 'Princess Coronation' class 50% of the reciprocating weights (i.e the coupling and connecting rods and the motion itself) are balanced, divided equally between the three coupled axles except for wheelsets with crank axles, where these are also taken account of.

Completed boiler ready to be lowered into the frames. (L.M.S./ 'The Railway Gazette')

MOTION

The Crewe Works drop forge was used to produce the coupling and connecting rod blanks from 'Vibrac' low alloy manganese molybdenum steel supplied by the Vickers Works of the English Steel Corporation. This steel had a breaking stress of between 50 and 60 tons per square inch. The 12 cwt rectangular billets used had to be heated up no less than five times to white hot heat to ensure that it remained malleable enough to be worked (hammered) to a rough forged shape to match a metal template. Once formed each item was then machined in the heavy machine shop, the fluted sides of the rods being milled out and a special circling milling machine being used to produce the eye end bores into which phosphor bronze bushes, with a white metal bearing surface would be pressed to complete the manufacuring process.

The many other forged motion parts went through similar processes, and all were stamped with the engine number and if necessary the handing of the part, i.e. 'R' for right hand side, 'L' for left hand side, `I' for inside, `O' for outside and 'D' for Driving. This system enabled easy identification of components when the engine returned to the shops for subsequent visits and overhauls.

ASSEMBLY

The final erection work could was completed in the main Erecting Shop South, where the main frame assembly had been moved and positioned on frame stands in its place on the production line. These stands, with adjustable screws, could be raised or lowered to ensure that the frame was absolutely level. With the slidebars, crosshead and reversing shaft in place, the completed boiler was one of the first major items to be fitted to the frames. Having been tranported from the boiler shop it was lowered into position using the overhead cranes.

One of the final assemblies to be fitted were the driving wheelsets and, with the frames hoisted aloft on the overhead cranes and the frame stands removed, these were rolled into position beneath the completed locomotive. A gang of men suitably positioned at each wheelset ensured that alignment was correct to ensure that the axleboxes entered the axlebox guides as the locomotive was slowly lowered. With wheelsets in the frame keeps were fitted followed by the axlebox underkeeps. The engine could be lowered onto the pit rails standing for the first time on its own wheels. Due to the concentrated nature of the final assembly, the bogie and pony truck were fitted later.

MOTION

The rods could now be fitted by slightly lifting the engine clear of the rails again and rotating the wheelsets to align the crank pins with the eyes in the coupling and connecting rods, and connecting the latter to the crosshead on each side. Once this was done

View showing the first engine with part of the streamlined casing fitted and the second engine with smokebox on behind.
(L.M.S./ 'The Railway Gazette')

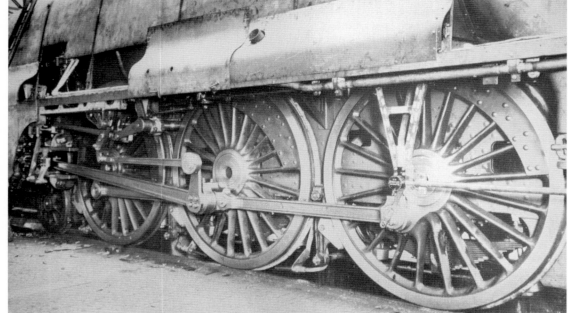

Close up of the driving wheels and motion on the first engine. The hollow axles saved 10 cwt. in weight.
(L.M.S./ 'The Railway Gazette')

and the pistons, valves and crosshead assembled, the process of valving could begin. This involved taking measurements of the position of the valves at various reversing gear settings and making sure that the valve travel was correct at each cut-off point. Usually a piece of tin plate was used with scribed lines marked in it, representing the various settings to give a total record.

CAB FITTINGS

The cab could now be fitted in position, and the various items of boiler fittings, injectors and pipework completed and connected up. Along with this work came the fitting of the streamlined casing which covered the boiler and cylinders and overlapped the running plates. These special sections were attached to profiled frames fitted over the boiler cladding. Access to the smokebox was provided by the 'gull-winged' half doors, hinged at the sides of the smokebox front ring, and once the doors were fully open a platform was revealed which could be used by staff working in that area.

View showing the coal pusher installation in the tender. (L.M.S./ 'The Railway Gazette')

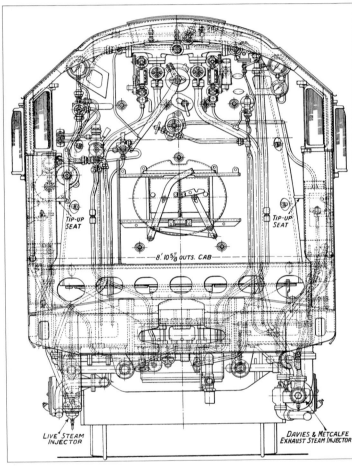

Drawing showing the arrangement of the driving cab. (L.M.S./ 'The Railway Gazette')

TENDER

The tender, which was meanwhile being built in the works tender shop, had a 4,000 gallon water tank and space for 10 tons of coal, and was of welded construction with the side sheets extended to align with the rear buffer faces to assist with the streamlining. At the footplate end, the first five tenders for locomotive Nos 6220-4 were roofed over to match the shape of the cab, and the intervening gap filled by rubber sheeting. As already mentioned, doors were provided to give access to the filling points, and the normal water pick-up apparatus, used to collect water without stopping from troughs between the lines during a run, was fitted with a deflector to minimise wastage. A coal pusher was also fitted, as described earlier. The tender fame was carried on three axles with 4 ft 3 in diameter wheelsets spaced equally on a total wheelbase of 15 feet.

Rear end of streamlined tender No. 9745, as fitted to engine No. 6227 'Duchess of Devonshire' showing wing plates, access ladder to water tank fillers and steam supply pipes and exhaust for the coal pusher. (L.M.S. Neg. DY 23882A. J.B. Radford Collection)

PAINTING

The final stage was the painting, and the engine, now coupled to its tender, was moved down the yard to the paint shop. Where it would receive various coats of primer, filling and stopping and top coats followed by varnishing to give a high quality finish to its final livery. The first five members of the class were painted blue with four silver stripes starting from a point just above the central lamp bracket and sweeping upwards and outwards to run horizontally along the sides of both engine and tender. The coaches were also being given the same horizontal lining, thus a matching train-set livery was achieved.

Subsequently the livery was varied, the next batch of streamlined engines being turned out in L.M.S. Crimson Lake (derived from the original Midland Railway Company's 'Lake' colour) with gold stripes, whilst the unstreamlined 'Duchess of Sutherland' and her four sisters carried a special Crimson Lake livery with gold leafed shaded lining. Full details of this livery plus the lettering and numbering are given in Appendix 6.

There is not room in this book to do full justice to the production of the components and the construction of these locomotives, but readers are referred to the two sections entitled 'The Streamliners' on p.27 and 'Building The Streamliners' on p118 of 'L.M.S. Reflections'. This book contains an excellent collection of photographs selected by Bob Essery and Nigel Harris from the Hulton-Deutsch collection and was published by Silver Link Publishing Ltd in 1986.

At this period Crewe Works employed over 6,500 men in total, and the great number of these would, at some stage or another, have had some hand in the manufacture of the parts and in the building and painting of a member of this fine class of locomotives, or in its subsequent repair and overhaul during a lifetime in service. In those days working on the railways, and particularly in the works, was very much a family tradition, and grandfather, father and son, plus uncles and cousins, worked for the company in their turn. In those days a job on the railways was a job for life, and staff were proud of such long traditions of service.

Now ready for service, the locomotive was then filled with water and coal and moved onto the Crewe weigh table so that the springs could be adjusted to give the correct setting for each axle in accordance with the design criteria. This weighbridge was situated in the old part of the works outside the smithy, but consisted of only five Pooley weigh tables, making it impossible to weigh a 4-6-2 type engine in one go. Accordingly, the outermost bogie wheels were left beyond the tables on a fixed pair of rails, it being assumed that the bogie might have an equally divided load. After the first weighing the engine was moved so that the bogie was fully on the tables but the pony truck was off them, and the weights taken again. Water levels and an estimate of the weight of coal in the firebox were also recorded. Throughout the whole life of the L.M.S.Pacifics, the weightable at Crewe remained the same. It remains quite astonishing that this was never modified to take a complete Pacific at one go, and so some inaccuracies in the readings must have been allowed to pass as a result.

It was now at last time to bring the engine to life for the first time. After lighting the fire in the firebox and gradually raising steam over a period of several hours, there would be a short trial run that would enable any minor faults to be identified and corrected. This would also show any steam leaks in the boiler, pipework or fittings that might need attention before the locomotive finally entered service.

Shrewsbury was the regular destination for a running in turn from Crewe, and it was a regular sight to see several engines coupled together being turned on the triangle at Shrewsbury before returning to Crewe. Following the running-in trials, all of the early locomotives of this class were allocated to the Camden motive power depot located just north of Euston station in London.

The first three streamlined locomotives lined up outside the paint shop in Crewe Works on 18th June, 1937 - Nos. 6220 'Coronation', 6221 'Queen Elizabeth' and 6222 'Queen Mary.' (L.M.S. Official/ J.B. Radford Collection)

Chapter Two

Into Service and More Building and Development

Official L.M.S. photograph DY. 22441 of the first locomotive of the class, 6220 'Coronation' posed in Crewe Works on 15th May, 1937. (L.M.S. official/ J. B. Radford Collection)

THE PRESS LAUNCH

The proposal to inaugurate the new 'Coronation Scot' trains had interestingly only been announced to shareholders of the L.M.S. by the Chairman, Sir Josiah Stamp, in his speech to them at the company's Annual General meeting on 26th February, 1937. The original authority to build five further Pacifics of the 'Princess Royal' class does not appear in the 1937 programme agreed on 27th July, 1936, nor were they mentioned in any later minutes of the Mechanical & Electrical Committee or of the Traffic Committee. The only mention is a marginal note in the minutes of that Board Meeting of 27th July, 1936 to the effect that "this minute also gave authority for the construction of an additional five Princess type locomotives." However, once the outcome of 1936 high-speed test runs was evaluated, and the Board had accepted the proposals for improved timings and thus the need for the new class of locomotives to meet the challenge, this authority was transferred to the building of five locomotives of the new 'Coronation' class. Design work in fact was already at an advanced stage, and the material ordering process well in hand.

Construction of the first of the new class of locomotives was achieved in record time, and on 5th June, 1937 No. 6220 'CORONATION' was ready for traffic, proudly carrying nameplates affixed to each side of the boiler and surmounted by a crown. Both locomotive and train were resplendent in a blue livery similar to the old Caledonian Railway colour but officially designated 'Coronation blue' with silver stripes as described in Chapter 1.

The specially designed matching train-set of nine carriages comprised of:-

Corridor first brake, corridor first, vestibule first diner, kitchen car, two vestibule thirds, a second kitchen car, another vestibule third and a corridor third brake. All had been built in the Wolverton Carriage Works of the L.M.S., with the special paint being supplied by Docker Brothers.

The complete train was introduced to the press by F.A. Lemon, the then Works Superintendent at Crewe, on Tuesday, 26th May, 1937, after which William Stanier himself welcomed the party to a special lunch at the Crewe Arms Hotel opposite Crewe station.

The first five locomotives were built to L.M.S. Lot No. 138 and Crewe Order No. 420, and were outshopped as follows:-

No.	Name	Completed
6220	'Coronation'	1st June, 1937
6221	'Queen Elizabeth'	14th June, 1937
6222	'Queen Mary'	22nd June, 1937
6223	'Princess Alice'	28th June, 1937
6224	'Princess Alexandra'	13th July 1937

Regarding the names, Stanier had written a letter dated 9th March, 1937 advising what the names for the other four engines should be, and followed it up with a further letter dated 1st April advising the agreed name for 6225, which was to be 'Duchess of Gloucester.' The use of royal names for members of the class had been specially agreed by His Majesty King George VI, 1937 being the year of His Coronation, after which of course the class was named. A later member of the class, No. 6244, originally named 'City of Leeds,' was eventually to be re-named in his honour in April, 1941, and had already been approved by the date of a list of proposed names got out by the C.M. & E.E. at the London Road Locomotive Drawing Office in Derby on 19th February, 1941, which will be referred to later.

INAUGURATION OF THE 'CORONATION SCOT' TRAIN.

The first public service trips of the new 'Coronation Scot' nine coach restaurant car train on its 6 1/2 hour schedule, ran between London Euston and Glasgow Central, calling only at Carlisle to set down passengers. on Monday, 5th July, 1937, but this was preceded on Tuesday, 29th June, 1937 by a special Press demonstration run for specially invited guests, using an eight coach train (one kitchen car having been left out) with a tare weight of 263 tons and hauled by No. 6220 'CORONATION'. This left Euston at 9.55 a.m. carrying reporting number 'W700,' but this was to be no ordinary special train, for it was during the down run to Crewe that the world speed record for steam traction of 113 m.p.h., held at the time by the L.N.E.R's Pacific No. 2512 'SILVER FOX', was broken with a speed of 114 m.p.h. at milepost 156 on the approaches to Crewe. Driver Tom J. Clarke was at the controls with Fireman J. Lewis, both from Crewe North shed, and with them was inspector S. Miller of Willesden and Robert A. Riddles, whose epic account of the event has been published many times.

This maximum speed achieved up to that date was not the maximum possible, but, as O.S. Nock, who was on board, observed "the utmost it was prudent to attempt in that particular locality," and in this case the locomotive was able to remain in service afterwards. He also later learned that the crew were asked to try for 120 m.p.h. R.A. Riddles, who was on the footplate at the time, eventually revealed the full story in his Presidential Address to the Junior Institution of Engineers in 1947 thus:-

"Again I was fortunate to be on the footplate, and with my diagrams laying down postulated speeds, all was set to make an attempt on the world's maximum record speed at Whitmore, where, after a short rise, we entered on a falling gradient down to Crewe 10 1/2 miles away. We had decided not to pick up water at Whitmore and so avoid reducing speed. The exhaust was humming with a continuous roar like that of an aeroplane engine. The white mileposts flashed past and the speedometer needle shot up through the '90's' into the '100's' to 100- 111-112-113-114 miles an hour, but beyond it - No! Basford Hall sidings 1 1/2 miles away now; spectators from Crewe coming into view at the lineside; and the train still hurtling along at 114 m.p.h.! On went the brakes; off the regulator; but on we sailed, with flames streaming from the tortured brake blocks. To my horror the signal was set for Platform No. 3 at Crewe, which has a reverse curve with a 20 m.p.h. restriction. We were doing 60 to 70 m.p.h. when we spotted the platform signal: down to 52 m.p.h. through the curve, the engine riding like the great lady she is: there wasn't a thing we could do about it but hold on and let her take it. And take it she did; with the crockery smashing in the dining car: past a sea of pallid faces on the platform: till we ground to a dead stand - safe and sound and still on the rails. We had set up a new world's speed record for the steam locomotive."

As they entered that reverse curve, back in the train F.A. Lemon, sitting opposite Stanier, said "We're for it now!" and put his feet up on the seat opposite to steady himself. Some appalling mis-judgments at Crewe had led to the train being switched to this difficult platform road, and it is probable that only the excellent quaility of the de Glehn bogie (copied by Churchward from the French Atlantics and brought to the L.M.S. by Stanier) had saved the train from disaster.

The L.M.S. had now secured the speed record from the L.N.E.R., but, although No. 6220 could probably have run a lot faster, there was no room to do it. Riddles own notes confirm that speed was

Full page advertisement from the L.M.S. 1937 summer timetable announcing the 'Coronation Scot' train services between London Euston and Glasgow Central.
(L.M.S./ J. B. Radford Collection)

The press demonstration run train, W700 headed by 6220 'Coronation' passes Kilburn No. 1 Box at around 60 m.p.h. on the way to her breaking the world record at 114 m.p.h. on 29th June, 1937.
(PRCLT Collection)

With a powerful blast of exhaust from the chimney, 6223 'Princess Alice' sets off from London Euston with the 'down' 'Coronation Scot' for Glasgow Central in 1937.
(J. B. Radford Collection)

still rising steadily on the 1 in 169 falling gradient right up to the moment that steam had to be shut off, and, given a little more track, 'CORONATION' could probably have reached 118-120 m.p.h. without difficulty on a longer down grade in A.J.Powell's view. The return trip turned out to be the fastest start-to-stop journey ever recorded up to that time between Crewe and Euston, the 158.1 miles being covered in a time of 119 minutes (scheduled for 135 mins.), giving and average speed of just over 80 m.p.h. for the whole journey. A speed of 100 m.p.h. was reached at Castlethorpe, near Wolverton and 99 m.p.h. at King's Langley.

In his book 'British Pacific Locomotives' published by Ian Allan in 1962, Cecil J. Allen states that on that famous occasion, in the company of D.S.M. Barrie, S.W. P. Corbett, and O.S. Nock, who were similarly engaged, he was timing the train as he had been on all previous L.N.E.R. record runs, and the excitement of these moments was intense. They recorded speeds by stopwatch over successive half-miles from milepost 148, half a mile north of Whitmore, where the speed was 85 m.p.h., and recorded 112.5 and 112.5 between posts 155 and 156. It was agreed that this could be interpreted as a peak of 113 m.p.h., exactly equal to the L.N.E.R. record, and "as the official 114 m.p.h. was taken off the engine speed indicator, which could hardly be regarded as a dead accurate method of recording, to this day it is by no means certain that the L.N.E.R. figure had been beaten." He adds that what might have been regarded as an optimistic booked time of 8 minutes for the 10.5 miles from Whitmore to Crewe was actually covered in the amazing time of six minutes and fifty-eight seconds. He also adds that the entry into Platform 3 was no mere single crossover - it consisted of a crossover leftwards from fast to slow, followed by a second double crossover to the left and then a right-handed crossover into the platform !

Concerning the smashed crockery, the L.M.S.R. Vice President, Sir Ernest Lemon remarked at the Press lunch afterwards "Of course, gentlemen, you realise that we shan't need to do this thing on every trip of the 'Coronation Scot !". Up to that point Sir Ernest had only quoted the 112.5 m.p.h. that the four observers had agreed, but then, as he read the paper, a broad smile spread over his face, and

he said "I have not been bribed, but I can now tell you that the maximum speed was 114 m.p.h.". The equipment then in use on locomotives of the class was of the Hasler type driven from the left trailing crankpin, and scrutiny of the speed recorder chart taken off the locomotive had confirmed the maximum speed, and thus the L.M.S.R. officially claimed the new record. Not only that but the engine continued in service afterwards without the need for repairs.

It is worth noting in passing that on the L.N.E.R. 'Silver Jubilee' streamlined train's run from Newcastle to London on 27th August, 1936, with 270 tons load, the 113 m.p.h. record with 'SILVER FOX' was gained at considerable cost to the engine, for at Hatfield the centre big end completely disintegrated and knocked out both cylinder ends and the engine limped into King's Cross on two cylinders. The later world record of 126 m.p.h. set by the L.N.E.R. Pacific No. 4468 'Mallard' on 3rd July, 1938 as she headed a 240 ton light seven coach train comprising three two-car twin sets and the ex N.E.R. dynamometer car, down a straight section of track on Stoke Bank between Grantham and Peterborough, was also achieved at some considerable cost to the locomotive. She had been worked at 40%-45% cut-off with full regulator opening, and this, coupled with the over-running of the middle valve-spindle, had caused the middle big-end to become damaged at such high speeds. She was subsequently run on slowly to the New England depot at Peterborough, and subsequently shopped at Doncaster works for repairs.

With a higher available drawbar horsepower, the 'Princess Coronation' class engine would have been quite capable of beating that record given the same circumstances. A top speed of 110 m.p.h. recorded by Driver Percy Wilson with No.6233 'DUCHESS OF SUTHERLAND' at the head of an ordinary Perth-Euston overnight sleeping car train whilst descending Shap during the war (c1942), and its subsequent performance on that run, which will be mentioned later, strongly supports that possibility. Of course, as railway enthusiasts and historians know, this particular debate has continued ever since 1937, and is likely to continue whilst there is any interest in steam locomotives in this country!

The 'up' 'Coronation Scot' headed by 6223 'Princess Alice' heads majestically southwards below a gantry of fine old signals near Preston on her way to London.
(Rev. E. Treacy)

A FURTHER BATCH

A further ten members of the class were ordered in late 1937 and built during 1938, the first five being streamlined and the last five non-streamlined. One visual detail difference with the details in the front running plate shape on the non streamlined is that it is continuous with a pleasurable radius down from high level to buffer beam level, which was of course omitted and in fact hidden from view in the streamlined version. The construction of these locomotives was approved as a result of a supplementary item approved for addition to the original 1938 Building Programme on 27th October, 1937 which was minuted by the Board as follows:-

"Minute No. 1276: With a view to meeting increasing demands for engine power likely to arise in 1938, it was recommended that 10 additional Class 7 4-6-2 express passenger tender locomotives (Coronation type) be built at an estimated cost of £138,000."

They were built to Lot No. 145 and Order E408 placed in October, 1937, the cost of each locomotive being estimated at £13,800. The manufacture of some component parts was carried out at Derby, the cost of this being covered by Order No. 311 dated 15th November, 1937.

There is no mention in the minutes of the fact that five of these were to be non-streamlined, although we know that Stanier wanted some to be built like this. Furthermore, there is no explanation as to why this requirement had not been originally included in the main programme for 1938 for building a total of 100 locomotives that had been agreed to earlier. This 100 comprised 15 Class 8F 2-8-0's, 20 class 5 4-6-0's, 30 class 4 0-6-0's and 35 class 4P 2-6-4T's. However it should be remembered that re-armament was already on the agenda, and that although the following modest progamme for 1939 also included a further 20 locomotives of the class, the last two were, in the event, cancelled in 1943. The order was only re-introduced later as part of the post-war building programme.

The first five locomotive of this batch were streamlined, but this time the batch was painted in L.M.S. red, identical to the old Midland Railway crimson lake, the lining-out being in gold leaf edged with vermillion, instead of straw, and gold scroll/serif num-

bering and lettering with vermillion shading. They were built at Crewe during 1938 and were named and numbered as follows:-

No.	Name	Completed
6225	'Duchess of Gloucester'	11th May, 1938
6226	'Duchess of Norfolk'	23rd May, 1938
6227	'Duchess of Devonshire'	7th June, 1938
6228	'Duchess of Rutland'	17th June, 1938
6229	'Duchess of Hamilton'	7th September, 1938

No. 6229 'DUCHESS OF HAMILTON' emerged from the works at a later date and out of build sequence, since she was held back to be fitted with the new design of deep drop firegrate and a hopper ashpan. In addition the port passages between the cylinders and the steam chests were streamlined in addition to the exhaust passages and piston heads. She was soon to exchange identities with No 6220 'CORONATION' for the duration of the L.M.S. Exhibition train tour of North America. For this period she remained in her red livery to match the carriages of the train, thereby leaving the original blue-liveried No. 6220 'CORONATION,' in the temporary guise of No. 6229, and so re-named, in service at home, much to the confusion of railway enthusiasts of the day.

The second batch, which were the non-streamlined locomotives was also turned out in the L.M.S. red but in a special livery lined out in black edged on the inside with gold edged in vermillion. A full painting specification is given in Appendix 6. They were turned out as follows:-

No.	Name	Completed
6230	'Duchess of Buccleuch'	27th June, 1938
6231	'Duchess of Atholl'	28th June, 1938
6232	'Duchess of Montrose'	1st July, 1938
6233	'Duchess of Sutherland'	18th July, 1938
6234	'Duchess of Abercorn'	4th August, 1938

With the permission of His Majesty the King, all this batch of engines carried names of Royal Duchesses with the last five being

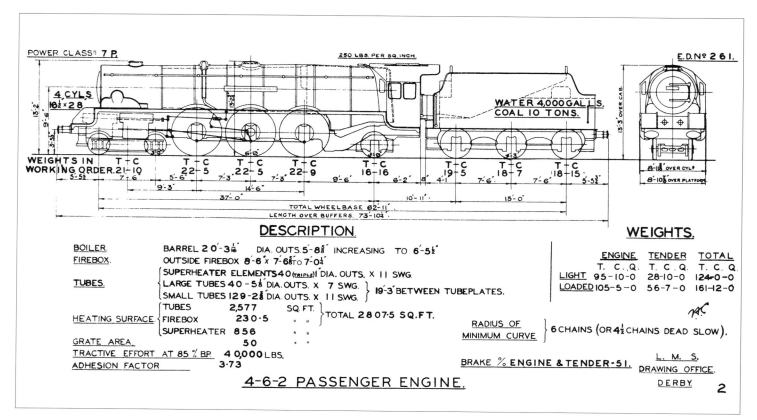

L.M.S. official diagram E.D. No. 261 prepared for the un-streamlined locomotives 6230-4 as originally built.
(L.M.S./J.B.Radford Collection)

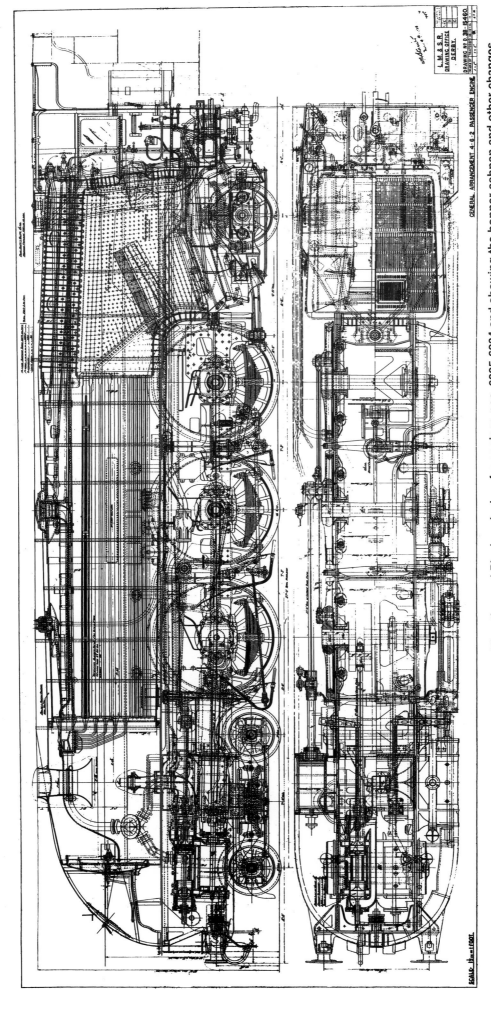

L.M.S. offical drawing No. D38-15460 'General Arrangement, Elevation and Plan' marked up for engines nos. 6225-6234 and showing the hopper ashpan and other changes. However, not all of those engines received the changes indicated. (L.M.S./ J.B. Radford Collection)

those holding Scottish titles. As a matter of interest the 'DUCHESS OF SUTHERLAND' locomotive was named after Lady Eileen Gwladys Butler, D.G.St.J.., J.P. who had served as Mistress of the Robes to Her Majesty Queen Mary from 1916-1921. She was the elder daughter of the 7th Earl of Lanesborough and had married George Granville Sutherland-Leveson-Gower, 5th Duke of Sutherland, K.T. on 1st April, 1912. She died on 24th August, 1943.

A new pair of general arrangement drawings was produced at Derby showing the second batch of streamlined engines Nos. D38-15460, showing the side elevation and plan views, and D38-15461 showing the end views and cross sections, and these were signed off by Stanier on 4th May, 1938. They were to cover engines Nos. 6225-6234 (despite the fact that Nos. 6230-6234 were un-streamlined) and took account of the changes necessary with the introduction of the new design of the deep drop firegrate and hopper ashpan with bottom doors, also fitted to 6229 as mentioned above. This change has been found to be necessary to ensure that the damper doors functioned properly and the openings did not become clogged up with ash as had occurred on the earlier engines. However locomotives Nos 6225 to 6233, with the exception of 6229 which was completed later and went on tour to North America, were not fitted when new with the drop grate. A new frame arrangement, D37-15173 was also produced together with new pipe and rod, lubrication drawings, and a new modified pony truck arrangement D38-15271.

The average cost per locomotive of this second batch of locomotives was engine £9,585, tender £1,509, total £11,094, as against the original estimate of £13,800. As to 'DUCHESS OF SUTHERLAND' herself, the official record card shows her actual original cost as being:- Engine:- £9,181, tender £1,478, total £10,659. The year of final depreciation to 'nil' value was to be 1968, thus predicting the standard life expectancy of 30 years. The 4,000 gallon tender attached to No. 6233 was numbered 9751, and this remains attached to the engine today. The principal dimensions and other technical details of these non-streamlined locomotives as originally built are shown on official diagram ED No. 261.

A fine colour plate of No. 6230 'DUCHESS OF BUCCLEUCH', taken from a painting by M. Secretan commissioned by the L.M.S., appeared in "The Locomotive Magazine' issue dated 15th June, 1938 and accurately depicts how these engines looked as new. It is reproduced here in this book by courtesy of that magazine. As to their appearance, although the streamlined engines of the class were undoubtedly impressive, and some would argue more attractive to look at than the wedge-shaped L.N.E.R. class A4 Pacifics, these non-streamlined locomotives were considered by many to be most impressive machines. C.Hamilton Ellis, in his book 'The Splendour of Steam,' offered his opinion that "The Duchess Pacific in its un-streamlined form was probably the most handsome express passenger locomotive ever to run on British Railways".

To complete this survey of the building of the class as a whole, early in 1939 a further order for twenty more was included in the Building Programme and approved the Board on 27th July, 1938, at an estimated total cost of £243,000. They were to be built as Lot No. 150, the first ten, numbered 6235-44 were all to be streamlined and were covered by Crewe Order No. 4114, with of the last ten, numbered 6245-54, to Crewe Order No. 415. In fact only Nos. 6245-8 were streamlined. With the intervention of the Second World War, the order for the last two was cancelled, and they were subsequently built after the war as part of Lot No. 184 under Crewe Order No. 464, along with a further three numbered 6255-7.

Reproduction of a painting by M. Secretan showing the special livery adopted for the five un-streamlined locomotives Nos. 6230-6234 when first built. This is the livery that 6233, as preserved in working order, carries today following her recent overhaul. (Courtesy 'The Locomotive Magazine')

This L.M.S. official photograph No. DY. 24028 was taken on 21st June, (33/1/02) 1938 and purports to show 6233 'Duchess of Sutherland' in 'shop grey' livery and 'as built' condition. It is in fact 6231 'Duchess of Atholl'. (see text) (L.M.S. official, courtesy the National Railway Museum)

NAMING AND OFFICIAL PHOTOGRAPHS.

As with the earlier streamlined engine No. 6220, a batch of six Derby negatives were produced at an official photographic session at Crewe Works on 10th June, 1938 and numbered DY 23955-60. These showed No. 6230 in shop grey livery as an official record of how the first of the five non-streamlined engines looked, and the locomotive was then painted in the full livery before it entered traffic. This was the common practice for all new locomotive types and variants, and one of the Chief Photographer's staff from Derby would travel to Crewe with his glass plate camera and tripod for the session. In prestige batches of engines it was also quite common for names and numbers to be changed on the first of the batch to produce a 'pseudo' photographic shot of each member of it. This resulted in negatives nos. DY24027-8, which are listed as No. 6233, actually being No.6231 'DUCHESS OF ATHOLL,' as were those purporting to be of Nos. 6232 and 6234. All were taken on 21st June, 1938, nameplates and cabside and smokebox numbers being changed as necessary.

Interestingly there were to be several changes of mind about the names to be used for the remaining engines, and it was originally decided that from No. 6245 onwards should be named after cities served by the L.M.S. system, in strictly alphabetical order, even though it was pointed out that not all of those chosen were accessible to the class due to gauging considerations on some routes! However, when 'CITY OF LEEDS' was re-named 'KING GEORGE VI' in April, 1941, as a patriotic gesture, the names chosen for the remaining cities of Leicester, Lichfield, Salford, Sheffield and Stoke-on-Trent, were allocated out of order, and in fact only No. 6246 'CITY OF LIVERPOOL' was numbered as originally intended.

Due to the many later changes, official photographs taken in advance using the first of a batch therefore showed wrong name and number combinations to those finally allocated for the remainder of the batch. This was made even worse in the case of illustrations of streamlined locomotives with names that were in fact later used for un-streamlined members of the class! For instance Derby negatives Nos. DY 26036-47 were taken in 1939 and purported to show No. 6246 'CITY OF MANCHESTER,' No.6250 'CITY OF NOTTINGHAM,' and No.6251 'CITY OF ST. ALBANS' in fully lined red livery. However, due to the intervention of the Second World War, like all of their later sister engines, they actually emerged from the works in unlined black. The locomotive used for this photographic session was actually No. 6235 'CITY OF BIRMINGHAM'.

The original instruction for allocating these names was dated 5th February, 1941 Refs. P/L.40 and K.8334, and seems not to have survived, but presumably referred to the change of name of No. 6244 mentioned above. However a list dated 19th February, 1941 has survived, as already mentioned, and lists the names a follows:-

6235 'City of Birmingham'	6236 'City of Bradford'
6237 'City of Bristol'	6238 'City of Carlisle'
6239 'City of Chester'	6240 'City of Coventry'
6241 'City of Edinburgh'	6242 'City of Glasgow'
6243 'City of Lancaster'	6244 'King George VI'

The intended names for engines not by then built are given as:-

6245 'City of Leeds'	6246 'City of Leicester'
6247 'City of Lichfield'	6248 'City of Liverpool'
6249 'City of London'	6250 'City of Manchester'
6251 'City of Nottingham'	6252 'City of St. Albans'
6253 'City of Sheffield'	6254 'City of Stoke-on-Trent'

However, Roland .C. Bond, then Locomotive Works Superintendent in the Chief Mechanical Engineer's Department at Crewe, sent a letter to Charles. E. Fairburn, at that time the Deputy Chief Mechanical Engineer at Derby, dated 22nd May, 1943 in which states that he had received instructions that the next 4-6-2 engines built at Crewe were to be named as follows:-

> "6245 'City of London'
> 6246 'City of Manchester'
> 6247 'City of Liverpool'
> 6248 'City of Leeds' "

Bond then wrote again on 9th October, 1943 stating:-

"With reference to your letter of the 21st September, the Vice-President has informed me that the four 4-6-2 locomotives, non-streamlined type, to be constructed in 1944 should be named as under:-

> 6249 'City of Sheffield'
> 6250 'City of Belfast'
> 6251 'City of Dublin'
> 6252 'City of Nottingham' ."

It is most interesting to note this idea of naming two of the locomotives after the capital cities of Northern Ireland and the Irish Republic, and it would appear to wish to reflect the L.M.S. Irish Sea ferry connections between Liverpool and Stranraer to Belfast and the service from Holhead to Dun Loaghaire. The L.M.S. also then owned railways inherited from the Midland and L.& N.W. Railway Companies.

However, the letter was soon countermanded a second time with a letter dated 23rd March, 1944, stating:-

"......The four locomotives in question are now to be named as follows, and I shall be glad if you will make the necessary arrangements accordingly.

> 6249 'City of Sheffield' (as already arranged)
> 6250 'City of Lichfield'
> 6251 'City of Nottingham'
> 6252 'City of Leicester'......"

Bond was asked to let the C.M.E. have a date that it was estimated that each engine would be completed as soon as possible, and later advise him approximately three weeks before completion of the date upon which each engine would be handed over to the Operating Department. The letter was again copied to Coleman, Chief Draughtsman at Derby.

A further letter, dated 21st June, 1946, from the C.M.E. at his Nelson Street offices in Derby to J. Rankin Crewe, also copied to Coleman, advised:-

NAMING OF LOCOMOTIVES
I give below particulars of the names allocated to the three 4-6-2 Passenger tender locomotives to be constructed during 1946 and shall be glad if you will arrange for the preparation of nameplates to be put in hand.

> Engine No. 6253 'City of St. Albans'
> Engine No. 6254 'City of Stoke-on Trent'
> Engine No. 6255 'City of Hereford'

Will you please let me know, as early as possible, the dates on which you anticipate each of these engines will be handed over to traffic with a view to ascertaining whether it is proposed to hold a naming ceremony."

These multiple changes must have caused a lot of confusion, especially for those involved in producing the necessary paperwork, preparing the drawings and also involved in the manufacture of the nameplates themselves.

L.M.S. official photograph No. DY. 27966 of 6244 in the red and gold livery. Originally named 'City of Leeds' it was taken after the locomotive had been re-named 'King George VI' in April, 1941 as a patriotic gesture during the Second World War.
(L.M.S. official/ J.B. Radford Collection)

Interesting view of Crewe Works Erecting Shop showing two 'Princess Coronation' class locomotives under construction. It must have been taken in late summer, 1939 and shows 6238 already painted in the red and gold livery and named 'City of Carlisle' but on frame stands. The engine in front nearing completion may be 6239 'City of Chester'.
(J.B. Radford Collection)

Details of the remaining locomotives as actually built and named were as follows:-

Lot. No. 150 Streamlined, red livery with gold lining, etc.

No.	Name	Completed
6235	'City of Birmingham'	27th June, 1939
6236	'City of Bradford'	27th July, 1939
6237	'City of Bristol'	9th August, 1939
6238	'City of Carlisle'	14th September, 1939
6239	'City of Chester'	29th August, 1939
6240	'City of Coventry'	27th March, 1940
6241	'City of Edinburgh'	3rd April, 1940
6242	'City of Glasgow'	15th May, 1940
6243	'City of Lancaster'	29th May, 1940
*6244	'City of Leeds'	12th July, 1940

*This engine was destined to be re-named 'King George VI', as already mentioned, and No. 6248 was in due course named 'City of Leeds' in its place.

As the photograph on page 27 shows there was clearly a problem with No. 6238 since, although finish-painted in the red and gold livery, she has had all her wheels removed and is on frame stands. What the problem was is not known, but she was accordingly late into service after No. 6239. Interestingly her official Engine History Card shows that she was 'stored serviceable five days' in 1939, but whether that was related is not known.

Lot No. 150 Streamlined, plain black livery:-

No.	Name	Completed
6245	'City of London'	26th June, 1943
6246	'City of Manchester'	11th August, 1943
6247	'City of Liverpool'	13th September, 1943
6248	'City of Leeds'	2nd October, 1943

Lot 150 Un-streamlined, plain black livery:-

No.	Name	Completed
6249	'City of Sheffield'	19th April, 1944
6250	'City of Lichfield'	20th May, 1944
6251	'City of Nottingham'	3rd June, 1944
6252	'City of Leicester'	24th June, 1944

This last batch had the full running plate curved to sweep down in front of the cylinders onto the lower level above the front buffer beam. However, all subsequent engines retained the split level which was a notable feature of streamlined members of the class when the streamlining was eventually removed. They were also turned out with tenders (Nos. 9812-15) still having the streamlined outline with extension plates at the trailing end of the tender tank side sheets.

The order for the final two locomotives, Nos. 6253 and 6254, having been cancelled in 1943, was included in the 1946 Building Programme approved on 23rd November, 1944 "to increase the fleet of these locomotives to 50 (sic) which it is considered will provide sufficient of the highest powered engines to meet post-war accelerations."

The estimated cost was put at £75,850 and they were built to Crewe Order No. 464, the first three being as follows:-

Part Lot 184 Un-streamlined, plain black livery:-

No.	Name	Completed
6253	'City of St. Albans'	14th September, 1946
6254	'City of Stoke-on-Trent	17th September, 1946
6255	'City of Hereford'	16th October, 1946

These engines had smoke deflectors from new, as did the final two members of the class, Nos. 6256 and 6257M, whose development is described later.

L.M.S. official photograph No. DY. 32485 taken in 1944 and showing the nameplate of the streamlined 6235 'City of Birmingham'. The locomotive has already been painted in wartime black livery, and the official naming ceremony took place the following year when the arms of the city were added above the nameplate.
(L.M.S. official/ J.B. Radford Collection)

L.M.S. official photograph DY. 31640 also taken in June, 1944 showing the nameplate of the un-streamlined 6252 'City of Leicester'. This locomotive was turned out in black livery as new, and the view shows the much easier access to the mechanical lubricators, oil reservoirs and sandbox fillers, etc. which was required for daily maintenance.
(L.M.S. official/ J.B. Radford Collection)

NAMING CEREMONIES

Being prestige locomotives, special naming ceremonies were arranged for many of these later locomotives, and these were all carried out in the cities after which they were named by the Lord Mayor or Mayor of the day. Known dates, taken mainly from the S.L.S. Journal, were as follows:-

No.	Name	Naming ceremony location and date
6235	'City of Birmingham' *(city arms added above)*	Birmingham New St. Station, 20th March, 1945
6240	'City of Coventry' *(city arms added above)*	Coventry Station, 6th November, 1945
6245	'City of London'	Euston Station, London, 20th July, 1945
6246	'City of Manchester'	Manchester Victoria Station, 3rd September, 1943
6247	'City of Liverpool'	Liverpool Lime Street Station, 21st September, 1943
6248	'City of Leeds'	Leeds City Station, 2nd December, 1943.
6249	'City of Sheffield'	Sheffield Midland Station, 1st November, 1944
6250	'City of Lichfield'	Lichfield Trent Valley Station, 20th June, 1944
6251	'City of Nottingham'	Nottingham Midland Station, 4th October, 1945
6252	'City of Leicester'	Leicester Midland Station, 10th October, 1945
6254	'City of Stoke-on-Trent' *(city arms added above)*	Stoke-on-Trent Station, 20th September, 1946

According to 'The Railway Magazine,' the driver selected to take No. 6245 'CITY OF LONDON', the first of the black streamlined locomotives, to her naming cermony was Driver Walter E. Freestone. He was a top link driver who was highly regarded, and had been awarded the British Empire Medal in 1941 for service during the blitz on London. Born in 1879 within the sound of Camden motive power depot, he signed for all of the main routes as far as Carlisle, and had been regularly driving on the Liverpool- London Euston services, often being in charge of Stanier's No. 6202 'The Turbomotive.'

Before the naming ceremony of No. 6235 'CITY OF BIRMINGHAM' clearance tests had to be undertaken on the route into New Street station, and locomotive travelled light from Crewe for that purpose on Monday, 19th February, 1944. This was the first time that a member of the class had visited the city.

The naming ceremony for No. 6248 'CITY OF LEEDS' was performed in that city by the then Lord Mayor of Leeds, Alderman Albert Hayes, and not at Euston station in London as often recorded, and No. 6250 CITY OF LICHFIELD' was named by the then Lady Mayor of Lichfield, Miss Agnes M. Thompson.

Mr Arthur Green of Chesterfield, who was taken by his father, Driver Arthur Green (of Staveley Shed) to the Sheffield naming ceremony of 'CITY OF SHEFFIELD' as a young man, records that the locomotive No. 6249 was hauled to Sheffield via the Hope Valley line. It was too heavy to enter Sheffield Station coupled to its tender due to a bridge loading restriction south of the station and the two had to be parted and then brought into the Station where they were re-united. The ceremony took place in the Bay Platform between Platforms 5 and 8.

Subsequently, in 1945, No. 6249 'CITY OF SHEFFIELD' was fitted with a set of stainless steel nameplates which replaced the original brass ones some two months after the first ceremony, these being supplied by Firth-Vickers Stainless Steels Ltd., a Sheffield firm.

The 'Railway Observer' reported that for the naming of No. 6251 'CITY OF NOTTINGHAM' a new type of nameplate was fitted, similar to the others members of the class but in polished brass with the background painted red, "which looks extremely smart against the black boiler." Unfortunately No. 6251 disgraced herself by becoming derailed at the Lincoln end of Nottingham Midland station immediately after the ceremony, causing considerable disruption to traffic in the station area.

FURTHER DESIGN PROPOSALS

To complete this brief resume of the history of the 'Princess Coronation' class it is necessary to record the various design proposals which were given consideration, some of which incorporated technical improvements intended to further enhance the performance of the class.

Inspired by Andre Chapelon's work in France, and in particular his design of the compound 4-6-2's for the Paris-Orleans line, the L.M.S. had continued to study the effects of improved draughting and increasing the temperature of the steam produced by the boiler up to a maximum of 750 degrees F., instead of the usual 600-620 degrees F. In 1938 the design team evolved a boiler for a proposed compound Pacific locomotive incorporating a combination of the French 'Houlet' superheater elements and thermic syphons in the firebox in order to boost the evaporative ability of the boiler. Inside high pressure and outside low pressure cylinders were part of the proposals, as well as oscillating cam poppet-valves and a 'Kylchap' double blast-pipe. The boiler was to be larger than that of the 'Coronation' type, and some detailed design calculations were done.

Stanier himself visited the Derby Locomotive Drawing Office on 5th November, 1941 to discuss the designs for this 4-6-2 compound engine, the main subjects raised being the use of 15 inch dia. high pressure cylinders and 23 inch dia. low pressure cylinders, giving a ratio of 2.35 to 1, with a stroke of 26 inches. The engine was to be started as a four-cylindered 'simple' using all four cylinders, with an intercepting and reducing valve, controlled from the reversing gear, to feed the low pressure cylinders and thereby equalise the load on all four pistons. In this case the tractive effort produced would be as for a four-cylindered simple engine, and at 85% boiler pressure would be 36,900 lb. By altering the diameter of the high pressure cylinders to 15⅝ inches a figure of 40,000 lbs could be achieved.

The second method considered for starting from rest would be as a simple, by admitting steam to the low pressure cylinder at 80% boiler pressure, no intercepting valve being employed, but with a small starting valve controlled from the reversing gear to admit steam to the low pressure cylinders for starting, with the high pressure cylinders 'floating.' This valve was to be closed as the engine was notched up by means of some pre-determined cut off.

A chart was produced by Arthur Edleston, a Senior Design Draughtsman in the Derby Locomotive Drawing Office, comparing four-cylindered simple and compound locomotives with the 'Coronation' class output of 40,000 lb. The proposed L.M.S. compound 4-6-2, with 15½ inches dia. high pressure cylinders and 23 inch dia. low pressure cylinders and a common stroke of 26 inches, could achieve 40,750 lb of tractive effort using the second method as opposed to 39,400 lb by the first.

An alternative design, reproduced in the 'Railway Gazette' issue dated 31st October, 1941, had high pressure cylinders 17¼ inches dia. and low pressure cylinders 25¼ inches dia., thereby achieving a calculated Tractive Effort. of 49,250 lbs with the second method

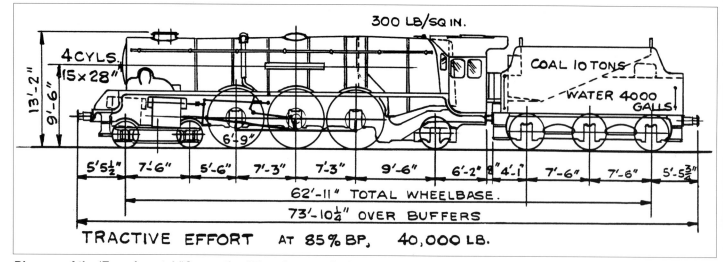

Diagram of the 'Experimental "Coronation" Type Locomotive' two of which had been authorised in 1939 for the 1940 Building Programme but were never actually built (see text). (J.B. Radford Collection)

and 48,750 lb. with the first. Five schemes were looked at in all, but none were proceeded with beyond the comparison chart stage, which also included figures for the 'Coronation' engines, the Paris-Orleans railway compound mentioned above, and the Horwich built compound 4-6-0 engine No. 10456, which incidentally had by then already been cut up in March, 1936. The chart is reproduced in full as Appendix 15.

In his book 'Stanier Pacifics At Work' the late John Powell records that in a letter to him Eric S. Cox described this compound proposal as 'the merest fiction' and continued 'Stanier may have seen it.... but his whole consistent locomotive policy was non-compound. He would never have entertained such a design.....because of doubts about its integrity.'

Be that as it may the chart itself shows that some considerable work had gone into examining the comparisons, for it was also proposed that in fact the basic 'Coronation' boiler could still be used, but working at the higher pressure of 300 lb./sq. in., thereby enabling the cylinder sizes to be reduced, and the compound system devoutly espoused by Chapelon was finally dropped.

The building of two such experimental 'Coronation' type locomotives had in fact been authorised in 1939 as part of the proposed 1940 Locomotive Building Programme. With a 300lb./sq.in. boiler pressure, a steel firebox with a thermic syphon, a higher degree of superheat and the steam circuit re-worked on the Chapelon principle from the regulator right through to the 'Kylchap' double exhaust pipe, the locomotives would otherwise have been identical to the existing locomotives. Four cylinders 15 in. dia. x 28 in. stroke were to be provided, and a diagram of the proposed 'Experimental 'Coronation' Type Locomotive' is reproduced below.

However, although none of the earlier schemes had been devel-

oped further than the preliminary stages, but it is interesting to record that in response to a request for information regarding the latter design Stanier himself had written to Edward H. Livesay in March, 1943 as follows:-

"You ask for some information with regard to the proposed Pacific engine which we have under construction for high pressure boilers. The whole intention with regard to these two engines, which were authorised in 1942, was to build them ready for carrying out a series of tests on the new locomotive testing plant which was in hand to satisfy ourselves as to the best arrangements for certain features. With this in view the cylinders and steam chests were to have liners so that the sizes could be varied; the boilers would have steel fireboxes, one with thermic syphons and the other with circulating arch tubes."

The locomotive testing plant referred to had been authorised in 1936, and was being built at Rugby as a joint project between the L.M.S and the L.N.E railway companies. However, due to the Second World War construction work was halted, and it was not to open until 19th October, 1948 as mentioned in a later chapter.

In an article in 'The Engineer' for 13th September, 1968, Livesay concludes that, from the above, it was evident that work on the two engines was actually begun, but that construction was halted until after the war. However, the locomotives were never in fact completed, but by the end of 1942 and into 1943 opportunities were available to look at the direction in which design might take once World War 2 hostilities were over.

Two larger streamlined Stanier engines of 4-6-4 and 4-8-4 wheel arrangement were looked at again, each with an eight-wheeled tender. The 'Improved Coronation 4-6-4,' as it was called, was intended to be capable of running non-stop from London to Glasgow with a 500 ton train in six hours, compared to the 'Coronation' class load

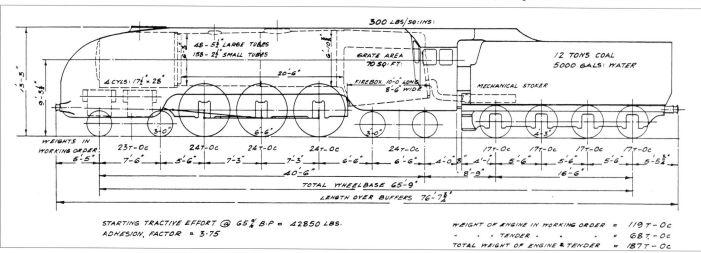

Diagram of the proposed 'Improved "Coronation" 4-6-4 Type Locomotive' with an eight-wheeled tender (see text).
(J.B. Radford Collection)

L.M.S. official photograph No. DY. 35934 of 6256 'Sir William A. Stanier, F.R.S.' as new turned out in Ivatt's 1946 black livery.
(L.M.S. official/ J.B. Radford Collection)

of 300 tons on a timing of six and a half hours. The details are shown on the diagram reproduced here at the bottom of page 30.

In the event, owing to the war these proposals were never taken further, but the last two engines of the class actually constructed, Nos. 6256 and 6257M, did incorporate some design changes and improvements arising from service experience. A number of these were designed to extend the period between shopping for repairs in an effort to try to attain 100,000 operating miles per annum.

Details of these locomotives are as follows:-
Part Lot 184 Unstreamlined, plain black livery:-

No.	Name	Completed
6256	'Sir William A. Stanier, F.R.S.'	13th December, 1947.
6257M	'City of Salford'	February, 1948, but not put into traffic until 19th May, 1948.

The last one built did not therefore enter traffic until after the Nationalisation of the railways on 1st January, 1948, and it therefore bore the number 6257M on the cabside but only 6257 on the smokebox numberplate, the tender being lettered 'BRITISH RAILWAYS.'

The new locomotives were fitted with roller-bearing axleboxes on all axles, those on the crank axle being by 'Skefco' and were separate boxes of the self-aligning grease lubricated type. The remainder of the driving wheel axles had 'Timken' tapered roller bearing split cannon type. Those on the bogie were of the split cannon type, housing the same size of axleboxes as had been used on No. 6202 the 'Turbomotive,' and those on the trailing truck and tender were also individual, and were of a type already used on other tenders. All axleboxes and axlebox guides had manganese steel bearing faces, and the frames below the guides had the clip type closures.

On the main frames, instead of the spliced extension, a two-inch thick semi-bar frame was rivetted on, supporting the rear buffer beam. A pair of support brackets, resting on spherical bearings sliding on top of the pony truck transferred the weight to a new and neater design, with a 'Delta' shaped one-piece cast-steel framing, embracing the pony truck wheels. Side control was effected by helical springs, the details of which were worked out by senior draughtsman Frank Carrier. In the space provided, a rocking grate was fitted, and the boiler was fitted with self-emptying ashpans, a self-cleaning smokebox and a double chimney. In the boiler the top-feed trays were eliminated by a new arrangement of deflector plates in the form of a saddle over the tube bank, which was introduced to allow the sludge carried over with the feed water to fall to the bottom of the barrel, clear of the tubes. The water de-aerating feature was retained, and in addition to blow-off cocks, an improved type of 5P4 superheater elements were introduced.

The self cleaning smokebox was of the 'Master Mechanics' type - This type of design had been seen originally by H.G.Ivatt in the USA and he was so impressed he brought the designs back with him. They were eventually used on all the British Railways Standard Locomotives built (999 in total) and on selected LMS locomotives. A few Class 5 Mixed traffic locomotives and six Princess Coronation Class were eventually fitted. Nos. 6256 and 6257M are the only two believed fitted from new.

The reason for fitting was principally a labour saving device with the smokeboxes only needing to be cleaned out on Boiler Inspection days. With the restoration of No. 6233 in 1999/2000 by The Princess Royal Class Locomotive Trust, a Master Mechanics smokebox self-cleaning apparatus has been fitted. In this case the need is principally for the containment of spark emissions, but does give the advantage of labour reduction in cleaning out the smokebox.

Other features included a new design of reversing screw, the bracket of which was mounted on the main frame near the reversing shaft, the screw being operated by a rotating shaft operated by a hand wheel in the cab. The cut-off indicator was on a revolving drum in front of the driver, a design feature later adopted for several of the British Railways series of Standard steam locomotives.

The motion was fitted with oil-lubricated steel bushes and case-hardened motion pins, and 'Skefco' roller bearings were fitted to the return cranks.

The tenders were of the standard 4,000 gallon type, with space for 10 tons of coal, although at the initial; design stages a diagram was produced showing the engine attached to a 5,000 gallon tender with space for 12 tons of coal and a coal pusher, thereby giving a longer range before the fuel ran out. In this case the tender wheelbase would have been 5ft 6in. between each wheelset, which had an axle load of 16 tons 5 cwt., totalling 65 tons in all. In that

L.M.S. official photograph No. DY. 38661 showing a detailed view of the rear end of 6256 with the 'delta' framed pony truck, modified cab and other detailed changes. *(L.M.S. official/ J.B. Radford Collection)*

case the overall length of the locomotive would have been increased to 76ft 0¾ in. all. As a matter of interest, during the recent general repair of 'DUCHESS OF SUTHERLAND' the opportunity was taken to modify the tender to increase the capacity of her tender to 5,000 gallons which affords better operating flexibility on today's railway which is of course now devoid of water troughs.

A new Engine Diagram No.278 was produced for these two locomotives as built. (opposite).

These new aspects of their design were down to Henry George Ivatt, the last C.M.E. of the L.M.S., and the son of H.A. Ivatt of Great Northern Railway fame. He had succeeded Charles Edward Fairburn, M.A., Stanier's deputy, on 1st February, 1946 following the latter's sudden death on 12th October, 1945. Upon Stanier's appointment as Scientific Adviser to the Ministry of Production in 1942 Fairburn had become Acting C.M.E., succeeding Stanier as C.M.E. on his retirement early in 1944.

The official description of these two locomotives states:-

"In order to obtain comparative data on the most modern developments in motive power, the L.M.S. has just completed Engine No. 6256 at Crewe Works, the first of two steam locomotives intended to compete with the 3,200 h.p. Double-Unit Diesel Electric locomotives shortly to be put into service on the Euston-Glasgow main line."

These, the first two main line diesel locomotives ever to run in Britain, were given the Nos. 10000 & 10001 and were designed in the Locomotive Drawing Office at Derby in conjunction with the English Electric Company, under Ivatt's overall direction. The outcome of the comparison trials is well documented elsewhere.

William Arthur Stanier had meanwhile become the only other British locomotive engineer, apart from George Stephenson, to be made a Fellow of the Royal Society, this honour being awarded him on 16th March, 1944. He was also further and rightly honoured by the naming of the new locomotive No. 6256 after him at a ceremony at Euston station in London on 17th December, 1947. After leaving the L.M.S. Sir William was to continue working elsewhere on engineering matters for a number of years, and died on 27th September, 1965 at the age of 89.

The last of the class, No. 6257M, was named 'CITY OF SALFORD' at Manchester Exchange station on 3rd June, 1948 by Alderman J. Brentnall, the then Mayor.

With regard to these last two 'Coronation' class locomotives, Eric Langridge interestingly recalled in correspondence:-

"The last two 'Coronations' were turned out with roller bearings and were to be costed against the 10000 and 10001 diesels. They were all right until H.G. Ivatt retired. The advent of an L.N.E.R. man in Harrison more or less spelt doom for L.M.S. ideas. He hated the 'Coronations' - said the repair figures were untrue, and thought there was nothing like a Gresley Pacific.... However, he calmed down a bit in due course and delighted in pulling my leg & discussing four v. three cylinders."

"When 'PRINCESS ANNE' (the rebuilt 'Turbomotive') got smashed up he had his chance, but I had to point out to him that if you want a Gresley engine you have to have his valve gear: Thompson had to have that elongated thing (he borrowed L.M.S. drawings for the job!) or Peppercorn had to come towards 'Coronation' style. So in the end it had Caprotti, the only then solution. He liked the 'Coronation' boiler strange to say. But the finished loco. the 'Duke' (B.R. Standard steam locomotive No. 71000 'Duke of Gloucester') didn't get a good name. What J.F.H. (Harrison) liked was to have the Gresley Pacifics working the Leeds-Carlisle jobs."

It is well recorded that this locomotive, 71000, was subsequently rescued by enthusiasts as a rusting hulk from Woodhams' Barry scrapyard after withdrawal, and has since been restored to full working order. One original outside set of Caprotti set of valve gear equipment from this locomotive had already been removed for display in the Science Museum in London before the locomotive was moved to the scrap yard, and this had to be replaced during the restoration process.

As to No. 6202 'Turbomotive,' mentioned above, after several mechanical failures, she was withdrawn in March, 1950 and permission given for her to be rebuilt as a conventional locomotive. Her boiler was overhauled, and by judicious use of existing material, the cost of conversion was kept to a modest £8,875. The original roller bearings were retained and the Derby Drawing Office produced a new essentially 'Coronation' front-end hybrid design, which overcame the weaknesses of the cylinder and inside valve gear arrangement. Permission was obtained to name the locomotive 'Princess Anne' after the daughter of Her Majesty Queen Elizabeth II and H.R.H. Prince Philip, Duke of Edinburgh, and the locomotive emerged from Crewe Works on 13th August, 1952.

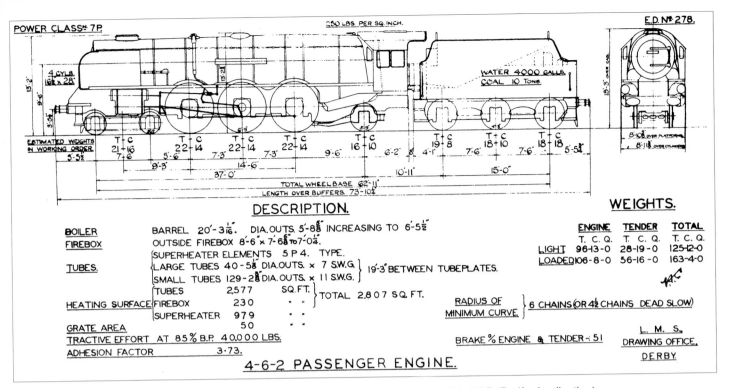

B.R. official diagram E.D. No. 278 produced for 46256 & 46257 as built. (B.R. official/ J.B. Radford collection)

On 28th August she returned to traffic on her old diagram, regularly working the 8.00 a.m. express from Euston to Liverpool, returning with the 5.25 p.m. 'Red Rose'

Tragically, only eight weeks later she was severely damaged on 8th October in the Harrow and Wealdstone disaster, having recorded only 11,443 service miles. Although another 'Coronation' class Pacific No. 46242 'CITY OF GLASGOW,' which was also badly damaged, was repaired, 46202 was more seriously damaged, and languished at Crewe for a considerable time before officially being withdrawn from traffic during the week ending 22nd May, 1954 and cut up for scrap.

The ill-fated 46202 'Princess Anne' rebuilt in 1952 from Stanier's 'Turbomotive' engine of 1935 with a hybrid 'Princess Coronation' front end design. (Photographer unknown/J.B. Radford Collection)

A brand new 6233 Duchess of Sutherland stands resplendent in her red LMS livery in July 1938 at Shrewsbury obviously on a running in turn from Crewe.
Courtesy National Railway Museum

34

Chapter Three

At Work for the L.M.S.

No. 6233 'DUCHESS OF SUTHERLAND,' was completed on Monday, 18th July, 1938 and then given a 'running in' turn between Crewe and Shrewsbury, as was the norm with newly built locomotives at Crewe. Upon satisfactory completion of this she was initially allocated (as in fact was the case with all other members of the class up to No. 6234 when new with the sole exception of No.6229) to the Camden motive power depot in London on 23rd July, 1938. The streamlined members of the class were principally working the `Coronation Scot' train, whereas for No. 6233 and the others of her batch their work was to haul other principal expresses. These were the 10.00 a.m. 'Royal Scot' restaurant car express with through coaches to both Glasgow and Edinburgh, the 2.00p.m. 'Midday

Scot' over the same route, the Edinburgh portion of which also included through coaches to Aberdeen, plus the reverse workings in the 'up' direction of course. The batch also worked beyond Glasgow as far as Perth, where No. 6233 was recorded on a working in 1939.

The earliest record of a run behind No. 6233 'DUCHESS OF SUTHERLAND' that we have located has been kindly loaned to the authors by G.A.M. Wood from his collection, and was recorded by Major A.P. le M. Sinkinson on 12th November, 1938 when No. 6233 worked the down 'Royal Scot' train with a load of 12 bogies equal to 375/400 tons. Major Sinkinson recorded many logs of timings, and recorded No. 6233 between Euston and Crewe, where he left the train, as his Run No. 113.

12th November 1938 (Saturday)
No. 6233 'DUCHESS OF SUTHERLAND'
Euston to Crewe on 'THE ROYAL SCOT'   Load 12   375 Tons tare   400 Tons gross

Distance	Station or mile post	Schedule	Actual minutes/ seconds	Speeds	Max/Min	Remarks
0	Euston	0	0			
1	1		3 57			
5	5		9 35			
5.4	Willesden	9	10 02	57.7	60/59	- 1'-2"
8	8		12 42	}		
10	10		14 44	59.1 }		
11.4	Harrow		16 07			
13	13		17 50	58.1	57	
15	15		19 55	57.6		
16	16		20 53	62.1	62	
17	17		21 48	65.4		
17.5	Watford	21	22 12		69	Watford – Rugby, 65.1 miles
18	18		22 40	69.2		in 57' 42" = 67.7 m.p.h.
20	20		24 31	64.9		
21	21		25 29	62.1		
24.5	Hemel Hempsted		28 55	61.1	60	
28	28		32 30	58.6		
30	30		34 30	60.0	58/61	
31	31		35 29	61.1		- 1' 4"
31.7	Tring	35	36 04			Tring – Bletchley in 12' 43"
32	32		36 28	61.1		
36	36		39 54	69.9	72/70/69	
40	40		43 20	69.9		Tring – Rugby, 50.9 miles
40.2	Leighton		43 32 }		75	in 43' 50" = 69.6 m.p.h.
46	46		48 18	72.5		- 1' 47"
46.7	Bletchley	47	48 47			Bletchley - Rugby
47	47		49 06	75.0 }		
52	52		53 00	76.9 }	79	35.9 miles in 31' 7" = 69.0
52.5	Wolverton		53 22			
53	53		53 46	78.8	79	
54	54		54 33	76.6		
55	55		55 20	76.6		
56	56		56 08	75.0		
57	57		56 59	70.3		
58	58		57 50	70.3	68	
59	59		58 43	67.9		
59.9	Roade	58	59 27		69	-1' 47"
60	60		59 35	69.2		

Distance	Station or mile post	Schedule	Actual minutes/ seconds	Speeds	Max/Min	Remarks
61	61		60 29	66.7	66 1/2	
62.8	Blisworth	61	62 00 }			- 1' 00'
69.5	Weedon		67 35 }	75.2		
70	70		67 52 }			
73	73		70 30	68.3		
74	74		71 25	65.4	65	
75	75		72 18	67.9	68/69	
75.2	Welton		72 31			
76	76		73 10 }	69.2		
	Kilsby		73 52 }			
	Kilsby Tunnel		75 00 }			
79	79		75 43 }	70.5 }		
80	80		76 31	75.0 }	75	
82	82		78 32	59.9		excellent example
82.6	Rugby	80	79 54		+ 6"	of perfect time-keeping
	stop	3 min	3 13		-13"	although liberties were taken
0	Rugby	0	0			with passing times.
1.1	83 3/4		3 03 }			
4.4	87		6 59 }	49.9		
5.4	88 (Brinklow)		8 00	59.1	62	
9.4	92		11 56	61.0		
10.4	93		12 55	61.0		
	Bulkington		13 23			
11.4	94		13 52	63.2		
14.5	Nuneaton	16	16 25	75		-0' 25"
15.4	98		17 13	71.6		
17.4	100		18 56	69.9	62	eased
19.8	Atherstone		21 12 }			
23.9	Polesworth		25 00 }			
24.4	107		25 28 }	65.9	71	-0' 3"
27.4	(110) Tamworth	28	28 03 }	69.0	71	Hademore
33.6	Lichfield	33	33 27 }		63	-0' 27"
38.5	Armitage		37 51 }			
41.6	Rugeley	40	40 25 }	68.9	77/75	-0' 25"
44.6	Colwich		42 40	78		
46.9	Milford and Brocton		44 35	76.3		23 miles in 19' 44"
47.4	130		45 00			= 70 m.p.h.
48.4	131		45 50	72.0	72	
49.4	132		46 40	72.0		brakes very fast on
50.4	133		47 47	53.7		undulating line
51.0	Stafford	49	48 42 }		36	+ 0' 18" beyond Rugby
56.3	Norton Bridge	55	55 07 }	48.3		- 0' 7"
58.4	141		57 10	61.4		
63.4	146		61 53	63.6	62/64	
65.0	Whitmore	64	63 20 }			+ 0' 40"
65.4	148		63 45 }	64.3	64/62	eased after summit
67.4	Madeley		65 40	62.1		eased
70.8	Betley Road		68 25	73.3	70/72/75	
74.4	157 (Basford Wood)		72 20	55.1 (sigs)	10	Slip, severe
75.5	Crewe	75	75 55			- 55" {+ 30"}

The timings show that 'DUCHESS OF SUTHERLAND' was fully able to cope with the task, providing an excellent example of perfect time-keeping, and she would apparently have arrived on schedule with her train but for the severe slip after the signal check on the approaches to Crewe. This problem with the locomotives of this class is discussed later on in this chapter.

THE 'CORONATION SCOT' ON THE NORTH AMERICAN TOUR.

The only exception to the aforementioned first allocation of engines to Camden motive power depot was No. 6229, which was initially allocated to Crewe North. This locomotive exchanged identities with No. 6220 for the tour of North America, in association with the New York World's Fair, that was to keep it in the U.S.A until 1942. On 30th November, 1938, No 6229 arrived in Glasgow painted in grey livery hauling the 'Coronation Scot' train, returning southwards the same day. She was back in the Crewe Works Erecting Shop where she was seen on 15th January, 1939 turned out in the crimson lake livery with gold leaf numbering, lettering and lining but all greased up and ready for her Trans-Atlantic trip. Now in the guise of No. 6220 'CORONATION,' she was worked up to Euston on 17th January and, after the whole exhibition train had been towed over the Southern Railway to Southampton by two locomotives, all were loaded on the Norwegian Christian-Smith Line ship the S.S. 'Belpamela' on 20th January 1939.

A red liveried 6229 'Duchess of Hamilton' renumbered and named 'Coronation' at South Kenton on her way from Crewe to London (Euston) with the American tour train on 17 January 1939, prior to being towed to Southampton.
(J.B. Radford Collection)

After a six-day delay due to rough seas, the train was unloaded on the quayside at Baltimore. Robert A. Riddles, then Mechanical & Electrical Engineer- Scotland, and in charge of the tour, having travelled across the Atlantic by liner, supervised the unloading and marshalling. The train was moved to the Baltimore & Ohio Railway workshops at Mount Clare. Here parts removed for the crossing were re-assembled and final preparations for the tour made. The train was put on display at a special viewing on 17th March before setting off with a press run the following day at the start of its 3,120 mile tour.

The tour has been well documented elsewhere, but in the event, due to the outbreak of the Second World War, it was to be 16th February, 1942 before the locomotive 'CORONATION' and its train arrived back in Cardiff docks. No. 6229, still in the guise of No. 6220 was then moved to Crewe, the nameplates were taken off and re-fitted to the correct locomotive and cabside numbers re-painted back. 'DUCHESS OF HAMILTON' survives today in the National Railway

Museum at York in her later un-streamlined form, in the interim having been saved, following her final withdrawal by British Railways, by Sir Billy Butlin for display at the Butlins holiday camp at Minehead.

For the USA tour Driver Fred Bishop and Fireman John Carswell were the chosen footplate crew, and Crewe Works Foreman F.W. Soden travelled as the mechanical assistant. Bishop christened him, the 'master mechanic,' in his personal and fascinating account of the tour in his book 'Queen Mary of the Iron Road' published by Jarrolds of London in 1946, which is highly recommended reading, giving, as it does, a real flavour of those times.

Apart from details of the special tour referred to above, Driver Bishop recounts his career with the L.M.S., and gives a most interesting description of a top link drivers' experiences with crack expresses like the 'Royal Scot' and the 'Coronation Scot,' writing as follows:-

"With a train like the 'Royal Scot' we have always a big 'gallery' at the London terminus. No sooner has the engine backed in than scores of old and young people gather around the footplate. There is a tendency on the part of some engine crews to be 'too busy' to talk to the public and I must admit, crowds can be overwhelming at times, but I have always made it a point, so far as I was able, of having a talk with the 'fans' and signing their autograph books when requested."

"Naturally enough, too, drivers are asked a lot of question by the gallery. Some people, judging by the questions they ask, seem to think that, in addition to driving the engine, the driver actually built it. Just think of that for a moment. You may be able to drive your car quite efficiently, but there are lots of technical questions about its construction you might not be able to answer. That, briefly, is the position of the engine driver. I usually delegated my fireman the job of answering questions and he acquitted himself nobly. One smart boy asked him the weight of the engine and tender. The fireman gave him a figure in

6229 (6220 'Coronation') stands at Hartford, Connecticut on 14 April 1939 with the 'Coronation Scot' North American tour train complete with the American regulatory headlight and bell. (J.B. Radford Collection)

round tons. Piped up the boy "And what?" He was referring to the odd hundredweights, which my fireman had purposely omitted. A cheeky boy but a smart 'un.'"

"Most people who come to look over locomotives are very friendly. Among our most frequent visitors for some reason or another are bishops and politicians. Ironically enough drivers get the biggest number of admirers after there has been a mishap - not necessarily on their own system. Such people, both men and women, sympathise with the drivers' responsibilities. My own reply to such well-wishers is that I am not afraid of my responsibilities, and that I, along with all other drivers, accept them as part and parcel of any big-time job."

"Some older fans are, in public life, clergymen, doctors, bank clerks and even farmers. They spend much of their leisure time travelling on trains. The majority are interested in engine performance. They note the engine crew,

Driver Fred Bishop and Fireman John Carswell on the footplate of 6220 'Coronation'. (Courtesy Jarrolds Ltd., London)

the number and type of locomotive and the tonnage of the train. They then get into a corner seat in some compartment on the side the mile-posts are to be seen, take out their stop watches, and then begin to time the speed of the train. At the end of the journey they come along to the engine crew and congratulate or commiserate with us as the case may be on a good or bad journey. They also tell the driver what kind of performance they have recorded on a similar type of engine."

"Crack expresses like the 'Royal Scot' are worked by what is known as a 'special link.' This consists of three drivers and three firemen. They take the trains between Euston and Carlisle and vice-versa. This will probably surprise many who imagine that one man - one man only - works the train from the starting point to the ultimate destination. Such a man, if he did exist, would need to be a superman. In fact he would not be driving for too long, for his services, I feel sure, would be greatly in demand as a physical training instructor - if he had any breath left in him."

'What happens is this: one hundred and forty miles is considered a working day for the engine crew and every fifteen miles above that is reckoned as an hour. Consequently, two round trips by members of this "special link" constitutes a working week. This leaves the crew with two clear rest days ahead which, I can honestly say, they need if they are to be fit and fresh for the job. Personally I like the work, but there are some drivers who dislike the strain of such long runs."

"When I am driving the 'Royal Scot' - and the same goes for the 'Coronation Scot' - I always get up at six o'clock in the morning. I have done this for years and the habit has grown on me. I like plenty of time to get myself dressed and the engine prepared. For more than thirty years I have done physical jerks in the morning. Now I would not miss them for anything. And I would like to mention in passing that I started them long before such things were considered fashionable, or the B.B.C. began to play musical accompaniments. These few simple exercises, performed directly after getting out of bed, have done me a tremendous amount of good. The outcome is that I feel half my age. The way I look at it is this: If a piece of mechanism requires care and attention for it to run properly, then the much more delicate machinery of the human body requires similar attention as well."

"Breakfast over I get ready to go to the engine sheds. Before leaving the house I make certain that my basket has been packed. I expect you have often seen these baskets, which are much the same as 'Mother's' only they have a lid on top. As we are to be away for two whole days, it means we have to take provisions to cover this

period. That isn't too difficult in the winter - although the war-time rationing makes it a problem at the best of times. In hot weather however, it is not such a simple matter. There isn't such a thing as a 'frig' (sic -fridge) on the engine and we have to select food that will be none the worse for the travelling in a constantly hot temperature."

"Strange as it may seem however, there is little time for eating on a long journey - not if you are the driver. I usually content myself with drinking a flask of hot coffee. Some drivers drink tea; others will be quite happy munching on a bar of chocolate. Alcohol of any description is strictly forbidden on the footplate or on railway premises, except for the passengers. Not until I reach my destination do I enjoy a proper meal. Then I make my way with my fireman to the enginemen's hostel, known to us as the "Barracks," where we are accommodated for the night. We sign the book just like any visitor at a luxury hotel. But there the similarity ceases."

"We have to get our own meal ready, so my fireman and I get busy. We cook meat (if we are lucky enough to have any left over from our weekly rations), peel and boil the potatoes and even go to the extent of making a milk pudding. I don't think we can be accused of being pampered. I might add this is not a wartime measure. We do it in peacetime as well. The journey usually gives us a good appetite and the fact that we have cooked a meal ourselves is like adding sauce to the dish. Then comes the wash and brush-up; the dirty begrimed men of the footplate are respectable citizens again - indistinguishable from the madding crowd."

"During the run of the 'Coronation Scot' from London to Carlisle the fireman has to handle about six tons of coal, as much in one six and a half hour journey as the average household consumes in a year. In addition it is his job to pick up water which, on the same run, the engine does no fewer than nine times. What a thirst these giant locomotives have....Why at each drinking place they think nothing of sending back 1,500 gallons at a crack."

"So you see that the fireman on a train like the 'Coronation Scot' is a pretty busy man. On this particular run he is fully occupied until about 37 miles south of Carlisle when he has usually got sufficient steam to carry him through to the border town. Even then he doesn't sit back and take things easy, but clears up and makes things tidy for the fresh crew who come on at Carlisle. They take the 'flyer' through to Glasgow."

The above extracts give a quite fascinating and detailed insight into the life of a top link engine driver working for the L.M.S, and Bishop's particular approach to his job. Driver Fred Bishop died at home on 29th September, 1944 aged 63.

THE PRESTIGE EXPRESS TRAINS.

The 'Royal Scot' express, mentioned by Bishop in the preceeding section, called for excellent enginemanship, for it ran non-stop to Carlisle where it was timed to arrive at 3.00 p.m., and was booked to arrive in Glasgow Central station at 5.00 p.m. and the other portion at Edinburgh at 5.05 p.m. In the return direction departure from both Glasgow and Edinburgh was at 10.00 a.m., but in this case the trains were worked separately, arriving in London Euston at 5.00 p.m. and 5.15 p.m. respectively. The train from Edinburgh, which had through coaches from Aberdeen and Dundee attached, called at Carlisle and departed from there at 12.15 p.m.

By 1939 the 'Royal Scot' was being regularly worked by the 'Princess Coronation' class, Nos. 6225-8, 6230 and 6233 herself all being reported in the Stephenson Locomotive Society Journal as hauling the prestige train in the spring of that year. She was photographed with that train passing Camden in September, 1938 and also south of Crewe that same year. 'The Railway Observer,' recorded that between November, 1938 and mid May, 1939 the non-streamlined members of the class had been in charge of the 'Royal Scot' train as follows:-

        6230 - 17 times
        6231 - 6 times
        6232 - 6 times
        6233 - 17 times
        6234 - 5 times.   (Total 51).

On occasions the streamlined stock of the 'Coronation Scot' was utilised for this train, particularly on Saturdays, but hauled by the non-streamlined members of the class as mentioned above.

Of the streamlined members of the class, Nos. 6221-4 and 6220 (actually still No. 6229 of course) had not been rostered to work that train, but had been reserved for working the actual 'Coronation Scot' service, the others being used as follows:-

        6225 - 35 times
        6226 - 30 times
        6227 - 30 times
        6228 - 22 times   (Total 117.)

Camden continued to be the first allocated depot for all of the class up until the emergence in April, 1944 of the unstreamlined No. 6249 'CITY OF SHEFFIELD', with the exception of Nos. 6235, 6238, 6240 and 6241 which went to Crewe North.

With the arrival of the 'Princess Coronations' the 'Princess Royal' class, with the exception of No. 6202, were gradually moved away from Camden, sometimes initially just briefly but eventually permanently, to such depots as Longsight in Manchester, Edge Hill in Liverpool and Crewe North where they were called upon to undertake new duties.

The 'Mid-day Scot' restaurant car express to Edinburgh left London Euston at 2.00 p.m., on weekdays, arrived at Crewe at 4.45 p.m., Preston at 6.00 p.m. and Carlisle at 7.44 p.m., with an arrival time in Edinburgh of 9.45 p.m. In the opposite direction, with a departure time of 1.40 p.m., Carlisle was left at 3.52 p.m. and Crewe at 6.49 p.m., with arrival in Euston at 9.30 p.m. The Saturday's only service was to a slightly different schedule.

This train had theoretically ceased to serve Glasgow with the inauguration of the 'Coronation Scot' in July, 1937, although it nevertheless had coaches for Glasgow to serve intermediate stations. The Glasgow portion, comprising of from four to six coaches and hauled by a Pacific, left five minutes after the 'Coronation Scot' joined the 10.05 a.m. express from Aberdeen, a four car restaurant set, at Law Junction, and finally linked up with the Edinburgh train at Symington.

The usual load for the 2.00 p.m. 'down' 'Mid-Day Scot' train from Euston to Glasgow in 1938 would be an Edinburgh portion com-

A red liveried 6225 'Duchess of Gloucester' storms through Bushey with the down 'Royal Scot' express circa 1938. Note the winged embellishment on the lamps carried by the streamlined 'Princess Coronation' class pacifics. (J.B. Radford Collection)

After having been in service two months, 6233 'Duchess of Sutherland' has charge of the down Royal Scot in September 1938 and is seen passing Camden near to the summit of the short but steep climb out of Euston. (E. Woods)

Making light work of the 1 in 175 gradient, 'Duchess of Sutherland' heads a remarkably light up 'Mid-Day Scot' at Calthwaite near Penrith in 1939. (E.E. Smith)

'Duchess of Sutherland' powers the 13 coach down Royal Scot past a bleak Shap Wells circa 1938/9. The 5 1/2 mile climb, mainly at 1 in 75, from Tebay to Shap summit was one of the factors in the introduction of the 'Princess Royal' and 'Princess Coronation' class pacifics. (Eric Treacy)

prising a 24 seat brake corridor third, a 30 seat semi-open first, a 30 seat restaurant third, a 42 seat open third, a 24 seat corridor brake third, and a Glasgow portion comprising an 18/24 seat corridor composite and a 24 seat corridor brake third. Attached at Crewe would be a through GWR corridor brake composite from Plymouth, and on Mondays and Fridays only, a 64 seat corridor third. Attached at Wigan would be the Manchester - Edinburgh through corridor brake composite coach and the Manchester-Glasgow portion (both ex Manchester 4.45 p.m.) comprising a 18/24 seat composite and a 24 corridor third, whilst the Liverpool-Glasgow portion, comprising an 18/24 seat composite and a 24 seat corridor third would be attached at Lancaster having left Liverpool at 5.00 p.m.

In 1938-9 'DUCHESS OF SUTHERLAND' was photographed climbing the bank near Calthwaite after leaving Carlisle with the up 'Mid-Day Scot', the load being two vans and nine coaches, which would present a lighter load than normal, the usual loads being up to fourteen or fifteen bogies.

During 1938 the Stanier Pacifics also began working through to Aberdeen. From Carlisle they worked the 10.50 p.m. from London Euston, returning with the 1.55 p.m. fish train for Broad Street, London as far as Crewe. The Camden based Pacifics were also working the up 'Postal' from Glasgow Central throughout, a train formerly taken forward from Preston by a 'Royal Scot' class 4-6-0 based there for the purpose.

Expresses from London Euston to Liverpool Lime Street were now also being worked by the new engines, and their duties from Liverpool included the working of the 10.10 a.m. 'Merseyside Express', a working on which 'DUCHESS OF SUTHERLAND' was photographed in September, 1939. They were also to be seen on expresses to Glasgow Central from the Liverpool terminus. 'DUCHESS OF SUTHERLAND' was photographed about that time on a working passing Acton Bridge at the head of what is thought to be a Glasgow - Euston express with a through GWR coach behind the tender.

Elsewhere the new Pacifics were in use on some trains from Euston to Manchester and back, and during the week ending 22nd July, 1939 they were used systematically to work the up 'Mancunian' at 9.45 a.m. and also on the down 'Lancastrian' leaving Euston at 6.00 p.m. However the Pacifics had to be turned at London Road station because at Longsight motive power depot, where they were serviced, there was no turntable long enough to accommodate them.

The range of Stanier's design work is clearly shown in this view taken at Rugby in 1939 as 'Duchess of Sutherland' heads a West Coast main line express whilst passing an unidentified Stanier class 4 tank, a type employed on local passenger train work. (Robert Humm Collection)

'Duchess of Sutherland' stands behind a streamlined 'Princess Coronation' class tender on Crewe North's electric turntable. When she entered service in 1938 she was fitted with a British Thomson-Houston (BTH) speed indicator but by 1941 an instruction had been given that these should be removed. However the supporting bracket can still be clearly seen by the rear driving wheel. (W. Whitworth Collection courtesy the National Railway Museum)

6226 'Duchess of Norfolk' nearing the end of an overnight journey from Scotland to London Euston as she passes Headstone Lane with the former London & North Western Railway's Royal Train on 2nd July, 1938. (C.R.L. Coles)

TESTS WITH NO. 6234 'DUCHESS OF ABERCORN.'

The performances turned in by these new locomotives was clearly of great interest, and important tests were carried out with No. 6234, now six months old, which had run some 50,107 miles since new, and 20,733 miles since a piston and valve examination. On 12th February, 1939, hauling an empty 20 coach train of some 604 tons, which included the ex L. & Y. No. 1 Dynamometer Car No. 45050, she made Test Run No. 811. Leaving Crewe at 8.10 a.m. and heading for Glasgow the train ran on 'Special Limit' timings equivalent to an overall London - Glasgow schedule of 7 hours. This showed up some problems with poor steaming, and resulted in the fitting of a twin blast pipe and chimney arrangement to try to improve sustainable power output.

Repeat return trip tests were made with the same locomotive, now fitted with a double blastpipe and chimney, and train on 26th February, 1939. Despite some operational problems during the first run, which had included a special stop at Symington for water, much better performances were achieved. Driver G. Garrett of Crewe North depot was at the controls from Crewe, and Driver J. Marshall of Polmadie depot in Glasgow took over at Carlisle. Firemen S. Farringdon of Crewe North, and D. Lynn of Polmadie, kept up a good head of steam throughout. On the return trip in the hands of Driver N. McLean and Fireman A Smith of Polmadie, the train reached Carlisle no less than 9½ minutes ahead of schedule, and had to wait for the clear road to proceed. Garrett and Farringdon took over again from Carlisle southwards.

For the outward of the two special runs, Run No. 812, No. 6234 left Crewe at 8.10 a.m. for Glasgow, starting back from there at 2.45

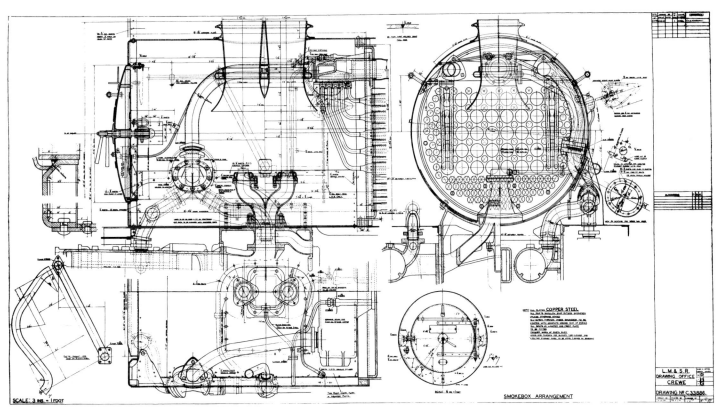

L.M.S. official Crewe drawing C.33886 'Smokebox Arrangement' showing the new double-chimney arrangement fitted to 6234 and subsequently to the rest of the class. (J.B. Radford Collection)

6234 'Duchess of Abercorn' arrives at Glasgow Central station with the No. 1 Dynamometer Car behind the tender after the test run on 26th February, 1939. (R.M. Tomkins Collection)

p.m, a distance of 487 miles, with only a two hour break in Glasgow. The train climbed both Shap and Beattock banks un-assisted with a minimum recorded speed of 30 m.p.h.. Coming south with Run No. 812A, the final two mile slog up the 1 in 99 incline to Beattock Summit, the culmination of a 23 mile rise from Carstairs, was covered at a steady 63 m.p.h.; the drawbar h.p. on this section reaching 2282 and the i.h.p an estimated 3333. These values were to be exceeded an hour later when accelerating away from Carlisle up the 3½ mile incline of 1 in 131 to Wreay, a speed of 42 m.p.h. being attained, an output of around 2511 max d.b.h.p. was recorded corresponding to a max. i.h.p. of 3348.

End to end running times were equal to speeds of between 55 and 58 m.p.h. over the different sections,

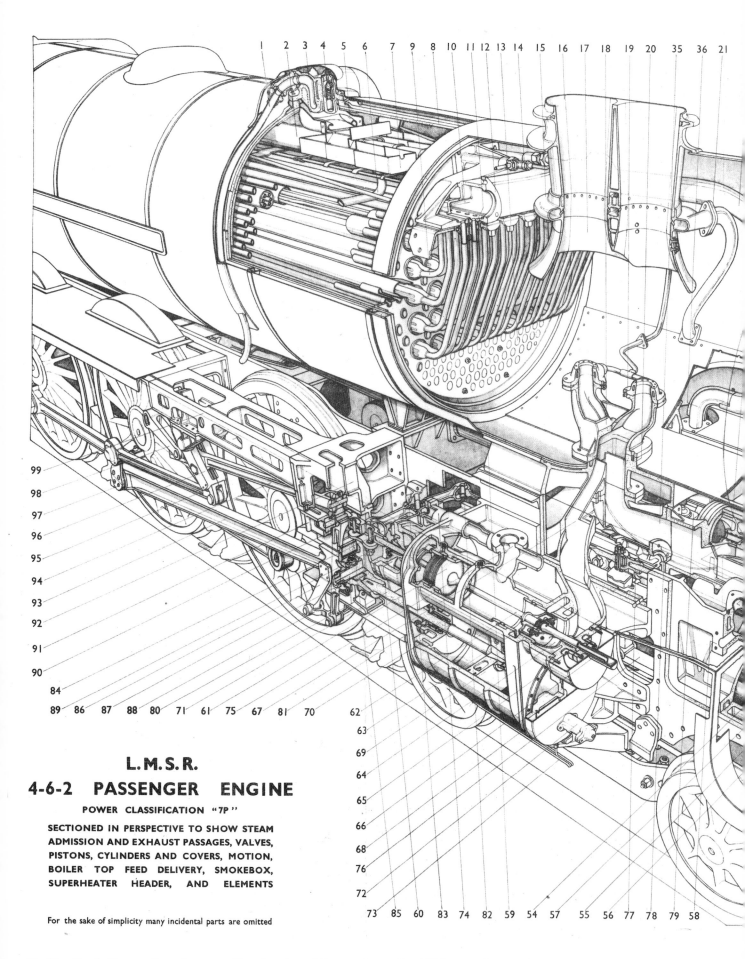

1 2 3 4 5 6 7 8 9 8 10 11 12 13 14 15 16 17 18 19 20 35 36 21

99
98
97
96
95
94
93
92
91
90
84
89 86 87 88 80 71 61 75 67 81 70 62
63
69
64
65
66
68
76
72
73 85 60 83 74 82 59 54 57 55 56 77 78 79 58

L.M.S.R.
4-6-2 PASSENGER ENGINE

POWER CLASSIFICATION "7P"

SECTIONED IN PERSPECTIVE TO SHOW STEAM
ADMISSION AND EXHAUST PASSAGES, VALVES,
PISTONS, CYLINDERS AND COVERS, MOTION,
BOILER TOP FEED DELIVERY, SMOKEBOX,
SUPERHEATER HEADER, AND ELEMENTS

For the sake of simplicity many incidental parts are omitted

Vic Stockton's fine sectioned perspective drawing of the un-streamlined 'Princess Coronation' class engines as fitted with the do

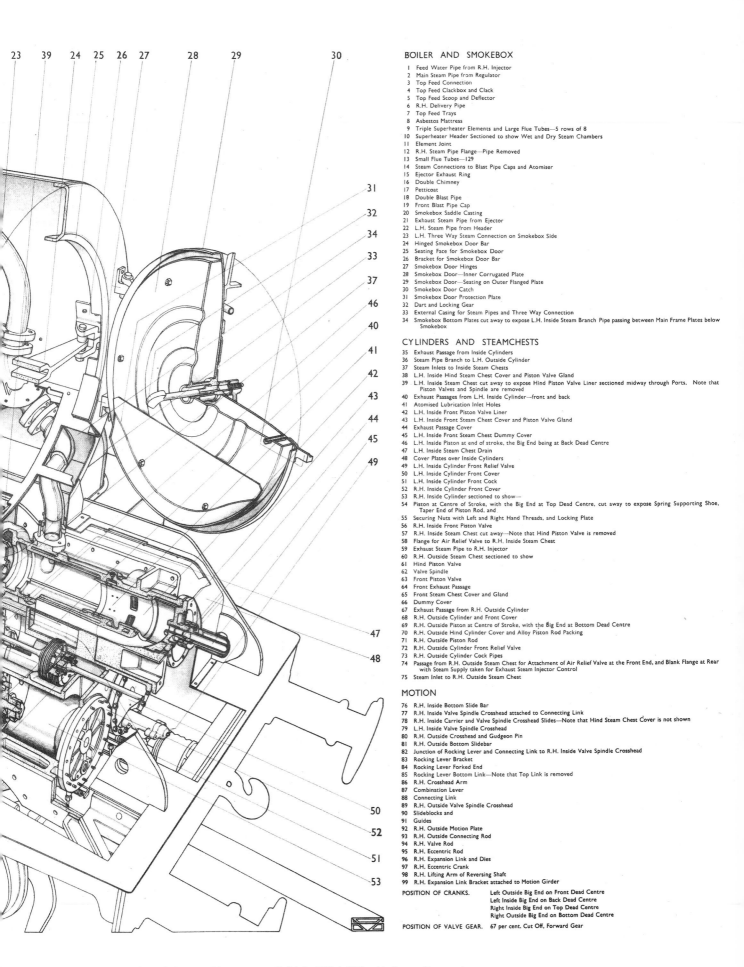

23 39 24 25 26 27   28   29   30

BOILER AND SMOKEBOX

1 Feed Water Pipe from R.H. Injector
2 Main Steam Pipe from Regulator
3 Top Feed Connection
4 Top Feed Clackbox and Clack
5 Top Feed Scoop and Deflector
6 R.H. Delivery Pipe
7 Top Feed Trays
8 Asbestos Mattress
9 Triple Superheater Elements and Large Flue Tubes—5 rows of 8
10 Superheater Header Sectioned to show Wet and Dry Steam Chambers
11 Element Joint
12 R.H. Steam Pipe Flange—Pipe Removed
13 Small Flue Tubes—129
14 Steam Connections to Blast Pipe Caps and Atomiser
15 Ejector Exhaust Ring
16 Double Chimney
17 Petticoat
18 Double Blast Pipe
19 Front Blast Pipe Cap
20 Smokebox Saddle Casting
21 Exhaust Steam Pipe from Ejector
22 L.H. Steam Pipe from Header
23 L.H. Three Way Steam Connection on Smokebox Side
24 Hinged Smokebox Door Bar
25 Seating Face for Smokebox Door
26 Bracket for Smokebox Door Bar
27 Smokebox Door Hinges
28 Smokebox Door—Inner Corrugated Plate
29 Smokebox Door—Seating on Outer Flanged Plate
30 Smokebox Door Catch
31 Smokebox Door Protection Plate
32 Dart and Locking Gear
33 External Casing for Steam Pipes and Three Way Connection
34 Smokebox Bottom Plates cut away to expose L.H. Inside Steam Branch Pipe passing between Main Frame Plates below Smokebox

CYLINDERS AND STEAMCHESTS

35 Exhaust Passage from Inside Cylinders
36 Steam Pipe Branch to L.H. Outside Cylinder
37 Steam Inlets to Inside Steam Chests
38 L.H. Inside Hind Steam Chest Cover and Piston Valve Gland
39 L.H. Inside Steam Chest cut away to expose Hind Piston Valve Liner sectioned midway through Ports. Note that Piston Valves and Spindle are removed
40 Exhaust Passages from L.H. Inside Cylinder—front and back
41 Atomised Lubrication Inlet Holes
42 L.H. Inside Front Piston Valve Liner
43 L.H. Inside Front Steam Chest Cover and Piston Valve Gland
44 Exhaust Passage Cover
45 L.H. Inside Front Steam Chest Dummy Cover
46 L.H. Inside Piston at end of stroke, the Big End being at Back Dead Centre
47 L.H. Inside Steam Chest Drain
48 Cover Plates over Inside Cylinders
49 L.H. Inside Cylinder Front Relief Valve
50 L.H. Inside Cylinder Front Cover
51 L.H. Inside Cylinder Front Cock
52 R.H. Inside Cylinder Front Cover
53 R.H. Inside Cylinder sectioned to show—
54 Piston at Centre of Stroke, with the Big End at Top Dead Centre, cut away to expose Spring Supporting Shoe, Taper End of Piston Rod, and
55 Securing Nuts with Left and Right Hand Threads, and Locking Plate
56 R.H. Inside Front Piston Valve
57 R.H. Inside Steam Chest cut away—Note that Hind Piston Valve is removed
58 Flange for Air Relief Valve to R.H. Inside Steam Chest
59 Exhaust Steam Pipe to R.H. Injector
60 R.H. Outside Steam Chest sectioned to show—
61 Hind Piston Valve
62 Valve Spindle
63 Front Piston Valve
64 Front Exhaust Passage
65 Front Steam Chest Cover and Gland
66 Dummy Cover
67 Exhaust Passage from R.H. Outside Cylinder
68 R.H. Outside Cylinder and Front Cover
69 R.H. Outside Piston at Centre of Stroke, with the Big End at Bottom Dead Centre
70 R.H. Outside Hind Cylinder Cover and Alloy Piston Rod Packing
71 R.H. Outside Piston Rod
72 R.H. Outside Cylinder Front Relief Valve
73 R.H. Outside Cylinder Cock Pipes
74 Passage from R.H. Outside Steam Chest for Attachment of Air Relief Valve at the Front End, and Blank Flange at Rear with Steam Supply taken for Exhaust Steam Injector Control
75 Steam Inlet to R.H. Outside Steam Chest

MOTION

76 R.H. Inside Bottom Slide Bar
77 R.H. Inside Valve Spindle Crosshead attached to Connecting Link
78 R.H. Inside Carrier and Valve Spindle Crosshead Slides—Note that Hind Steam Chest Cover is not shown
79 L.H. Inside Valve Spindle Crosshead
80 R.H. Outside Crosshead and Gudgeon Pin
81 R.H. Outside Bottom Slidebar
82 Junction of Rocking Lever and Connecting Link to R.H. Inside Valve Spindle Crosshead
83 Rocking Lever Bracket
84 Rocking Lever Forked End
85 Rocking Lever Bottom Link—Note that Top Link is removed
86 R.H. Crosshead Arm
87 Combination Lever
88 Connecting Link
89 R.H. Outside Valve Spindle Crosshead
90 Slideblocks and
91 Guides
92 R.H. Outside Motion Plate
93 R.H. Outside Connecting Rod
94 R.H. Valve Rod
95 R.H. Eccentric Rod
96 R.H. Expansion Link and Dies
97 R.H. Eccentric Crank
98 R.H. Lifting Arm of Reversing Shaft
99 R.H. Expansion Link Bracket attached to Motion Girder

POSITION OF CRANKS.   Left Outside Big End on Front Dead Centre
                       Left Inside Big End on Back Dead Centre
                       Right Inside Big End on Top Dead Centre
                       Right Outside Big End on Bottom Dead Centre

POSITION OF VALVE GEAR.   67 per cent. Cut Off, Forward Gear

...imney showing full details of the working parts. (L.M.S. Official/The Railway Gazette)

The fireman of 6233 keeps a watchful eye of the road ahead as 'Duchess of Sutherland' passes Acton Bridge with what is believed to be a Glasgow-Euston Express circa. 1938. The leading G.W.R. through coach would have been detached at Crewe.
(Rail Archive Stephenson)

A relatively new 'Duchess of Sutherland' backs onto the 10.10am Merseyside Express at Liverpool Lime Street station on a date given by the photographer as being either the 2nd or 9th September 1938. Arrival at Euston was at 1.26pm, 4 minutes early. (R. Moss)

The unmistakable outline of Glasgow's Polmadie depot shows behind as 6233 is prepared for a southbound return working. Although several members of the class were allocated to Polmadie, 6233 was allocated to English depot's throughout her career. (J.L. Stevenson)

and coal consumption over the round trip was 68.7 lb./mile, equal to a firing rate of 75.7 lb./sq. ft./hour, average evaporation being 7.58lb. of water /lb. of coal. The full details appeared in due course as Official Test Report No. 80 dated 23rd March, 1939, that analysed the findings in detail. The power output figures calculated during the two performances showed that No.6234 sustained 3,300 i.h.p. for about five minutes, and achieved momentary peak outputs of 3,348 i.h.p. This level of performance has never been equalled by any other class of British locomotive, and therefore the 'Princess Coronations' can justifiably be considered to be the most powerful express locomotive class ever to run in Britain.

As a result of these tests, all members of the class were subsequently fitted with the double blast pipe and chimney at the next General Repair under Job No. 5205 issued on 6th April, 1940. Later members of the Class had the modified design fitted when built. 'DUCHESS OF SUTHERLAND' received the modification during her first heavy general overhaul in Crewe Works, the locomotive being in the works from 5th February to 8th March, 1941. By then No. 6233 had already notched up an impressive 225,944 miles, having already had two visits into Crewe Works for light service repairs in July, 1939 after completing 97,450 miles, and in July, 1940 after accumulating 183,347 miles.

As a matter of record the other engines then running with a single chimney were altered to double chimney and blast pipe form as follows:-

6220	31/12/44	6227	31/12/40
6221	30/11/40	6228	17/9/40
6222	7/8/43	6229	20/4/43
6223	1/11/41	6230	11/10/40
6224	29/5/40	6231	1/6/40
6225	24/6/43	6232	21/1/43
6226	25/7/42	6233	22/3/41

In this form the L.M.S. had produced a fine cut-away perspective drawing made of the front end of the un-streamlined version of the class. (see pages 44 & 45). This was drawn by Victor C. Stockton, an excellent technical draughtsman then working as a Technical Assistant in the Locomotive Drawing Office at Derby, and shows very

clearly the innermost component parts of the locomotive. It was subsequently used as part of an official L.M.S. poster entitled "The L.M.S. In Perspective No. 5" along with the photograph of No 6231 passing Tamworth.

Having completed several of these superb drawings of various L.M.S. engines, and despite verbal promises that he would be promoted, this was denied him, and he was most upset after all of the excellent work that he had put in. He therefore had a small rubber stamp made which he carried in his pocket along with a stamp pad, and whenever he came across a copy of the offending poster on stations or other L.M.S. premises he would overstamp it with the words:- "THIS DRAWING WAS DONE UNDER FALSE PRETENCES."

However the fitting of a double chimney exacerbated the problem of smoke blowing down in front of the driver's vision, as shown in the official photograph of No. 6231 at Tamworth. It eventually brought about the fitting of smoke deflectors either side of the smokebox to create an upward current of air to lift the exhaust well clear of the smokebox, boiler top and cab of the engine. No. 6233 was later to be so fitted during a heavy service at Crewe Works she being in Crewe Works from 3rd to 24th August, 1946, to be mentioned later, the whole class being eventually fitted with one or other of two types.

The design of these smoke deflector plates for the non-streamlined members of the class took into account further work in the wind tunnel at Derby following full scale trials at the National Physical Laboratory by Dr. Johansen, and investigated a large number of devices. The accompanying illustrations from Denis Peacock's Paper No. 506 on the work, presented to the Institution of Locomotive Engineers in 1951, show three practicable solutions that did not involve radical changes to the engine. With the objective of keeping the smoke well above the boiler by promoting a flow of clean air along the boiler sides, they show the effect of a head wind on the flow as built and with three different types of deflector. There was no such problem with the streamlined engines, the smoke flowing smoothly over the top of the boiler.

The first set of official photographs of 'DUCHESS OF SUTHERLAND' were actually taken on 20th April, 1942 at Crewe following a light service repair, and show her still in the original special crimson lake livery, as opposed to the usual shop grey, before the smoke

6231 'Duchess of Abercorn' passing Tamworth at the head of an Aberdeen bound train from London Euston on 21st December, 1939. This photograph clearly illustrates how the exhaust smoke and steam tended to cling to the locomotive and train before the fitting of smoke deflectors. (L.M.S. Official/ J.B. Radford Collection)

deflectors were fitted but with the double chimney. These Derby negatives were numbered as follows:-

DY 28752 Side view,
DY 28753 L.H. side 3/4 view,
DY 28754 L.H. front 3/4 view,
DY 28755 Front view.

An earlier set of photographs taken on 21st June, 1938 had included two, Nos. DY 24027 Side view and DY 24028 R.H. 3/4 view, purporting to be No. 6233 in original condition. In actual fact the whole sequence for the last four non-streamlined locomotives were actually of No. 6231 'DUCHESS OF ATHOLL' sporting the different nameplate and numbers on the side that was photographed only!

That doyen of railway artists, C. Hamilton Ellis, painted No. 6233 in this condition, and, in reproducing the picture as Plate II in his book 'The Splendour Of Steam' published by George Allen and Unwin Ltd. in 1965, waxed lyrical about this form of the 'Princess Coronation' class of locomotives, saying that the painting:-
"....shows what I consider to have been the most handsome of British steam locomotives in their later and most glorious years: Sir William Stanier's second series of Pacific type express engines without their streamlined casing, and painted in that red, though it was not the true Midland red although it was supposed to be, still became the engine very well. Who, as a mere beholder, could resist these superb locomotives, whether one saw them in the smoke-swirling Gehenna at Euston at night, or roaring up the Lune valley in the teeth of a mountain squall, or racing across the smiling shires in sunshine at high noon?"

"Why this engine should be thought so beautiful, it is hard to state in academic terms. But it had mechanical balance, always a lovely thing, and it had balance in the eyes of the artist... That was

The model of the non-streamlined engines used in wind tunnel tests. Top to bottom: the smoke flow as built, with the deflector plates design as eventually fitted, with deflector plates and cross vane, and with the N.P.L. drum type deflector.
(L.M.S. Official, courtesy I. Loc. E.)

the outcome of ...the coincidence of aesthetic and functional beauty... The Stanier Pacific was, to my eye, at its best with a double blast-pipe and corresponding chimney, and so I have painted 'DUCHESS OF SUTHERLAND' thus."

The locomotive was depicted posed on Camden shed alongside an ex L. & N.W.R. eight coupled coal engine.

THE PROBLEM OF SLIPPING.

As the S.L.S. Journal for June, 1939 records, the new 'Princes Coronation' class were on occasions prone to bouts of slipping, as witnessed when No. 6234 'DUCHESS OF ABERCORN' got into a violent slip at Watford Junction on Saturday, 8th April, 1939 whilst in charge of the 12.05 p.m. Euston - Crewe express. With the regulator jammed open she slipped for fully five minutes at high speed, wearing away the top web of the railhead. Eventually she was moved a yard or so, but then began to slip once more for a further three minutes until a valve spindle broke.

A second disturbing incident was recorded on Tuesday, 31st October, 1939 (Sunday the 29th according to the S.L.S. Journal) to a streamlined member of the class when No. 6228 'DUCHESS OF RUTLAND' in charge of the 9.25 a.m. from Euston, 'The Irish Mail', came to a stand at a permanent way slack at Headstone Lane and the driver could not close the regulator. With the train remaining stationary, "for nearly ten minutes the engine pounded away with the wheels revolving.. and the blast roaring out of the chimney, with brakes hard on. It was a sight worth seeing." After it was eventually brought under control and got away two lengths of rail had to be replaced before normal traffic could resume.

The run of No 6233 on 12th November, 1938, between Euston and Crewe, recorded by Major A. P. le M. Sinkinson, and fully documented earlier in this chapter, also records an extended period of slipping after she was brought to a halt by signals just beyond Basford Wood on the approaches to Crewe, which caused a 55 second late arrival.

As John Powell has observed in his book 'Stanier Pacifics At Work,' with a high tractive effort amounting to 26.8% of the diagram adhesive weight, sensitive handling of the regulator was essential if slipping was to be avoided. The volume of uncontrollable steam in the passages beyond the regulator was very large, and drivers adopted various methods to avoid a slip, including opening the regulator and closing it again several times when starting. Although a modification was made to the main regulator valve that stopped the problem occurring, uncontrolled slipping due to serious water carry-over remained a problem throughout the life of the class and even under test conditions, when the engine was being worked in a well controlled manner, as will be referred to again later.

MAINTENANCE AND OVERHAUL STRATEGY.

Apart from daily examinations at pre-determined intervals, the pattern of major overhaul was based loosely on miles run, and standards were laid down in document MP 11 'Standard Examination Schedule' issued by the Superintendent of Motive Power at Euston. Normal shed maintenance for locomotives such as No. 6233 involved a daily examination and an examination 'in steam' every six to eight days, which involved a check on every moving and operational part. The firebox had to be examined for defects, which involved cooling the boiler down by passing water through it at a prescribed rate, and the boiler was washed out every twelve to sixteen days. Other on-shed exams involved a three to five week inspection of gauge frames and glasses and the ejectors, the train-heating valve and hoses.

At seven to nine weeks the firebox fusible plugs were changed and the driver's brake valve and injectors checked, whilst at between nine and fifteen week intervals the safety valves were examined and checked to ensure the correct relief pressure of between 245 and 255lb./sq. in.

As to the moving parts, apart from the driver's own checks before each run, the second group of requirements were based upon miles actually run in service, and were mainly concerned with the condition of the component parts subject to mechanical wear and the satisfactory performance of the functional items. Wheels and tyres were examined and tender tanks check for leaks at multiples of 5-6,000 miles, whilst every 10,000 to 12,000 miles the motion was examined and some parts dismantled, crank axles inspected for movement, piston rings changed, axlebox pads and the general lubrication system checked and drawgear examined. Most parts were however examined in position up to and including the 15,000 to 18,000 mile exam.

At between 20,000 and 24,000 miles piston rings had to be changed and at 30,000 to 36,000 miles (designated the No. 6 Exam) engine and tender had to be separated to examine drawgear and rubbing plates. The inside and outside cylinders were opened up and pistons and piston valves withdrawn and checked and rings renewed, steam and exhaust ports cleaned by chipping off carbon deposits to open up their full cross sectional area, and crankpins examined. In addition the motion on Pacific class engines was stripped down and sent to Crewe Works for attention. This caused delays in the transportation of materials to and from the works, and it was therefore normal post-war practice at this point for the examination and stripping work to be done at Crewe North motive power depot, irrespective of the home depot, to reduce such delays. Time out of traffic was thus kept to a minimum, and it was expected that a locomotive would be back in traffic within 24 hours unless boiler or other repairs were required.

It was the responsibility of the Mechanical Foreman on each depot to submit a Shopping Proposal for the engine to be shopped again at main works once the engine had worked for eight months since the last classified repair. The Shopping Bureau would normally accept the proposal rather than risk running further mileage, but the Shopping Bureau Inspector always had the last word, and would personally examine any engines where there was doubt. John Powell records that about half of all shoppings of the 'Princess Coronation' class locomotives for General or Intermediate Repairs was on account of valve or piston examination.

The shopping record of the class as a whole was better than the 'Princess Royals,' and an average mileage of 190,897 was being achieved in the 1940-5 period of the Second World War for the 'Princess Coronations' as compared to 160,900 for the former. This rose to 205,255 in the 1945-50 period whereas the older class of locomotives dropped back to 139,132.

The main scheduled classified repair work was undertaken at Crewe Works, except for some isolated visits of Scottish based engines to St. Rollox Works, Glasgow for casual repairs, and was undertaken every eight months or so. A heavy general repair always involved a boiler change and extensive stripping down of the engine to its frames, all component parts being sent off to the various shops for re-conditioning. A heavy repair involved a combination of new tyres for the wheels, new cylinders if required, repair and re-tubing of the boiler and motion and brake gear overhaul., whilst a light repair involved one of the above and a variety of other repair jobs, including work for which locomotives had to be called into shops specially to have done, including essential modifications to either engine or tender. Heavy and Light Repairs were also designated 'Intermediate' or 'General,' the boiler remaining 'in situ' for the former category, although other work might put it in the 'Heavy Intermediate' category. Intervals between these two types were nominally eight months, but it depended upon the need to attend to an item not done at 'Intermediate' repair which, especially in the case of the boiler, dictated the date of the next 'Heavy Repair.' Because of higher mileages, locomotives working express passenger traffic tended to be shopped much more frequently for attention than other types.

Three official LMS photographs of
6233 taken after the fitting of the
double blast and chimney
on 22 March 1941.
The supporting bracket for the
previously fitted BTH speed
indicator has been retained.
Note that a war time- time
restriction required the cabside
windows to be 'blacked out'.
(L.M.S. Official/J.B. Radford
Collection)

WARTIME TRAFFIC REQUIREMENTS AND ALLOCATIONS.

By the end of July, 1939 the allocation of the engines of the class was:-

Camden: 6220-8, 6230-4, 6236.
Crewe North: *6229 (in the U.S.A.) and 6235 (on loan)

However, following the outbreak of the Second World War in September, 1939 all of the fastest trains quickly disappeared, and many of the Stanier Pacifics then at Camden were re-allocated as a matter of urgency, although No. 6233 was one exception. Nos. 6220 (still temporarily re-numbered 6229) and 6221-4 moved to Polmadie depot in Glasgow (coded 27A) in November, and unstreamlined engines followed in 1940, with Nos. 6225-7 finding themselves briefly at Holyhead (coded 7C) on 21st October, 1939 in order to work the "Irish Mail" expresses and other additional wartime traffic to Holyhead, No. 6226 having briefly been allocated to Speke Junction depot from 16th September. However, on 9th December, 1939 No. 6226 returned to Camden depot and on 6th April, 1940 Nos. 6225 and 6227 returned to Crewe North

Those of the class working on the West Coast main line were put on 'Full Load' trains running to less tight schedules at speeds up to a maximum of 75 m.p.h., the number of coaches being increased according to the needs of the traffic. These easier schedules saved on both fuel and maintenance costs. On 4th December, 1939 a new train was initiated leaving Euston at 10.00 a.m. for Glasgow Central, becoming the wartime equivalent of the "Royal Scot.' This train was usually hauled by a streamlined member of the class, and continued to run until 17th June, 1944.

As an example of the more relaxed timings, by 1941 this train was slowed to give a later 6.45 p.m. arrival in Glasgow, with stops at Rugby (arr. 11.40 a.m.), Crewe (arr. 1.15 p.m), and Carlisle (arr. 4.24 p.m.). Engines were changed at Crewe and the train worked forward to Carlisle by Polmadie men. In the reverse direction the 10.00 a.m. from Glasgow now made stops at Carlisle, which it left at 12.23 p.m., arriving in Crewe at 3.31 p.m. and then running from there to Euston non-stop, arriving at 6.50 p.m.

The 'Mid-day Scot' continued to run, with some interruptions, throughout the war, hauled by locomotives of the class, although the train ceased to serve Edinburgh. It was regularly loaded to fifteen or more bogies, more often than not all crowded to capacity. Leaving Euston at 1.00 p.m. and stopping only at Rugby, Crewe and Carstairs, where it provided connections to Edinburgh, Perth and North Scotland, and also to Motherwell, it arrived in Glasgow Central at 9.58 p.m. In the reverse direction it left at 1.00 p.m. and called at the same places on the up journey, with the addition of Watford to set down passengers, and was booked to arrive into London Euston at 9.56 p.m.

During the 1940's members of the class allocated to Crewe North were working through to Perth daily arriving at 6.16 a.m. They then worked the 8.48 a.m. to Glasgow Buchanan Street station, arriving at 1.40 p.m., and then worked back to Crewe at 8.35 p.m.

By mid 1940 the allocations were: Camden: 6233-4, Crewe North: 6225-28, Polmadie: 6220-4 and 6230-2.

'DUCHESS OF SUTHERLAND' remained at Camden for most of the war and was in regular use on the more heavily loaded timetabled trains and on war effort specials such as troop trains. With her sisters No. 6233 worked trains to Glasgow, Liverpool, Manchester and Holyhead.

By 1941 both classes of Stanier Pacifics, including the streamlined members, were working regularly into Aberdeen. These were again normally those engines allocated to Crewe North depot which had worked the overnight sleeping car train from London Euston to Inverness as far as Perth. To fill in their day before the return working they were employed hauling the 9.20 a.m. Perth to Aberdeen passenger train which arrived at 11.35 a.m., returning with the 1.10 p.m. Aberdeen to Perth ariving at 3.26 p.m. Nos. 6225-8 are recorded on that diagram along with'Princess Royal' class engines Nos. 6205, 6207 & 6208.

During the latter months of 1941 Stanier Pacifics began using the Nuneaton and Coventry line, and both 6200 'THE PRINCESS ROYAL' and 6233 'DUCHESS OF SUTHERLAND' were observed working Liverpool Lime Street - London Euston expresses on that route on 7th September, 1941. By mid 1943 this had become a very heavily loaded train of up to 17 bogies.

Early in 1942 there was a change from the established pattern of workings for the 12 noon and 1.00 p.m. expresses from London Euston. Instead of working through to Glasgow the Pacific now worked the express for Windermere partway, whilst the Glasgow train was worked forward by an Edge Hill (Liverpool) 'Royal Scot' class 4-6-0, usually after an engine change at Crewe. This arrangement proved to be only a short term measure since it was reversed again from May, 1943 until the withdrawal of the service.

On 29th July, 1942 'DUCHESS OF SUTHERLAND' was recorded by Vic R. Webster working the 8.40 a.m. Birmingham to Euston express with a load of 13 bogies. In a contribution to the April, 1943 issue of the S.L.S. Journal he reported boarding the train at Rugby and, following a p.w.s. at Kilsby, Weedon, 12.9 miles away, was passed in 17 mins, whilst Wolverton was passed in 32½ mins for a distance of 30.2 miles. A severe signal check caused the 5¾ miles to Bletchley to take no less than 9½ mins. And further delays caused by the p.w.s. in force from Leighton Buzzard to Cheddington. Corresponding times were Tring 50.9 miles in 61 mins., and Watford, where a stop was made, a distance of 65.2 miles covered in a total time of 75 mins. The 17.4 miles to Euston took 23 minutes giving a net time of little more than 65 mins. for the 77 miles.

Further runs of 6233 during this year have been sent in by Gavin R. Whitelaw, and are listed below.

On Friday, 21st August, 1942 she was timed working the 9.38 p.m. from Glasgow Central as far as Carlisle:-

	Arr.	Dep.	Late	Load (tons)
Glasgow	-	9.38	-	488
Motherwell	10.00	10.03	2	
Carstairs	10.34		4	
Symington				
Summit	11.07		-	
Beattock	11.18		1 early	
Gretna	11.58		-	
Carlisle	12.14 No.12		3	

Delays:- 3 minutes signals Carlisle No. 3 & 4, 2 minutes p.w.s. Newton, 2 mins p.w.s. Law Jctn.

On Saturday, 29th August, 1942 she was timed working the 4.55 a.m. down train between Carlisle and Glasgow:-

	Arr.	Dep.	Late	Load (tons)
Carlisle		6.16	81	459
Lockerbie	6.58	7.02	90	
Beattock	7.22	7.29	95	
Summit	7.53		95	
Symington				
Carstairs	8.22	8.27	95	
Motherwell	8.50	8.53	96	
Glasgow	9.22		102	

Delays:- 4 mins. sigs Carlisle No. 4 & Kingmoor, 3 mins. Quintishill, 2 mins. at Castlemilk, 3 mins. Beattock South, 6 mins Uddingston to Gateside (8.50 a.m. Bothwell), 4 mins sigs and drawing up Beattock, 1 min p.w.s. Law Jctn.

Also on Saturday, 29th August, 1942 she was timed working the 7.29 p.m. up train between Carlisle and Glasgow as follows:-

	Arr.	Dep.	Late	Load (tons)
Carlisle		9.07	98	510
Lockerbie				
Beattock	10.05		110	
Summit	10.27		112	
Symington				
Carstairs	10.51	11.04	114	
Motherwell	11.27		117	
Glasgow	11.44		115	

Delays:- 9 mins water, drawing up, B.E. Beattock, 6 min traffic Carstairs, 3 min p.w.s. Law Jctn. 3 min running to Beattock.

On Monday, 31st August, 1942 6233 was timed working the 7.29 p.m. departure from Carlisle to Glasgow Central as follows:-

	Arr.	Dep.	Late	Load (tons)
Carlisle	7.38	7.45	16	514
Lockerbie				
Beattock		8.38	28	
Summit	9.03		28	
Symington				
Carstairs	9.31	9.44	34	
Motherwell				
Glasgow	10.25		36	

Delays:- 7 mins. Wamphray & Murthat freight, 2 min. traffic at Carlisle, 5 mins. water B.E. Beattock, 6 min Dr. up & traffic Carstairs, 2 mins. p.w.s. Law Jctn.

These runs clearly document the lengthy delays suffered by trains running to the wartime timetable. Other runs by 'Princess Coronation' class Pacifics and other locomotives sent in by Mr. Whitelaw show that No. 6233 was not alone in meeting great delays on that summer Saturday, and Nos. 6223, 6231, 6240 and 6243 also feature during that same weekend period.

HIGH SPEED RUNNING WITH AN 'UP' SLEEPING CAR TRAIN.

In response to requests for information for this book, the authors received a most interesting communication from Mr Brian Barlow of Wigan which relates to a sterling performance put in by No. 6233 at the head of the overnight sleeping car train from Perth to London Euston. The locomotive was in the hands of Driver Percy Wilson, who is still alive at 102 and who also lives in Wigan. Percy was born at Cowan Bridge, a village situated between Ingleton and Kirby Lonsdale on 14th August, 1899 and began his working life in 1913 at the age of 14, working at Tebay as an engine cleaner for the London & North Western Railway. His great grandfather had helped to build the main line from Lancaster to Carlisle over Shap, and his grandfather and father were also railwaymen. During the First World War he enlisted with the Border Regiment at the age of 18, but returned to the railway after the Armistice. In 1998 he was awarded the Legion d'Honneur in recognition of his service in France.

Percy moved to Springs Branch depot at Wigan in August, 1921, which at that time boasted 540 sets of men, i.e. drivers and firemen. Percy had lodgings at Lower Ince. Drivers from that depot were reluctant to work into Carlisle Citadel station and would not sign for the road, preferring to get home at night, even though that turn of duty brought in extra money. This was also because of the poor facilities at the enginemens' hostel at Carlisle, including poor food and sharing a small dormitory with their fireman with just a flimsy curtain between them. However Percy became one of the youngest drivers at Springs Branch in 1932, and did sign for the road, and was never happier than when pounding up and down the West Coast main line between Crewe and Carlisle.

One night, about 1942, when he was living and working in Carlisle, he found himself 'knocked up' in the early hours to go to Citadel station and relieve Perth men who had brought the Up Express in from the North. This was the Perth to Euston overnight sleeper which he had to work to Crewe because there were no Crewe North men available to work the train south, the section being diagrammed in both 'Up' and 'Down' directions for men from that depot. Percy recalls :-

"When I got to the station, I found that the loco. was 6233 'DUCHESS OF SUTHERLAND'. As I boarded the footplate the Station Manager came up. "This train is over-loaded, Driver. You've nearly 600 tons." The Fireman looked at me. "Do you think we can manage Percy?" I replied "With this engine? Certainly. We left Carlisle on time and topped Shap Summit in 31 minutes." Arrival at Wigan, the one intermediate stop, was 7 minutes early. "As we were going down Shap I nudged the fireman and pointed to the speedometer - 110 m.p.h!" Departing Wigan on time, Percy remembering clearly that it was 3.03 a.m., Crewe was reached in 32 minutes.

Percy recalls that his fireman had not fired a 'Princess Coronation' class engine before, and also that "6233 was one of a batch of five engines, 6230-34 and it was the best of the batch." So the speed record of 114 m.p.h. set up by 6220 'CORONATION' on 29th June, 1937 could almost be equalled in service by a member of the class with a very heavily loaded train, albeit downhill and as indicated by the British Thomson-Houston speed indicating equipment then fitted to 6233.

Percy retired in 1964, but is still visited by his fireman, whom he refers to as his 'Lad', although he is now himself 74 years old!

REPAIRS AND MODIFICATIONS.

No. 6233 had been shopped briefly for a light repair to her tender from 5th to 18th June, 1941 and had had both a light and a heavy service repair in 1942. The first causing her to be out of traffic for 25 days from 25th March to 22nd April, and the second for 25 days from 16th October to 13th November. However, her second heavy general repair took place in 1943, and she was shopped on 2nd July for an overhaul that kept her out of traffic for 32 days. Whilst in shops she had her boiler exchanged for No. 10287, which had been taken off streamlined engine No. 6235 'CITY OF BIRMINGHAM'. This had been to the Crewe boiler shop for heavy overhaul during which the 'Monel' metal firebox stays replaced steel ones under Order No. 5495. 'DUCHESS OF SUTHERLAND' was returned to traffic on 7th August, 1943.

No. 6233 was also fitted with the improved type of piston head and rod, which also required the fitting of new front cylinder covers. Job. No. 5329 had been issued on 16th February, 1943 and engines were to be called onto works specially when the material was available. This involved securing the piston rod to the head by means of two nuts; one with right hand thread and one with a left hand thread, with a locking plate between, an improvement designed to lessen the risk of the piston head becoming loose whilst in traffic. No. 6233 was so fitted during the period ending 3rd October, 1943.

Further shopping of 'DUCHESS OF SUTHERLAND' occurred in 1944, and from 5th January to 10th February a light overhaul was carried out to the engine. From 16th May to 2nd June she was in Crewe shops for more tender repairs following which she was re-allocated to Crewe North motive power depot. Another light service repair was carried out at Crewe between 12th October and 3rd November 1944.

In April, 1944 the class were distributed as follows:- Nos. 6220-24 and 6230-32 were still at Polmadie, Nos. 6225-9, 6233 and 6235-48 were at Camden and No. 6234 was the sole representative at Crewe North. However by July, 1944 Nos. 6233-36 and 6252 were at Crewe North and No. 6242 moved to Polmadie along with Nos. 6249-51. In 1946 Nos. 6226-8 (ex Camden) and Nos. 6249-51 (ex Polmadie) were moved to Carlisle Upperby and No. 6238 moved from Camden to join them in May of the following year. More engines were re-

Although partially obscured by the trailing exhaust 6233, now fitted with a double chimney, is seen passing Henry Casserley's house at Berkhampsted with the 6.50am departure from Euston to Windermere on 12 June 1944.
(H.C. Casserley)

allocated to Crewe North, No. 6225 from Camden arriving in June, 1946, but it returned in October, 1947 and was replaced by Nos. 6227 and 6229, both from Carlisle Upperby. Nos. 6253-5 were allocated when new to Camden in September and October, 1946, and No. 6256 to Crewe North upon entering traffic on 13th December, 1947.

As to 'DUCHESS OF SUTHERLAND' herself, Henry Casserley photographed her as she sped past his home at Berkhamsted on 12th June, 1944 with the 6.50 a.m. Euston to Windermere express. He was to record her again working south with an up express on 3rd April, 1946, when she was held at signals right opposite his bedroom window. Many such workings were recorded on film over his long and active life, and, as a much valued recorder of the railway scene, his collection of negatives today form a most valuable archive of past scenes, now in the hands of his son Richard.

The S.L.S. Journal for September, 1944 records that there were then two night expresses from Perth to London Euston leaving at 8.20 p.m. and 8.55 p.m., both of which were worked by Crewe North based Pacifics as far as Crewe. Recently recorded on those duties had been 'Princess Royal' class Nos. 6205-12 and 'Princess Coronation' class No. 6233 'DUCHESS OF SUTHERLAND' as well as No. 6235 and recently delivered members of the class, including No. 6249 on 22nd May, 6250 on 28th June, 6251 on 15th June and 6252 on 17th July.

ACCIDENTS AND OTHER INCIDENTS.

Two early incidents in which the driver had difficulty in closing the regulator have already been recorded, but there were other problems in service.

On 10th September, 1940 there was a boiler explosion on No. 6224 'PRINCESS ALEXANDRA' in which the fireman was killed. Due to the booked crew not arriving in time to take the 'Royal Scot' southwards from Glasgow because of enemy action, a passed fireman and a passed cleaner were substituted at short notice, arriving on the engine only three minutes before the booked starting time. Neither of them had been in charge of such a large locomotive before. The train got as far as Carluke where it became necessary for the crew to stop for a 'blow-up.' Clearly the water level in the boiler was still too low and, with a sharp change in gradient on the climb to Craigenhall between Cleghorn and Carstairs, the fusible plugs melted. This went un-noticed and was very soon followed by the firebox crown becoming plastic and collapsing, the young passed cleaner paying for it with his life as scalding hot steam was discharged onto the footplate. The boiler involved was No. 9937 which had been the original boiler fitted to 6220 'CORONATION' when new, and which had been fitted to 6224 when outshopped on 25th May, 1940 after a heavy general repair at Crewe.

By remarkable coincidence the same engine was again involved in a similar incident on 7th March, 1948, this time due to the faulty fitting of the water gauge links. The 9.25 p.m. Glasgow to Euston had run 13 miles to Lamington when the firebox crown collapsed, killing the driver. A previous driver had reported a discrepancy between the readings on the two water gauge glasses the day before, but the fitter could not find the fault, despite the fact that the right hand side of one of the cock levers was incorrectly fitted on the square, so that when the bottom cock was open the top one was shut. Despite the stop at Carstairs and the shed foreman and two fitter's examination of an audible steam blow in the boiler, obviously caused by a melted fusible plug, no fault was found in the cock levers, and the train proceeded. On the falling gradient to Lamington the firebox crown collapsed with fatal results. The Polmadie fitter was held to be responsible, and steps were taken to ensure that in future such a mistake in fitting up the gauge cocks and linkage could not occur.

Duchess of Sutherland climbing towards Shap Summit with an up express between the dates August 1946 and October 1948. (R. Humm Collection)

On 16th November, 1940 No. 6232 'DUCHESS OF MONTROSE' was damaged after running into fallen girders brought down by enemy action at Berkhamsted, but fortunately no-one was killed in the incident.

There were two major incidents involving passing signals set at danger, the first being on 6th October, 1940 when No. 6230 'DUCHESS OF BUCCLEUCH,' heading the 9.25 p.m. Euston to Glasgow, ran into the back of a freight train at Hartford at about 50 m.p.h. Fortunately no-one was killed and damage was relatively limited.

However, the second incident, on 21st July, 1945, was much more serious and involved sister engine No. 6231 'DUCHESS OF ATHOLL' at the head of the 1.00 p.m. express from Glasgow Central to London Euston. At Ecclefechan the train collided with a freight train whilst it was being shunted into the up refuge siding, and both driver and fireman were killed outright, the position of the controls afterwards suggesting that the driver missed the distant signal set at danger, and only realised his mistake on sighting the home signal, by which time it was, of course, too late to stop. Despite considerable damage to the locomotive and the stock, no passengers died as a result.

A third incident occurred on 18th May, 1947 at Lambrigg Crossing on Grayrigg Bank when the driver of No. 6235 'CITY OF BIRMINGHAM,' at the head of the 1.00 p.m. Glasgow Central to London Euston express, ran through signals instead of stopping at the Lambrigg Crossing signalbox, where his train should have been reversed onto the down line because the up line was blocked for repairs. Despite a collision with Class 2P 4-4-0 No. 565, there were no serious injuries, even though the incident happened on the high Docker Viaduct.

In this period there were also two serious incidents involving track in poor condition. The first occurred on 15th April, 1944 at Mossband signalbox near Gretna and involved the 8.40 p.m. down sleeping car train from Euston, which was put on mainly for servicemen. The locomotive was No. 6225 'DUCHESS OF GLOUCESTER' which became derailed on bad track whilst travelling at about 55 m.p.h. A torn up rail completely demolished the signalbox and three passengers were killed as a result.

The second incident occurred only a few weeks later and involved No. 6244 'KING GEORGE VI' whilst it was working the 8.30 a.m. express from London Euston to Liverpool Lime Street on 21st July, 1944. As the train was

travelling round the curve at Grendon, between Atherstone and Polesworth, at about 65 to 70 m.p.h., the track gave way and the locomotive was completely derailed. It was recorded that the track at this point was nearing the end of its life, being due for renewal in 1948, and its deterioration, particularly the track gauge on the curve, was the cause. Sadly five passengers died as a result.

One further incident should also be mentioned which involved No. 6224 'PRINCESS ALEXANDRA' yet again. This time she was working the 1.00 p.m. express from Glasgow Central to London Euston on 17th November, 1945, and, whilst running between Rugby and Nuneaton, the engine struck an object fouling the gauge of the running line at the site of some permanent way repairs. The streamlined casing was cut into pieces and the nearside cylinder casing ripped completely off. In addition, on the motion the nearside crosshead lever was wrapped around itself. After lineside attention, No. 6224 limped into Nuneaton using only its offside two cylinders. Fortunately no-one was injured.

A list of all of these incidents is included in the Appendix 8, and later incidents from 1948 onwards will be referred to in Chapter Four.

6233 'DUCHESS OF SUTHERLAND' ON TEST

Official tests were carried out over the years with various members of the class, and included in these were tests with No. 6233. The dynamometer car used for these was the ex Lancashire & Yorkshire Railway Dynamometer car M45050, that has been preserved at the Midland Railway Centre and which is due to be put on display by the Princess Royal Class Locomotive Trust in the future.

These tests with No. 6233 took place in 1945, and were part of a series comparing different classes of locomotive. 'DUCHESS OF SUTHERLAND' had just undergone her third Heavy General Repair at Crewe, which lasted from 18th April to 19th May, during which she was unavailable for traffic for 27 days. At this repair she had been fitted with boiler No. 10297 ex No. 6234 'DUCHESS OF ATHOLL.' She had run a further 152,745 miles since her previous general repair, and clearly her wartime mileage was rather less than that in peacetime.

TEST RUN DETAILS

Run No. 829 (two runs) from Crewe to Carlisle and back took place as follows:-
    30th October 1945 :- Train: 1.34 p.m. Crewe to Carlisle with a load of 530 tons
    31st October1945 :- Train: 12.42 p.m. Carlisle to Crewe with a load of 524 tons

Run No. 830 (two runs) from Crewe to Carlisle and back took place as follows:-
    1st November 1945 :- Train: 1.34 p.m.Crewe to Carlisle with a load of 535 tons
    2nd November1945 :- Train: 12.42 p.m. Carlisle to Crewe with a load of 525 tons

The coal used was Barnborough, which was much inferior to the Grimethorpe coal used on the pre-war tests, and an average coal consumption of 3.87 lb./d.b.h.p./hr. compared poorly with the 3.12 lb./d.b.h.p./hr. achieved in the tests with 'DUCHESS OF ABERCORN' in 1939 already referred to.

The purpose of the tests was "to ascertain the coal and water consumption of the 4-6-2 type engine when working similar trains to those worked by the engine reviewed in Report No. 82 with special reference to engine No. 6131. Particulars of steam chest and exhaust steam temperatures were also obtained."

The mileage of No. 6233 since service repair was approximately 20,000, these being accumulated between May and October of that year and which meant that she was in a 'nicely run-in' condition. The general weather conditions were "similar throughout the tests with the exception of the run on November 1st, when there was a certain amount of fog between Crewe and Wigan, which did not however cause any delay in working."

The other tests referred to had been carried out on the same route starting on 12th & 13th December, 1944 with 'Royal Scot' class 4-6-0 No. 6131 'THE ROYAL WARWICKSHIRE REGIMENT' with a trailing load of 442 tons, on 14th & 15th December with a trailing load of 449 tons, and on 6th March & 8th March, 1945 on the 1.34 p.m. Crewe to Carlisle with trailing loads of 448 tons and 449 tons respectively.

'Jubilee' class 4-6-0 No. 5736 'PHOENIX,' rebuilt with a double chimney and a larger Class 2A boiler, was tested on the same route - out on 1st May, 1945 with 449 tons and back on 2nd May with 439 tons, and on run No: 826 it did the out and back in one day with the same trains as No. 6233 on 3rd May with a load of 444 tons out and 440 tons back.

In 1945 another 'Royal Scot' class 4-6-0 No. 6162 'QUEEN'S WESTMINSTER RIFLEMAN' repeated the tests on 29th May (out) and 30th May (return) with loads of 456 tons and 471 tons, and again on 31st May/1st June with 447 tons and 464 tons respectively.

The results of the tests with 'DUCHESS OF SUTHERLAND' were set out in Report No. 83. Barnborough coal from Manvers Colliery Main Seam was used, and, although the steaming of the engine was found to be "not satisfactory."

"A pressure of 200-210 lb./sq. in. was maintained on the level and easier gradients, and an average pressure of 225 lb./sq. in. on Shap Bank. The safety valves were lifting at 210 lb./sq. in., the volume of steam increasing in intensity to 240 lb./sq. in. The engine was worked consistently throughout the test with full regulator whenever practicable, and the firing was quite satisfactory. An Inspector from the Motive Power Department, and a footplate observer rode on the footplate during each day's test, and the engine was handled very efficiently. The engine was worked at an average cut-off of 15% on the level and easier gradients, with a maximum of 35% on Shap Bank."

Combustion appeared to be satisfactory, and the exhaust quite clear, but there was evidence of the formation of hard clinker on the grate at the end of each days test. The engine was thoroughly examined, including checking the elements and chimney for alignment, etc., and given a water test at the conclusion of the trials, and no defects were found to account for the poor steaming.

However, when later analysing the coal used, it was found that the Barnboro' coal was very much inferior in quality to the Grimethorpe coal used in 1934 tests. The moisture, ash and sulphur contents being greater, and the calculated calorific values of 12,850 and 11,950 B.Th.U's on the two runs much lower as compared with 14,450 for the Grimethorpe. The moisture contents of 5.5% and 5.7% respectively, the ash contents of 5.7% and 11.0% compared to 2.8% and the sulphur contents were 1.2% and 2.6% compared to 0.8%. The fusion point of the ash was also low, and that coal would therefore have a tendency to produce a greater volume of clinker.

On timekeeping the report says "The test runs were rather spoilt by traffic delays. On the first day, when working the 1.34 p.m. Crewe-Carlisle train, a derailment north of Warrington resulted in a signal stop of 11 minutes, and subsequent signal checks and permanent way restrictions accounted for a total loss of 24 minutes on

actual running time. A delay of 61 minutes at the start of the test run on 1st November due to a broken rail at Milford and Brockton, resulted in the train running out of path and a total delay of 21 minutes on actual booked time resulted. However, in spite of indifferent steaming, booked sectional running times were maintained over the most severe portions of the route."

A copy of the data from the Dynamometer Car during the test runs is given as Appendix 7. The combined average of all four runs gave an average speed of 42.6 m.p.h. with a power output of 1.82 Horse Power min./ton mile, excluding the engine. Coal consumption was 62.1 lb./mile, 0.091 lb./ton mile including the engine, giving a figure of 3.87 lb/D.B.H.P. Water consumption was 44.9 gallons per mile, 28.1 lb./D.B.H.P. and 7.22l lb/lb of coal.

"The coal consumption figure of 3.86 lb./D.B.H.P. is considerably higher than the figure obtained from this class of engine using Grimethorpe coal, and the increase can be largely attributed to the inferior quality of the Barnboro' coal. On account of the poor steaming, and the traffic delays, it was decided to repeat the tests with an engine of the same class."

After the tests with 'DUCHESS OF SUTHERLAND' further tests were therefore carried out using the then relatively new No. 6252 'CITY OF LEICESTER' on 4th-7th December, 1945, and these can be referred to at the National Railway Museum in Test Report No. 83. Finally more tests were done with 'Royal Scot' class 4-6-0 No. 6131 from 11th-14th December. A memo dated 21st September, 1945 drew attention to the fact that recent tests with these engines had shown:- "that the 'Royal Scot' class used 20% more water per D.B.H.P. as compared to the latest 4-6-2 engines, and this was put down to a combination of variations in the design of cylinders, valve gear and valve events, the differences in the superheat of the steam fed into the cylinders and variations in the test conditions. Superheat figures for the 4-6-2's were thought to be about 50 degrees higher than on the converted 'Royal Scots,' possibly saving between 8% and 10% in water consumption. More tests comparing the two classes of engine were therefore called for, when it was expeced that the latter engines' water consumption might come down to 27-28 lb of water per D.B.H.P. as compared to a figure of 24.15 lb (including blowdown) for the latest 4-6-2, for which the higher degree of superheat was thought to be responsible.

ALLOCATIONS

With more locomotives of the class being completed and put into service, the allocations to the various depots were changed to meet traffic requirements, and by the end of 1944 the 33 engines then in service were dispersed as follows:-

Camden:	6225-9, 6238-41 & 6243-8	(Total 15)
Crewe North:	6233, 6235-6, 6252	(Total 4)
Edge Hill:	6234 (on loan)	(Total 1)
Polmadie:	6220-4, 6230-2, 6237, 6242 (on loan), 6249-51 (on loan)	(Total 13)

REMOVAL OF THE STREAMLINED CASING

The streamlined casing had proved to be of little benefit in improving performance in practical terms. The inconvenience it caused in restricting access, plus the fact that some sections had to be removed for some heavy daily maintenance procedures, caused a decision to remove it to be taken at the M. & E.E. Committee meeting on 24th October, 1945. This was after Stanier had faded from the scene, and H.G. Ivatt, as Acting C.M.E., stated that the streamlining casing "was a disadvantage both from the point of view of its maintenance and the inaccessibility of the engine generally resulting in increased maintenance expenditure." With the concurrence of the Chief Operating Manager, he recommended that it be removed and that side smoke deflector plates be fitted at an estimated cost of £5,527. Job No. 5434 was issued on 28th December, 1945 to cover the work, and it was completed on 6th September, 1949. This involved removing the casing and light framing and fitting new boiler cladding as used with the non-streamlined engines. However its removal now revealed the tapered top section to the smokebox wrapper which had been necessary to clear the nose end streamlined casing, and this unique feature remained until the engines required new smokeboxes. In addition the gap in the running plate as it dropped to the lower level in front of the outside cylinders was also exposed. No. 6235 'CITY OF BIRMINGHAM' was the first to loose its streamlined casing on 24th April, 1946, and the last was No. 6243 on 6th September, 1949. The full list is as follows:-

> 1946: 6220-4, 6227, 6235, 6246, 6248.
> 1947: 6225, 6228, 6236-8, 6239-42, 6244-5, 6247.
> 1948: 6226, 6229.
> 1949: 6243.

One formerly streamlined member of the class, No. 46242 'CITY OF GLASGOW', was unique in that it was later to be fitted with the full running plate during the very heavy repair and rebuilding following the Harrow and Wealdstone crash of 8th October, 1952, during which the locomotive was severely damaged. She was out of service for more than a year.

THE FITTING OF SMOKE DEFLECTOR PLATES.

For the existing unstreamlined members of the class, the fitting of smoke deflectors from 1945 onwards, referred to above, changed the appearance of the locomotives considerably, and many would say for the worst. Two of them were so fitted under Experiment C/LD/1277 dated July, 1944 (Nos. 6232 on 24th February, 1945 and 6252 on 9th March, 1945) before the general instruction covering all nine engines was issued to New Works Order No. 8826 as Job No. 5429 on 4th December, 1945. The reason given was "There is a tendency on this class of engine for the smoke to envelope the boiler and cab when running at speed and thus interfering with the driver's vision." The work was officially completed on 24th October, 1947.

The dates of leaving shops to return to traffic after the work had been done were:-

6230 14/9/46,	6249 19/9/46,
6231 22/8/46,	6250 28/2/46,
6232 24/2/45,	6251 17/8/46,
6233 24/8/46,	6252 9/3/45.
6234 16/3/46,	

When first fitted the smoke deflectors on Nos. 6230-4 and 6249-52 did not have footholds on the upper level of the running plate since, unlike the streamlined members of the class, they had the full curved section of running plate sweeping upwards just in front of the outside cylinders to link the lower and upper sections.

'DUCHESS OF SUTHERLAND' was shopped for a light overhaul on 15th February, 1946 and left the works on 7th March. She was back in works again for a heavy service repair on 3rd August, 1946, and this lasted 19 days, during which she was fitted with her smoke deflectors. She returned to traffic still in the original red special livery that the five un-streamlined members of the class received when brand new, and she was photographed in this condition by Will Whitworth. As a matter of record, following her recent overhaul in the West Shed by The Princess Royal Class Locomotive Trust, it was in this authentic original livery that she was outshopped.

A CHANGE OF LIVERIES.

In 1946 changes of livery were being considered by the new Chief Mechanical Engineer, Henry George Ivatt. Both the S.L.S. Journal and 'The Railway Observer' reported that No. 6234 'DUCHESS OF ABERCORN' and 'Jubilee' class 4-6-0 No. 5594 'BHOPAL' were exhibited in Platform No. 7 at Euston station in London on 28th March, 1946 painted in experimental liveries, along with two carriages, for examination by the Directors of the L.M.S. No. 6234 'DUCHESS OF ABERCORN', then with smoke deflectors, appeared in a "light grey with a bluish tint" lined out in gold and crimson lake with lettering in unshaded gold and with the nameplate background also in the crimson lake colour. There were different crests on the tender sides, the alternative to the normal one being a design incoporating the Doric Arch of Euston station. Henry Casserley, that doyen of railway photographers, observed that the other side of the locomotive had red edging to the yellow lining as opposed to the black on the other, and the rear of the tender was finished in a 'half and half' fashion. 'BHOPAL' on the other hand was turned out in crimson lake, and it was observed that these liveries were "most dazzling to the eyes after six years of drabness and austerity."

In March, 1946 'The Railway Observer' reported that No. 6234 had now been fitted with smoke deflectors and had been painted in "experimental blue livery with a two inch wide crimson lake band," and in May, 1946 the newly de-streamlined No. 6222 was observed in a "greyish black with yellow lining having a red edging," the S.L.S. Journal continuing:- ".....she worked a local train to Chester on 14th December, 1946 and on the 21st was booked to work the Euston - Perth express." She had followed No. 6235 'CITY OF BIRMINGHAM' as the second to be painted in the smart new L.M.S. black livery, following the trials with No. 6234 mentioned above.

After these experiments to determine the durability, economy and appearance of the trial liveries, the L.M.S. settled on a standard postwar colour scheme for its locomotives, namely that all should be painted black, but that express passenger locomotives should also be lined out in maroon and straw. All members of the 'Princess Coronation' class were so painted between April, 1946 and December, 1947 with the sole exception of No. 6234 which retained her experimental livery except that the trial tender crests were replaced with the standard 'LMS' lettering. Full details are given in Appendix 6.

THE LAST L.M.S. REPAIRS TO 'DUCHESS OF SUTHERLAND.'

No. 6233 had her last L.M.S. heavy general repair between 26th July and 28th October, 1947, during which she was out of traffic for an exceptional 81 days. The record card does not enlighten us as to why this was so, but she was fitted with repaired boiler No. 10646 taken off No. 6250 'CITY OF LICHFIELD,' that had accumulated some 241,411 miles of running since having the boiler fitted as new on 20th May, 1944. At this shopping No. 6233 was repainted in the new, fully lined-out black livery. She was photographed in this livery leaving Lichfield Trent Valley station on Saturday, 24th April, 1948 with the 11.37 a.m. semi-fast from London Euston and the following day was photographed heading the diverted Sunday 'Royal Scot' at Roe Green Junction, between Manchester and Wigan and again at Sanderson Sidings, Worsley.

However, she was soon back in works again after accumulating only 484 miles in service since the heavy general for a repair to her tender, and it took eleven days, from 3rd to 14th November, 1947, to effect it. The recently acquired third individual Engine Record Card for 6233, shows that this was for the rectification of a hot box. This type of card accompanied a locomotive when it was transferred to a new depot as opposed to the master Engine History Card which was retained and kept up to date at the C.M.E. headquarters (see Appendix 1).

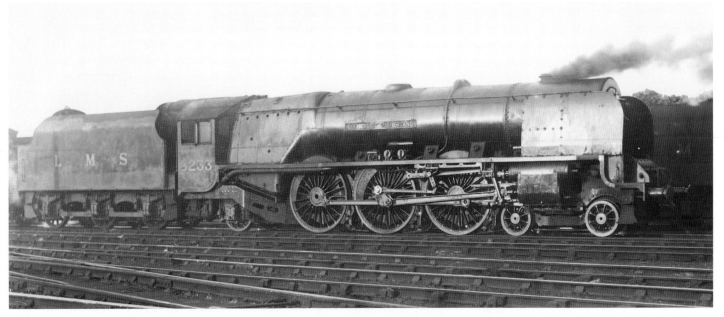

Fitting of smoke deflectors to 6233 was completed on 24th August 1946 and the locomotive is pictured so fitted at what is thought to be Crewe North depot Note that the original deflectors had neither hand grab holds nor foot hole fitted.
(W. Whitworth courtesy National Railway Museum)

A classic photograph of LMS liveried Duchess of Sutherland taken at Crewe dated between August 1946 and October 1947. Hand grab holes have by now been inserted into the smoke deflectors.
(W. Whitworth Collection courtesy the National Railway Museum)

At the end of her years of working for the L.M.S. engine No. 6233 had accumulated a total mileage of 666,642 as follows:-

Year	Miles run	Weekdays out of service			
		Heavy/light repairs	Running repairs	Days not required	Total
1938	46,599	2	20	1	23
1939	89,436	16	70	1	87
1940	82,750	14	71	-	85
1941	74,992	40	43	1	84
1942	54,163	50	63	1	114
1943	89,591	32	30	1	63
1944	60,844	68	41	1	110
1945	58,840	27	70	1	98
1946	68,480	37	38	-	75
1947	40,947	81	54	-	135

In all she had undergone four heavy general repairs, two heavy service repairs, four light service repairs and two light overhauls, and full details of these are shown on the Engine Record Cards reproduced as Appendix 1.

On 28 October 1947 6233 left Crewe Works painted in 1946 LMS black livery with straw lining. The locomotive is pictured with this livery on 24 April 1948 leaving Lichfield Trent Valley with the 11.37am ex Euston express. (HMRS/ E.S. Russell Collection courtesy LNWR Society)

Some four months after nationalisation, 6233 is still in the 1946 LMS livery of black with straw lining whilst passing Sanderson Sidings at Worsley with the down Royal Scot on Sunday 25 April 1948. The train had been diverted via Manchester and Wigan because of the Winsford crash which had occurred on the 16 April. (W.D. Cooper Collection)

Shed staff at Crewe North prepare to clean Duchess of Sutherland. Although undated, the photograph must have been taken between August, 1946 (fitting of smoke deflectors) and 2nd October 1948 when 6233 was re-numbered 46233 after nationalisation. (A.G. Ellis Collection)

The driver of 6233 Duchess of Sutherland keeps a watchful eye on the photographer whilst departing Carlisle with the W98 train, the 10.05a.m. Glasgow – Birmingham express. Another 'Princess Coronation' class pacific can be seen in the distance waiting to follow on behind. (H. Gordon Tidey courtesy the National Railway Museum)

Although not as steep as the northbound climb to Shap Summit, the southbound approach was still a challenge, especially to a cold locomotive from a Carlisle start. 6233 is pictured storming towards the summit on the 1 in 125 gradient with an 'up' express. (E. Treacy courtesy the National Railway Museum)

Chapter Four

Working for British Railways

The four major railway companies, namely the London, Midland & Scottish, the London & North Eastern, the Southern, and the Great Western Railways were nationalised and brought together on 1st January, 1948 to form the new organisation 'British Railways.' Soon afterwards tests were carried out to compare the performance of the latest locomotives of each company as a prelude to deciding which elements of the various designs should be adopted and built into the design of a new range of British Railways Standard steam locomotives.

On being taken into the British Railways stock of locomotives the locomotives of the 'Princess Coronation' class were gradually all renumbered by adding 40,000 to their existing numbers, an exercise which began with No. 46236 'CITY OF BRADFORD' on 17th April, 1948, and was finally completed on 17th October, 1949 when No. 6253 was renumbered No. 46253. Two of the class temporarily carried an 'M' prefix smokebox numberplate, and cabside numbers with an 'M' below, these being M6230 'DUCHESS OF BUCCLEUCH' (until 29/5/48) and M6236 'CITY OF BRADFORD' (until 17/4/48). No. 6257, the last of the class, was completed in February 1948 but was not put into service until 19th May that year, and as originally outshopped had an 'M' suffix below the cabside number but only 6257 on the smokebox. She was re-numbered before finally being put into traffic.

A grubby 46233 climbs the 1 in 75 gradient at Scout Green, Shap, with a load of 13 vehicles. The fireman has clearly been working hard judging by the volcanic smokescreen being laid across the Westmorland fells. (E. Treacy/NRM)

Duchess of Sutherland, in LMS lined out black livery, stands at Crewe North, dated between October 1948 and May 1950.
(P.R. Wethersett/NRM)

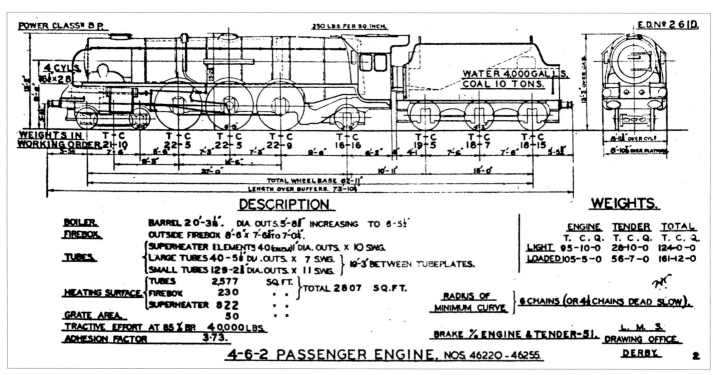

LMS official diagram E.D. No. 261D prepared to show the final form of the 'Princess Coronation' class of locomotives except for the last two. (LMS Official/J.B. Radford Collection))

EXCHANGE TRIALS AND OTHER COMPETITION.

The Stanier "Princess Coronation' class 4-6-2 locomotive chosen to take part in the comparison trials mentioned above was No. 46236 'CITY OF BRADFORD' and she was tested on the Western, Southern and Eastern Regions of the new British Railways. Her last previous general repair had been completed at Crewe on 27th February, 1948, and was selected as having run the specified 15-20,000 miles since. Throughout the tests she was allocated to Camden and the footplate crew were Driver Byford and Fireman Saint from that depot. Her performance on the Western Region between 19th and 21st May was seldom good and on the steep South Devon banks poor, which was put down to driver inexperience, unlike the awesome performance put up by 6233 'DUCHESS OF SUTHERLAND' over the same route, following her restoration, in October 2001.

46236 was ranked second in coal economy behind the Eastern Region's Gresley A4 Pacifics, the differences only being such as might be explained by the errors of margins in the test procedures. Other types tested included the rebuilt 'Royal Scot' class of the LMS, Southern Region 'Merchant Navy' class Pacifics and Western Region 'King' class 4-6-0's.

However, the performances did not in fact measure up to those of the 1930's, although late arrivals and other delays were usually caused by operational difficulties and poor coal. The heaviest train loads in Britain were then to be found on the West Coast main line, and loads south of Crewe commonly consisted of up to seventeen bogies.

As mentioned at the end of Chapter Two, the portents of a future threat in terms of other types of motive power were already showing. The first main line diesel electric Co-Co locomotive No. 10000 having emerged from Derby Locomotive Works on 5th December, 1947, was soon to be joined by sister locomotive No. 10001 which emerged from the No. 10A diesel shop at Derby on 10th July, 1948. The two were to be tried on the Anglo-Scottish services and, quoting from the official C.M.E meeting minute:-

"in competition with the two 4-6-2's built in the 1946 Programme which it is intended will be built with roller bearings and other modifications. In addition it is intended that a diesel locomotive should be split into separate units and subsequently tried out on intermediate and mixed-traffic services in order to explore the possibilities of diesel traction in those fields."

The two 4-6-2's were Nos. 6256, afterwards named 'SIR WILLIAM A. STANIER F.R.S', and 6257M 'CITY OF SALFORD'.

After an extensive trial period, which included a test run from Euston to Carlisle on 5th October, 1948, when the twin 1,600 horsepower diesel-electric units performed most impressively, an inaugural run was set up for the new diesels with the 'Royal Scot' train running non-stop from London Euston to Glasgow Central on 1st June, 1949 on an 8 hour 25 minute schedule and with a trailing load of some 545 tons, making a total train load of some 800 tons. Cecil J. Allen refers in detail to this trial in his 'British Locomotive Practice and Performance' article in the September/October issue of 'The Railway Magazine,' and records that the train reached Glasgow three minutes early. Clearly this form of motive power had a great future, and these two prototype diesel units continued to share these duties with both classes of Stanier Pacifics for a number of years. However, it was to be another ten years or so before this form of traction went into serious production following the proposals made in the 1955 plan to modernise British Railways. It was to be 1958 before the first of the type 4 diesel-electric locomotives was to emerge and begin to seriously threaten the future of steam.

On 1st January, 1948 the allocation of the 'Princess Coronation' class locomotives was as follows:-

Camden, London:-	6225, 6237, 6239-41, 6243-8 and 6253-5.
Crewe North:-	6227, 6229, 6233-6, 6252 and 6256
Upperby, Carlisle:-	6226, 6228, 6238 and 6249-51
Polmadie, Glasgow:-	6220-4, 6230-2 and 6242.

When No. 6257M 'CITY OF SALFORD' finally entered traffic on 19th May, 1948 it had already been re-numbered 46257 and was allocated to Camden motive power depot.

'DUCHESS OF SUTHERLAND' was shopped at Crewe on 19th August, 1948 for a light service repair which took no less than 36 days, having run 59,249 miles since her last heavy general repair of October, 1947. The repair is shown as having been completed on 29th September, but records show that there followed a further period in shops for work described as 'not classified.' This is shown on the Engine Record Card as being for a 'hot box', ie. a defective axle box bearing which had to be rectified. She eventually left the shops on 20th October, still in the Ivatt pre-nationalisation fully lined black livery, with the 'L.M.S.' lettering on the tender but having however been renumbered 46233 in the interim on 2nd October, 1948.

Locomotives of the 'Princess Royal' and 'Princess Coronation' classes were called upon from time to time to work the Royal Train, although these were much more frequently headed by a pair of Stanier 'Black Five' 4-6-0's. Two locomotives gave the Motive Power department more comfort in the rare, but nevertheless possible, event of a locomotive failure. However, No. 46225 'DUCHESS OF GLOUCESTER' did work such a train on 6th August, 1948 and was seen passing Watford about 7.40 p.m. in the evening.

THE NEW BRITISH RAILWAYS LIVERIES.

At a meeting of the Railway Executive on 17th January, 1949, and in response to a letter from the British Transport Commission dated 11th January, 1949, a minute recorded that blue should be adopted as a livery colour for some two hundred passenger locomotives, including the top link Stanier 4-6-2 express locomotives. This followed trails with variations of the actual shade of the colour, for No. 46244 'KING GEORGE VI' had emerged from Crewe Works on 27th August, 1948 in a lighter shade of 'Coronation' blue with black and yellow lining. Elsewhere this was described as being 'L.N.E.R. garter blue' when it was seen on Camden motive power depot on 7th November, 1948. The lining-out was later changed to black and white, which was eventually the scheme adopted, and the same locomotive was displayed for inspection at Addison Road station on 10th January, 1949 for a final decision to be made. 'Real Photographs' picture No. 2541 shows 46244 in this blue livery with the tender having a wheel crossed by the words 'BRITISH RAILWAYS' and a rather indistinct lion above.

A further light intermediate repair was carried out to No. 46233 between 18th July and 12th August, 1949, after 55,700 miles run since the previous repair. Then, on 12th April, 1950 she entered Crewe Works for her fifth heavy general repair, remaining on the works until 19th May. Repaired boiler No. 10645, ex. No. 46229 'DUCHESS OF HAMILTON,' was fitted, and No. 46233 emerged from the shops in this new 'Caledonian blue' livery lined out in black and white, and with the first large-sized British Railways 'lion and wheel' emblem on the tender sides. A photographic study of her was taken by W. Whitworth on 19th May.

During this period No. 46233 was regularly to be found hauling the 'Royal Scot' and 'The Mid-Day Scot' expresses between London Euston and Glasgow, on the Glasgow - Birmingham expresses in both directions and also on the Manchester to the West of England services, upon which Gordon Coultas recorded her on camera on 3rd June. The inimitable Eric Treacy also took a fine photographic study of her at Euston station waiting to depart with a down express in this livery.

During this period the Crewe North based 'Princess Coronations' were working the Crewe - Perth sections of the Highland sleeping car train route, and had begun to make their appearance on the up "Postal" between Aberdeen and Perth. In his regular article on "British Locomotive Practice And Performance" in 'The Railway Magazine' of January, 1951 Cecil J. Allen published a number of logs he had received of part of this working between Forfar and Perth, including one by No. 46233. In the article he comments that

Ex works in an immaculate B.R. blue livery, 46233 reverses with drain taps open on Crewe North MPD in May 1950. (W. Whitworth/NRM)

64

'DUCHESS OF SUTHERLAND' was "so energetic in getting away from Forfar that speed actually rose to 80½ m.p.h. - a rare event - between Glamis and Essie, giving a time of 13 min. 20 secs. For the first 14.2 miles to Ardler. After a check, and a relatively slow recovery, speeds were 79 m.p.h. at the bridge over the Tay, and 70½ before and 75½ after Stanley; net time on this run was 29¾ min with a ten coach train. The other runs by 46225 and 46229 were unremarkable. (See accompanying table).

After another light casual repair from 14th March to 10th April, 1951 at Crewe, 46233 was back in the shops on 19th December, 1951 for a heavy intermediate repair which lasted until 24th January, 1952, having run 115,835 miles in service since the previous heavy general repair. Whilst in shops she was fitted with the 'tell-tale' device to give warning of excessive heating on the big ends. A notice was affixed to the inside of the cab roof above the driver to indicate the locomotive was so fitted.

46233 'DUCHESS OF SUTHERLAND' was recorded on camera by Eric Bruton heading the down 'Mid-Day Scot' at Northchurch on 16th August, 1952.

He commented thus:-

"A little top lighting from a bald and sunless sky helps to brighten up this shot near Northchurch signalbox of the down 'Mid-Day Scot' in the charge of Stanier 8P 'Princess Coronation' class 4-6-2 No. 46233 'DUCHESS OF SUTHERLAND' as it heads for Tring Summit at 50 m.p.h. with 14 corridor coaches on. All bar the third coach - still in L.M.S. red - in the newer B.R. carmine and cream livery introduced some time in 1950 and starting the process of elimination and change. Taken at 2.07 p.m. on August 16th, 1952. The livery of the locomotive was not noted, so was probably dirty post-war black."

SCOTTISH REGION : FORFAR-PERTH								
	Wheel arrangement			4-6-0			4-6-2		
	Engine No.			45714	45581	44677	46225	46233	46229
	Engine Class			5XP	5XP	5	7P	7P	7P
	Load, coaches			8	8	10	8	10	10
	„ tons tare			240	251	309	243	298	304
D st.	„ „ gross		Sch ed.	255	265	325	255	315	320
miles			min.	min. sec.	min. sec.	min. sec.	min. sec.	min. sec.	min. sec.
0.0	FORFAR		0	0 00	0 00	0 00	0 00	0 00	0 00
2.9	Kirriemuir Junction		4	4 33	4 25	4 23	4 14	4 22	4 13
5.7	Glamis			7 05	6 51	7 15	6 44	6 49	6 57
				sigs.					
7.9	Eassie		—	9 21	8 36	9 14	8 34	8 27	8 50
12.0	ALYTH JUNCTION		12	13 14	11 56	12 56	11 51	11 35	12 23
14.2	Ardler		—	15 08	13 47	14 53	13 39	13 20	14 14
					p.w.s.	p.w.s.	p.w.s.	p.w.s.	p.w.s.
16.7	COUPAR ANGUS		16	17 05	16 54	17 47	16 36	16 25	17 03
18.9	Burrelton		—	18 53	20 21	20 27	19 19	19 57	19 43
21.2	Cargill		—	20 46	22 36	23 01	21 30	22 15	21 57
23.1	Ballathie		—	22 11	24 07	24 46	22 59	23 44	23 24
25.3	STANLEY JUNCTION		24	23 57	25 57	26 56	24 52	25 33	25 12
				sigs.*					
27.4	Strathord		—	25 42	27 39	28 42	26 39	27 09	26 48
				sigs.*					
28.3	Luncarty		—	26 33	28 26	29 33	27 31	27 58	27 36
30.9	Almond Valley Junction		30	28 56	30 42	31 43	29 57	30 08	29 44
32.5	PERTH		34	32 24	33 39	34 29	32 54	32 55	33 20
32.5	Net times (min.)		34	29½	30	32½	30	29¾	30¼

*Very slight check

In fact, as we can tell from the date, she was then in the blue livery, not only not very clean but also by now showing some wear and tear, as also evidenced by a photograph of her taking water in the centre road at Shrewsbury station on 1st October, 1952.

46233 'DUCHESS OF SUTHERLAND' returned to Crewe Works again on 15th October, 1952 and, after five days waiting works, went into shops for her next heavy general repair which lasted for a further 24 days. She had run 68,756 miles since her last intermediate repair. Outshopped without the sandguns and associated equipment removed to New Works Order No. E.2194 and fitted with cast steel inside cylinders at a total cost of £703 to N.W. Order No. 2212. She returned to traffic on the 29th November, resplendent in the new Brunswick Green livery, lined out in orange and black, and with the British Railways lion and wheel emblem on her tender.

During this period No 46233 was often working 'The Mid-Day Scot'

Still in B.R. blue livery, 46233 stands at Platform 13 at Euston awaiting departure with a northbound express. (E. Treacy/NRM)

Passing Northchurch signal box with the down 'Mid-Day Scot' on 16 August 1952, Eric Bruton's wonderful description of the photograph is contained in the text. (E.D. Bruton/NRM)

With water cascading from the tender, Duchess of Sutherland thunders over Rugeley troughs with the down 'Mid-Day Scot' in the early 1950's. (H. G. Tidey/NRM)

On a summers day in the early 1950's, a green liveried 46233 is captured hauling a train of mixed liveried stock on the northern approach to Shap. (E. Treacy/NRM)

46233, now in green livery, passes Tebay No 2 signal box on 3rd August 1953 with the up 'Mid-Day Scot'. The photographer has been positioned on the Tebay down starter and NER junction signal gantry. (A.G. Ellis collection)

With safety valves feathering, 46233 awaits departure from Platform 4 at Carlisle on Saturday 31st January 1953 with the up 'Mid-Day Scot' which it will work on to Crewe. Only two months out of Crewe Works, the locomotive is in B.R. green livery. (F. Alcock)

train in both directions, and a fine photograph from the A.G. Ellis Collection shows her passing Tebay No. 2 signal box with an up 'Mid-Day Scot' on 3rd August, 1953. She was recorded on Polmadie depot on 2nd October, 1953 complete with 'The Mid-Day Scot' headboard.

She was also regularly being booked to work the Glasgow - Birmingham expresses at this time as recorded in her 'Known Service Workings' (see Appendix 13). On 13th June 1953 she took over the 11.25 a.m. Birmingham New Street to Glasgow Central express at Crewe, and with a load of fifteen bogies, managed to arrive in Carlisle four minutes early. J E Wilkinson recorded 'DUCHESS OF SUTHERLAND' on camera with the 11.15 a.m. Birmingham-Glasgow at Scout Green on 28th May, 1953 in her new green livery, although looking none too clean.

ACCIDENTS AND INCIDENTS.

Whilst still on the works 46233 was joined by another member of the class; the ill-fated 46242 'CITY OF GLASGOW,' which had been severely damaged in the Harrow and Wealdstone accident mentioned earlier in connection with the rebuilt 46202 'PRINCESS ANNE.' On the morning of Wednesday, 8th October, 1952 when, at the head of the Tuesday evening up 8.15 p.m.sleeper from Perth to London, and running ninety minutes late, she ran into the rear of an up local train in the platform. The wreckage was then run into by 46202 piloted by 'Jubilee' class 4-6-0 No. 45637 'WINDWARD ISLANDS' heading the 7.55 a.m. express from Euston to Liverpool running at around 60 m.p.h. 112 passengers and train crew died. Extricated from the wreckage 46242 was hauled to Crewe shortly afterwards, and, after waiting works for 33 days for a decision on her future, she spent an official record of 291 days in shops. She underwent a major repair, including the fitting of new front end frames, with unusually the curved section of running plate in front of the cylinders, normally only a feature of the unstreamlined members of the class, and a repaired boiler (ex 46235) fitted on 4th August, 1953. She was put back into service on 26th October, 1953, and saw a further decade of service, until finally withdrawn during the week end-

ing 19th October, 1963.

An earlier incident also involved a member of the class when, at about 5.30 a.m. on the morning of Monday, 19th November, 1951, 46252 'CITY OF LEICESTER,' hauling the 10.30 p.m. express from Glasgow to London Euston. The locomotive became derailed on the facing points, crossing from the fast to the slow lines, at Polesworth near Tamworth, which it took at 55 m.p.h., the driver having missed the distant signal. The locomotive was left on its side, half-buried in the stationmaster's allotment garden, and the up lines were blocked. Fortunately there were no fatalities, and only one passenger was badly hurt. The locomotive was shopped for a heavy general repair after waiting 12 days, and returned to traffic on 29th January, 1952.

Some other incidents involving members of the class had occurred by this date, the first, and most serious, happened at 12.17 a.m. on Saturday, 17th April, 1949 when 46251 'CITY OF NOTTINGHAM,' hauling the up 'Postal', ran into the rear of the Friday evening 5.40 p.m. express from Glasgow Central to London Euston hauled by 'Princess Royal' class 4-6-2 locomotive 46207 'PRINCESS ARTHUR OF CONNAUGHT' which had come to a stand after someone had pulled the communication cord. The offender was a young soldier who had recklessly tried to shorten his journey home rather than be carried on to Crewe, with the tragic result that eighteen passengers were killed outright, and six others succumbed to their injuries later in hospital.

The signalman was found to be at fault in clearing his block instruments for the section, even though he had not seen the passenger train pass the Winsford station box. The result was that 46251 and her 625 ton Glasgow to Euston 'Postal' train had ploughed, at a speed of about 45 m.p.h., into the back of the passenger train, which had by then been standing for some 17 minutes.

46251 suffered heavy front end damage, but was shopped at Crewe for a heavy general repair. Fitted with repaired boiler No. 10300 (ex 46234) on 8th April, she was back available for traffic on 19th May.

Just over a month later, on Thursday, 26th May, 1949, another incident occurred, this time involving 46230 'DUCHESS OF BUCCLEUCH' at the head of the 10.10 p.m. express from Glasgow Central to London Euston, which was derailed at points at Douglas Park, south of Uddingston. The signalman had left the distant signal showing 'line clear,' but put the home signal back and moved the facing points into the loop. The train could not be stopped within the sighting distance given by the home signal and became derailed, although fortunately no-one was killed. Only a light casual repair was required, but she was not shopped until 13th November. After 24 days on works she was ready for traffic once more on 29th December.

The next incident, which occurred shortly before the Harrow and Wealdstone crash mentioned above, happened at Etterby Junction on Saturday, 16th August, 1952 and involved No 46224 'PRINCESS ALEXANDRA,' which was travelling light, tender first, on her way to Carlisle Kingmoor motive power depot. She ran into the 11.40 p.m. Newcastle to Stranraer train which had stopped at the home signal. Fortunately no-one was killed.

A further incident, this time involving buckled track, occurred at Abingdon on Saturday, 8th August, 1953 as No. 46231 'DUCHESS OF ATHOLL' was passing with the down 'Royal Scot.' The last seven coaches of the train were derailed, but fortunately yet again no-one was killed. The incident was put down to the high ambient temperature causing excessive expansion of the rails and resulting in deformation of the track alignment.

The final incident in this period happened on Wednesday, 3rd February, 1954 at Watford Tunnel and involved 46250 'CITY OF LICHFIELD' as she was working the up 'Royal Scot.' A broken rail, which actually may have fractured as the train passed over it, caused the derailment of the last bogie of the eighth coach whilst the train was running at 65 m.p.h. Despite the communication cord being pulled, the train continued for a further 1½ miles to Watford Junction. At the north end of the station, the ninth and tenth coaches became derailed at the crossover from the fast to the slow lines,

and the train finally came to a belated halt. Fortunately, and quite extraordinarily, yet again there were no casualties. The subsequent investigation revealed that the right hand rail had been deteriorating over a long period, and the chairs and sleepers under it were also in a poor condition. The cause was put down to the extensive discharges of water from the continuous blowdown valves deposited by many locomotives which had passed over it in the preceding long period of use. As a result, this discharge was diverted into the ashpan under an alteration covered by the modification procedure.

Much later, on Tuesday, 13th January, 1960 there was yet another incident involving a member of the class, when 46231 'DUCHESS OF ATHOLL' collided heavily with the rear of the 11.00 a.m. Birmingham - Glasgow Central express train standing in the platform at Carlisle station, although there was no loss of life. This was the third major incident she had been involved in, having previously been in a collision at Ecclefechan in 1945 and the derailment at Abington in 1953. However, she was shopped at Crewe for a light casual repair on 5th May and returned to service on 18th June for a final two years of active life.

WEST COAST MAIN LINE TRAFFIC.

Following the ending of the Second World War, despite the fact that the L.M.S. was once more operating in a peacetime situation, the fast pre-war timings introduced in 1939 were not re-introduced, and sadly this was to remain the situation right up until the nationalisation of the railways in 1948. However, in 1953 big changes were made to the West Coast schedules of the London Midland Region, and a serious start was made in bringing the fastest expresses up to 'Special Limit' timings south of Crewe. This was followed in 1954 by further improvements to the 'XL limit' over the same stretch of line.

Taken from Tebay No 2 signal box window on Saturday 8th August 1953, 46233 rushes (minus headboard) through Tebay in pouring rain with the down 'Mid-Day Scot'. A number of steam blows show a defective inside cylinder drain tap and left hand outside piston gland packing. (J. E. Wilkinson)

L.M.R.: CARLISLE-LANCASTER

Dist.	Run No. / Engine, 4-6-2 No. / Load, coaches / ,, tons tare / ,, ,, ,,		1 / 46233 / 14 / 453 / 495		2 / 46243 / 15 / 474 / 510		3 / 46231 / 15 / 477 / 510		4 / 46243 / 17 / 531 / 570		4 / 46212 / 17 / 542 / 580	
Miles		min.	m. s.	m.p.h.	m. s.	m.p.h.	m. s.	m.p.h.	m. s.	m.p.h.	m. s.	m.p.h.
0.0	CARLISLE ...	0	0 00	—	0 00	—	0 00	—	0 00	—	0 00	—
1.4	*Carlisle No. 13* ...	—	3 49	36	3 30	33	3 39	31	4 07	29	—	—
4.9	Wreay	—	9 06	46	9 00	43	9 23	41	11 10	31	10 31	33
7.0	Southwaite ...	—	11 40	60½	11 40	53	12 14	50	14 47	42	14 03	41
10.7	Calthwaite ...	—	15 28	60/56	15 33	59/55½	16 25	53/51	19 43	45/41	19 11	43½/40½
12.8	Plumpton ...	21	17 50	64	17 52	64½	18 58	60	22 48	52½	22 17	52
17.9	PENRITH ...	27	22 47	60/71	22 43	55	24 08	55/61½	28 40	48½/60	28 15	47/56½
21.1	*Eden Valley Jc.* ...	—	25 52	62	26 09	60	27 29	55½	32 04	55½	31 51	52
							p.w.s.	*30				
22.6	*Milepost* 46½ ...	—	27 24	53	27 48	52	—	—	33 52	46½	33 52	42
23.6	,, 45½ ...	—	28 36	49	28 59	49	30 58	35	35 15	41½	35 26	36
24.6	,, 44½ ...	—	29 54	45½	30 14	47	32 33	39	36 45	38½	37 08	34½
25.6	,, 43½ ...	—	31 15	44	31 33	45	34 03	41	38 21	37	38 53	34
26.6	,, 42½ ...	—	32 38	43½	32 56	42½	35 29	43½	40 02	35½	40 37	34½
27.6	,, 41½ ...	—	34 01	43½	34 22	41½	36 49	45½	41 42	36	42 19	35½
28.6	,, 40½ ...	—	35 23	44	35 47	44/50	38 06	46	43 18	38	43 56	38
29.4	Shap	—	36 24	49	36 49	47½	39 09	47	44 27	44½	45 04	44
31.4	*Shap Summit* ...	48	39 02	45/85	39 20	47½	42 17	35	47 24	40½	48 04	38
36.9	Tebay	54	44 06	*70	44 10	86	47 52	80½	52 23	82	52 58	82
			sigs.	*20	sig. stop							
42.9	Grayrigg ...	—	51 37	45	54 16	38	54 00	48	57 24	65	57 57	66/77½
50.0	OXENHOLME ...	66	58 30	78/*70	61 25	72	60 29	74	63 06	79/80½	63 47	*71
55.5	Milnthorpe ...	—	63 00	77½	66 11	80½	65 25	69	67 25	76	68 20	78½
59.6	*Milepost* 9½ ...	—	66 23	67	69 25	69	69 25	53	71 02	61½	71 38	65½
62.8	CARNFORTH ...	78	68 55	86	72 01	79/72½	72 31	69½/61	73 49	76/68½	74 16	76/71
66.0	Hest Bank ...	—	71 14	84	74 36	76	75 35	64½	76 33	71	76 53	73
69.1	LANCASTER ...	85	74 39	—	78 26	—	79 31	—	80 12	—	80 21	—
69.1	Net times (min.)	85	72	—	72	—	77½	—	80½	—	80¼	—

*Speed restriction

SCOTTISH REGION : CARSTAIRS-CARLISLE

Distance	Run No. / Engine No. / ,, type / Load, coaches / ,, tons tare / ,, ,, gross	Schedule	1 / 45455(a) / 4-6-0 / 9 / 251 / 270		2 / 46233(b) / 4-6-2 / 14 / 453 / 495		3 / 46201(c) / 4-6-2 / 14 / 448 / 490		4 / 46233(b) / 4-6-2 / 15 / 473 / 510		5 / 46104(d) / 4-6-0 / 16 / 499 / 550	
Miles		min.	m. s.	m.p.h.	m. s.	m.p.h.	m. s.	m.p.h.	m. s.	m.p.h.	m. s.	m.p.h.
0.0	CARSTAIRS ...	0	0 00	—	0 00	—	0 00	—	0 00	—	0 00	—
3.5	*Leggatfoot* ...	—	6 03	41/55	6 17	39/63	6 03	42/58	6 36	36/56½	6 50	35/55
6.6	SYMINGTON	9	9 52	47	9 58	49	9 48	46	10 29	46	10 46	44½
10.3	Lamington ...	—	13 35	63	13 24	80	13 39	67	14 08	74	14 45	65
			p.w.s.	40	p.w.s.	20						
15.7	Abington ...	—	19 58	54	20 57	62	18 50	59	18 55	62/63½	20 10	56/57½
18.2	Crawford ...	—	22 42	58/51	23 24	64/59	21 28	57½/53	21 20	59/55½	22 55	55/51
20.9	Elvanfoot ...	—	25 24	58	26 07	65½	24 24	60	24 08	61½	25 57	59
23.8	*Summit* ...	28	28 47	47	29 07	52	27 48	44	27 21	47	29 34	38
28.1	*Greskine* ...	—	32 47	74/66	32 57	80/72	31 43	83/90	31 16	84/96	33 46	78½/68
									p.w.s.	10		
33.8	BEATTOCK ...	38	37 40	74	37 29	82	35 43	82/85	36 11	62½	38 25	70/77
			p.w.s.	45	p.w.s.	35						
39.0	Wamphray ...	—	43 03	61	42 58	60	39 31	72½	42 46	70½	42 44	68½/72½
44.8	Nethercleugh	—	48 26	68	48 15	74	44 10	75	47 46	75	47 45	70½
47.7	LOCKERBIE ...	50	51 04	65	50 45	69½	46 42	69	50 15	68	50 23	65
50.8	*Castlemilk* ...	—	53 58	61	53 33	67	49 32	60	53 09	60	53 34	54
							p.w.s.	30				
53.4	Ecclefechan ...	—	56 17	69	55 46	74	52 32	—	55 29	72	56 08	65
56.8	Kirtlebridge ...	—	58 58	76/65	58 20	85/77	56 36	62½/58	58 04	83½	59 00	74½
60.5	Kirkpatrick ...	—	62 08	68	61 10	80½	60 11	72	60 55	74	62 16	65½/72
64.9	GRETNA ...	65	65 47	77	64 51	70	63 59	68/76	64 07	76/86	66 08	65
69.5	Rockcliffe ...	—	69 33	64	69 00	65	67 51	65½	67 44	65½	70 50	57
			sigs.		sigs.		sigs.		sigs.			
73.5	CARLISLE ...	75	75 02	—	77 45	—	76 34	—	74 33	—	76 52	—
73.5	Net times (min.)	75	72¼	—	69	—	70½	—	69½	—	76¾	—

Notes: (*a*) Class "5" 4-6-0; (*b*) *Duchess of Sutherland*; (*c*) *Princess Elizabeth*; (*d*) "Royal Scot," *Scottish Borderer.*

The 13.30 'Mid-Day Scot' departure from Euston now had maximum loadings of up to 17 coaches between Crewe and Carlisle typically comprising a G.W.R. Plymouth-Glasgow corridor composite attached at Crewe, brake van, L.M. corridor third, L.M. corridor brake third, two more B.R. corridor thirds and two open thirds, an L.M. kitchen car, B.R. open and corridor firsts, a B.R. corridor composite, a B.R. brake van, and a section detached at Carlisle comprising corridor composite, brake third and two corridor thirds L.M. vehicles.

In his book 'Stanier Pacifics At Work,' John Powell records that further north it was then normal practice to de-rate the trains on the climbs to Shap summit, thus allowing for a through load of some 500 tons, with a further 100 tons allowed for strengthening on the more easily graded and busier sections of the route.

PERFORMANCES TO IMPROVED SERVICE TIMINGS.

North of the border some very hard running was called for in the 1950's, and with heavy loads and tight timings, 'The Mid-Day Scot' was allowed 86 minutes from Carlisle to Carstairs, a distance of 73.5 miles against the grade. Southbound it was some 75 minutes. The Stanier Pacifics took the brunt of these improvements.

A number of runs in this period, timed by W. Robertson, were published, and on one of these 'DUCHESS OF SUTHERLAND' took a 15 coach train, 474 tons tare, 510 tons gross, up Beattock, topping the first 1 in 200 stretch at 63½ m.p.h., the second at 66 m.p.h. and earlier in the run achieving 79 m.p.h at Lockerbie. The start to stop run from Carlisle to Beattock was completed in 38 min. 5 sec. for the 39.7 miles. A vigorous ascent was then made of the climb, with a 2-6-4T at the rear, and a speed of 37 m.p.h was reached from a standing start. Despite standing for 4½ minutes waiting for the banker to come on, and possibly also taking water, the summit was passed before time, and the train arrived at Symington 3¾ minutes early.

In the other direction, two runs behind 46233 hauling the 1.30 p.m. up 'Mid-Day Scot' from Glasgow Central to London Euston (Limited Load), with a fourteen coach formation of 453 tons tare and 495 tons gross, have been recorded. The performance on the section from Carstairs through Carlisle to Lancaster was logged by an informant with the pen-name 'Goliath' and reproduced by Cecil J. Allen in his series 'British Locomotive Practice and Performance' in 'The Railway Magazine' issues dated December, 1954 and February, 1955. The tables, which also include runs by other locomotives, are reproduced by kind permission of that journal. Driver Latham was in charge with A. Clarke of Crewe North depot making up the crew and, in his performance evaluation, written for Docherty's 'The L.M.S. Duchesses' book, published by Model and Allied Publications Ltd. in 1973, John Powell comments; "that these runs were some of the hardest turns that the 'Duchesses' were called upon to tackle in the 1950's". He also comments that the run "typified the sound, steady enginemanship with none of the 'starve-and-burst' attitude that one often saw."

Column 2 in the February article details the performance of 46233 against an overall timing of 8 hours and 15 minutes that allowed for six intermediate stops. She reached her first 80 m.p.h.after only 10.3 miles at Lamington. There was then such a good recovery from a 20 m.p.h. permanent way slack that, up a 1 in 294 gradient, she had accelerated to 64 m.p.h. by the time she reached Crawford, with a minimum speed of 59 m.p.h. thereafter. The two mile climb up the final incline of 1 in 99 to Beattock Summit saw the speed fall off from 65½ to 52 m.p.h. as she breasted the summit. Powell calculates an E.D.B.H.P. output of a full 1,885. 80 m.p.h was achieved at Greskine, where a permanent way restriction of 72 m.p.h was in force. Lockerbie was passed less than a minute behind schedule in 50 minutes 45 seconds, and a maximum speed of 85 m.p.h. was achieved at Kirtlebridge. Gretna Junction was taken at 70 m.p.h., slightly early, and Rockcliffe was passed at 65 m.p.h. in 63½ minutes net. Here 46233 was delayed by the usual signal check, giving an eventual arrival in Carlisle in 77 minutes 45 seconds and a net time of 69 minutes for the 73½ miles. A punctual arrival within the booked time of 75 minutes had clearly been possible.

At Polmadie 46233 awaits her crew before backing down to Glasgow Central on Saturday 2nd October 1953 to work the up 'Mid-Day Scot' as far as Crewe. (J. Robertson/Transport Treasury)

On an unidentified express, Duchess of Sutherland passes Victoria Colliery Sidings signal box on the West Coast main line between Standish and Boars Head on Saturday 1st May 1954 (R. Hinton)

Approaching Rugby in the mid 1950's with a down express from London Euston. The train is comprised of LMS and BR stock in carmine and cream livery. (T. E. Williams/NRM)

Easing forward on Crewe North depot on Saturday 14 May 1955 one week after leaving Crewe Works following a heavy intermediate overhaul. (J.E. Wilkinson)

72

Leaving Carlisle eight minutes behind schedule, 'DUCHESS OF SUTHERLAND' set about her task in Driver Latham's capable hands. Good acceleration up to 36 m.p.h achieved up the 1 in 131 to Wreay was a fine performance with this load, and even better was the further acceleration up to 60½ m.p.h. climbing the 1 in 228 to Southwaite and the maintained 58½ m.p.h. up the rising grade of 1 in 172 to 1 in 114 past Calthwaite. 60 m.p.h. was achieved on the level past Plumpton and 56 m.p.h. minimum up the two miles of 1 in 186 immediately beyond. Penrith was reached over four minutes early; but the outstanding feat was the rapid acceleration to 71 m.p.h. on the short, level stretch beyond. The next seven miles at 1 in 125 to milepost 41½ was taken at a sustained speed of 43 - 44 m.p.h. and Shap Summit was breasted at 45 m.p.h., almost nine minutes early. This, Powell observes, showed a similarly good performance as that to Beattock Summit, with a D.B.H.P. output of between 1,780 and 1,940. 85 m.p.h. was reached on the approach to Tebay, which was passed two minutes early. The express had the signals against it whilst an up freight was looped at Grayrigg, but then, with a clear road ahead, 46233 reached 86 m.p.h. just before Carnforth. Lancaster was reached just over two minutes early in 74 minutes 39 seconds and a net time of 72 minutes for the 69.1 miles from Carlisle, 13 minutes less than the schedule, and a truly stirling perfomance.

A further run between Carstairs and Carlisle also appears in the table of the February article as column 4. The driver's name is not recorded, but as Cecil J. Allen remarks he was "evidently partial to high speed !" He further remarks that "as far as Symington the brakes appear to have been dragging on slightly, but even so, time was slightly improved to the Summit, after which came a most rousing descent of Beattock Bank, with the highest speed on it that I have ever known." The table shows the speed increasing from 44 m.p.h. when breasting the summit to a maximum of 96 m.p.h. at Greskine, followed immediately by severe braking to 10 m.p.h. for a permanent way slack due to track repairs at Beattock Station, after which the brakes appeared to be dragging again. The remainder of the run included even more high speed running, with a maximum of 86 m.p.h at Floriston, Although there was the usual slowing for signals on the approach to Carlisle, an arrival 'on time' was achieved. The net time for the 73.7 miles with the 510 tons train was 69½ minutes.

The article of December, 1954 also included a series of runs southwards over Shap with loads varying from 495 to 580 tons. The schedule was 48 minutes for the 31.4 miles from Carlisle to the Summit, and the fastest climb was that recorded with 'DUCHESS OF SUTHERLAND' with 495 tons trailing, when the Summit was passed in only 39 minutes 2 seconds, as described above.

On 16th October, 1954 No 46233 took over the up 'Mid-Day Scot' and arrived at Carlisle a minute early. She was not replaced, and had to continue on to Glasgow Central with the train, as had been the practice with the previous years' timetable.

Further north still, at the most northerly location to which the Stanier Pacifics worked, 'DUCHESS OF SUTHERLAND' was to be found at Aberdeen on a number of occasions, having worked north with the 7.15 a.m. from Glasgow Buchanan Street, leaving Perth at 9.20 a.m. for Aberdeen. She was on this working on 20th December, 1952, and returned south at 3.30 p.m. with the up 'Postal.'

At this time members of the class were also occasionally to be seen heading 'The Saint Mungo', the 9.35 a.m. express from Aberdeen to Glasgow, but there is no record of 46233 being on this turn of duty so far as is known.

However, 'DUCHESS OF SUTHERLAND' did certainly work into Edinburgh, and Stuart Sellar recorded her at Princes Street station on 15th June, 1955 with a train of carmine and cream liveried stock.

CHANGES OF ALLOCATION.

During early July, 1952 three members of the class had been moved from Crewe North depot to Camden in London, 46225 and 46252 on the 5th and 46229 on the 7th. Further changes followed, so that by January, 1954 the allocation was as follows:-

Camden (1B) :-	46229, 46236-7, 46239-41, 46244-5, 46247, 46249-50, 46253-4 and 46256-7
Crewe North (5A) :-	46225, 46233-5, 46242-3, 46246, 46248 and 46252.
Carlisle Upperby (12A) :-	46226, 46228, 46238, 46251, 46255.
Polmadie (66A) :-	46220-4, 46227, 46230-2, 46244-5.

Presumably borrowed by Polmadie for a fill-in turn, Duchess of Sutherland stands in unfamiliar territory at Edinburgh Princes Street awaiting departure with a Glasgow bound express on Wednesday 15 June 1955. (W.S. Sellar)

46233 'DUCHESS OF SUTHERLAND'S REPAIR HISTORY - 1953-6.

46233 was not shopped at all in 1953, during which she ran 90,220 miles, but on 16th January, 1954 she entered Crewe Works for a light intermediate overhaul, and was on works for 20 days, after waiting to go in for only one day. Her next heavy intermediate repair followed her being taken out of traffic on 14th March, 1955, and after eight days awaiting a decision, it was to be a further five days before she was shopped at Crewe, finally emerging on 7th May after having had £2,791 spent on her. A further light casual 'engine only' repair followed, causing her to be out of traffic from 31st August to 3rd October, 1955, during which she was fitted with a modified piston for the continuous blowdown valves to Order No. E.3329. A further casual repair followed from 25th December, 1955 to 30th January, 1956.

The end of 1956 saw her seventh heavy general repair for which she was taken out of traffic on 25th October. Having run 101,032 miles since her last heavy intermediate repair, and with a day waiting for a decision and eight days waiting works, she was back at Crewe and emerged on 8th December having been fitted with repaired boiler No. 9937. This was the original boiler that had been fitted to No. 6220 'CORONATION' when first built. 46233 was also fitted with strengthened axlebox guides under Order No. E.3869, and to Job. No. 5755, at a cost of £171-7s-3d. This had become necessary as a result of trouble experienced with broken guides and loose rivets at the leading and intermediate driving wheel positions, and the necessity of removing the wheelsets at motive power depots at the No. 6 examination to effect repairs. This work also covered the 'Princess Royal' class engines, but of course excluded Nos. 46256-7 with their roller bearing axleboxes.

VARIATIONS IN LIVERY

During the first six months of 1953 members of the class were recorded by 'The Railway Observer' exhibiting a variety of liveries. 46228 was in blue but changed to green by 8/55; 46229 was in green; 46236 was in black; 46237 in blue but green by 8/55; 46239 was green; 46240, 46243 and 46244 were blue; 46245 was changed from black to green early in 1953; 46246 was still in black lined in maroon and straw; 46247 was in black changed to green by 3/54; 46248 was in lined black; 46249 in blue but changed to green by 3/54; 46250 was in green; 46251 in lined black; 46253 in black changed to green by 3/54; 46254 was in blue; 46255 in green; 46256 was in blue and 46257 in green.

INTRODUCTION OF 'THE CALEDONIAN' EXPRESS.

By the winter of 1955-6 the two long established named trains were on a 111 minute timing from Glasgow to Carlisle, and these were held until the introduction of 'The Caledonian' express in June, 1957. With this came a move away from the very heavily loaded Anglo-Scottish expresses such as 'The Mid-Day Scot', with its splitting and joining-up at Crewe, Carlisle and Symington, all of which was time consuming, and 12-14 coach train formations now became the norm for the 'Royal Scot.' The former had continued to be heavily loaded until the winter of 1954, when the down train ran as a Glasgow only service on the 'XL limit' timings to Crewe and special limit timings onwards to Carnforth.

The first down 'Caledonian' express, with its horizontally lettered headboard, was appropriately hauled by No 46242 'CITY OF GLASGOW' and the first up run by 46229 'DUCHESS OF HAMILTON,' both then Camden engines. 46229 arrived at Euston two minutes early, and the following day 46242 was seven minutes early on its return working.

The introduction of 'The Caledonian' express provided a service somewhat resembling the pre-war 'Coronation Scot' but without the supplementary fare. The new service started on 17th June, 1957. It was a lightly loaded train up to a maximum of 280 tons, equivalent to eight B.R. coaches, and typical train formation for the afternoon Euston departure being a BR Mk 1 corridor brake second, three Mk.1 open seconds, an ex LMS kitchen car, two BR Mk 1 open firsts and an ex LMS corridor brake first.

It had a 6 hour 40 minute overall schedule to meet, and was timed to leave Glasgow at 8.30 a.m. with a later afternoon return from Euston at 4.15 p.m. it stopped only at Carlisle for two minutes, and overall running times were 291 minutes and 107 minutes in each direction. This was an improvement on all of the 1956 timings with the sole exception of the East Coast 'Elizabethan', which ran non-stop during the summer. The new 'Caledonian' had an average speed of just over a mile-a-minute, and was to a schedule only ten minutes slower than the old 'Coronation Scot.'

In response, the Eastern Region commenced operating the new 'Morning Talisman' express in competition between London Kings' Cross and Edinburgh via the East Coast main line. Trains left at 4 p.m., the former taking the time of the old L.N.E.R. 'Coronation' express.

The Modernisation Plan of 1955, mentioned earlier, had already raised the spectre of an ultimate threat to the supremacy of steam on these routes, but progress was to be relatively slow, and it would be 1958 before sufficient of the Type 4 English Electric diesel-electric 1Co-Co1 locomotives were available to first threaten and then cause the ultimate demise of Stanier's Pacific locomotives.

On a running in turn following a visit to Crewe Works, 46233 hauls a three coach local train near Shrewsbury. (G. Coltas)

With a full head of steam 46233 eases out of London Euston with the down 'Mid-Day Scot' on Monday 21st May 1956. The smoke deflectors are now fitted with footholds which were probably added during the light casual repair in January of that year. (P.H. Groom)

Rather late in their working life a number of tests were carried out life a number of tests were carried out with members of the class including performance with test trains and static tests at the Rugby Locomotive Testing Station which had been officially opened by the then Minister of Transport, Alfred Barnes, M.P. on 19th October, 1948. A locomotive test plant for all four main companies had been advocated as early as 1927 in a paper presented by Sir Nigel Gresley, but in 1936, with strong support from Stanier, the L.M.S. agreed to join the L.N.E.R. in a joint scheme which did not come to fruition until after the war. Sir William A. Stanier was present at the opening along with the 'Princess Coronation' class locomotive 46256 named after him, and the late Sir Nigel Gresley was represented by the Class A4 Pacific locomotive bearing his name.

Having regard to the important role played by the 'Princess Coronation' class on the West Coast main line, static tests were carried out at Rugby with 46225 'DUCHESS OF GLOUCESTER' at speeds up to 100 m.p.h. in May 1955, after she had had a general repair. After a heavy intermediate repair and running in, subsequent tests were carried out between March and May, 1956 with a 640 ton train on the Settle-Carlisle line between Carlisle and Skipton at controlled speeds between 20 and 80 m.p.h. at increments of 5 m.p.h., using the L.M.R. Dynamometer Car No. 3 controlling the Mobile Test Units. These tests proved that at 70 m.p.h. the i.h.p. reached 2,100 and the drawbar horsepower 1,570 with a firing rate of 3,820 lb./hour. A drawbar horsepower of 2,250 was achieved, but requiring a firing rate well beyond a fireman's capabilities except for short bursts. The result of these tests were written up in Report R13, which quoted:-

"Steaming rates using the live steam injector, range from 14,640 to 41,500 lb/hr on the test plant and from 15,000 to 40,000 lb./hr on the line, the upper limits being set by the liability to slipping, but also, on the line, by limited water capacity of the tender, which was designed for..... a route exceptionally equipped with water troughs, and by the difficulty of handling bagged coal at a sufficient rate in the confined space of a coal bunker."

The Interim Report L.109 stated in its observations that "it was evident that the locomotive was exceptionally free steaming and had a large evaporative capacity. The cylinder efficiency and overall efficiency, as reflected by the coal consumption per I.H.P. hour and per D.B.H.P. hour respectively compared very well with other locomotives of modern design." Another observation was that with the valves set to give equal leads there was a difference of approximately 17% in M.E.P. between the front and back cylinder ends. By setting the valves back by $^{1}/_{16}$ inch this difference was reduced to approximately 2%, and it was recommended that the practice of setting valves back slightly be extended to this class of locomotive.

Earlier tests in 1955 using the ex G.W. R. dynamometer car on the Western Region between Paddington and Plymouth enabled a comparison to be drawn between the performance of 46237 'CITY OF BRISTOL' and a modified 'King' class 4-6-0 with enlarged superheater and a double chimney. The Stanier Pacific proved its superiority in starting and hill climbing, and although the two locomotives had virtually the same theoretical tractive effort, the Pacific was capable of developing the greater horsepower.

'The Mid-Day Scot' was a frequent working for 46233 whilst allocated to Crewe North and she is again seen in charge of a down train at Lichfield Trent Valley. A blow of steam at the front indicates a defective cylinder drain tap. (G. W. Sharpe)

Duchess of Sutherland replenishes her tender at Glasgow St. Rollox shed on Saturday 9th July 1955.
(J. Robertson/Transport Treasury)

A MAGNIFICENT PERFORMANCE WITH 46244 'KING GEORGE VI'

In a bid to improve train timings still further, two special runs were made in the autumn of 1957 on which the timing of the up train beyond Crewe was cut by fifteen minutes, giving an arrival time in Euston of 2.55 p.m., a total time of only 130 minutes for the 158 miles. On August 7th 46229 'DUCHESS OF HAMILTON,' driven by William Thomas 'Bill' Starvis and with A.W. Wills as Fireman, both from Camden depot, worked a train to this schedule, thereby cutting the overall time from Glasgow to Euston to 6 hours and 27 minutes. Although an excellent performance, it was by no means an all-time record for, quite apart from the exploits of 'Princess Royal' class 4-6-2 No 6201 'PRINCESS ELIZABETH' in 1936, there had been numerous instances of the pre-war 'Coronation Scot' bettering its schedule by more than three minutes. The fifteen minutes taken off the overall time required an average speed of 74.1 m.p.h. to be achieved over the 158 miles, start to stop.

However, an even better performance occurred the following month on Thursday, 5th September, 1957 when the train locomotive was 46244 'KING GEORGE VI'. Starvis was again the driver and John Tumilty the fireman, with Inspector J.H. Woodruffe keeping a watching brief. The 8.30 a.m. 'Caledonian' from Glasgow Central left Carlisle one minute late at 10.19 a.m. and the 141 miles to Crewe were covered in 135 minutes, 113 minutes net, despite three delays at Penrith for signals, a p.w.s. at Hest Bank and a signal check at Norton Crossing near Acton Bridge, which accounted for some eight minutes in all. With Crewe passed 12 minutes early 46244 finally came to a stand at Euston station no less than 37 minutes early at 2.33 p.m. instead of a booked arrival time of 3.10 p.m. This gave an overall time of 6 hours and 3 minutes for the 401 miles, and therefore 'KING GEORGE VI' had beaten the 1936 record set up by 'Princess Royal' class locomotive 6201 'PRINCESS ELIZABETH' between Crewe and Euston by no less than 13 minutes.

Bill Starvis had been asked by his Superintendent to get the 'Caly' into Euston 'about fifteen minutes early' and there were clearly no half measures in his response to the edict, the exit from Carlisle being distinctly fast. Once underway 46244 was heading for Shap summit 10 minutes early. However, the signalman at Penrith was clearly unprepared to accept the "Caledonain" 6 minutes early, and, after crawling up to Penrith No. 1 Signal Box, matters rested for a full 3 minutes. Once the signals were pulled off the engine was set to it working hard, and Shap Summit was passed 4 minutes early in 36.5 minutes, 29 minutes net. After negotiating various moderate restrictions following a signal check at Scout Green, 46244 improved on 'PRINCESS ELIZABETH's' time between Oxenholme and Carnforth by over a minute, a hundred or so being attained in the vicinity of Hincaster Junction, the latter's maximum at this point having been 86 m.p.h.. Crewe was passed 13 minutes early, a net time of 124 minutes from Carlisle.

In conversation with Douglas Landau in 1969 Bill Starvis recalled "I doubt whether the speed was as high as ninety-six at Tring Summit, more like ninety-two. The exact time from Bletchley to Tring was nine minutes and forty seconds. After eighty through the Wolverton slack we were up to about eighty-eight through Bletchley and over ninety by Leighton, then we opened her out a bit and went over the top without falling below ninety." He was unable to throw any light on how the reported minumum of 96 m.p.h at Tring emanated, the time of 9 minutes 40 seconds, giving an average speed of 93.2 m.p.h. accords with the minimum of 91 or 92. Onwards from Tring, judging from 'Coronation's' times and speeds, 'KING GEORGE VI' attained a hundred or more at King's Langley

and Wembley before coming to rest in Euston 37 minutes early. The run from Carlisle had been made in 253 minutes, 242 net, giving actual and net average speeds of 70.8 and 74.0 m.p.h., start to stop. Perhaps the most exciting average speed of the trip was that of 92.0 m.p.h. set up over 54.5 miles between Roade and Willesden. 'Coronation's' average over this section was 89.3 m.p.h.

Bill Starvis himself summed it up by saying *"Number forty-four was the pick of a very good bunch, the weather was favourable and the coal was good, although not the best. But when an engine is driven hard over 400 miles, things have to be managed with care. On a shorter journey I think the run from Crewe could have been made in a hundred and fifteen minutes. Given today's signalling, possibly a trifle less."*

The Inspector's Log, which was published as part of a most interesting article by John Clarke in the August, 1996 edition of 'Steam World' is given below:-

	BOOKED TIMES		ACTUAL TIMES		MINUTES		CAUSE
Motive Power Dept., London Midland Region. 5th September, 1957. Weather favourable.							
REPORT OF INSPECTOR J.H. Woodruffe ON THE RUNNING OF THE 8.30 a.m. Passenger train from Glasgow to Euston as between Carlisle & Euston. on 5th September, 1957.							
STATIONS	Arr.	Dep.	Arr.	Dep.	Lost	Recov'd	
Carlisle		10.19		10.20	1		
Plumpton	37		33			5	
Penrith	42		41		3		Sgls
Shap Summit	58		55			2	
Tebay	11.04		11.00			1	Sgls
Scout Green							
Oxenholme	16		12				
Carnforth	27		20			3	
Lancaster	32		28		3		P.w.s
Garstang	42		36			2	
Preston	52		46			2	
Euxton Jctn	59		53				
Wigan	12.13		12.02			5	Lib. Allow.
Warrington	25		12			2	for p.w. ops. Vic. Co. sdg.
Weaver Jctn	32		21			2	
Winsford	38		27				
Crewe	47		35			1	
Whitmore	57		45				
Norton Bridge	1.04		50			2	
Stafford	09		55				
Milford & Brockton	13		59				
Rugeley	17		1.03				
Tamworth	27		13				
Nuneaton	38		22			2	
Rugby	50		33			1	
Roade	2.07		50				
Bletchley	16		59				
Tring	28		2.09			2	
Watford	38		18			1	
Willesden	47		25			2	
Euston	2.55		2.33				

It should be noted that the above arrival time of 2.55 p.m. in Euston is that shown in the working timetable and not the public timetabled time of arrival.

At the end of the run both Starvis and Tumilty were photographed standing in front of 46244 by a 'Daily Express' cameraman, and Bill later received a letter from Mr. E.H. Baker, the Divisonal Motive Power Superintendent at Crewe which read:-

"Dear Mr. Starvis,

I have received a letter of congratulation on the excellent run you made with the Up "Caledonian" on Thursday last, September 5th.

This notable achievement on your part has brought credit to the Western Division in general and to the Motive Power Department in particular, and I am pleased to be able to send you this congratulatory message, at the same time adding my personal thanks for a very successful performance.

Yours sincerely,
(signed) E.H. Baker."

Starvis had begun his career as a call boy and cleaner at Camden in 1913 working for the old London & North Western Railway, his then ambition being to drive 'The Corridor' express which later became the 'Mid-Day Scot' and also to drive the Royal Train. He worked as a passed fireman with both Laurie Earle and Bert Smith, before passing out as a driver with the L.M.S. in 1933. In July, 1951 he was passed out to drive the diesel-electric locomotives 10000 and 10001, and ten years later his diesel turns exceeded his steam ones. His last turn was working 46252 'CITY OF LEICESTER' on the 1.05 p.m. Euston to Carlisle on 17th April, 1962, but even after retirement he kept up his acquaintance with steam by visiting Butlin's holiday camp at Skegness to tell visitors to the footplate of preserved 'Royal Scot' class 4-6-0 No. 6100 'ROYAL SCOT' of his days as a top link driver. He died in March, 1975.

As Cecil J. Allen observed in his article in the November, 1957 issue of 'The Railway Magazine' "although the broadcast announcements of what happened, including the televised interview with Driver Starvis, not to mention the newspaper references on the following morning, seemed designed to make it appear that this was something done quite easily, it is obvious that nothing of this kind would have been possible without considerable pre-arrangement." He adds that several trains would have had to be held at various points on the route in order to give 46244 the required path.

The article produced logs of the run compared to that of 6201 and also 6220 'CORONATION' herself some thirty years earlier on the day of the 'Coronation Scot' press trip of 29th June, 1937, when the overall time from Crewe to Euston was the same - 119 minutes start to stop, although 46244 had the advantage of running through Crewe without stopping, worth up to a 1 1/2 minute saving as opposed to the dead start of 6220.

In an article in 'Trains Seventy One,' published by Ian Allan Ltd., D.H. Landau described the run in further detail and produced a log of the run taken from Bill Starvis's own notes and the guard's log. In an editorial piece headed 'East v West', the November 1957 issue of 'Trains Illustrated' comments "The guard's journal time of 9 1/2 minutes for the 15 miles from Bletchley to Tring may sound optimistic, but we have it on good authority that some heroic driving methods saw the summit topped with a blast of sound and fury at 96 m.p.h." Nearly 100 m.p.h. uphill is a magnificent achievement, and this is undoubtedly one of the best runs ever recorded with a 'Princess Coronation' class locomotive. The majority of passing times were only taken to the nearest minute, and therefore an error of up to 1/2 minute is possible at any point on the run, with a maximum accumulated error of 1 minute.

From 9th June, 1958 'The Caledonian' service was effectively doubled, with an additional early morning 'down' train leaving Euston at 10.45 a.m. and a later afternoon 'up' train leaving Glasgow at 4.00 p.m. Both these trains made additional stops at Crewe northbound and Stafford southbound with good connections for Birmingham and the Midlands. Arrival times were 2.30 p.m. and 10.45 p.m. respectively. The 'up' train had the fastest scheduled booked time on the London Midland Region, being only given 120 minutes for the 133.6 miles from Stafford to Euston, giving an average speed of 66.8 m.p.h. start to stop. The new 'down' train was also on a mile-a-minute schedule between Euston and Crewe, 158 miles in 147 minutes, averaging 64.5 m.p.h. The inaugural trains were worked by No 46224 'PRINCESS ALEXANDRA' from Euston and 46232 'DUCHESS OF MONTROSE' from Glasgow. Unhappily there was a lack of interest from the travelling public, and the trains disappeared from the winter timetable of 1958-9, the last up afternoon train being worked by 46224 on 12th September, 1958.

Another change to services was that the Perth portion of the 10.10 a.m. from Euston, which now included through coaches to

Driver Bill Starvis and fireman John Tumilty pose with 46244 after their run on September 5th 1957.

Aberdeen, was worked forward as an extra train arriving at 10.15 p.m. The balanced return working was provided by the 10.20 a.m. departure which joined the 12.20 p.m. train from Perth to Euston, arriving at 9.46 p.m. 'The Mid-Day Scot' also began running on Sundays from that date.

However, as Cecil J. Allen observed, the pre-war best times for the fastest express services were never achieved again, and the 1939 timing of 3 hours 20 minutes for the Liverpool to Euston stood at 3 hours 50 minutes in the 'up' direction, only two minutes better than the 'down'. Even the 'Royal Scot' was on a 7 hour 55 minute schedule from Euston to Glasgow as compared with 7 hours 20 minutes pre-war. By contrast the timings north of the border between Glasgow and Aberdeen were considerably faster, and with more frequent services into the bargain.

Other workings for members of the class included the 3.30 p.m. 'Up Postal' to London Euston which was occasionally worked all the way to Crewe by a Crewe North allocated engine, and 'DUCHESS OF SUTHERLAND' would have found herself on this working again at some time in this period, as she had already been in December, 1952 as mentioned earlier.

The 1957 decision to change engines at Crewe and at Carlisle on expresses running between London Euston and Glasgow Central, further reinforced by the need to have Stanier 'Pacifics' allocated to the depots at Crewe North and Carlisle Upperby at the expense of both Camden and Polmadie depots. By that October the class were split between Crewe North with twelve, Polmadie with nine, Carlisle Upperby with just three and Camden with fourteen. Allocated to Crewe North depot, 46233 had also continued working 'The Mid-Day Scot' and Glasgow-Birmingham expresses right through the 1950's, but on 14th June, 1958 she was briefly involved in the new stategy and re-allocated to Carlisle Upperby. With her went 46236 'CITY OF BRADFORD,' 46237 'CITY OF BRISTOL,'

46243 'CITY OF LANCASTER', 46244 'KING GEORGE VI' and 46250 'CITY OF LICHFIELD.' By 5th July, 1958 the "Princess Coronation" class was distributed between the various depots as follows:-

London Camden:-	46229, 46239-42, 46245, 46247, 46254, 46256-7. (10).
Crewe North:-	46220-1, 46225, 46228, 46234-5, 46246, 46248-9, 46251-3 (12).
Carlisle Upperby:-	46226, 46233, 46236-8, 46243-4, 46250, 46255 (9).
Glasgow Polmadie:-	46222-4, 46227, 46230-2 (7)

As to repairs, 46233 had been shopped specially between 10th and 23rd October, 1957 for an unclassified repair during which she was fitted with Smith-Stone speed indicating equipment under order No. R7461 and Job No. 5794 issued on 20th August. This Order covered all members of both Stanier 'Pacific' classes except Nos. 46256 and 46257 which were already so fitted, the work being considered to be necessary "in view of the number of high speed trains now operating in this (London Midland) region."

A heavy intermediate repair followed, and from 24th February, 1958 'DUCHESS OF SUTHERLAND' was out of traffic for a total of 40 days, having run 92,569 miles since her last heavy general repair. She spent 38 days in the works, and was outshopped and returned to Crewe North depot ready for service on 12th April.

'DUCHESS OF SUTHERLAND' was re-allocated to the Crewe North depot again on 20th September, 1958.

Carlisle was of course a 'mecca' for the Stanier Pacific fan, and the class were to be seen throughout the day on the various express workings passing through the station en route between England and Scotland. A photograph by Gordon Coultas captures the essence of this place, and shows 46233 entering Platform 4 with an un-named up express around 1958-9, since the view shows the new

station roof which was a 1958 addition. Passengers and staff and a lot of parcels fill the platform, and the time shown on the clock is 3.38 p.m., assuming it is working!

ANOTHER CHANGE OF LIVERY FOR THE CLASS.

With the introduction of the summer services of 1956, the first train-sets painted in maroon livery had appeared on the 'Royal Scot' and also on 'The Merseyside Express' running between London Euston and Liverpool Lime Street.

Following this change, a decision was taken late in 1957 to return to the crimson lake livery, with black and yellow lining out, for a number of London Midland Region based Stanier 'Pacifics'. No 46245 'CITY OF LONDON' was selected for trial, and was displayed in the new livery at Euston station in London on 8th January, 1958 alongside No. 46250 'CITY OF LICHFIELD' in a 'Brunswick Green' livery, lined out in orange and black, for comparison purposes. The crimson lake livery was approved and twenty locomotives, including some from Princess Royal Class were repainted. The Princess Coronations were as follows:-

46225 (9/8/58), 46226 (26/11/58), 46228 (21/6/58),
46229 (17/5/58), 46236 (2/7/58), 46238 (20/6/58),
46240 (11/7/58), 46243 (11/10/58), 46244 (24/10/58),
46245 (28/12/57), 46246 (11/10/58), 46247 (24/5/58),
46248 (7/6/58), 46251 (22/11/58), 46254 (6/9/58), 46256 (17/5/58).

Of these it was reported in the railway press that both 46226 'DUCHESS OF NORFOLK' and 46240 'CITY OF COVENTRY' had a different B.R. style of lining out instead of the L.M.S. style of black edging yellow which the previous repaints had received.

With the climb from Carlisle to Shap Summit completed, the fireman takes the opportunity to move coal forward with the aid of the steam operated coal pusher, its use being indicated by the plume of steam at the rear of the tender (P. Conolly)

Duchess of Sutherland threads her way through the Clyde Valley between Abington and Crawford on the climb to Beattock Summit with an up express in May 1957.
(W.J.V. Anderson/Rail Archive Stevenson)

46233 heads a Glasgow to Birmingham express out of Lancaster on Saturday 14 September 1957. The gradient of 1 in 98 appears to have been taken with little effort on the part of the fireman. (N. A. Machell)

With a train of BR MK1 maroon stock, Duchess of Sutherland attacks the 1 in 75 climb to Shap Summit at Greenholme with the down 'Royal Scot' from London Euston. The tender is already well down on coal, the locomotive having covered some 263 miles from Euston. (E. Treacy/NRM)

Running towards Tebay past Tebay No 1 box, 46233 heads a London Euston to Carlisle express on Monday 11th August 1958. (G. Morrison)

For a 3 month period during 1958, 46233 was allocated to Carlisle Upperby and is seen sporting a 12B shed plate passing Ribble Sidings south of Preston with a W74 reporting number indicating a Carlisle to London Euston express. The Smith-Stone speed indicator fitted to the trailing driving wheel had been added in November 1957. (W. Ashcroft)

Amid the bustle of a busy Carlisle Citadel station, Duchess of Sutherland arrives on platform 4 with an up express, circa 1958. Station staff and passengers can be seen preparing for the train to come to a stand. (G. Coltas)

The locomotives selected were all allocated to Camden, Crewe North or Carlisle Upperby motive power depots at the time. However, because the requisite number of locomotives had been repainted in the new livery by the time she was shopped for her next heavy repair on 1st August, 1959, 46233 remained in the Brunswick Green livery. At that time she still retained the old style 'lion and wheel' emblem on the tender. Four 'Princess Royal' class locomotives allocated to Edge Hill motive power depot in Liverpool were also re-liveried in crimson lake at the time, these being Nos. 46200, 46204, 46207 and 46208, presumably in their case also for working the 'Merseyside Express'.

1959 saw the 'Royal Scot' and 'Mid-Day Scot' trains brought up to the same overall timings, and O.S. Nock includes details of a number of timed runs behind 'Princess Coronation' class locomotives in his article 'British Locomotive Practice and Performance' in the March, 1960 issue of the 'Railway Magazine', although none these involved 46233.

Another factor affecting the duties of all Stanier Pacifics was the steady progress of electrification on the route from Euston to Manchester. Due to the number of speed restrictions caused by essential engineering work, large recovery times were built into the schedules from the winter of 1958-9. The general plan was to start trains ten minutes earlier from Euston so that they passed through Crewe more or less at the original timings so as to cause as little disruption as possible. Even the 'Royal Scot' was so re-timed from 10.00 a.m., and both that and the up 'Mid-Day Scot' took 15 minutes longer, whilst the down 'Mid-Day Scot' was decelerated by no less than 28 minutes. The 12.20 p.m. from Perth to Euston, normally a Stanier Pacific working, was the train least affected by the changes, being promoted from 'Special Limit' to 'XL Limit' status, arriving in London only seven minutes later at 9.52 p.m. Most of the up Anglo-Scottish expresses, already having liberal recovery times, retained their Euston arrival times, but the 'Irish Mail' was also retimed to

give a later arrival.

The down morning and up evening 'Caledonians' having disappeared, the complimentary workings leaving Glasgow at 8.30 a.m. and Euston at 4.05 p.m. were both allowed an extra 15 minutes, giving an overall journey time of 6 hours and 55 minutes.

FINAL HEAVY REPAIRS TO 46233.

After having run some 101,590 miles since her previous heavy intermediate repair at Crewe 'DUCHESS OF SUTHERLAND' was taken out of traffic on 1st August, 1959 and, having waited four days for a repair decision. This was the last time she was shopped at Crewe for a heavy general repair in B.R. days. This involved replacing the existing boiler No. 9937 and replacing it with repaired boiler No. 10641 which she still retains as a preserved locomotive today. This had come from 46252 'CITY OF LEICESTER' and had originally been fitted as new to 6238 'CITY OF CARLISLE'. It had subsequently been used on 6230 'DUCHESS OF BUCCLEUCH', 6235 'CITY OF BIRMINGHAM' and 46248 'CITY OF LEEDS'. At this repair 46233 was also fitted with the B.R. Automatic Train Control system under Order No. E.4983 at a capital cost of £302-9s-0d.

She emerged from the works on 26th September, 1959 still in the Brunswick Green livery, but with her tender now sporting the new B.R. emblem which now included the words 'British Railways'.

At the end of 1959 the L.M. Region made a revolutionary change by reducing the formations of both the 'Royal Scot' and 'Mid-Day Scot' trains to precisely the same eight coach, 270 ton formation as the 'Caledonian,'and all three now covered the journey to and from London and Glasgow in precisely the same time, i.e. 7 hours 15 minutes, with 326 minutes allowed for the 299.1 miles from Euston to Carlisle. No recovery times were allowed north of Preston, but

Summer 1959 at Cheddington sees 46233 heading towards London Euston. Almost exactly four years later, this location was to be the scene of the great train robbery. (M. Welch)

thirty odd minutes were allowed south of that point in both directions. Pre-booking of seats was now strongly recommended, for standing was not allowed. These trains now left Euston at 9.05 a.m., a big acceleration for the historic 'Royal Scot', and 1.05 p.m. respectively, the up 'Mid-Day Scot' now starting from Glasgow at 1.15 p.m. which brought its arrival time in Euston forward to a more satisfactory 8.30 p.m. instead of 9.10 p.m.

However, a 9.50 a.m. departure from Euston remained in the form of a greatly accelerated version of the previous winters service to Perth. It did not now call at Rugby, and ran forward from Crewe independently of the 10.55 a.m. Birmingham to Glasgow, being allowed a 32 minute recovery time up to Crewe. Leaving Carlisle at 3.56 p.m., and with stops at Motherwell, Larbert and Stirling only, it arrived in Perth at 7.12 p.m., an overall acceleration of no less than 58 minutes. Afternoon passengers now had only the slackly-timed 1.05 p.m. (formerly the 1.25 p.m.) from Euston to Perth which included a portion for Glasgow worked forwards ahead of the Perth section of the train, and arriving at 10.40 p.m.

One interesting effect of the 1959-60 timetable was the diversion of the 4.00 p.m. from Liverpool Lime Street to Euston via Northampton, even though not booked to stop there! This was done merely to clear a path for the up 'Mid-Day Scot' from Glasgow, and the Liverpool train did not now arrive in London until 9.00 p.m. compared to the former arrival time of 8.22 p.m. The fastest time from

Liverpool to London was now four hours.

On the Sundays 15th and 22nd November, 1959 the West Coast main line was shut at Garstang and Carnforth for engineering work, and through Anglo-Scottish traffic was re-routed. The 'Royal Scot' still had to make its booked call at Penrith to pick up passengers, and therefore then took the Ingleton line from Low Gill. 'DUCHESS OF SUTHERLAND' was booked to work the up 'Royal Scot' on 22nd November, and was photographed crossing Clapham Common, Yorkshire on the Low-Gill - Clapham branch, a most unusual location for a Stanier Pacific. This is recorded in a photograph taken by Peter Sunderland and published in Trains Illustrated February 1960.

Up to the end of 1949 'DUCHESS OF SUTHERLAND' had already accumulated some 805,002 miles in service, and during the next

Year	Miles run	Weekdays out of service						
		Waiting Repair Decision	Waiting Works	On Works	Total	Running Repairs & Exams	Not Req'd	Total
1950	65,291	Figures not recorded						
1951	67,088	-	5	25	30	61	-	91
1952	74,461	4	3	53	60	41	-	101
1953	90,220	-	-	-	-	61	-	61
1954	76,890	-	1	20	21	39	2	62
1955	51,530	10	13	55	78	25	4	107
1956	61,490	1	9	52	62	46	2	110
1957	75,897	-	-	-	-	66	1	67
1958	63,439	-	2	38	40	39	1	80
1959	70,258	-	4	44	48	Not recorded		

TOTAL MILEAGE 1950 to 1960 696,564.

Tuesday 6th October 1959 and Duchess of Sutherland heads past Strickland Wood on the climb to Shap with the up 'Mid-Day Scot'. The locomotive is less than two weeks out of works following a heavy general overhaul when the AWS equipment was fitted. (D.M.C. Hepburne-Scott/RAS)

Following the heavy general overhaul completed on 26 September 1959 46233 is seen at Shrewsbury after working a running in turn on a Crewe – Shrewsbury train. The locomotive then returned to Crewe where the AWS apparatus was fitted. (G.W. Sharpe)

decade had accumulated a further impressive mileage as follows:-

The official records show that 'DUCHESS OF SUTHERLAND' had remained at Crewe North depot except for two short periods at Carlisle Upperby from 14th June to 20th September, 1958 (already mentioned) and from 2nd to 23rd April, 1960. She returned to Crewe North again for just a week before being re-allocated to Camden depot in London, along with 46220 and 46256, where she was to remain for four and a half months available to work the express passenger traffic out of Euston to the north.

During this period she was back working the 'Royal Scot' and 'Mid-Day Scot' trains, and was photographed on both services. Perhaps the most interesting photographs were two taken by Eric Treacy, since at that time the "Royal Scot" was advertised as being non-stop, but in fact did pause to make a crew change at Carlisle Kingmoor shed in the 'down' direction and at Carlisle Upperby in the 'up' direction. The photographs are reproduced on pages 88 & 89.

A timed run behind 'DUCHESS OF SUTHERLAND' from Carlisle to Euston, in the hands of Driver Wilson (Carlisle Upperby), was documented by Paul Irving on Friday, 29th July, 1960 as she headed the 'up' 10.00 a.m. 'The Royal Scot'. The load was 8 vehicles, 277 tons tare, 290 tons gross. He writes:-

"I found myself travelling behind 'Sutherland' by default. In those days the August Bank Holiday weekend was at the start of the month and I had omitted to note that my intended train, the 10.19 a.m. up 'Caledonian' did not run on Bank Holidays ! So it was that the next advertised service to London was at 12.57 p.m., the 9.00 a.m. Perth-Euston, as the 'Royal Scot' was nominally non-stop Glasgow-Euston. It did, however, have to stop at Carlisle No. 12 Box, opposite Upperby shed, for crew relief. Frequently the train would call at Carlisle station for water as the troughs at Floriston, six miles north, were notoriously unreliable. So my hope was that the 'Scot' would call for water, and it duly did! A brief explanation to the Guard and I was aboard. A short hop to No. 12 Box and we were away non-stop to Euston."

"Already running a few minutes late approaching Carlisle, the un-booked stop for water made us 14 minutes late departing No. 12 after locomen's relief. The early stage of the run to Preston was unspectacular but efficient insofar as we absorbed the loss of time incurred by two temporary speed restrictions (TSR's) up to

Carnforth. The signals at Hest Bank and River Lune IBS (intermediate block signal) however caused a further 5 min. loss by Garstang, passed at an energetic 86 m.p.h. on a slightly falling gradient."

"Preston was passed 17 mins. late, the ongoing subsidence TSR at Standish Junct. had little effect on time recovery (every train had 3 mins. recovery time for this) and with speeds in the high 70's we were only 9 1/2 mins. late passing Crewe. The long series of TSR's through Stafford-Milford-Colwich for remodelling were well compensated for by adequate recovery times and with energetic running up the Trent Valley, we passed through Nuneaton over two minutes early. Evidently Driver Wilson then looked at his watch and speed fell sharply up the rise to Bulkington IBS and onwards to Shilton. Again a generous recovery time saw us pass Roade summit 7 mins. early despite further checks between Rugby and Kilsby Tunnel. A lovely climb saw Bletchley-Tring covered in 12 min. 32 sec. with a maximum of 81 in the slight dip at Sear's Crossing. So we passed Tring seven minutes early and with only one further TSR at Hemel Hempstead, the job was 'in the bag.'

" It really was a case of filling in time and for the fireman to have a leisurely half-hour after his labours, savouring the north London scenery. Slight signal checks approaching Euston did not prevent asnarrival time 4 minutes early at 17.11 p.m. Neat job from Carlisle, a job well done."

"I calculate delays cost 25 3/4 min. Deducting this from the overall time leaves a net time of 280 mins. seven minutes less than the nett schedule (324 mins. minus 37 min. recovery time). Given that the 'Duchess' took things easily after regaining her path at Nuneaton and on the descent from Tring, I think perhaps she could have knocked up to seven more minutes off this but it was not required as we were running punctually."

"By way of comparison, when Bill Starvis took 46244 'King George VI' on the up 'Caledonian' on its record trip in 1958, she left Carlisle at 10.20 and arrived Euston at 14.33 including a signal stop at Penrith. This would represent a nett time of around 238 minutes for the 299.1 miles."

A second run behind 46233 was detailed by Mr. Irving when, in the hands of Driver Flanaghan, also of Carlisle Upperby depot, she was working the 13.15 Glasgow-Euston, the up 'Mid-Day Scot', on

After a spell allocated to Crewe North, 46233 was transferred back to Carlisle Upperby on 2nd April 1960 but the allocation to the Border City was only for a mere 3 weeks, and it is during this period that Eric Treacy has recorded a classic picture of the locomotive on the northern fells. (E. Treacy/NRM)

Awaiting to take over a southbound express, the fireman is busy preparing 46233 at Carlisle Citadel on Monday 18 April 1960. Judging by the size of the coal in the tender he should have few problems keeping the back corners of the firebox well filled. (D. Forsyth)

The relieving crew cast a critical eye over Duchess of Sutherland as the locomotive on the up 'Royal Scot' comes to a halt outside Carlisle Upperby depot for a crew change.   Eric Treacy, albeit a brilliant photographer, never recorded dates of his photographs but the AWS and the 1B shed plate date this photograph between 30th April and 16th September 1960.
(E. Treacy/NRM)

1st August, 1960. The load was 8 vehicles again, 268 tons tare, 280 tons gross, and he writes:-

" *When the Anglo-Scottish expresses were reduced to eight coach formations in 1960 to minimise the decelerations due to electrification work, the three main trains were all booked non-stop Euston to Carlisle and vice-versa. But it was soon recognised that the 'Mid-Day Scot' should have its Crewe stop re-instated. So I was able to join it there, where booked departue was 17.39. This is the reason why another Carlisle man was at the regulator, where hitherto this train had been the domain of Crewe North and Polmadie men.*"

"*Driver Flanaghan had a bit of a reputation as a speed merchant, though I had never timed any runs behind him, prior to this. The late start of 10 mins. provided the incentive for some early energy, passing Great Bridgeford in even time from Crewe start with speed already into the eighties, and recovering six minutes by Stafford, albeit four of it recovery time.*"

"*Signal checks through the Trent Valley from an empty stock train (turned slow line at Nuneaton and overhauled near Shilton) were a hindrance but we couldt complain as passage through Rugby was over two minutes early. Signal and TSR's meant that the journey was one of checks interspersed by checks, but passing Roade Jn. at 80 mph certainly showed the 'Duchesses' capability. A costly series of checks on the descent towards Watford and in from Willesden interspersed by 86 mph approaching Wembley, saw the 'Mid-Day' nicely set for a punctual arrival. And so it was despite a short stop at the last signal before the terminus. Delays cost a total of 29 1/2 mins. leaving a net time of 136 mins. as against 144 mins. net schedule*"

Mr Irving's detailed combined log of the two runs is reproduced on page 93 with his kind permission:-

On 17th September, 1960 No 46233 was re-allocated to what was to be her final shed, the motive power depot at Edge Hill, Liverpool, also at that time the home of 'Princess Royal' class locomotives 46204 'PRINCESS LOUISE' and 46208 'PRINCESS HELENA VICTORIA'. 46233 was joined there briefly by 46236 'CITY OF BRADFORD' from 25th January to 25th March, 1961, but also by 46229 'DUCHESS OF HAMILTON', 46241 'CITY OF EDINBURGH' and 46243 'CITY OF LANCASTER' from p.e. 25th March, 1961, all of which were to have the depot as their final home. Although members of the class had been allocated to the shed from time to time since May, 1944, 'DUCHESS OF SUTHERLAND' was to become the member of the class allocated to the depot for the longest continuous period of time.

Her new duties, along with her sisters, included working the restaurant car expresses to London such as 'The Merseyside Express', 'The Manxman', 'The Shamrock' and also 'The Red Rose', an express service introduced in 1951 to mark the 'Festival of Britain' held that year.

'The Merseyside Express' with a restaurant car service, a train originally introduced in 1927 by the London & North Western Railway Company as the 'London-Merseyside Express', left Lime Street station at 10.00 a.m. arriving in Euston at 2.00 p.m. on weekdays and 2.15 p.m on Saturdays. The return train left at 6.20 p.m. on weekdays and called at Mossley Hill on the outskirts of Liverpool at 10.17 p.m., arriving in Lime Street at 10.35 p.m. On Saturdays there was an earlier departure at 6.00 p.m., arriving Mossley Hill at 9.49 p.m. and Lime Street at 10.10 p.m. Provision was made for a through coach which continued to Southport Chapel Street station, worked by another engine.

After the brief stop, the 'Royal Scot' is re-started from Carlisle Upperby. The safety valves feather as the fireman starts to prepare for the 30 mile climb to Shap Summit. The quantity of coal remaining in the tender has to get the train 298 miles to Euston. (E. Treacy/NRM)

Right: Duchess of Sutherland awaits departure from London Euston with the 'Royal Scot' on Saturday 7th May 1960. (G.Rixon)

Top Left: Carrying 'The Royal Scot' blue-backed headboard, Duchess of Sutherland storms past Bay Horse, south of Lancaster, with the up express in 1960.
(A. E. R. Cope/Colour Rail)

Middle Left: 46233 passing over Bushey troughs with a down 1Z10 special express working in the early 1960's.
(P. Riley/Colour Rail)

Bottom Left: Powering through Oxenholme at speed the Duchess of Sutherland heads the down 'Royal Scot' on Saturday 30th April 1960.
(Colour Rail)

Below: Small boys always seemed to be fascinated by steam locomotives, and this one clearly is as he looks at 46233 preparing to depart with the down 'Royal Scot' from London Euston on Saturday 7th May 1960.
(G. Rixon)

46233 with the up 'Royal Scot' sweeps through Lichfield at speed on Monday 13th June 1960. (E. R. Morten)

With steam to spare Duchess of Sutherland passes Greskine box on the climb to Beattock Summit with the down 'Royal Scot' on Saturday 30 July 1960. Being banked by Fairburn 2-6-4T 42192, the train is running some 40 minutes late. (W.A.C. Smith)

CARLISLE TO EUSTON

Loco: "Princess Coronation" No. 46233, "Duchess of Sutherland".
Load: 8 vehicles, 277 tons tare, 290 tons gross.
Train: 10.00 Glasgow to Euston, "The Royal Scot", 29 July 1960.
Driver: Wilson, Carlisle Upperby.

Miles	Timing Points	Sched. mins.	Actual m. sec.	Speeds. mph.
0.00	CARLISLE No.12 Signal Box	0	0 00	14 LATE
0.55	Carlisle No.13		1 46	
3.95	Wreay		7 12	42
6.45	Southwaite		10 02	58
9.85	Calthwaite		14 02	50
12.10	Plumpton	17	16 24	60
14.25	Kitchen Hill I.B.S.		18 35	58
17.00	Penrith	22	21 23	60/TRS 28
20.30	Eden Valley Jn.		26 30	47
25.35	Thrimby Grange		32 42	51
28.55	Shap		36 31	50/58
33.15	Shap Summit	38	38 48	54
33.15	Scout Green		41 11	72
36.15	Tebay	44	43 31	83
40.35	Low Gill		47 03	65
42.10	Grayrigg		48 40	65
43.95	Lambrigg Xing		50 10	80/85
49.15	Oxenholme	56	54 01	TSR 24
52.80	Hincaster Jn.		58 52	70
57.50	Burton & Holme		62 50	72
62.00	Carnforth	67	66 23	78
63.80	Bolton-le-Sands		67 48	74
65.15	Hest Bank		69 37	SIGS 28/24
68.25	LANCASTER	72	76 11	42
69.35	Lancaster No.1		72 47	40
74.00	Bay Horse		82 25	70
79.75	Garstang & Catterall	82	86.58	86
87.90	Oxheys	89	93.19	54
89.25	PRESTON	92	95 22	32
91.55	Farington		98 40	52
93.25	Leyland		100 28	60
94.70	Euxton Jn.	99	102 01	55/65
101.10	Standish Jn.	106	108 36	TSR 38
		(*3)		
104.35	WIGAN NW	113	112 55	57/67
111.05	Golborne Jn.		119 22	55
112.60	Winwick Jn.	121	121 00	60/62
116.10	WARRINGTON	125	124 31	58
118.10	Acton Grange Jn.	127	126 41	54
123.95	Weaver Jn.	132	131 43	74
125.75	Acton Bridge		133 11	74
128.40	Hartford		135 23	71
131.45	Winsford Jn.	138	137 50	79
135.35	Minshull Vernon	(4*)	141 03	71
137.40	Coppenhall Jn.	147	142 40	79
140.25	CREWE	151	146 28	SIGS 14
142.00	Basford Hall Jn.		149 27	47
145.00	Betley Road		152 40	64
148.20	Madeley		155.36	67
150.60	Whitmore	163	157 38	72
154.85	Standon Bridge		161 02	79
159.40	Norton Bridge	170	164 24	83
161.40	Great Bridgeford	(3*)	165 52	80
164.70	STAFFORD	178	168 52	TSR 58/50
168.70	Milford & Brocton	182	173 22	TSR 55
171.10	Colwich	(4*)	176 41	TSR 32
173.95	Rugeley Trent Valley	191	180 20	62
177.25	Armitage		183 15	78
182.00	Lichfield Trent Valley	197	187 12	66
184.75	Hademore Crossing		189 36	80
188.25	Tamworth	203	192 18	75
191.75	Polesworth		195 08	74/79
195.95	Atherstone	(4*)	198 25	75
201.15	NUNEATON T.V.	219	202 42	72
204.75	Bulkington I.B.S.		206 18	58
206.85	Shilton	(4*)	208 33	55
210.15	Brinklow		211 49	74
213.25	Newbold		214 21	72
215.70	RUGBY MIDLAND	237	217 33	SIGS 24
217.95	Hillmorton		221 38	TSR 46
219.85	Kilsby Tunnel North		223 44	TSR 60/52
222.95	Welton	(4*)	226 48	77/83
228.55	Weedon	252	231 08	72
235.40	Blisworth	257	236 34	77
238.35	ROADE JN.	260	239 08	67
243.50	Castlethorpe	(4*)	246 02	TSR 28
245.85	Wolverton		249 25	70/65
251.60	BLETCHLEY	275	254 29	75
253.75	Stoke Hammond		256 12	75
258.05	Leighton Buzzard		259 51	68
260.20	Sear's Crossing		261 31	81
262.15	Cheddington		263 09	70
264.30	Tring Cutting Box		265 01	68
266.60	TRING	288	267 01	70/72
270.30	Berkhamsted	(4*)	270 10	69
273.75	Hemel Hempstead		274 21	TSR 31
275.15	Apsley		277 16	55
277.30	King's Langley		279 34	58
280.80	WATFORD JN.	303	283 08	57
282.25	Bushey & Oxhey	(3*)	284 48	50
284.95	Hatch End		287 52	55
286.85	Harrow & Wealdstone		289 41	67
290.20	Wembley Central		292 49	63
292.85	Willesden Jn.	316	295 28	53
295.85	South Hampstead		300 05	SIGS 30
297.15	Camden No.1		302 40	30
	Euston Box.			SIGS 12
298.25	EUSTON	324	305 53	4 EARLY
	Nett times: (mins)	287	280	

(*4) etc. = recovery time (minutes).
TSR = Temporary speed restriction.
SIGS = Signal check.
I.B.S. = Intermediate block signal

CREWE TO EUSTON

Loco: "Princess Coronation" No. 46233, "Duchess of Sutherland".
Load: 8 vehicles, 268 tons tare, 280 tons gross.
Train: 13.15 Glasgow to Euston, "The Midday Scot", 1 August 1960.
Driver: Flanaghan, Carlisle Upperby.

Miles	Timing Points	Sched. mins.	Actual m. sec.	Speeds. mph.
0.00	CREWE	0	0 00	10 LATE
1.75	Basford Hall Jn.		3 15	50
4.75	Betley Road		6 44	58
7.95	Madley		9 55	61
10.35	Whitmore	13	11 59	70
14.60	Standon Bridge		15 24	78
19.15	Norton Bridge	20	18 40	86
21.15	Great Bridgeford	(4*)	20 08	80
24.45	STAFFORD	29	22 58	TSR 57
28.45	Milford & Brocton	33	28 23	TSR 40
30.85	Colwich	(4*)	32 35	TSR 30
33.70	Rugeley Trent Valley	42	36 36	70
37.00	Armitage		39 16	78/85
41.75	Lichfield Trent Valley	48	43 24	SIGS 63
44.50	Hademore Crossing		45 30	81
48.00	Tamworth	54	48 08	79
51.50	Polesworth		51 28	SIGS 28
55.70	Atherstone	(4*)	56 00	65/72
60.90	NUNEATON T.V.	70	61 10	SIGS 53
64.50	Bulkington I.B.S.		64 43	58
66.60	Shilton	(3*)	66 51	69
69.90	Brinklow		69 36	74
73 00	Newbold		72 11	70
75.45	RUGBY MIDLAND	87	74 41	51
77.70	Hillmorton		77 30	TSR 46
79.60	Kilsby Tunnel North		79 47	TSR 53
82.70	Welton	(5*)	82 53	TSR 64
88.30	Weedon	103	87 56	73
95.15	Blisworth	108	93 20	81
98.10	ROADE JN.	111	95 32	80/TSR 37
103.25	Castlethorpe	(4*)	101 29	62
105.60	Wolverton		103 42	69
	Denbigh Hall			SIGS 56
111.35	BLETCHLEY	126	109 28	63
113.50	Stoke Hammond		111 29	65
117.80	Leighton Buzzard		115 23	67/73
119.95	Sear's Crossing		117 13	69
121.90	Cheddington		119 29	SIGS 44
124.05	Tring Cutting Box		122 07	56
126.35	TRING	139	124 27	63/75
130.05	Berkhamsted	(4*)	128 21	TSR 45
	Bourne End Box			SIGS 31
133.50	Hemel Hempstead		133 30	SIGS 39
134.90	Apsley		136 08	TSR 30
137.05	King's Langley		140 04	SIGS 2/52
140.55	WATFORD JN.	154	144 52	TSR 35
142.00	Bushey & Oxhey	(4*)	146 23	63
144.70	Hatch End		148 52	68
146.60	Harrow & Wealdstone		150 21	83/86
149.95	Wembley Central		152 50	75
152.60	Willesden Jn.	168	155 22	SIGS 50
155.60	South Hampstead		159 19	SIGS 40
156.90	Camden No.1		161 22	SIGS 25
	Euston Box		162.34	SIG
			163 00	STOP
158.00	EUSTON	176	165 35	" EARLY
	Nett times: (mins)	144	136	

(*4) etc. = recovery time (minutes).
TSR = Temporary speed restriction.
SIGS = Signal check.
I.B.S. = Intermediate block signal

With the revised timetable there was now a service in the reverse direction, leaving Euston at 12.15 p.m. and arriving in Liverpool at 4.15 p.m., ten minutes later on Saturdays. The return service left at 5.15 p.m. and called at Crewe at 6.15 p.m., with arrival time in Euston booked for 9.10 p.m., again ten minutes later on Saturdays.

6233 was recorded passing Speke with 'The Merseyside Express' on 13th September, 1962.

It was on 'The Merseyside Express' O.S. Nock observed a particularly bad bout of slipping on one occasion when an un-recorded Stanier 'Duchess', with a 500 ton trailing load and no banking assistance at the rear, slipped to a standstill every time she tried to start the train up the 1 in 101 followed by 1 in 83 incline out of Lime Street station. However the driver stuck to his task, and struggled for nearly an hour before he finally got the train out of the platform. This tendency to slip has been referred to earlier, and these engines needed all of a driver's skills to avoid the problem. His article, in the March, 1960 issue of 'The Railway Magazine', which also gives details of other timed runs which he made in 1959 between Carlisle and Glasgow, does not feature 46233.

Climbing at an average of 1 in 75 for 10 miles, the driver of 46233 seems content to allow the rear end banker to do most of the work as the down 'Royal Scot' climbs Beattock Bank during the summer of 1960. (W.J.V. Anderson/RAS)

'The Manxman', another named express, only ran in summer in conjunction with the sailings of the Isle of Man Steam Packet Company's services to and from Douglas, and left Lime Street at 2.00 p.m., calling only at Rugby Midland, with booked arrival in Euston at 6.05 p.m. after a very fast run, whilst on Saturdays a five minute earlier start gave a London arrival time of 6.00 p.m. In the 'down' direction a 10.20 a.m. weekday departure time, with a stop at Crewe at 1.31 p.m., had a booked arrival in Liverpool of 2.30 p.m. in good time for the afternoon sailing. The Saturday departure time was five minutes later, and there was no stop at Crewe, giving an arrival time of 2.40 p.m. Seats were reservable at 2s 0d. each.

'The Shamrock', another express worked by Edge Hill engines, was timed to connect with the Belfast Steamship and the British & Irish Steam Packet Companies' sailings to and from Belfast and

Above:
Duchess of Sutherland was transferred from Camden to Liverpool Edge Hill depot on 17th September 1960 and is pictured at her new home in the company of 46245 City of London and Jubilees, 45552 Silver Jubilee and 45583 Assam.
(J. Carter)

Right:
Liverpool Edge Hill with Princess Coronations 46233 and 46245 awaiting their next duty.
(J. Carter)

As a result of the transfer to Edge Hill, 46233 began to appear in charge of Euston-Liverpool workings and is seen at the head of the 'The Merseyside Express' at Stafford circa 1962. (N.E. Preedy)

Dublin. On Mondays to Fridays it left Lime Street at 8.05 a.m. with overnight boat passengers and, calling at Mossley Hill at 8.17 a.m. only to set down passengers (8.28 a.m. on Saturdays), it called at Crewe at 9.06 a.m. (9.17 a.m. on Saturdays) and Bletchley at 11.18 a.m. (11.33 a.m.), reaching Euston at 12.15 p.m. In the opposite direction, and also in connection with the overnight sailings, 'The Shamrock' left Euston at 4.55 p.m. and ran non-stop all the way to

Liverpool, arriving at 8.55 p.m. (9.00 p.m. on Fridays). On Saturdays, with a 4.30 p.m. departure, it called at Rugby Midland at 6.12 p.m. and Crewe at 8.02 p.m., arriving in Liverpool at 9.00 p.m. There was no Sunday service. Stanier Pacifics worked both of these trains, and also their reliefs if required.

Other boat train duties included the 'Empress Voyager', and 46241 'CITY OF EDINBURGH' was allocated to Edge Hill depot

Duchess of Sutherland stands at London Euston as passengers board the 1Z60 to Liverpool Lime Street on Friday 20th October 1961. (M. Welch)

specifically to work this service from p.e. 25th March, 1961. 'DUCHESS OF SUTHERLAND' herself worked this in the 'up' direction on 9th August, 1962. In addition the Edge Hill Pacifics were called upon to work the night sleeping car trains from Liverpool to Glasgow in place of the rebuilt 'Patriot' and 'Royal Scot' class locomotives used formerly.

OTHER CASES OF LOCOMOTIVES SLIPPING.

Further to the case of a 'Princess Coronation' class Pacific slipping on trying to start unaided out of Liverpool Lime Street station with the 'The Merseyside Express' mentioned above, O.S. Nock reported a similar incident in 1959 when he was travelling behind a member of the class on a journey northwards from Carlisle. The Pacific, with a trailing load of 430 tons, and despite permanent way slacks causing a delay of 32¼ minutes to Lockerbie, passed Beattock at full speed and began to climb the bank. However he continues "as early as Auchencastle I felt an ominous surge in the train, indicative of a slip, and to cut a long and dismal story short, we took no less than 28 minutes to struggle up the ten miles from Beattock to the Summit box. That was not all. The continuous slipping had so depleted the water supply that the diver felt constrained to stop at the summit to take water. Ultimately, with one stop at Carstairs, we took a total of 151 minutes from Carlisle to Glasgow central, 102.3 miles...As the driver said sorrowfully to me

at Glasgow "She wouldn't have it!"

Perhaps the most alarming incident involving a member of the class during this period occurred in 1961 when a driver, whilst restarting the overnight sleeping car train from Kilmarnock station, got 46222 'QUEEN MARY' into a violent slip. To make matters worse the boiler was full and water surged through the valves. Making it impossible for the driver to close the regulator. Eyewitness accounts describe how the engine slipped uncontrollably for some 15 minutes without moving a foot! The noise was heard all over the town, and it was a miracle that the engine stayed on the track. Derek Cross visited the scene some two hours later and saw that the rail had been burnt right through to expose the rail web!. Two similar incidents of the same kind had occurred much earlier in the life of the class in 1939, as already mentioned, and a modification to the main regulator valve had been put in hand. However, in this particular incident, as John Powell has observed, the serious carry-over of water would have prevented the combination of a full brake application and winding the reverser into mid position from stopping the slip, thereby allowing the regulator to be closed.

Given the 'right away', 46233 departs Euston with the 2.05 pm to Liverpool Lime Street on Friday 20th October 1961. (M. Welch)

97

CLASS ALLOCATIONS AND WORK IN THE 1960's.

By 5th November, 1960 the 'Princess Coronation' class were allocated as follows:-

Camden:- 46239-40, 46242-3, 46245-7.
Crewe North:- 46220-1, 46229, 46235, 46241, 46248-9, 46251, 46253-4, 46256.
Edge Hill:- 46233
Carlisle Upperby:- 46225-6, 46228, 46234, 46236-8, 46244, 46250, 46252, 46255, 46257
Polmadie:- 46222-4, 46227, 46230-2.

By this date the English Electric Type 4 1-Co-Co-1 diesel-electric locomotives, which had originally been passed to work between London Euston and Carlisle and between Crewe and Liverpool Lime Street from July, 1959, had also largely taken over the regular working of expresses between Liverpool and London. Stanier Pacifics only filled in on these duties at weekends and, as and when required by failures. By September, 1959 only the 2.20 p.m. Euston - Liverpool and the 4.00 p.m. in the reverse direction were regularly steam hauled, and from 2nd November, 1959 steam haulage was officially, in theory at least, to have finished altogether on the Liverpool - London services. In actual fact it was to be a few more years before this actually happened, for the new diesels were plagued with a number of technical problems, not least of which was with the train heating boilers.

Electric traction working under the 25 K.V., overhead system was also taking over on parts of the Stanier Pacifics territories, the section from Crewe to Manchester being energised in September, 1960 and later that from Liverpool to Weaver Junction (on the same route) in January, 1962. Further north electrification came too late to affect the class.

At the end of 1960 Stanier Pacifics were still regularly being used as motive power for hauling the 9.30 a.m. Crewe-Holyhead service, Nos. 46226, 46229 and 46257 being noted on this working. During the following Christmas period the extra boat trains attracted others, including 46251 of Crewe North. 'The Irish Mail' and its counterpart and slower named train, 'The Emerald Isle Express', were regular boat train workings in connection with the 8.40 p.m. sailings to and from Dun Laoghaire; the former being the overnight express leaving Holyhead at 1.10 a.m. and arriving in Euston at 6.55 a.m. The latter was the early morning train to London Euston starting from Holyhead at 7.30 a.m. In the 'down' direction the latter left Euston at 5.35 p.m. whilst 'The Irish Mail' had a later 8.40 p.m. departure, in both cases providing an arrival time for passengers on the ferry sailing into Dun Laoghaire harbour of 6.40 a.m. the following morning. 'Princess Coronation' class engines were to be regularly seen on these workings, with 46245 being in charge of 'The Emerald Isle Express' throughout on 9th October, 1961 and arriving in Euston on time.

THE LAST BRITISH RAILWAYS REPAIRS TO 46233

On 18th January, 1961 'DUCHESS OF SUTHERLAND' was taken out of service and is shown as 'Waiting Repair Decision' for five days. She then entered Crewe Works for a heavy intermediate repair that took a further 24 days, having run 98,848 since her previous heavy general overhaul from which she had been out-shopped on 26th September, 1959. This was to be her last heavy repair before her withdrawal from traffic apart from a light casual repair between 10th July and 24th August of the same year, with no less than eight days standing out of use awaiting a decision. Other running repairs would of course have been additionally undertaken at the Edge Hill depot as and when found to be necessary in order to keep her in

service. It was in fact to be a further 38 years before her next heavy general repair was to be started in 1998 as will be recounted in a later chapter.

At the beginning of 1961, apart from the Edge Hill allocation previously mentioned, there was a re-allocation of the class generally to meet the ever changing motive power requirement for workings both north and south of the border until the end of the summer timetable. The English Electric diesel-electric locomotives had by then taken over most of the 'Royal Scot', 'The Mid-Day Scot', 'The Caledonian' and West Coast Postal train workings.

As part of these changes the two Carlisle depots received three more engines of the class, 46220 went there from Crewe North and 46236 from Edge Hill to Upperby during p.e. 25th February and 25th March, 1961 respectively. 46221 moved to Kingmoor from Crewe North at the latter date. She was later joined there by 46226, 46237, 46244, 46252, 46255 and 46257 which were all moved across from Upperby, and during p.e. 17th June 46247 joined them. The Polmadie allocation was increased by the addition of 46242 from Camden and 46249 from Crewe North in March, 1961, although the latter was only on loan until 23rd June when the transfer was made permanent.

Among the trains now worked by Kingmoor's new fleet was the 9.20 a.m. Crewe-Perth express, the return working being the 12.20 p.m. Perth - London Euston, the 9.50 a.m. Perth - Euston and the 12.15 p.m. Perth - Euston, the Kingmoor engines only being used north of Carlisle. The heaviest of these trains was normally limited to eleven bogies and the class therefore usually kept excellent time. The locomotives also found use hauling the 2.40 p.m. and 4.25 p.m. (ex Aberdeen) 'Fish Special' trains from Perth southwards, engines recorded on those workings including 46221, 46226, 46244, 46252, 46255 and 46257.

There was also a working over the Carlisle G&SW line, one of the new arrivals being used to work the 3.21 a.m. Carlisle-Kilmarnock and the 7.21 a.m. Kilmarnock-Glasgow St. Enoch station via Dalry, the return working being the 5.30 p.m. from St. Enoch. Nos. 46221, 46226, 46237, 46244 and 46252 were seen during the first month or so.

Other less prestigious work now fell to the 'Princess Coronation' class in their 'Indian Summer', although they continued to be used on express passenger services between Liverpool and Manchester and Glasgow, but restrictions at Bank Hall and Bolton prevented them from being regularly rostered on these turns, and the E.E. Co. Type 4 diesel-electrics took over most of these workings in 1961. The Stanier Pacifics were by now mostly employed north of Preston, but occasionally worked right through, and in fact continued to deputise for diesel failures until the end of their lives.

An even humbler working was the 4.30 p.m. milk train from Carlisle to Willesden, London, and with loadings up to 600 tons the use of such a large locomotive was justified. Both 46238 and 46255 were seen on this duty on 11th and 18th March, 1961 respectively.

One unusual booked working was with 46238 at the head of the expected 7.19 p.m. arrival from Glasgow at Liverpool Exchange station. However, on leaving Ormskirk 'CITY OF CARLISLE' slipped violently and then failed completely at Town Green, Aughton. An ex War Department 2-8-0 No. 90712 was sent from Aintree depot to bring the train into the terminus tender first. The last previously recorded visit of a member of the class to that location had been in 1947 when 46232 was the locomotive in question.

However, the class was also still called upon on occasions for the most prestigious work of all, that of hauling the Royal Train. One such was on the evening of 29th September, 1961 when 46246 'CITY OF MANCHESTER' was the train engine which worked from London Euston to Carlisle. Standby engines were 46239 at Euston and 46254 at Crewe.

Members of the class were still to be seen working such trains as the 'Lakes Express' from Euston as far as Penrith, particularly on Saturdays, and also at the head of Euston to Glasgow overnight sleeping car trains which used the former Glasgow & South Western Railway route via Kilmarnock, terminating in St. Enoch station in

Five days after leaving Crewe Works following a heavy intermediate overhaul, 46233 stands in the semi-roundhouse at Crewe North on Sunday 26 February 1961 in the company of 46105 Cameron Highlander, 46228 Duchess of Rutland, and 46254 City of Stoke-on-Trent. (S.D. Wainwright)

On her last service visit to Crewe Works when she received a Light Casual repair, 46233 stands in the works yard on Tuesday 3rd August 1961. (B. Hoper collection)

Glasgow. They were still to be found on the 'West Coast Postal' trains to and from London. Workings to Perth continued, and Polmadie allocated engines also worked the fast express service between Glasgow and Edinburgh quite frequently, and 'Princess Coronations' were also seen working between Edinburgh and Perth, and at unlikely places such as Callender and Grangemouth.

The following year, still allocated to Edge Hill depot, 46233's work now also became more varied. She was still to be seen at work on express passenger services, and on 17th February, 1962 she was recorded by John Edgington at Birmingham New Street station as she worked the 8.45 a.m. Euston to Wolverhampton express.

One lower status duty for 'DUCHESS OF SUTHERLAND' was hauling the 4.15 p.m. southbound stopping train from Carlisle, and O.S. Nock's article in his 'British Locomotive Practice and Performance' series in the January, 1963 issue of 'The Railway Magazine' contained a table of eight runs between Penrith and Oxenholme submitted by Mr. H.G. Ellison of Penrith, a regular traveller. Column 6 features 46233 in which her performance is compared to the Caledonian Railway 4-6-0 No. 903 'Cardean' during trials between Carlisle and Crewe in 1909. O.S. Nock observes that 'Cardean' must have been worked to her limits, for her performance was, in his words, "phenomenal. Certainly in her daily round from Glasgow to Carlisle and back she was never called upon to do such work."

As to the performance of 'DUCHESS OF SUTHERLAND', Mr Ellison considered that it "showed considerable superiority over all other classes of locomotive concerned in his own records" but adds that it was quite typical of 'Duchess' work during the years immediately before the superceding of steam. At the time of this particular run the train had an additional stop at Tebay; but this was so smartly made that the time to Oxenholme was still 4 1/4 minutes inside the 46 minute schedule.

In the same article O.S. Nock also refers to his own experience of 46225 'DUCHESS OF GLOUCESTER' slipping during adverse weather conditions, when he was on a footplate trip. She slowed to 2 m.p.h. at Sedgwick signalbox from which she could not recover. The on-board Inspector deciding to stop at Oxenholme for assistance at

the rear in the shape of a 2-6-4T, the net time from Milnthorpe to Grayrigg being 34¾ minutes for the 12.6 miles.

During the summer of 1962 the class continued to deputise for diesel locomotives on principal express services, especially at weekends, but were also increasingly seen on short formation stopping services, milk, parcels and express freight trains, duties which of course did not exert them at all.

There were a few further transfers during 1962, 46221 and 46237 moving from Kingmoor to Upperby depot in Carlisle p.e. 7th April, and 46252 went south from Kingmoor to Camden p.e. 22nd September. Finally 46236 moved across from Upperby to Kingmoor p.e. 3rd November, 1962. At the end of 1962 Polmadie depot lost three members of the class, 46227, 46231 and 46232, on their withdrawal from traffic, the first members of the class to go. Others had been put into store in November, these being 46221 and 46237 at Upperby. Further withdrawals followed in January, 1963, these being 46234 (with a cracked frame) from Upperby, 46246 from Camden and 46253 from Crewe North, whilst 46256 was merely put into store there.

From this time on any members of the class found to require extensive repair work, such as on boilers, frame fractures, collision damage or other remedial work were withdrawn from service. Many members of the class were also officially put into store for long periods at their home depots, and it is clear that the political will was not there to continue to use the class any more on a longer term basis, as is referred to later.

However, one late special duty for two members of the class occurred in connection with Her Majesty The Queen's visit to Merseyside. On 13th December, 1962 46248 'CITY OF LEEDS' was called up at short notice in lieu of a Type 4 diesel electric and brought out of store at Crewe North to work the Royal Train from Euston to its overnight stabling point in South Lancashire. The honour of working the Royal Train into Liverpool Lime Street station the following day fell to 46220 'CORONATION', she having worked light from Edge Hill depot to Lowton Junction to take on the task. Afterwards 46248 'CITY OF LEEDS' re-appeared to work the train from Lime Street to Watford Junction where the royal party

Saturday 24th March 1962 at Birmingham New Street, 46233 departs with the 5.00 pm Euston train. (S. Creer)

Saturday 3rd March 1962 and Duchess of Sutherland is climbing the 1 in 135 gradient past Brisco, south of Carlisle, with a Glasgow to Birmingham train. The leading vehicle is a through coach to Penzance and a milk tanker is attached to the rear of the train. (A.R. Thompson)

The same train as the preceding photograph is seen near Morecambe South Junction. (N. A. Machell)

A classic British Railways era scene is captured at Rugby as Duchess of Sutherland heads the 9.35am Wolverhampton to London Euston express on Saturday 7th April 1962. (Peter Fitton)

de-trained for a road trip to Windsor. 46220 was put into store again, but returned to traffic in January, 1963, being observed working between Crewe and Carlisle, and on 22nd January was seen on Warrington depot in steam and ready to work the 8.20 a.m. fitted freight to Carlisle.

During 1963, due to the unavailability of diesel-electric motive power, other members of the class were still to be found working the occasional 'Royal Scot', 'The Caledonian' and 'The Mid-Day Scot' daytime and the overnight sleeping car services between London Euston and Glasgow, as well as the 10.05 a.m. Glasgow Central to Birmingham and similar express trains to Manchester and Liverpool. They also occasionally worked the 'Thames-Clyde Express' to and from Glasgow as far as Carlisle, and even also headed 'The Waverley' from Edinburgh over that route as far as Carlisle.

'DUCHESS OF SUTHERLAND' was officially stored as serviceable from 6th October, 1962 until 2nd February, 1963, being, like many of the class, again called into use for what was to be in her case her final official year of active life as part of the now much depleted stock of British Railways' steam locomotive. However she was in fact observed working the 10.10 a.m. up 'Merseyside Express' on Wednesday, 30th January, 1963. She was also, like the rest of the class, now being given less prestigious work hauling fitted freight trains etc., and was recorded on such a working at two locations at Brisco, south of Carlisle and again further south climbing Shap near Clifton & Lowther with an up perishables freight train, which included six loaded cattle wagons, on 13th April, 1963. 46233 worked throughout the year on a variety of similar duties, but was also to be noted at the head of Glasgow-Birmingham and Glasgow-Euston services. On 1st June, 1963 she was photographed working the 1M25 9.56 a.m. up relief 'Royal Scot' express from Glasgow Central to London Euston which she took over at Carlisle.

A little later that summer she was photographed working a 1X85 up relief at Berkhamsted on 6th August, on a down Euston-Liverpool 'Merseyside Express' at Kilburn High Road on 9th August, and again on the 1Z10 Euston-Liverpool 'Empress Voyager' boat train service on 31st August at Aston Heath near Warrington. In each case there would have been a balanced outward or return working back to Edge Hill depot.

Norman Preedy observed her passing Blisworth with a northbound passenger train on 6th September, and she was photographed on Carlisle Kingmoor depot with a chalked 1X37 number on the smokebox door on 30th September, 1963.

At Carlisle Kingmoor two of the stored 'Princess Coronations' were put back into service during the week ending 2nd February, 1963 to deputise

WEST COAST ROUTE: PENRITH-OXENHOLME									
Run No.		1	2	3	4	5	6	7	8
Engine No.		45506	45718	45593	72003	903	46233	45599	72001
Engine name		The Royal Pioneer Corps	Dread-nought	Kolhapur	Clan Fraser	Cardean	Duchess of Suther-land	Bech-uanaland	Clan Cameron
Engine type		4-6-0P	4-6-0S	4-6-0S	4-6-2A	4-6-0M	4-6-2D	4-6-0S	4-6-2A
Load, tons (e/f)		282/295	302/320	307/335	342/370	367/390	373/400	413/440	429/470
Dist.		Sch.	Actual	Actual	Actual	Actual	Actual	Actual	Actual	Actual
Miles		min.	m. s.	m. s.	m. s.	m. s.	m. s.	m. s.	m. s.	m. s.
0.0	PENRITH	0	0 00	0 00	0 00	0 00	0 00	0 00	0 00	0 00
1.1	Eamont Jc.		2 55	2 57	2 50	2 54	2 50	2 56	3 01	3 30
4.3	Milepost 47		7 19	7 17	7 07	7 13	6 49	6 49	7 52	8 35
6.3	Milepost 45		10 47	10 12	10 06	10 17	9 12	9 27	12 13	12 42
8.3	Milepost 43		14 21	13 07	13 06	13 28	11 45	12 08	16 56	17 05
11.6	Shap		19 50	17 42	17 56	18 33	16 05	16 20	23 23	24 42
			—	—	—	—		—	—	27 06
13.6	Shap Summit	27	22 52	20 23	20 43	21 23	18 30	18 47	26 44	33 05
19.1	Tebay	33	28 22	25 42	25 34	27 31	23 45	25 03	31 28	38 22
								25 40		—
25.1	Grayrigg		34 56	32 12	30 44	33 56	—	33 45	36 13	43 33
28.7	Hay Fell Box		38 01	35 42	33 56	37 26	—	37 14	39 03	46 49
					sigs.			—		—
32.2	OXENHOLME	46	41 22	40 28	38 18	42 00	37 30	41 46	42 54	50 23
Net times, min.			41¼	40½	37½	42	38 to stop	37½	43	43¼
Speeds, m.p.h.										
Eden Valley Jc.			47	48	49	49	54	53	43	44
Min. before Shap			34	41¼	39¼	36	44	45	24	27
Max. Shap Station			42	49	48	43	53	54	41	stop
Shap Summit			38	42	43	39	48	48	33	25
Max. on descent			80	77	80	69	73½	77	87	80

Engine classes: A = "Clan" class "BR6"; D = "Duchess"; M = McIntosh Caledonian type; P = "Patriot" class; S = Stanier "Jubilee"

After rounding the curve out of Chester, 46233 accelerates away from Chester No. 6 box with the 9.20am Crewe to Holyhead express on Saturday 28th April 1962. (J. Carter)

for more failed Type 4 diesel electrics. These were 46221 and 46237 which had been mothballed during the w.e. 29th October, 1962. Another significant change was the re-allocation of members of the class to Carlisle Kingmoor for working trains to the north, particularly Perth, also being made available to deputise for failed E.E. Co. Type 4 diesel electrics. Nos. 46226, 46236, 46244, 46255 and 46257 were the engines involved.

The Carlisle based 'Princess Coronations' were also often in use during that summer of 1963 on the 5.30 p.m. from Glasgow St. Enoch over the former G. & S.W. R. route to Carlisle, 46244 and 46255 both being observed on the working during the week ending 26th October. It continued to be a favourite turn for the Kingmoor based engines right into 1964. One member of the class was pressed into service by Corkerhill depot on 27th May, 1963 when 46224 worked a local passenger service to Ayr and back - said to be the first visit of a member of the class to that particular location, but more followed including 46223 and 46249.

On Sunday, 8th September, 1963, the last day of the summer services, 46254 'CITY OF STOKE-ON-TRENT', immaculately clean and in maroon livery, worked the up 'Royal Scot'. Although it was thought that this might be the last time one of the class worked this prestige train, they continued to work it until the end of the year, together with 'The Mid-Day Scot' and in fact right through the following summer of 1964.

The class also continued to work the "Irish Mail" regularly between London and Holyhead, and unusually 46239 'CITY OF CHESTER' was briefly re-allocated to the Holyhead

depot from Willesden for that purpose on 24th August, 1963, remaining there until 4th October before returning again to Willesden.. The engine record card is silent on this latter move, as it is on its final move to Crewe North during the period ending 5th September, 1964 just before its withdrawal. As a matter of interest Camden depot had been officially closed to steam from 11th September, 1961 and completely on 9th September, 1963, the other two of its engines 46240 and 46245 not being officially re-allocated to Willesden until that latter date. 46252 had languished in store alongside the coaling plant at Camden for some twelve months, but was then sent to Crewe Works to be cut up.

After a period 'in store' at Edge Hill, 46233 has been returned to traffic and is seen at that depot on Saturday 23rd March 1963. (J. Corkhill)

Relegated to freight duties, 46233 is seen climbing away from Carlisle at Brisco with a freight train comprising of six loaded cattle wagons behind the locomotive in a long fitted freight train. Rarely can cattle have experienced haulage by such prestigious motive power.
(S.C. Crook)

On the same day, Saturday 13th April 1963, the train is seen south of Penrith at Clifton and Lowther.
(J.S. Whiteley)

In final B.R. green livery, 46233 heads southbound near Clifton Road Junction with the 14.05 Liverpool Lime St.- London Euston express in April 1963.
(D. Smith/Colour Rail)

Deputising for a failed English Electric Type 4 diesel, Duchess of Sutherland powers the down Merseyside Express past Kilburn High Road on Friday 9th August 1963.
(M. Welch)

On Saturday 1st June 1963, Duchess of Sutherland was captured on no less than three occasions on the 1M25 relief to the 'Royal Scot' between Carlisle and London. The first view shows the locomotive backing on to the train at Carlisle Citadel station. (H.R. Davies)

Well into her stride, 46233 rounds the curve at Bessie Ghyll on the climb to Shap Summit. (P.J. Robinson)

Climbing the 1 in 98 gradient south out of Lancaster.
(N.A. Machell)

Below:
Three days later and 46233 is still displaying the 1M25 reporting number whilst stabled on Willesden depot.
(P.H. Groom)

46233 Duchess of Sutherland passes Standish Junction with a down fitted freight, 31st May 1963. (Bob Maxwell)

SPECIAL RAILTOURS.

At this late period a few members of the class worked a number of special excursions, and 46245 'CITY OF LONDON' worked a Home Counties Railway Society special tour on 9th June, 1963 between Doncaster and London King's Cross.

The former Midland Railway Company's main line from Settle Junction to Carlisle featured as the route for other specials, and on Sunday, 30th June, 1963, "Three Summits Railtour', organised by the Railway Travel and Correspondence Society, ran from Leeds City station over the Settle-Carlisle line and then on to Carstairs, returning via Dumfries, Shap and the Clapham to Tebay line and thence back to Leeds. Taking over from ex L.& N.E.R. Class A4 Pacific 60023 which had brought the train from Leeds, 46255 'CITY OF HERE-FORD' took the train forwards from Carlisle to Carstairs and, despite operating difficulties, gave an excellent account of herself.

One of the most frequently used locomotives was 46238 'CITY OF CARLISLE' in her smart crimson lake livery, and on 27th September, 1963 she was in charge of the joint R.C.T.S./S.L.S. 'North Eastern Tour 1963' special from Skipton and over the line to Carlisle as part of a five day itinerary.

To commemorate the apparently imminent demise of the class, the R.C.T.S. organised a 'Duchess Commemorative Tour' which took place on 5th October, 1963 and was to have featured 46256 'SIR WILLIAM A. STANIER, F.R.S.'. In the event a bogie fault on 46256 caused another member of the class No. 46251 'CITY OF NOT-TINGHAM' to be substituted on the route from Crewe to Edinburgh (Princes Street) and back to Crewe. She had been taken out of store specially to work this train and was returned to storage immediately afterwards.

LAST DAYS FOR DUCHESS OF SUTHERLAND

The more mundane work on the London Midland Region continued for these magnificent engines particularly on busy Saturdays. One such regular working was the 6.00 a.m. Warrington to Carlisle slow passenger train, known colloquially as `The Lulu' that arrived in Carlisle at 10.02 a.m., the return working being the 7.11pm Carlisle-Warrington slow, due in at 10.30 p.m. Needless to say this was a very easy diagram for such a powerful locomotives, and 46233 worked this train on a number of occasions, being noted on it on 16th,19th and 20th July 1963, very late in her service career.

Another working which the 'Princess Coronations' were found a late use for was hauling the unofficially named 'Maiden Lane', a train conveying foodstuffs and perishables from Carlisle to Maiden Lane Goods Yard for distribution to the London markets. 'DUCHESS OF SUTHERLAND' was recorded being prepared for this train at Carlisle Kingmoor on 30th September 1963 and then on the train near Salterwath, the train that day comprising of loaded cattle trucks and mixed vans.

The end for 'DUCHESS OF SUTHERLAND' and her sisters at Edge Hill and elsewhere following the handing over to the English Electric Type 4 1Co-Co1 diesel electrics of the principal expresses with the introduction of the winter timetable on 9th September, 1963. With increasing diesel haulage of the many other services on which they might have still been used on the Lancaster and Carlisle line and elsewhere, their work just petered out.

THE WITHDRAWAL FROM SERVICE OF 46233 'DUCHESS OF SUTHERLAND'

At the close of that busy season 'DUCHESS OF SUTHERLAND' had once more been put into store as serviceable on 14th October, 1963. She was not taken out of store until Monday, 3rd February, 1964, finally being withdrawn from service during that week ending Saturday, 8th February. Whether she was used at all after officially being taken out of storage on the 3rd is unclear. The authors' opinion is that she was not steamed again, and the official records point to her being immediately withdrawn.

Officially withdrawn on the same date as 46233 was 46229 'DUCHESS OF HAMILTON', both locomotives being covered by the London Midland Region's 1963 withdrawal programme. However, most fortuitously Billy Butlin had earlier taken a decision that he wanted some withdrawn locomotives for display at his holiday camps, and both of them were in fact purchased by him with a view to restoring them for static display as part of the collection he had already purchased for that purpose. This is discussed fully in the next chapter, but already preserved under that plan had been 6203 'PRINCESS MARGARET ROSE' of the 'Princess Royal' class, which had been placed at his Pwllheli holiday camp as a visitor attraction in early May, 1963.

Tuesday 16 July 1963 and Duchess of Sutherland's driver awaits the guard's whistle for departure from Lancaster with the 6.00 a.m. Warrington to Carlisle stopping train colloquially known as the 'Lulu'.
(P. Rowlands)

Tebay on a summers evening as 46233 departs with the 'Lulu'- the 7.11 p.m. Carlisle to Warrington stopping train.
(P. Conolly)

Standing at Carlisle Kingmoor depot on Monday 30th September 1963, Duchess of Sutherland waits her next turn of duty. See next photo. (R. Helm)

Still displaying the chalked reporting number seen at Kingmoor, Duchess of Sutherland is seen on one of her last known workings coasting down Shap with the unofficially named goods train the 'Maiden Lane' conveying foodstuffs and perishables to Londons' markets. 46233 was placed into store at Edge Hill on 14th October 1963, being officially withdrawn from service during the week ending 8th February 1964. (D. Cross)

In their final months of service Coronation Pacific's were seen increasingly on freight work, a task they were wholly unsuitable for. 46233 is seen passing Lancaster circa 1963 with a long unfitted freight. (R. Helm)

With the left hand outside piston gland blowing, 46233 Duchess of Sutherland heads the 1Z10 London Euston to Liverpool 'Empress Voyager' boat train at Aston Heath on Saturday 31st August 1963. (P. Claxton)

During her final years of service 46233 amassed many more miles in service as follows:-

1960   77,402
1961   38,464
1962   26,839
1963   Mileage not recorded.

This gives a total recorded mileage covered over her lifetime of 1,644,271 as shown on the last Engine History Card. To this must be added an additional calculated mileage for the year 1963 arrived at by summating the total mileage covered for known workings over that year which comes to approximately 13,000. This gives a maximum total mileage of approximately 1,657,270.

46233 is first recorded in 'The Railway Observer' as being in the Crewe Works arrival sidings on 14th June 1964 where she was photographed by Norman Preedy. However, most interestingly, 46229 'DUCHESS OF HAMILTON' was already in the Paint Shop in Crewe Works ready for repainting in a representative L.M.S. livery as early as 25th March, 1964 bearing her original number 6229, and the work had been completed and she was on Crewe North depot ready to be moved to the Minehead holiday camp on 18th April, 1964.

All of Edge Hill's allocation were recorded as being in store on 20th October, 1963, these by then being 46229, 46233, 46241 and 46243, whilst a visitor on shed was 46249 'CITY OF SHEFFIELD' from Polmadie depot.

Members of the class stored at Crewe North on 10th November 1963 were 46228, 46235, 46248, 46251, 46254 and 46256, whilst 46250 was in steam, and on Crewe South depot was 46227. Nos 46231 and 46232 awaited their fate at the hands of the cutters' oxyacetylene torches in the nearby works.

By the end of that summer of 1963 the working members of the class were becoming thinner on the ground everywhere, and by the end of November Polmadie depot in Glasgow had lost all of its allocation of 'Princess Coronations'. 46223 was withdrawn during the 4 week period ending 5th October, 46222, 46224 and 46242 went during p.e. 2nd November. Nos 46230 and 46249 during p.e. 23rd November, the latter having been seen still in steam on the nearby Corkerhill depot only two days before withdrawal on 5th November.

Wintertime duties for the remainder in service included some passenger, parcels, freight and mixed trains. Carlisle's members of the class continued to work up to Glasgow and were occasionally still to be seen working the 'Royal Scot', often replacing other engines at Carlisle. A 'Princess Coronation' was often pressed into service in favour of any other type of motive power by die-hard depot staff there, and Crewe North based locomotives also on rarer occasions worked that prestige service into and out of Euston and Glasgow Central. They were also still to be seen at work on Kilmarnock-Glasgow Central local passenger trains. The Christmas period traffic brought these still useful Stanier Pacifics into their own again on 'Royal Scot' and 'Mid-Day Scot' services and their reliefs, whilst Kingmoor's newly acquired members of the class were pressed into work hauling postal specials.

An unusual proposal was made at his time to extend the life of the class by putting them to work on the Southern Region hauling the London Waterloo-Bournemouth expresses, but the scheme was abandoned due to clearance problems in the Southampton area.

Withdrawn from traffic, 46233 stands in Crewe Works on Sunday 14th June 1964 with motion taken down awaiting cosmetic restoration. One week later she was inside the paint shop. (N.E. Preedy)

EMBER DAYS - THE FINAL YEAR OF 1964.

The final year of operation for the class began in much the same way as 1963, with members of the class working both named and relief expresses as well as stopping services on the West Coast main line into both Euston and Glasgow, although many were to remain in store. Changes of engines at Carlisle resulted in a 'Princess Coronation' deliberately being pressed into use as before, and by the middle of February 46225, 46238 and 46250 of Upperby and 46236 and 46255 of Kingmoor were in action. 46244 and 46257, neither in such good condition mechanically and stored at the latter depot, were moved to Upperby yard to join 46226 and 'Princess Royal' class locomotive 46200 in store there. However, 46237 and 46257 were back in service yet again by March. Members of the class were still to be seen occasionally in Birmingham and working trains to Liverpool and Holyhead.

A number of the class however remained in service for one last season, some being used the early part of 1964 due to the continued unavailability of the E.E.Co. Type 4 diesels yet again. The 'Princess Coronations' continued to be used on a mixture of trains - express and local passenger, fitted freights, fish, newspaper and parcels trains, car/sleeper services but also even on the most humble duties of hauling cattle wagons and coal empties - surely a most ignoble end for such a prestigious class of locomotives.

Apart from regular use in the Carlisle and Glasgow areas on local trains and freight workings, they were still very occasionally to be seen on the 'The Mid-Day Scot' and other Euston-Glasgow workings including sleeping car services, and the Birmingham-Glasgows. They were also regularly used in Scotland, particularly on the 9.25 a.m. Crewe-Perth northwards from Carlisle, the 12.25 p.m. (S.O.) Glasgow-Lockerbie, and the 11.00 a.m. Carlisle-Glasgow St. Enoch and the 5.30 p.m. Glasgow St. Enoch - Carlisle, both of the latter running over the old G & S.W.R. route.

Further south they were also still to be seen on their old stamping grounds in the Liverpool, Manchester, Birmingham and Coventry areas, as far west as Holyhead on the services from Crewe, and of course in the London area. Four members of the class, 46239, 46228, 46251 and 46240, were assembled at Euston on Grand National Day to work early morning specials to Liverpool, but were taken off at Crewe and replaced by Britannias. Two others, 46245 and 46256 were also prepared for the specials but not used.

However, the final blow came with the issue in July, 1964 of an instruction which went to all depots with members of the class still allocated. This stated that all Class 8 passenger engines of ex L.M.S. design were to be withdrawn as from 12th September, 1964 on which date they were to be worked to their home shed and the name and number plates removed. As a result the last depot transfers made were of 46245, which moved from Willesden to Crewe North during the p.e. 8th August, and 46239 and 46240 which made the same move during the following period ending 5th September.

Enthusiasts were naturally keen to pay their last respects to this magnificent class of locomotives, and on 9th May, 1964 the R.C.T.S. organised the 'East Midlander No.7' special over the former Great Central line from Nottingham to Didcot hauled by 46251. 'CITY OF NOTTINGHAM' of Crewe North depot, and on 21st June she worked another special, this time over a most unusual route from Shrewsbury to Paddington station in London. She returned as far as Rugby where she was held as standby engine for a Royal Train working to Scotland, but not being needed, returned to Crewe North depot on a parcels train on 23rd June.

Then, on 12th July, 1964 two Stanier Pacifics were involved in the Stephenson Locomotive Society 'Pennine Three Summits' rail tour. 46251 worked the train from Birmingham New Street to Carlisle via Shap. 46255 'CITY OF HEREFORD' then took over for the run over the former Midland Railway line via Settle Junction to Leeds, where 'Jubilee' class 4-6-0 45647 'Sturdee' was waiting for the final section over Standedge Summit and then back to Birmingham via Stockport and Crewe.

Stanier Pacifics were still much in evidence on Shap during the two weekends 23rd -25th July and 31st July-2nd August when, from the Friday evening to the Sunday eight and seventeen members of the class respectively were observed working passenger and freight trains. The class also remained very frequent visitors to Glasgow right through that summer, and twelve members of the class were seen there in August. Steam working of the 'Mid-day Scot' continued until the end of the summer timetable, 46254 being observed on the working on 29th August. The class were banned from working south of Crewe from 1st September, but continued to work trains north of that station until 10th September.

The first few days of September, 1964 saw the disappearance of the Stanier Pacifics from the West Coast main line, and also the last runs of 'The Caledonian'. The last down 'Caledonian' on Friday, 4th September, 1964 was fittingly worked by 46238 'CITY OF CARLISLE', a prestige engine as far as the staff at its Upperby home depot were concerned, and its demise shortly afterwards evoked a sense of deep mourning in their ranks, such as is only normally engendered by the loss of a close and very dear friend!

A little earlier, on 1st September, 46243 'CITY OF LANCASTER' of Edge Hill depot, Liverpool worked the 11.30 a.m. Birmingham-Edinburgh, returning the following day with the 10.10 a.m. Edinburgh-Birmingham; almost certainly the last of the class seen in the Scottish capital. During the first two weeks of September those still at work included 46250 of Upperby depot on a Crewe-Glasgow on the 4th, 46239 of Crewe North on a Euston-Carlisle passenger, plus 46240 on a down freight on the 7th and 46228 on a parcels train on the 8th, both also of Crewe North. 46250 was seen again on a Euston-Perth on the 9th and 46256 on a Carlisle-Euston on the 9th plus 46228 again on a relief special on the 11th, all being seen at Preston. Three of the class were seen at work in the Tebay area on Saturday, 12th, these being 46238, 46245, 46251 in addition to an un-identified green liveried one.

The last of the class to work into Glasgow Central was 46228 'DUCHESS OF RUTLAND', that worked a relief into that station on 11th September, and, although booked to work the 22.45 hours relief train as far as Crewe, this was taken on by 'Royal Scot' class 4-6-0 46166 'LONDON RIFLE BRIGADE.' 46228 was still in steam on Polmadie depot on Sunday, 13th September, and sister engine 46244 'KING GEORGE VI' was also in Scotland at the same time, having worked a train to Perth.

All of the remaining members of the class were officially withdrawn during the first two weeks of September, 1964, with the sole exception of 46256 'SIR WILLIAM A. STANIER, F.R.S.'. This locomotive was required for a special train later, but all of the remainder should have been out of service by 12th September, although a few continued to work for a few days beyond that cut-off date.

This last special working of 46256 took place on 26th September when she worked the R.C.T.S. 'The Scottish Lowlander' from Crewe to Carlisle, where Gresley Class A4 Pacific No 60007 took the train over the Waverley route to Edinburgh. 60009 replaced her at Niddrie Junction for the run via the Edinburgh suburban line to Glasgow St. John's and then, via Kilmarnock, to Carlisle. Here 46256 was waiting to take over for the final leg back to Crewe.

The final withdrawals now took place, 46241 having been withdrawn from Edge Hill and 46248 from Crewe North during the p.e. 5th September, with 46239 and 46240 moving to the latter depot. The following period ending 3rd October saw the withdrawal of the rest of the class from the following depots:-

Crewe North:-	46228, 46235, 46239, 46240, 46245, 46251, 46254, 46256.
Liverpool Edge Hill:-	46243.
Carlisle Kingmoor:-	46226, 46244, 46255, 46257.
Carlisle Upperby:-	46225, 46237, 46238, 46250.

It should be noted that some of these last allocations were never recorded on the official engine record cards.

One of this last batch to be withdrawn, 46235 'CITY OF BIRMINGHAM', was in fact also set aside for preservation, and was chosen to represent the class as part of the National Collection on the basis that accommodation for it was offered by the city of that name. It remains on display there, painted in the Brunswick green B.R. livery, and in 2001 the locomotive was moved to new accommodation at Birmingham's new Museum of Science and Discovery at Millennium Point from its first home in the city's original Museum of Science and Industry.

The first arrivals of engines at the Carlisle Upperby storage sidings were 46225/6/38 and 46250 noted there on 19th September, to be joined by 46244 and 46255 by the 27th of that month. The full list of disposals is given in Appendix 11.

It has been suggested by some commentators that the 'Princess Coronation' Pacifics were in fact ushered out of use with indecent haste under a policy generated by those in positions of power, who had special affections for the Gresley Pacifics and who were determined to see these outlast what many consider to be the finest express passenger locomotives ever to run on the national system of this country. Eric Langridge referred to this in his remarks included in Chapter Two. Certainly the engines that replaced them were in every way inferior in terms of sheer power output, and many on the London Midland Region were outraged when the final members of the class were prematurely withdrawn taking into consideration design life and mechanical condition as well as ability.

As Derek Cross has observed, the Carlisle men soon exploded the theory that the 'Britannia's' would be able to do the work of the 'Duchesses'. "The summer traffic of 1966/7 had found the L.M.R. in a very poor position for motive power, the 'Britannias' having to be double-headed on anything like a heavy train..... many having to revert to two (Stanier) class 5's.... What is certain is that by 1964 the L.M.R. had too many large engines... What is also certain is that the Stanier Pacifics were cut down in their prime without any blemish in their design or mechanical ability. To many of us who knew these mighty engines the end of steam came not on 11th August, 1968 but on 12th September, 1964. The trout had gone, only the tiddlers remained."

One of the bright spots of this period was the sight of 6233, replendent in L.M.S. livery albeit with incorrect detail, just out of Crewe Works and ready to be moved to Butlin's holiday camp at Heads of Ayr. That story and what followed is recounted in our next chapters.

The scene on Carlisle Upperby shed in October 1964 as 46238 'City of Carlisle' and 46250 'City of Lichfield' await their fate. Climbing into the cab of 46250 is a young Howard Routledge, now a Trustee of The Princess Royal Class Locomotive Trust, who has been responsible for collecting together the majority of the action photographs of 'Duchess of Sutherland' used in this book. (G.W. Routledge)

Chapter Five

Saved for Preservation

As already mentioned, unlike most of the class who were fated to be dispatched and cut up for scrap, as listed in Appendix 9, 46233 'DUCHESS OF SUTHERLAND' was one of only three survivors, along with 46229 'DUCHESS OF HAMILTON' and 46235 'CITY OF BIRMINGHAM'.

Both 46233 and 46229 were to be saved and preserved by Billy Butlin as part of his scheme to exhibit steam locomotives at his holiday camps, and in our previous book "6203 'PRINCESS MARGARET ROSE' - The First Production Stanier Pacific", published by Platform 5 in 1992, we referred to the series of events resulting in 'Princess Royal' class locomotive 46203 being preserved and put on display at Butlin's holiday camp at Pwllheli in Wales in 1963. We related the facts as then known, and the request from Butlins to Mr.A.B.Macleod, then the London Midland Region Stores Controller, to purchase 46201 'PRINCESS ELIZABETH', which had already been sold to the 'Princess Elizabeth Society', and how 46203 was offered instead and the offer accepted.

What we were unaware of at the time of writing that book was the invaluable part played by Mr. Brian Walker, a very pro-active railway enthusiast at that time, and then living in Reading, who was moved to try to save "some of the most important steam locomotives" from the cutter's torch and hopefully into posterity.

On 5th February, 1963 Brian Walker wrote to Sheffield City Council suggesting that they purchase 46249 `CITY OF SHEFFIELD' "as a `Monument of the Iron and Steel Industry of Sheffield`, but the Director of the City Museum wrote in reply on 4th March 1963 to advise that the proposal had been considered by the City Council who unanimously turned it down, stating "it would be quite impractical to install and maintain this relic, either at the railway station or in this Museum, for the benefit of the very small minority of people to whom it would appeal."

He wrote another letter on 19th February, 1963 to the Clerk to the Borough Council at Crewe, suggesting the establishment of a Heritage Centre there as an important L.M.S. Railway town which would include representative preserved locomotives. This too was turned down following a discussion that took place just between the Town Clerk and the Leader of the Council! A further letter was sent by him to the council authorities in London regarding 46245 'CITY OF LONDON', and to both Leeds City Council and Eric Treacy about saving 'Jubilee' class 4-6-0 No. 45562 'ALBERTA', which at the time had been allocated to the Holbeck motive power depot there for over 30 continuous years. Again there was insufficient interest.

As part of his personal campaign, on 16th January, 1963 he had written a letter to Mr. Billy Butlin at the Butlin's Holidays headquarters in Oxford St., London advising them that an official society, The 'Princess Elizabeth' and 'Royal Scot' Preservation Society',

Duchess of Sutherland stands outside the paintshop in Crewe Works August/September 1964 after her cosmetic overhaul. (see text re incorrect livery) (W .Potter)

had been formed and were endeavouring to raise sufficient funds to purchase those two steam locomotives, and pleading for the holiday firms' financial assistance in helping save both. Almost enough money had been raised to purchase 46201 'PRINCESS ELIZABETH' -the sum being £2,160, but not for 46100 'Royal Scot', for which B.R. required £1,900. He went on to suggest in his letter that Butlins might also help to "make it possible for a place be found to display them in a museum or "at one of your many holiday camps." He included a brief potted history of both locomotives, including the fact that in 1933 46100 'ROYAL SCOT' had travelled by ship across the Atlantic to the Chicago World Fair and afterwards made a 12,000 mile tour of the North American Continent including the unassisted crossing of the Rockies. As to 46201, he stated that her claim to fame was her world-record non-stop run from Euston to Glasgow, covering the 401.4 miles in 344.5 minutes giving an average speed of 70 m.p.h., and paving the way for the pre-war 'Coronation Scot' service.

Initially there was an encouraging response by Butlins Ltd. In a letter, dated 23rd January 1963, from Mr G.S. Ogg, an Assistant Managing Director, that was copied to Mr. Walker but written to Mr. R Bell of the 'Princess Elizabeth Locomotive Society', which had meanwhile succeeded in raising sufficient funds for the purchase of 46201, Mr Ogg stated that "British Railways serve all our Holiday Camps, and in fact at three of our sites the Railway Station is actually on our Camp grounds. We would be prepared to provide space at our Camps for these Locomotives to be on permanent display where they could be seen by thousands of people every year. If necessary, a plaque or board could be erected giving the history of the Locomotive and the facts of how they were purchased to enable them to be preserved. The locomotives would be on free show to all our Campers and our day visitors."

However, when the Butlin's Board considered the proposal at its 14th February meeting, they turned it down on the grounds of a likely total capital outlay of £15,000. Not to be deterred, and to his immense credit, Brian Walker wrote again on 19th February 1963 pleading that at least 46100 'ROYAL SCOT' be considered for any scheme, for by then, following the initial setback, Mr Ogg had continued to show interest. His enthusiasm for the idea, and his determination that there should be a successful outcome `turned the tide' and led to Butlins having a change of heart, and they now agreed to follow up Brian Walker's suggestions with actions of their own.

At that stage they were only interested in large passenger locomotives, preferably with some significant history. With 46201 'PRINCESS ELIZABETH' now sold to the `Princess Elizabeth Society', moves were made by Butlins to purchase another 'Princess Royal' class Pacific locomotive. It should be remembered that by this time in early 1963 all of the 'Princess Royals' had already been withdrawn, whereas the 'Princess Coronations' still had some months left in service. Consequently it was initially to the 'Princess Royals' that Butlins' interest again turned, and the locomotive selected was 'PRINCESS MARGARET ROSE', which, as Brian Walker pointed out, was the first production member of the class. Having already been withdrawn during the week ending 20th October, 1962 the locomotive was immediately available, and also Princess Margaret was a popular and high-ranking member of the Royal Family, and was in fact married in 1963.

Furthermore Butlins also owned a 21 inch gauge steam outline, but diesel driven, locomotive with the same name. Curiously, after the arrival of the full sized 'Princess Margaret Rose' they re-named the miniature locomotive 'Queen Elizabeth', and so in one way achieved their original objective of having a locomotive named after Her Majesty The Queen ! As we told in our book on 'PRINCESS MARGARET ROSE', this diminutive locomotive is also now owed by The Princess Royal Class Locomotive Trust, and has recently been restored to full working order after being recovered by the Trust from a scrapyard in the early 1990s.

On 1st May, 1963 Mr. Ogg, of Butlins, wrote again to Mr Walker advising him that they had now purchased 46203, and that the locomotive would be exhibited at the Butlins' camp at Pwllheli. He added that they were "negotiating too for 'ROYAL SCOT' which is earmarked for our camp at Skegness, but arrangements for this have not yet been finalised." A further letter from Mr Ogg dated 23rd May, 1963 advised "we have been successful in obtaining the 'ROYAL SCOT' which will be positioned at our Skegness Camp in about three weeks time."

As to other locomotives, Mr Walker was later advised that money was going to become available to purchase and display a locomotive at their No. 1 Camp at Minehead and also the camp at Ayr in Scotland.

Butlins approached the Eastern Region of British Railways to acquire ex L. & N.E.R. Class A4 Pacific 'SILVER LINK', which at the time was languishing in Doncaster Works. However the asking price was well above the normal scrap price and Butlins would not agree to this 'inflated' figure. 60014 was sadly therefore duly cut up for scrap.

It also now appears that, unknown to Mr Walker, Butlins had also made an approach to the Western Region to purchase 'King' class 4-6-0 6018 'King Henry VI' with the intention of displaying it at their Minehead holiday camp. Once again the asking price was well above the scrap price and Butlin's declined to meet the figure.

Following Mr. Ogg's failure to secure the purchase of 'SILVER LINK', his interest then centered on 46220 'CORONATION' for the Minehead camp, but when Mr. Walker wrote back to advise that in fact it was (4)6229 'DUCHESS OF HAMILTON' that had made the historic 1939 trip to North America in the guise of 6220, it was that locomotive that was then chosen. She was therefore purchased and moved to Crewe Locomotive Works for cosmetic restoration, and on 25th March 1964 she was in the Paint Shop being repainted in a representation of the original L.M.S. crimson lake livery. She was on Crewe North motive power depot on 18th April and was subsequently moved southwards on the 24th April, travelling via Birmingham Snow Hill, and shortly afterwards put on static display in the Minehead Holiday Camp.

Mr Walker had originally suggested that 46242 'CITY OF GLASGOW' would be appropriate for the Heads of Ayr Holiday Camp, since she was the only locomotive involved in the 1952 Harrow and Wealdstone crash to have been rebuilt and returned to service. For reasons unknown she was not selected, and the chosen locomotive was 46233 'DUCHESS OF SUTHERLAND' which had lain out of use at Edge Hill since her withdrawal. Her purchase negotiated with Mr. A.B. Macleod, the then London Midland Region Stores Controller for around £2,500.

Why she was chosen is not known, but one can speculate that it was partly because she did carry a title with strong Scottish connections, which were in keeping with the location of the camp but mainly because she was available at the right time. It would seem that the negotiations for her purchase must have been carried out at a later date than those for 46229, which would account for her much later move to Crewe for restoration.

It is appropriate therefore that the efforts of both Mr B.Walker, as a dedicated, persistent and far-sighted railway enthusiast, and Mr G.S. Ogg, for so positively championing the proposal within the Butlins organisation, should now go on record for their sterling efforts at that crucial time. They both played a critical role in the sequence of events that resulted in the preservation of both of the Stanier Pacifics that are now in the ownership The Princess Royal Class Locomotive Trust , 'DUCHESS OF HAMILTON' now at the National Railway Museum at York, and of course 'ROYAL SCOT' now at Bressingham. Since their return to steam all three of the Pacific locomotives have afforded the chance for thousands of the present generation to take great pleasure from seeing them hard at work on their old stamping grounds, and also on new and unfamiliar territory, and their absence today from the list of preserved locomotives would have left a massive void. At the time of writing this book work has commenced on the overhaul of No. 6100 'ROYAL SCOT' to full mainline running condition, so in the future all of those locomotives saved through Mr Brian Walker's efforts will have graced the main line once again.

Once the purchase arrangements had been completed 'DUCHESS OF SUTHERLAND' was subsequently moved by rail from Liverpool, and photographed in the arrival sidings at Crewe Works by Norman Preedy on 14th June, 1964, still complete with name and numberplates but with coupling and connecting rods removed. Once in the shops her smoke deflectors were removed and her B.R. '46233' smokebox numberplate was replaced with an L.M.S. style one bearing her original number '6233'.

The old numberplate was discarded for scrap, but was fortuitously recovered from a scrap bin, along with that of 46229, by an Inspector. By a stroke of good fortune on 15th June, 2002 that numberplate (together with that of 46229) was sold at a Sheffield Railwayana Auction and, thanks to a most generous donation, No. 6233's was purchased for £5,800 by The Princess Royal Class Locomotive Trust, by then the owners of 'DUCHESS OF SUTHERLAND'. It has thus found its rightful place back with the locomotive and completed the collection.

By 12th August, 1964 6233 was in the Paint Shop ready for repainting. As with No. 6229, she too was to be turned out in a representative, though not strictly accurate, early L.M.S. crimson lake livery. The lining out colours of black and straw were used and the cabside numbers were not as originally used by the L.M.S in 1938.

By 30th August she was complete, and was photographed by Norman Preedy, appropriately carrying a 5A (Crewe North) shedplate, outside the paint shop in the old location formerly used for all Crewe Works official photographs.

THE MOVE TO BUTLIN'S HEADS OF AYR HOLIDAY CAMP.

6233's move to the Butlin's holiday camp at Heads of Ayr was covered by an excellent article by the late Derek Cross in the Ian Allan 'Trains Annual' for 1966 from which we are pleased to be able to quote. After referring to the fact that it was originally intended that she be moved into position over temporary track, he continued:-

".. owing to the steepness - and to a lesser extent - the soft nature of the clay soils around the site, this idea had to be abandoned. Instead, very difficult and involved road/rail operations had to be planned."

"The site of Butlin's camp at Heads of Ayr falls steeply from the A719 Ayr-Turnberry coast road to the bay lying between the rocky headlands of Heads of Ayr and Longhill Point. The difference in altitude between the road at the camp entrance and the shore is 165 feet and the camp is spread out between these two points. At the front of the camp is a small area of flat ground and on this, some of the offices and dance halls for the camp are built; it was on this flat area that it was decided to exhibit the locomotives. The station serving the camp is sited approximately on the 100 foot contour and was built on the old Ayr, Dunure & Maidens Light Railway. It consists of a long concrete platform and a loop for running round, and is now the terminus of the Ayr - Maidens line, which has been lifted beyond this point. Unfortunately this station is on an embankment, and so could not be used as a suitable point for unloading such a heavy locomotive."

When the camp closed at the end of the summer season in September, 1964, a short length of temporary track was laid in the rose gardens between the dance halls and the main road, for it was then known that, in addition to 6233, restored 'Terrier' tank engine No. 32662, formerly ex L.B. & S.C.R. No. 62 'Martello', was also to be displayed there.

Derek Cross continues:-
" 'DUCHESS OF SUTHERLAND' meanwhile had been withdrawn from service in May (sic) and, suitably restored, left Crewe on the morning of Tuesday, 15th September as a special 'out-of-gauge' goods train hauled, according to a witness, by a Stanier Class 5 that was just about as dirty as the Pacific was clean."

Approaching Greenbank Sidings Signal Box (Preston) LMS Class 5 45026, with reporting no 6Z02, hauls the Duchess north. (W.Ashcroft**)**

A contrast in appearances as an immaculate 6233 is hauled by a workstained Class 5 No. 45026 at Greenbank Sidings Signal Box on the journey from Crewe Works to Ayr on 15th September 1964. (W. Ashcroft)

Duchess of Sutherland minus her tender is hauled through Ayr Station on 21st October 1964 on the journey from Ayr mpd to Greenan Siding. (D. Cross)

This Stanier Class 5 was in fact 4-6-0 No. 45026. After a short stop in Kingmoor Yard at Carlisle, she continued northwards, again hauled by another Stanier 'Black Five', arriving in the early hours of Wednesday, 16th September.

The plan to lay a spur into the site in the camp was abandoned, and it was decided to work the engines into Greenan Siding on the Heads of Ayr Branch, a single siding facing towards Ayr, that lay adjacent to the main road about 3/4 mile from the camp. As there were no heavy gradients this would enable the locomotives to be hauled a minimum distance by road. The siding was stable and needed only steel plates to be laid down to take heavy point loadings. The local highway authorities had forbidden the 'Duchess' from passing over either of the two road bridges in the area!

Until the preparation work had been completed, 6233 was stored in the diesel railcar maintenance shed at Ayr motive power depot, but the 'Terrier', which had contrived to become lost on the Western Region in transit from Eastleigh Works from where it had left, loaded onto a 'Lowmac' flat vehicle, at the same time as 'DUCHESS OF SUTHERLAND' left Crewe. It finally arrived on 28th September, having lodged at Liverpool and Tebay en route! Pickfords, with whom the road move had been contracted, had suffered problems over the delay in preparing the site, and the idea of towing both locomotives to Greenan Siding was abandoned.

Derek Cross continues:-

"So it was on the morning of Monday, 19th October that a strange cavalcade left Ayr m.p.d. for Townhead Siding and initiated a week of bizarre railway and road activity. It comprised diesel shunter D3206, 'Terrier' No. 32662 and the tender of 'Duchess' No. 6233. In order to have these two facing the most suitable way for Pickfords to load, the train left the sheds facing north towards Glasgow, ran onto the main line at Newton-on-Ayr station, and then reversed itself round the Blackhouse-Hawkhill triangle. Once back on the Ayr-Girvan main line, the train moved very slowly through Ayr station, provoking one of the most delightful comments of the whole operation, when an aged bystander on the Ayr platform remarked to a porter: "Man, that's surely an awful big tender for a wee engine.""

Cross records that after the train had been reversed into the Townhead coal siding, the diesel uncoupled and the same two 25 ton cranes which had unloaded and re-railed the 'Terrier' some three weeks previously, re-loaded her again onto a Pickfords 40 ton road trailer. Shortly after lunch the engine was towed out to the camp without incident and at a very brisk pace and then lifted off and placed in position on the tracks that had been laid on the exhibition site the previous day. The following morning the exercise was repeated for the tender of the 'Duchess', the only hitch being the damage to overhanging trees on the different route taken because of the height of the load, the tender therefore arriving on site with a number of branches adorning it.

"All this was a curtain raiser to moving 'DUCHESS OF SUTHERLAND'. This operation fell into two distinct phases: towing her by

rail to Greenan siding, then loading and taking her by road to the Butlin's camp. Even the rail part of the journey was not simple, for the biggest locomotive allowed down the branch from Alloway Junction to Heads of Ayr are Class 5's or their equivalent, though on occasion 'Jubilee' Class 4-6-0's and on one rare occasion a 'Clan' Pacific, have been down. Also Class 7P's and 8P's are not normally allowed on the main line south of Ayr ....the main snags for big engines are the restricted clearance through overhead bridges and above all through the short but narrow and curved tunnel at Alloway. The picturesque stone viaduct over the Doon at Alloway is subject to a fairly strict weight restriction, although this was waived on account of the 'Duchess' running with an empty boiler and the low speed (5 m.p.h.) allowed her on the branch. Another unexpected snag arose as a result of the tender having been taken off the locomotive and transported by road, which left 118 tons of locomotive without any operative brake at all. The Heads of Ayr branch is steeply graded down from Alloway Junction to the Doon viaduct 1½ miles away, so it was decided that there would have to be a diesel shunter at each end of No. 6233, in case of a coupling failure between the Pacific and a single propelling diesel. Ayr m.p.d. devised a linkage to fit through the arm normally used to join the locomotive to her tender that would couple onto a second diesel shunter to be used purely as an emergency brake."

Not only did the depot devise the above coupling to the engine's drawbar pin, but William Bennett, then the Shed Master at Ayr, had greased and lubricated when 6233 was on Ayr m.p.d. Consequently she went onto her display plinth with some valuable protection on many of her hidden parts. He did this out of pride for the locomotive and his training as a locomotive fitter. Another important factor that assisted in the well being of the locomotive was that prior to the move from Crewe to Ayr, with the motion remaining in position, liberal amounts of thick oil were poured down the blast pipe. This, although principally for the move to Ayr, also ensured that all inside surfaces were well coated with oil for what turned out to be the eight years that the locomotive was to remain on display in the open air and in the seaside environment of the holiday camp. All of this care, and handsome measure of good fortune was to pay dividends in later years.

Derek Cross continues:-

" 'DUCHESS OF SUTHERLAND' was booked to leave Ayr. m.p.d. at 10 a.m. on Wednesday, October 21st for her last run on B.R. metals. With her cab towards Glasgow, she was drawn out of the shed by Barclay diesel shunter No. D2434. At this stage No. D3005, booked to propel the Pacific to Greenan, developed a faulty injector pump, and by the time this was rectified it was 11 a.m. As with the 'Terrier' and the tender, 6233 had to be turned on the Blackhouse-Hawkhill triangle, and it was 11.15 a.m. when the special made its way on to the Glasgow-Girvan main line."

"At the eastern mouth of Alloway Tunnel the train stopped, and an inspector walked through the tunnel on foot checking clearances, but there was no cause for worry; in fact I was told afterwards that she had plenty of clearance in the tunnel and that the tightest part was through the bridge carrying a minor road over the branch between Alloway Junction and the tunnel. The need for the

The short but unusual train passes Alloway. (D. Cross)

The two diesels haul 6233 back to Greenan Sidings. (D. Cross)

Duchess of Sutherland being winched onto the Pickford's low loader trailer at Greenan Sidings after her front bogie had been removed. Note the steel plates laid to run the low loader across the soft ground.
Thursday 22nd October 1964 (D. Cross)

The first tractor unit reverses on to the low loader trailer (Bill Hamilton)

The front wheels of the low loader trailer are positioned (Bill Hamilton)

6233 is eased away from Greenan sidings (Bill Hamilton)

Running on steel plates, the abnormal load turns onto the exit from Greenan Sidings site. (Bill Hamilton)

The steel hawser is fixed between the two tractor units. (Bill Hamilton)

The convoy moves up the incline and towards the main road. (Bill Hamilton)

The highway is reached at last. (Bill Hamilton)

The arrival at Ayr Camp, and with a Police presence, the low loader trailer carrying 6233 is pushed into the camp. (D. Cross)

With bogie truck in position the locomotive is lowered down using the two mobile cranes. (D. Cross)

121

front diesel as an emergency brake resulted in the train having to run right out to Heads of Ayr station, for as soon as No. 6233 was positioned at Greenan Siding the track had to be lifted in front of her, and this would have entailed No. D2434 being trapped at Greenan for some days. As the line from Heads of Ayr to Greenan is flat, it was decided to take 'DUCHESS OF SUTHERLAND' out to Heads of Ayr station to allow the Barclay diesel to run round and attach in front of No. D3005. They could then both tow No. 6233 back to Greenan and couple off to return light to Ayr. The whole journey from Ayr was accomplished without incident on a day of glorious autumn sunshine and by 12.30 p.m. No. 6233 was in position at Greenan with the permanent way gang lifting three lengths of track to allow Pickfords to get their heaviest trailer in for loading."

"The only trailer available in Scotland to shift a load the weight of 'DUCHESS OF SUTHERLAND' was one that Pickfords had in Glasgow, originally built in 1923 to convey locomotives from the North British Locomotive Company's works to the docks, and which I can remember seeing in Glasgow before the war hauled by two traction engines. On 'DUCHESS OF SUTHERLAND's' last journey this trailer was hauled by a very large Scammell tractor, assisted out of Greenan by the slightly smaller Scammell used to shift her tender and the 'Terrier'. The trailer, though fit to take the weight of No.6233, was not long enough, and the front of the engine had to overhang the back of the trailer; to obtain clearance for this the front bogie had to be removed. This operation was completed on the afternoon of Thursday, October 22nd by lifting the locomotive with the two 25-ton mobile cranes, aided by two jacks; the bogie was drawn out with a winch and lifted onto the lorry by a third, lighter mobile crane. The lorry then drove with the bogie to the camp."

"The morning of Friday, October 23rd was taken up levelling the track bed where the rails had been lifted in front of the engine; this piece of ground was then covered with steel plates. The trailer was backed into position and its front bogie and draw-gear detached. A short length of temporary track was laid from the cut end of the main line to connect with the rails that form part of the integral structure of the trailer by the Scammell tractor. With the Pacific now secured in place, the trailer was raised by jack and its front bogie unit was replaced ready for the road journey."

Derek Cross continued by describing the laying of steel plates in the yard, which took the rest of Saturday and Sunday morning; the short push up the 40 yards onto the main road needed both tractor units, the smaller one being stationed on the main road pulling on a steel hawser. The procession over the 3/4 mile to the camp taken at walking pace; the transfer of steel plates from the rail siding to the camp, and laying them down to form an unloading platform, taking the rest of Sunday and all of Monday.

It was not therefore until Tuesday, 27th October that everything was in place for the final phase of the operation, but unfortunately the weather had turned to rain. The trailer was propelled into position some ten feet from the end of the display track, its front bogie and towing equipment removed and, using six-roller skate units at each front corner of the trailer frame, it was winched forwards until the track connected with a short length of temporary track, itself connected to the permanent display length of track. Derek felt that this was the trickiest part of the operation, since the only control came from steering the back bogies of the trailer with the requirement that the front of it must connect up with the short temporary track first time, a repeat being a major operation.

He concluded the article by saying:-

"All went well, and by early afternoon 'DUCHESS OF SUTHERLAND' was man-handled off the trailer and onto the track that was to be her final home. It is a fitting tribute to the standard of workmanship that Crewe had put into restoring her mechanically as well as externally, that two men with pinch bars and six men pushing were able to shift nearly 120 tons of locomotive along a level track without too great an effort - I know - I helped to push! All that now remained was for the front bogie to be replaced, which was done in a similar manner to the way it had been removed five days earlier. The bogie was lifted by a crane and was placed on the short length of temporary track .... The front of the locomotive was then lifted by the two 25-ton mobile cranes and the bogie slid into place underneath. Then she was man-handled back to rejoin the tender, and the steps, sandpipes and various other small parts which had been removed to avoid damage when loading and unloading....were replaced."

Once in position 'DUCHESS OF SUTHERLAND' and her diminutive sister, the 'Terrier' tank 'MARTELLO', were to become attractions for the thousands of visitors who flocked to the holiday camp during each successive season. Provided with a set of access steps, the footplate of 6233 became the chosen venue for children and grown-ups of all ages, who could lower themselves into the driver's seat, handle the controls, and imagine themselves in charge of this giant of steam as she thundered at high speed along the main line in charge of a named express in times now gone by. From time to time Butlins would engage former drivers of the class to stand in the cab and described the work of the footplate staff as they set about their demanding and taxing work. She was also visited by many railway enthusiasts who made the pilgrimage to Ayr just to see and photograph her, now as a preserved locomotive and a Stanier Pacific that had escaped the fate of all but five from a field of fifty remaining in the early 1960s.

However, 'DUCHESS OF SUTHERLAND' was not fated to remain a mere static exhibit for too many years.

Duchess of Sutherland in her new residence with Martello.
(S. Sellar)

Chapter Six

Butlins to Bressingham Steam Museum

The movement of 6233 'DUCHESS OF SUTHERLAND' from the Heads of Ayr holiday camp to the Bressingham Steam Museum near Diss in Norfolk was part of a decision of Butlins Ltd. to release all of the locomotives that had been put on display at their camps as visitor attractions. By 1970 they were all badly in need of some conservation care, their paintwork and bright parts showing signs of weathering as a result of standing outside, and thus the actions of salt in the air with them being at seaside resorts. Furthermore since the mid-1960s times had moved on. Man had gone to the Moon in 1969 and from what may have been icons of their day from the 1930s to the 1960s, express steam locomotives were now consigned to history. Space rockets and supersonic aeroplanes were now the fashion. The `Butlin` locomotives had outlived their initial useful purpose as attractions, and considerable expenditure was now required to keep them presentable.

The acquisition of ex L.M.S. 4-6-0 6100 'ROYAL SCOT' by Alan Bloom, the owner of the Bressingham Steam Museum, is worth recording, since this then started the pattern of events in respect of 6233 herself.

Initiator of the moves to Bressingham was Geoffrey Sands, who had left British Railways in 1970 and joined the staff at Bressingham. Geoff's father had been Chief Traction Inspector in the Norwich District so Geoff had developed and interest in railways from an early age. He had formerly been the Shed Master at Stoke before moving to Crewe North motive power depot, a post he had been given in 1961 at the early age of 33. He had remained in the post until 1964, thus being responsible for the day-to-day maintenance, repair and servicing of a large number of locomotives, including 6233 herself and other members of the class. Following a move to Salisbury, where he became Area Manager, he left BR and became the manager of the museum at Bressingham.

During a visit to the recently closed B.R. East Lincolnshire line to look for items for display in the museum, as suggested by the late Dr. John Scholes, then Curator of Historical Relics for the British Transport Commission, Sands called in at the Butlins Skegness holiday camp to see `an old friend' 6100 'ROYAL SCOT'. Following a conversation with the manager of the camp it was suggested that Sands might like to contact the Butlins Board of Directors with a view to getting them to release the locomotive into the care of Bressingham, they being an organisation that knew how to care for and preserve locomotives.

Upon his return to Bressingham, Sands told Alan Bloom "I'd dearly love to see it here. The man in charge says it's a nuisance - standing there rusting away with people tampering with it - an eyesore rather than an attraction." An initial approach that Bloom had made in 1968 had not been fruitful, but in October, 1970 he wrote again to Butlins suggesting that it might now be an idea to move their locomotives away from the coast to stop further deterioration. He advised that Bressingham had skilled locomotive engineers and equipment available so that they could be well looked after.

This approach by Alan Bloom could well have been the trigger for action, for within a short time the Butlin's Board had decided that the time had come to release all of the locomotives on display at their various camps, since they had now become somewhat of a liability. Following a visit to Bressingham by a Butlin's Director in November, 1970 the company agreed that it would be an ideal place for the engines, and that they could have their choice of all of the locomotives for permanent display at their museum, provided that they paid all transport and restoration costs and maintained them in

good condition. However Trevor Watts, the Butlin's representative, expressly wished to keep the matter confidential, and asked Alan Bloom's advice as how best to place those locomotives which Bressingham could not deal with. Bloom's suggestion was to bring in the Transport Trust as a suitable body, since he had already had dealings with, and was associated to it.

A site meeting was held at Skegness to discuss movement problems, and then, on 22nd December, 1970 a formal application for 6100 'ROYAL SCOT', 6203 'PRINCESS MARGARET ROSE' and 6233 'DUCHESS OF SUTHERLAND' plus 0-6-0T 32662 'MARTELLO' was made by Bressingham, 6100 being specifically promised subject to a satisfactory agreement being reached. It was then discovered that Butlins had advertised both 6229 'DUCHESS OF HAMILTON', located at their Minehead camp, and 6203 PRINCESS MARGARET ROSE' at their Pwllheli camp, in their 1971 brochure, and therefore they could not be moved until the end of the summer season for fear of falling foul of the Trades Description Act. That left only the locomotives at the Skegness and Heads of Ayr camps able to be moved, i.e. 'ROYAL SCOT' and 'DUCHESS OF SUTHERLAND' plus a small tank engine at each place, and these could be moved in the spring of 1971.

Specific negotiations resulted in an agreement on 9th February, 1971 that 6100 and 6233 should go to Bressingham. The prospect of having to cope with four large locomotives and four smaller ones was rather more than they could hope to deal with, and at Alan Bloom's instigation the availability of the other six locomotives was made known to other preservation bodies. The item was placed on the Agenda of the Association of Railway Preservation Societies Annual General Meeting held on 23rd January, 1971, but by that date Butlins has already placed the disposal of the other locomotives in the hands of the Transport Trust.

It should be mentioned that as early as 1967 Alan Bloom had considered turning his venture at Bressingham into a Trust in its own right. However rules governing donations to charitable causes had resulted in him endeavouring to come under the wing of the Transport Trust as an already existing Charitable Body. On 24th June, 1972 Alan had handed over the relevant documents, still incomplete, comprising the Agreement and the Deed of Gift to General Lonsdale of the Trust. However further delays in completing them, plus a relaxation in the Law relating to private museums holding collections of historical and educational importance, fortuitously gave time for Alan to go ahead with his original plan and form a separate Charitable Trust for the Bressingham Collection.

6100 'ROYAL SCOT' had originally been purchased by Butlins upon withdrawal from traffic, and then cosmetically restored at Crewe Works in L.M.S. crimson lake livery, a colour not in fact historically accurate in its then rebuilt condition, and with a plate bearing the words 'THE ROYAL SCOT' on its smokebox door. The locomotive had then been moved by rail to Boston on 12th June, 1963, and thence by low loader to the Skegness holiday camp. As a matter of interest, and some reflective amusement, the locomotive was paraded through the town en route to the camp headed by a line of elephants !

After a draft loan agreement based upon that for locomotives in the National Collection had been agreed between Butlins and Alan Bloom, he was able to announce on 16th March, 1971 that not only 6100 'ROYAL SCOT' but also 6233 'DUCHESS OF SUTHERLAND' had been placed on permanent loan to his museum, and over a period of time they were to be moved to Bressingham. 6100 arrived first on 18th March, 1971. Two small Southern Railway Class A1X 0-6-0T 32662 'MARTELLO' tank engines from Skegness, and ex L.& S.W.R. class B4 0-4-0 dock tank 102 'GRANVILLE' from Ayr, were subsequently moved to Bressingham just for storage to enable Butlins to clear the two camp sites. Subsequently they too became part of the agreement, following Butlins decision not to move 6229 and 6203, at Minehead and Pwllheli respectively, for the time being.

THE TASK OF MOVING 'DUCHESS OF SUTHERLAND'.

A preliminary inspection of 6233 was carried out at Ayr on 11th February, 1971 and on 23rd February the nominated haulage contractor, Messrs Sunter Brothers Ltd. of Northallerton, moved into the camp with their 64 wheeled transporter unit. The following day the engine and tender were split and loaded onto units for transportation from the camp site to the re-railing site on British Railways' metals.

It was at this point that the forethought of William Bennett, the Shed Master at Newton-on-Ayr motive power depot, in well greasing every exposed part of 6233 before she had been placed on display, plus the copious quantities of oil poured down the blast pipe during the journey from Crewe to Ayr, paid off, for it was found that the reversing gear could be wound from full forward to full reverse positions without difficulty. And when the engine was being slowly winched onto the low loader unit, there was no groaning from the pistons as they moved in the cylinders, the grease on the piston rods and valve spindles having also ensured that they had not become pitted during the eight years or so that they had been exposed to the salt in the seaside air.

Bennett had also kindly offered to make all other necessary preparations of the locomotive for her second long-haul rail journey, this time from Ayr to Norfolk, arranging especially for the removal of the cylinder relief valves and fully lubricating all the moving parts, paying special attention to the oil feeds to the valves and pistons prior to the move.

According to local newspaper reports at the time, steam enthusiasts from all over the south-west of Scotland plus two pipers from the Argyll and Sutherland Highlanders turned out to watch the engine and tender being loaded on Wednesday, 24th February to permit the road transfer from the camp to British Railways' Townhead sidings. Also present to say farewell was Pat Turner, a local resident, who had grown accustomed to seeing the 33 years old aristocrat on the rails at the camp. Photographs of Pat, attired in the then fashionable sweater, 'hot pants' and long white boots, standing on the running plate of 6233, accompanied various newspaper stories, and under

The abnormal load moves off from Heads of Ayr holiday camp. (D. Cross)

the headline "Hot pants girl takes last look at the Duchess", the 'Scottish Daily Mail' reported:-

"Steam engine nostalgia lives on. Yesterday university student Pat Turner turned up to bid farewell to one of Britain's greatest steam engines, about to start life all over again. The "Duchess of Sutherland", forced into retirement six years ago, left a holiday camp at Heads of Ayr to start a 400 mile journey to Bressingham Live Steam Museum near Diss, Norfolk. But there will be no majestic return. There are no watering places or coaling stages, so the 4-6-2 Pacific class steam loco. will be towed by diesel. Pat, 20, wore hot pants for the occasion. The Duchess had to be content with her old London, Midland & Scottish Railway livery."

After passing through the suburbs of Ayr, where she excited some interest, 'DUCHESS OF SUTHERLAND' duly arrived in British Railway's Townhead coal yard, and the following day, the 25th, she was off-loaded onto B.R. metals once more and re-united with her tender. The `Duchess' was then propelled through Ayr station the following day by Class 08 diesel shunter D3278 and into the motive power depot.

Derek Cross, the well known railway photographer, made a record of these events, and commented that during this re-railing exercise not only was it a very dull day, but also, at the very time 6233 was being slowly lowered down the ramp connecting the low loader bed with B.R. metals, there was a partial eclipse of the sun resulting in his photographs not being quite up to his usual high standards !

Mr D. W. 'Bill' Harvey, who until his then recent retirement had been manager of British Railways' running and maintenance depot at Norwich, was put in charge of all the arrangements for the actual movement of 'DUCHESS OF SUTHERLAND'. The move was almost entirely done on her own wheels by rail from Ayr to Bressingham, a distance of almost 400 miles. The locomotive had originally made a trouble-free movement north from Crewe in 1964 with all the motion in place, and although the regulations now required the motion and coupling rods of any steam locomotive to be taken down when any movement was made in 'dead' condition, i.e. not in steam, over a greater distance than 25 miles, it was decided that they could be safely left in position for this second trip. There can be no doubt that the recommendations of Bill Harvey played a major role in this decision for he still commanded the respect of the decision makers in B.R. despite being in retirement.

As is good practice when moving locomotives dead, oil was poured down the blastpipe orifice in order to lubricate the piston valves and in turn, the main cylinders.

An amusing report in the 24th February, 1971 issue of the 'Eastern Daily Express' newspaper recorded that a startled Norwich shopkeeper had been surprised to receive a request from a man flourishing an empty squash bottle for "a pint of castor oil for the Duchess please." The report adds that "he might have added that the Duchess in question weighs 164 tons and is about to face a 400 mile journey on which the castor oil would be a vital necessity. She

Wednesday 24th February 1971, complete with a banner proclaiming her destination, 6233 is ready to be loaded onto the low loader at Ayr Holiday camp. (D. Cross)

A Hillman Imp Police van gives rear escort at the junction of Doonfoot Road and Racecourse View, Ayr. (D. Cross)

Thursday 25th February 1971. D3278 moves 6233 away from Townhead Coal Sidings. (D. Cross)

The Ayr police keep an eye on the movement as 6233 is turned past Ayr Grammar School into Townhead Coal Sidings yard. (D. Cross)

Now re-united with her tender, 6233 stands on the spur between Blackhouse Junction and Newton Junction before being propelled into Ayr mpd. (D. Cross)

Arrival in Townhead Coal Sidings yard. (D. Cross)

Duchess of Sutherland stands on Ayr mpd on Thursday 25th February 1971. (D. Cross)

is in fact the "Duchess of Sutherland" - the biggest express passenger steam locomotive ever used on the railways of this country. For several years now she has been idling away her retirement on show at Butlin's holiday camp at Ayr.......Sadly after so long out of action she cannot make the trip under her own steam... And that is where the castor oil comes in. "There is nothing like it," declares Mr Harvey, "for lubricating bearings which otherwise might seize up." "You can't beat it" he said enthusiastically, as he set off to get his squash bottle filled.

6233 left Ayr by rail at 12.58 p.m. on Monday, 1st March, 1971,

marshalled between two brake vans and hauled by B.R.C. & W. 1,250 h.p. Type 2 Bo-Bo diesel-electric No. D5355, bearing the headcode 9X51. She was accompanied from Ayr by Bill Harvey and David Ward, then the London Midland Region's Passenger Marketing Manager at Euston, and also by John Scholes, then Curator of Historical Relics for the British Railways Board, who travelled with the locomotive as far as Doncaster. The latter had experienced considerable difficulty and cost in dismantling the motion on British Railways' preserved locomotives before moving them, and he was keen to learn from the experience.

'DUCHESS OF SUTHERLAND' was hauled at a restricted maximum speed of 10 m.p.h. from Ayr to Mauchline Junction, where an examination found that all of the bearings were still cool. Thereafter the maximum permitted speed was to be 25 m.p.h. with reductions to 10 m.p.h. or less at specific overbridges.

Bill Harvey recorded that a steady speed of 25 m.p.h. was kept on the journey southwards from Ayr, as required by the regulations, and the cylinders, which had been previously charged with 10 gallons of lubricating oil, were topped up by pouring another half-gallon or so down the blast pipes every succeeding 100 miles. Indication that more lubricant was required was a slight loss of crispness in the exhaust beat and on the last occasion by a smell of hot oil. The inside big ends were topped up every 50 miles and these, like all of the other bearings, ran cool throughout the journey. The reversing gear was set initially at 40% cut-off, but this was brought back to 25% in order to reduce the rubbing speed, despite an increase in compression.

Geoffrey Sands, went onto the footplate as relief when the cavalcade reached Leeds (Hunslet) at 03.00 hours, in the early morning of 2nd March. Alan Bloom himself joined the locomotive at Ely North Junction, and was delighted that all was still going to plan.

David Ward wrote a most interesting contemporary account of the movement for the Norfolk Railway Society's News Letter, and this is reproduced here, courtesy of the author:-

"MOVING L.M.S. 6233 'DUCHESS OF SUTHERLAND' FROM AYR TO NORWICH" - by D.H. WARD

"After three months of consideration it was finally confirmed on Tuesday, 9th February, that this fine locomotive, which is representative of the most powerful express engines ever to work in this country, was to be allocated to the Bressingham Steam Museum. During the consideration period, tentative thought had been given to the practicability, price and method of movement and it was decided that because of the long trunk haul, rail would have to be used between Ayr and Thetford, with Messrs. Sunter of Northallerton doing the collection and delivery to and from the railheads. Diss could not be used as a terminal because the locomotive was too high to pass under the railway bridge to the south of the station which carried the London-Norwich main line over the branch."

"So it was that on Thursday, 11th February, only two days after the decision had been made, that Bill Harvey and I set off for Ayr on the Euston-Stranraer sleeper. We had friends in the General Manager's Office, Glasgow whom we knew would help all they could, and a site meeting was arranged with them for the Friday morning. Bill and I wished to give the locomotive a good look over before the meeting, because we reckoned on having to be responsible for splitting the engine and tender and re-coupling, supervising loading and unloading and preparation of the locomotive for its 400 mile journey. This would obviously be a considerable task as the locomotive had been on exhibition in the open since October, 1964. Experience with 'THUNDERSLEY' (the preserved ex L.T. & S.R. 4-4-2 tank engine, which had been moved from Attleboro' to Diss with its motion up in August, 1968) had taught us the effects of years of neglect, and we both had considerable apprehension about the task ahead. Questions which had been passing through our minds included what pieces would be missing, what was the mechanical state of the motion, valves, pistons and axleboxes, and would we find vital moving parts completely seized up ? We knew that the engine had been prepared for movement with its motion up when it was restored at Crewe, and we had been told that either the piston heads had been removed or had had holes drilled in them !"

"First impressions were that superficially the locomotive appeared in fairly good order. The paintwork, although beginning to flake and crack, was in much better condition than we could have hoped for

With D5355, Duchess of Sutherland awaits departure from Ayr on Monday 1st March 1971 (D. Cross)

David Ward looks back from the veranda of the leading brake van as 6233 passes Annbank Junction.
(D. Cross)

after seven years in a sea atmosphere. The boiler clothing appeared in reasonable order and, apart from the inside of the tender, there was no serious corrosion apparent. Apart from broken glass in the steam heater gauge, four missing nuts on the driver's brake valve (the governor was subsequently found to be missing), absence of a driver's seat, brick arch and back half of the grate (the latter two had obviously not been replaced when the locomotive was restored), the locomotive appeared to be 100% complete, which seemed most remarkable and augured well for the task ahead."

"Bill Harvey's first task was to try the reversing lever. He knew that if he could move this from full back to full forward gear the piston valves had not seized. Although rather stiff, there was no trouble with this test. Similarly the handbrake was found in good working order. The regulator was, however, jammed, but the footboarding had been so designed to stop anyone opening the cylinder cocks and this had retained oil in the cylinders which had been put there on the run from Crewe after restoration."

"External examination was very promising. The outside motion was well greased, the valve spindles and slide bars appeared to be well oiled, but the inside piston rods and slide bars were well rusted. The motion gave the appearance of having been completely overhauled at the time of restoration. Examination between the frames showed a fairly hopeful picture, apart from two disconnected lubricator pipes to driving wheel axleboxes. Oil wells and lubricators seemed clean but trimmings were all missing."

"Behind the Duchess stood Terrier Tank 32662 'MARTELLO'. The rail price for movement of 6233 included 32662 for no extra cost, but examination of this pretty little engine soon showed that, although she was complete and apparently in good order, it would be foolhardy to attempt dragging her 400 miles on her own wheels. The fact that she had been sent from Brighton on a wagon was enough to tell us that this would have to be a road job throughout."

"After an hour's examination we held our meeting with the Scottish Region officials in the cab of 6233. Here we met Mr. W.A. Bennett, Depot Engineer, Ayr who had been in charge of placing the locomotive into the camp in 1964. He immediately expressed the view that the locomotive was fit for the long journey if properly prepared, offered to split the engine and tender, prepare the locomotive and supervise loading, etc. onto the road vehicle. This was a most generous offer, and over the succeeding days until the movement commenced on 1st March, nobody could have done more to ensure a trouble free journey. Nothing was too much trouble, every detail was looked after and the co-operation we received was beyond praise."

"The following list, which is by no means complete, gives some idea of the work which Mr. Bennett undertook:-

(a) Splitting engine and tender and re-coupling.

(b) Supervising loading and unloading to road vehicle.

(c) Making and fitting new oil trimmings, charging and working by hand for considerable periods the mechanical lubricators

(d) Withdrawing axlebox underkeeps, examining journals, cleaning pads, etc.

(e) Removing one cylinder relief valve to ascertain what modifications had been carried out to the pistons. This showed that the cylinders were well lubricated. The piston heads were complete and release and compression had been provided by removing the valves themselves from the relief valve bodies.

(f) Removing the piston packing to release build-up of compression.

(g) Freeing the regulator - to enable air to be released by the boiler if it should build up in the cylinders.

(h) Putting 10 gallons of oil in the cylinders down the blast pipes, putting cocks in the cylinder relief valves and dragging the engine up and down the locomotive yard to squirt oil well round the valves and pistons.

(i) Giving the engine and tender a thorough clean to bring up the paintwork.

(j) Supplying oil and other materials for the journey.

(k) Fitting vacuum and steam heater pipes."

"The special train was timed to leave Ayr at 12.58 on the 1st of March, and Bill Harvey and I went down on the 23.00 'Night Limited' sleeper from Euston the night before. We had specially asked that we should have daylight for the first few hours of the run because this would be the crucial period. On arrival at Ayr we were escorted into the diesel shed by Mr. Bennett, and it was soon apparent what a magnificent job he had done. The red L.M.S. livery gleamed, the brass on the nameplates had been cleaned up and mechanically everything had been done. Even Bill Harvey could not find anything that had been overlooked, although he was naturally apprehensive about how the journey would go, especially as it had been agreed that the motion should remain up. This in itself was a generous gesture on the part of the Scottish Region officials. Imagine putting up coupling and connecting rods on a four-cylinder six-coupled engine at Bressingham without a pit, with the crank pins all out of phase !"

"Mr. Bennett's generosity did not finish at this late hour. He insisted on us having lunch with him and even supplied footplate passes in a special plastic case. He also ensured that we had a good supply of coal in the brake van and after we left kept in touch with our progress. The only thing he did not organise well was the weather ! This was attrocious - it rained and snowed from the time we got out of the sleeper at Glasgow until we got beyond Leeds in the early hours of Tuesday morning."

"Of the journey itself there is not much to relate. The first 50 miles would obviously be crucial, but Mr. Bennett's preparation had made sure that nothing got warmer than blood temperature apart from the inside slide bars, but as soon as these cleaned up

with movement their temperature dropped to normal. The train left Ayr on time and arrived in Norwich on time, and during the latter parts of the journey the locomotive was running so well that it was not necessary to make all the examination stops."

"The journey time was exactly 28 hours and continuous apart from the stops for examination and to change the hauling locomotive or the men. The hauling of the locomotive after 7 years retirement did her a power of good and she now runs like a sewing machine. Superficially the boiler and firebox appear in good order, but we will have to wait for the Boiler Inspector's report. It will be surprising if re-tubing is not required."

"In conclusion I think we should record our admiration for Bill Harvey. Not only did he undertake 30 hours continuous duty in terrible weather but he also accepted and carried out most successfully the responsibility for the movement over 400 miles of a large four-cylindered locomotive which had not turned a wheel for 7 years. Taking everything into consideration this was one of the most remarkable 'dead' steam locomotive moves ever made, and a positive contribution to live steam preservation."

The route from Ayr to Norwich took 'DUCHESS OF SUTHERLAND' via Mauchline, Sanquhar, Dumfries and Gretna Junction to Carlisle, and thence via the former Midland Railway's route to Settle Junction and Skipton, Leeds, Doncaster, Boultham Junction, Sleaford South Junction, Spalding, Ely North and Thetford. Geoffrey Sands, Curator of the Bressingham Steam Museum, went on the footplate as relief at Leeds Hunslet, and waiting anxiously at Ely North Junction was Alan Bloom, the owner of the Bressingham railway centre. A maximum speed of 25 miles per hour applied throughout, and stops were made every 25 miles for examination of

The ensemble pass the site of Mossblown Junction
(D.Cross)

At 8.00 p.m. the special train stands in Carlisle Station.
(Peter Robinson)

With the weather getting colder and snow on the ground, the train passes Spalding on Tuesday 2nd March 1971 (John H. Meredith)

the bearings and other moving parts.

As already mentioned, departure from Ayr was scheduled for 12.58 p.m. on Monday, 1st March, 1971 with arrival in Norwich scheduled for 4.58 p.m. the following day, where she arrived exactly on time. A copy of the British Railway's 'Special Notice' for this unique movement and the actual timings appear as Appendix 14 at the end of this book.

In an interesting letter to David Ward dated 15th March, 1971 Bill Harvey wrote:-

"I would like you to know how much I appreciate all the excellent arrangements you made for the movement of 6233 and our comfort, especially our "Caboose.""

"No.954710 will long remain in my memory - especially midnight at Blea Moor waiting for the soup to heat up and enjoying the excellent company I was in. I have never known the small hours pass so quickly as I did on that occasion. John Scholes seemed to enjoy himself; I was delighted that he was able to join us - partly so that he could see for himself what is involved in moving dead steam engines and for the pleasure of his company. As you remarked at the time we made a first class team..."

"I understand that depending on Sunter's movements, 6233 will go to Thetford on Fri. - I shall ride with her of course.

Yours ever,   Bill."

THE DUCHESS BECOMES 'A WARD OF COURT.'

However one particular event occurred during the movement which has not so far been mentioned, for, whilst still en route, 6233 became a 'Ward of Court.' The first that Alan Bloom knew of this was a phone call from Norwich depot at 23.00 hours on March 2nd stating that a solicitor was on his way with an injunction, and at 00.30 on March 3rd a further telephone call confirmed that solicitor Roger Hill had arrived and attached a legal document to the cabside of 6233 as she rested in the shed. The injunction also applied to the 4-6-0 No. 6100 'ROYAL SCOT', which was then still at Butlin's holiday camp at Skegness on the owner's property !

The legal move was made by Dr. Peter Beet, on behalf of the Lakeside Railway Estates, Carnforth and was supported by Geoffey Drury of the Blue Peter Preservation Society. According to a press report, they alleged that the decision on a new home for 6233 should have been the subject of a postal ballot arranged by the Transport Trust, the body that had been invited to make recommendations as to the disposal of the remaining Butlin's locomotives but, because of a postal strike, this had not proved possible. The writ was issued against the Transport Trust, and the move came as a complete surprise to Alan Bloom. A Butlin's spokesman wryly commented at the time "We can't see why anyone else should

determine what should happened to our property!"

However, on 10th March, the day set for the hearing in Leeds, the objection was withdrawn at a hearing in chambers at Leeds Assize Court. The parties and individuals involved by then had been advised by their legal representatives that it was a lost cause and the injunction was lifted, enabling the locomotive to continue its movement to Bressingham. However, and very regrettably, it was this action that somewhat prejudiced the future allocation of the other locomotives by the Transport Trust, since Butlin's had now become all too aware that they were valuable items. They accordingly placed the whole process on hold, but Alan Bloom did manage to agree terms for the allocation to Bressingham of the two smaller engines at Ayr and Skegness already mentioned.

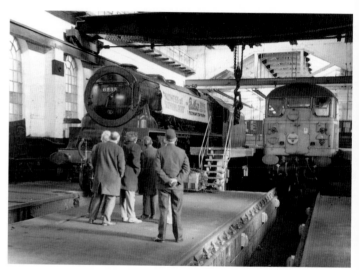

Duchess of Sutherland at Norwich M.P.D. on Saturday 6th March 1971 stands next to D5523. Alan Bloom is on the left in the group of five onlookers with John Crawley from the Transport Trust fourth from the left.
(G. R. Mortimer)

The writ attached to the cab side. (G.R.Mortimer)

Duchess of Sutherland reverses into Euston (the Suffolk village !) en route to Bressingham by road on Sunday 21st March 1971. (G.R. Mortimer)

This delay very sadly meant that it was not to be until 1974 that custody of 6229 'DUCHESS OF HAMILTON' was offered to the National Railway Museum at York and that of 6203 'PRINCESS MARGARET ROSE' to the Midland Railway Centre.

As originally planned, 6233 was initially towed by rail to Norwich, and was stabled there temporarily in the erecting shop at the motive power depot for security reasons, there to await the availability of Sunter's tractor and low-loader unit. Whilst there 'DUCHESS OF SUTHERLAND' was put on display to the public on Saturday, 6th March at Norwich Thorpe station in the 'Royal Dock', the platform at the extreme right hand side of the station, from 10.00 a.m. to 1.00 p.m., a small charge being made for admission.

The locomotive was then moved from Norwich to Thetford by rail, and following delivery of 6100 'ROYAL SCOT' to the Bressingham Museum, 6233 was again split up into engine and tender units and loaded up to complete her journey to her new home by road on Sunter's low loader unit, arriving there on 21st March, 1971. All previous locomotive deliveries by rail had been to Diss station from whence they completed the journey by road, and this had included that of B.R. Standard 'Britannia' class 7MT 70013 'OLIVER CROMWELL'. However, the greater height of 6233 when on the low loader made this impracticable because of limited clearance under a rail overbridge carrying the London-Norwich main line immediately to the south of Diss station.

That this move from Ayr to Bressingham was so successfully completed reflects great credit on all who were involved, particularly Bill Harvey. John Scholes, the then Curator of Historical Relics, sent

Duchess of Sutherland turns in the yard of her new home at Bressingam and is re-united with 32662 Martello. Alan Bloom with hands in pockets, stands surveying his acquisition. (G.R.Mortimer)

Mr.T.C.B. Miller, then Chief Mechanical & Electrical Engineer for the British Railways Board, a copy of Harvey's report on the move of 6233 in the hope that when he was involved in similar movements of steam locomotives in his care, a sympathetic view would be taken in the future. The reply from Terry Miller indicated that such a relaxed view of the requirements in not taking down the motion, etc. did not have his approval because of the possible consequences of serious delays should there be a problem, and that in future the regulations would be strictly applied.

After arrival 'DUCHESS OF SUTHERLAND' was cleaned up and placed on static display in the new shed, where she became the object of much attention from visiting members of the public. Alan Bloom obtained the services of retired B.R. engine drivers who were on hand to provide first hand accounts of driving locomotives of this class in service.

RETURN TO STEAM.

Subsequently, and to the delight of many fans of this class of locomotive, 6233 was painstakingly returned to full working order between 1972 and 1974, the first of the class to receive the restoration treatment. Most of the locomotive was in good working order, but the boiler in particular required major repairs. The inner firebox lap plates were badly wasted in places, as were the laps in the combustion chamber, which had to be studded. The back flange was repaired, the stay nuts renewed and new firebars and a brick arch were fitted. The small boiler tubes were renewed, and the last of the superheater flues were removed in October, 1972, their ends being renewed before they were re-used. The old superheater elements were repaired or replaced as required according to their condition.

With smokebox door removed, flue tubes are lifted out of the boiler. (S.A.Fenn)

It was found on examination that the smokebox door ring was wasted completely through adjacent to the hinges, and required a plating repair, whilst the firebox cladding sheets were found to be badly corroded, and were renewed. Other miscellaneous items also required attention, and in his book 'Steam Engines At Bressingham', published by Faber & Faber Ltd. in a revised edition in 1976, Alan Bloom records that "all kinds of snags were encountered, often because spare parts and replacements were by then virtually non-existent". He quotes the case of a die nut (sic - expander?) of an odd size needed to ensure that small tubes had a good fit in the firebox end of the boiler. Extensive enquiries were made over a period of months, but a new one had eventually to be specially made at a cost of £47 for a small item weighing only 4 ounces.

6100, in steam, hauls 6233 out of the shed for another days work by the restoration team on the Duchess in the yard at Bressingham. (S.A.Fenn)

The official Bressingham repair sheet record shows the work done on 6233 thus:-

Date	Repairs
27/3/72	Defective superheater flue removed for repair.
30/6/72	Remove blast pipe vacuum exhaust cowl.
	Remove smokebox door.
	Withdraw small tubes.
	Remove all element tubes.
	Remove all superheater flue tubes.
	Clean boiler barrel.
	All inspection doors and plugs to be removed, new joints fitted when replacing.
	Clean water ways.
	Examine firebox.
	Back-head laps to be repaired as instructed
	Rear section firebars to be renew.
	Remove water gauge columns.
	Clear water spaces.
	Re-pack gauge cocks and re-fit.
3/1/73	Repairs to tender platework
21/3/73	Re-set safety valves
3/1/74	Cleaning and painting inside tender with 'Inolac' black paint.
28/5/74	Loco. steamed O.K.
17/6/74	Regulator valve re-bedded.
21/6/74	Repairs completed
9/7/74	Boiler washout.
1/8/74	Safety valve adjusted. Left hand rear screwed up 1/2 inch.
14/10/74	Boiler washout for winter layout.
15/10/74	Repairs completed

Alan Bloom stated at the time that the task of restoring the 'Duchess', having been started, had to proceed regardless, and at the end of the exercise he wrote an article which appeared in 'The Railway Magazine' issue dated July, 1974 in which he spoke of the trap which preservationists fall into when they see in their mind's eye how the locomotive will appear when completed, "however forlorn rusty and lifeless it is when taken over, especially if it happens to be one of a famous class." He continues:-

"With the locomotives (6100 and 6233) here at Bressingham, we were able to make a closer inspection of their condition, and decided to tackle 'ROYAL SCOT' first. Expense had to be studied because funds depended on what visitors pay on open days, and it was obvious that the 'Duchess' would be the more costly of the two. I'd estimated in glib ignorance that the 'Scot' would cost around £3,000 and the 'Duchess' £5,000 pounds to restore. But it was purely guesswork, for as the work began so more faults were revealed."

In the event No. 6100 cost just over £10,000 and Bloom decided that nothing less would do for No. 6233, and continues:-

"During the summer of 1972 the tedious task of removing all tubes took place. This was one of the first essentials, knowing that replacements would take time to procure..... having been withdrawn from service in 1962 (sic), it was certain that all 198 small tubes would be useless. The superheater tubes appeared to be in fair order, but the only way to test their flue tubes was to have all forty of them out for inspection. They had to be cut out and, though good enough to go back, it was a costly business to weld on the ends again 14 in. long and have them taper threaded for re-insertion. This alone was a very tedious and expensive process. Meanwhile, a start was made on the formidable task of the de-rusting of all exterior surfaces, but the underparts of both engine and tender were so bad and so difficult to access that it would be beyond almost anyone's patience to accomplish."

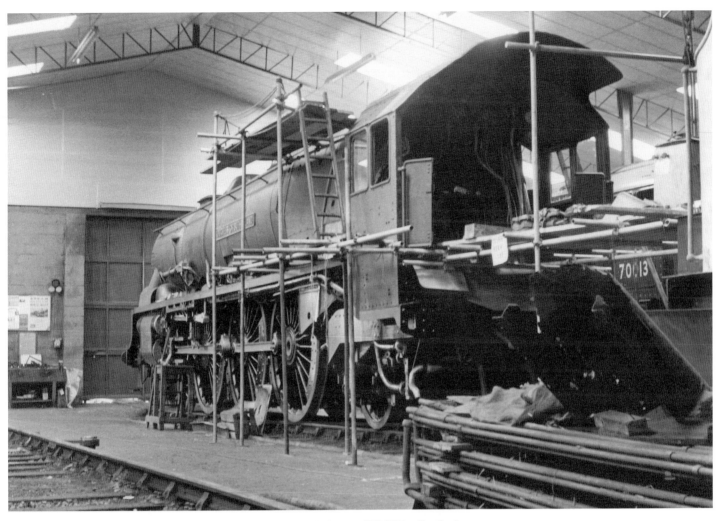

6233 undergoing her overhaul in the Bressingham workshops. (PRCLT collection)

With a scaffold platform erected inside the shed at Bressingham, sand blasting has commenced on the firebox and cab roof. (PRCLT collection)

The tender repairs start as shotblasting reveals life expired platework on the tender side sheeting. (PRCLT collection)

"Someone suggested sand-blasting. It seemed a good idea. What it would cost by hand over a period of months could be done by blasting in a very few days at no greater final cost, so we were told. A huge plastic-sheeted cocoon was erected over hoops to cover engine and tender, and the contractors came along with their gear and 12 tons of special sand. For a few days it was all hell let loose. Holes appeared in the plastic covering, allowing dust to settle on every other locomotive in the shed, and ankle deep in places nearby. It was a shambles, but where this stuff had done its work the surface was scoured down to bare metal."

"It was not until weeks later, when the job of applying preservative paint began, that we discovered how ineffective sand-blasting

was for a job like this. The underparts of a locomotive have far too many facets, nooks, crannies and variable surfaces, and the operator simply cannot see what he's aiming his nozzle at, protected as he is from almost lethal dust. The net result - after a cost of about £800 - was that a large amount of hard work still had to be done."

In paying the bill Alan Bloom resolved that never again would he use this 'hit-and-miss' method on other locomotives. Don Hubbard had had the unenviable task of doing this work, having already done similar work on other locomotives, and Alan Bloom records that he was dismayed at the thought of so much still to do, in cramped, dark and dirty conditions.

"The front of the smokebox was holed through wastage, making

it dangerous to open the door. New insertions had to be cut and welded in, and this involved a large amount of work before the door fitted snugly. The firebox was reasonably sound, but new stay bolt heads, caulking and minor repairs all took time. All injectors, blower, lubrication and other pipework were removed with replacements where necessary, and likewise all cab fittings. The regulator rod was badly wasted and parts of the firebox casing were renewed, as were the cylinder casings. Firebars were amongst the missing items on arrival, and there was the expense of making new patterns as well as the casting of the bars. Such items, and many more, are relatively small, but all take time and add to costs which it is not possible to estimate in advance."

"The tender of No. 6233 was in a poor state. Having made the seized-up (through rust) coal pusher work again, and de-scaled the water tank, the bottom was found to be too thin in places to pass. Above, the incurving tender sides also had wasted and were badly bulged from contact with coal. Sections of each side. 16 ft. long and 2 ft. 6 in wide, were cut out and beaded afresh before welding back into position and grinding off ready for painting."

"Painting has been a task in itself. All under-parts had three coats of metal preservative, undercoat and top coat, but for most of the exposed surfaces a total of eight coats was applied before the rich LMS maroon showed sufficient depth for lining out. Between each coat on the boiler casing there was a rub down with 'wet and dry' and wherever pitting, however small, had occurred filler was scraped in and rubbed off."

The person charged with the painting work on 6233 was Bob Rolfe, who lived nearby and who had already been employed in the final painting of the Burrell showman's engine 'Black Prince' and the other Butlin's main line express locomotive 6100 'ROYAL SCOT'. He did the work "more for love than money" as Bloom put it ! Once he was satisfied that the prepared metal surface could take them, he began by applying the four undercoats, followed by the top coat, lettering and lining out. Having researched every detail of the livery of 6233, Bob Rolfe applied the exact shade of L.M.S. crimson lake as this final coat. The livery was unique to the five engines Nos. 6230-4, and the correct size and positioning of the LMS letters and numerals, plus the special lining-out using real gold leaf as used originally, gave an immaculate finished appearance. A press report stated that some 20 gallons of paint were used in all, and Alan Bloom himself put the cost of the painting and gilding as "well over £500, but since the total cost of restoration had already passed £16,000, it would have been inexcusable to skimp anything now !"

The article concludes by recording that, thanks to the preparation work carried out at Ayr before the move,

"...having taken down the motion and checked on the piston rings, we had nothing more to do but re-burnish and replace the rods. ... It is true to say that the 'Duchess' has received a major overhaul, perhaps ranking as one of the most thorough undertaken by a private concern. For us it is a matter of pride in a job well done, especially as the total cost of rather more than £15,000 has all been paid for. It could have cost far more if, for example, extensive firebox repairs had been needed. We can but be thankful for this, but those intent on restoration work would do well to allow far more for the unexpected than appears needed on first examination of locomotives which have been long neglected."

Alan Bloom has recorded elswhere that the restoration work in fact took around 20,000 man hours of effort to achieve the standard reached.

Thus it was that on Tuesday 28th May, 1974 'DUCHESS OF SUTHERLAND' was hauled out of the shed and her fire lit again for the first time. The repair record shows "Steamed ok". The Thursday of that week was the first open day of the season, and she went into service giving footplate rides to visitors, but not for long ! As so often happens with freshly steamed locomotives after heavy repairs, full water circulation and steam pressure, plus the movement along the short length of track, dislodged odd particles of scale, some of which settled beneath the clack box valve and prevented the injectors from functioning, allowing steam to escape. It was galling that despite best efforts, the same fault occurred again

the following Sunday.

On that same 'return to steam' day Alan Bloom had invited the Countess of Sutherland, then rather appropriately Chairman of the Trentham Horticulural Centre near Stoke-on-Trent and sharing with him a passion for horticulture, to carry out a simple un-veiling ceremony in the form of climbing up into the cab and blowing the whistle. A press report accompanying a photograph of the event in the Eastern Daily Press newspaper issue dated 31st May, 1974 reported it as follows:-

"FAMILY SEND-OFF FOR THE DUCHESS"

"The Countess of Sutherland met the Duchess of Sutherland for the first time at Bressingham yesterday. But it was not a family event, as the Duchess in question is a 164-ton steam locomotive in steam for the first time at Mr. Alan Bloom's museum.

The Countess, a cousin of the present Duke, travelled 550 miles from her home in Scotland to 'launch' the giant engine. She went onto the footplate and blew the whistle of the gleaming locomotive, an example of Stanier's famous 'Duchess' Pacific class which hauled expresses on the London to Glasgow run.

The former London, Midland & Scottish Railway locomotive has been at Mr Bloom's museum for three years, and it had required two years work to prepare it for its first 'live' appearance.

Like the Royal Scot, another ex L.M.S. locomotive at Bressingham, the Duchess is owned by Butlins and came to Norfolk from a holiday camp. The Duchess was on show at Ayr and the Royal Scot came from Skegness. Both are now on permanent loan to Mr Bloom. The Royal Scot cost 10,000 pounds to restore and the Duchess £16,000. Over 19,000 man-hours went into the restoration of the latter, said Mr Bloom.

Mr Bloom now has 38 rail and road steam engines at his museum - the most comprehensive private collection in the country."

Having made that first public debut, the 'DUCHESS OF SUTHER-LAND' ran for about two years during the season over the five hundred yard section of standard gauge track laid in the Bressingham Gardens. This had been specially re-aligned and extended from its

The Countess of Sutherland stands with Alan Bloom to officially re-dedicate the locomotive on Thursday 30th May 1974 (Eastern Daily Press)

Royal Scot 6100 renews acquaintances with 6233 Duchess of Sutherland as they raise steam together alongside LMS 3 cylinder Stanier tank locomotive No. 2500. (PRCLT collection)

On the official first day back in steam Duchess of Sutherland is posed for the photographers at Bressingham on Thursday 30th May 1974. (Geoff Rixon)

original two hundred yard length for the purpose, thus giving more extended footplate trips to visitors on open days during the season.

However 6233's active service was to be shortlived as she was withdrawn from use again in 1976, due mainly to the condition of the firebox tubeplate which had developed a severe steam blow that was thought to be bridge fractures. A new tubeplate was considered to be necessary to solve the problem, but the estimated cost of this work and other necessary repairs to the boiler was considered to be around £12,000. The locomotive was therefore returned to static display only, and in 1977 Butlins were approached asking if they would be willing to assist with the cost of repairs. The response from Mr.T.H. North of Butlins was that they were not in a position to do so, and so 'DUCHESS OF SUTHERLAND' was destined to remain on static display in the exhibition hall for the foreseeable future.

When the recent heavy overhaul was carried out by The Princess Royal Class Locomotive Trust, armed with the knowledge and views of the Bressingham Staff from 1976, close inspections was carried out on the firebox tubeplate. In the event it was decided to renew it principally due to bulging and large size tube holes. No bridge fractures were found, and it is now believed that the severe steam blow was a lap seam opening up, as in fact the one in the boiler of (4)6203 had done when that was steamed again in 1990 after a 27 year period out of steam. The repair to 46203 was done in one day by caulking, and so it would appear that 6233 could have been 'repaired' in 1976 by that relatively simple means. However, it has to be said that knowledge and experience of working with locomotive boilers in preservation has moved on considerably since 1976, and what was a difficult and very disappointing decision for them at that time was clearly taken in the interests of safety and the locomotive. Today it is academic in any case.

6233 was to remain on static display on for the next 25 years. She was still one of the principal exhibits at Bressingham and continued to attract many visitors. As the years went by she was eclipsed by the plans of the National Railway Museum to allow the restoration of `DUCHESS OF HAMILTON 'to full main line working order by the Friends of the National Railway Museum.

With 125 lbs of steam on the pressure gauge, the Countess of Sutherland blows the Stanier hooter.
(Eastern Daily Press)

BRESSINGHAM PURCHASES 'DUCHESS OF SUTHERLAND'

Rank Leisure Industries, which had in the meantime taken over Butlin's Ltd., subsequently decided to sell off all of the locomotives purchased from British Railways and formerly on display at their holiday camps. Accordingly 6233, along with the other three locomotives now at Bressingham, including 6100 'ROYAL SCOT', were offered to Alan Bloom in May, 1989 and to the other custodians of the other locomotives - they being the National Railway Museum for 6229 and the Midland Railway Trust for 6203.

Tough negotiations followed between Mr. A Creighton Miller, the Managing Director of the Leisure Division of Butlins and Mr David Ward, representing the Trustees of the Bressingham Steam Museum. Rank initially refused to acknowledge the validity of the permanent loan agreement, and said that their price for the four locomotives was £250,000. However, after taking Counsel's opinion and studying the correspondence of 1973, and in particular a letter signed by a Butlin's Director quite explicitly stating that the locomotives would not be removed unless Bressingham defaulted on the loan conditions, Ranks re-considered the position and placed a price of £100,000 pounds on the 'DUCHESS OF SUTHERLAND' alone, offering the three other locomotives free of charge. The Bressingham Trustees decided to go ahead, Rank kindly offering to accept staged payments, and the negotiations that had started out in a tough manner were thus concluded on a most amicable basis, thereby securing all four locomotives for the Bressingham Museum.

LOAN TO THE EAST LANCASHIRE RAILWAY.

The locomotive remained at Bressingham until 2nd August, 1993 when, in return for a payment of £4,000 pounds, it left under a four week hire agreement to be placed on static display as one of the exhibits at the East Lancashire Railway's "Steam Railway Festival." This was held every weekend between 7th & 8th and 28th & 29th August to mark the 25th anniversary of the steam finale of main line steam workings in the north west. 6233 'DUCHESS OF SUTHERLAND' took pride of place among the exhibits on static display in their former B.R. five road electric train shed at Buckley Wells. The festival also featured trains worked by other visiting preserved steam locomotives, including the ex S.& D.J.R. 2-8-0 No. 13809 from the Midland Railway Centre.

Whilst there 6233 was temporarily re-named 'CITY OF MANCHESTER' and re-numbered 2000 for a local publicity stunt in connection with that city's bid to host the Olympic Games in the year 2000, which in the event failed. Further temporary changes were made to her appearance with the transformation into B.R. 46246 'CITY OF MANCHESTER' complete with front numberplate and 1B shedcode and diagonal yellow cabside stripe (i.e. used by B.R. to denote "Not to work south of Crewe" following electrification) when she appeared at Bury Bolton Street station sporting a headboard 'The Caledonian' with a rake of maroon stock behind the tender. As mentioned elsewhere, these temporary changes did not have the prior approval of the Bressingham authorities, and David Ward has indicated that they would not have been approved had an approach been made.

The East Lancashire Railway Directors had it in mind to try and negotiate either the purchase or long term loan of the locomotive in order to justify the expense of returning it to working order for use on their line and possibly also on the B.R. main line. They offered £100,000 for the outright purchase, but the Bressingham Trustees were not prepared to sell, and certainly not at that price. Negotiations therefore commenced for a ten year lease plus two to three years to carry out the overhaul, and the E.L.R. commissioned a technical survey from the Intercity Fleet Engineer at the Railway Technical Centre at Derby. Locomotive Inspectors Brian Penney and

Sam Foster examined the locomotive on 5th October, 1993 at the request of Ian Riley, the Chief Mechanical Engineer of the E.L.R.

The report identified that, apart from normal overhaul work, essential boiler repairs would have to include cutting out and replacing wasted firebox doorplate lap joints; repair or possible removal of the distorted firebox tubeplate and also the roof stays; rolling a new smokebox; fitting new main steam pipes in the boiler and smokebox and providing a full set of new superheater elements, superheater flues and small tubes. A new ashpan would also be needed, and in addition the blue asbestos boiler lagging would have to be removed by specialists working under new tight H.S.E. regulations.

After costing the work identified, it was estimated by the E.L.R. that the expenditure on the restoration would be around £162,000 in total, for which the railway hoped to attract sponsorship. However, this did not materialise and it was not considered practicable to meet a Bressingham hire fee of £25,000 pounds out of likely revenue receipts. Accordingly 6233 was returned by road to Bressingham on 18th July, 1994 using Alleley's transporter units, where she was put on static display once again. Although the original one month loan had thereby been extended to nearly a year as a result of the negotiations, this had suited both parties. The Bressingham Gardens had a closed season lasting from November to April and the absence of 'DUCHESS OF SUTHERLAND' had avoided the need to leave her out in the open since by remaining at the E.L.R. she was able to remain under cover.

The £25,000 hiring fee was criticised by some as being excessive, but in fact such a figure merely represents no more than the inter-

David Ward proudly poses in the cab of 6233 now restored in correct LMS livery. (PRCLT collection)

6233's boiler sheeting is polished prior to another day on display and in steam at Bressingham in 1974. (PRCLT collection)

est on the capital value of such an important locomotive, together with a contribution towards the depreciation that would have occurred from ten years use. A ten-year loan would also have meant that Bressingham would not have been able to realise the capital value during this period unless they had paid a pro-rata contribution for the un-used part of the life of the ten year overhaul, which would have been greater than its actual value to Bressingham.

Alan Bloom drives an ex Penrhyn Quarry narrow gauge locomotive on a double headed train past the magnificent display of standard gauge locomotives with a traction engine being turned in the yard. 6233 is not in steam. This scene illustrates the wonderful collection at Bressingham that no other museum could match at that time. (PRCLT collection)

Chapter Seven

Purchase by
The Princess Royal Class Locomotive Trust

Towards the end of 1994 the Bressingham Trustees asked The Princess Royal Class Locomotive Trust if there was anyone interested in purchasing their 9½ inch gauge 'Garden Railway' that ran round the garden at the north end of the Bressingham site. Plans were in hand at Bressingham to replace this railway with a new 10¼ inch gauge layout. The old railway had as its motive power a 4-6-2 named 'PRINCESS' which bore some resemblance to the 'Princess Royal' class, although with a G.W.R. style copper-capped chimney! Brell Ewart, Chairman of the P. R.C.L.T. already owned another 9½ inch gauge freelance locomotive which formerly ran in the Hall Leys Gardens at Matlock in Derbyshire, and the thoughts at the time were that they might both be used on a narrow gauge line linking the West Shed headquarters of the P. R.C.L.T. with the centre of the main Midland Railway Centre site at Swanwick Junction.

After some discussions Mr Eric Hackett, a member of the Midland Railway Trust, expressed an interest, the sale of the complete railway including the locomotive 'Princess' was completed in January, 1995 and all items transferred to the Midland Railway Centre. During the visits to Bressingham associated with the 9½ inch gauge railway Brell Ewart assisted Eric Hackett, and the regular contact Brell Ewart had with David Ward, conversations digressed onto 6233 'DUCHESS OF SUTHERLAND'. Its likely market value was raised, although at that time the Bressingham Trustees did not have an intention to sell her.

Throughout 1995 Brell Ewart and David Ward regularly returned to the discussion of 6233. It was clear that the Bressingham Trustees were having an internal debate as to the merits of retaining 6233 as a static exhibit or alternatively selling the locomotive to bring in cash that could be very usefully used for future developments at Bressingham.

In the autumn of 1995 the Bressingham Trustees received an approach from the Great Central Railway for the loan of 6233 for static display. The loan was not turned down completely, although the experience with the loan of the locomotive to the East Lancashire Railway had shown that there was very little advantage to Bressingham in such a move. Such loan moves were viewed in some quarters as the start of a process to eventually take ownership of the locomotive, almost by attrition, in that once on another site and faced with costs of road transport and all that goes with such moves, ways could be found for permanent acquisition.

Meanwhile the Bressingham Trustees had made a decision to sell 6233 and Brell Ewart, Chairman of The Princess Royal Class Locomotive Trust, was immediately contacted. Brell Ewart recalls:-

"I received a telephone call from David Ward stating that the Trustees (Bressingham) had met and agreed, albeit somewhat reluctantly, to sell 'DUCHESS OF SUTHERLAND'. David said that they all wanted The Princess Royal Class Locomotive Trust to have 6233 in view of the facilities they had and also their track record with the earlier general overhaul and restoration of 46203 'Princess Margaret Rose' to main line running condition. What did I think?"

"I replied I had not really ever thought about it, but if that was what they (Bressingham) thought then we had better say yes." That was the extent of the conversation: it was done as quickly as that, and no figure was mentioned at that stage.

In the following days and weeks a purchase figure was provisionally agreed and the definite position of giving us first refusal was agreed."

The G.C.R. proposed loan deal was not yet dead and buried, and out of the blue an offer was made in excess of the provisionally agreed figure with Brell Ewart for the locomotive, but in the earlier negotiations mentioned above the P. R.C.L.T. had already been given the first option to purchase. Brell Ewart therefore agreed to match the offer from the G.C.R.

The Bressingham Trustees held a special meeting early in November, 1995 to discuss the position, and made the decision to sell the locomotive to the P. R.C.L.T., their decision being based on the following facts:-

a) The P. R.C.L.T. had a proven track record with Stanier Pacific 6203 'PRINCESS MARGARET ROSE' in restoring and maintaining a large Pacific locomotive to the highest standards for mainline operations.

b) The P. R.C.L.T. was a Trust with a long term future, and they were just completing a large new locomotive shed to the highest standards which could house 6233 permanently in the best possible conditions.

c) Historically 6233 would be a very suitable partner for 6203.

d) Covered space at Bressingham was at a premium, and 6233, although housed under cover, could not be displayed effectively.

e) Now that the Health and Safety Executive had prohibited footplate rides, the Bressingham Trustees could not justify the cost of returning 6233 to working order.

f) The sale would provide for the removal of asbestos boiler cladding and cylinder insulation that would become a liability to Bressingham.

g) 6233 represented a considerable capital asset that, as an attraction, did not earn its value in additional receipts at Bressingham.

h) The capital raised by the sale would enable other, much more beneficial Bressingham projects to be funded.

The Bressingham Trustees therefore viewed the sale as being in the best interests of the future of 6233 'DUCHESS OF SUTHERLAND' and both Trusts.

In the following week arrangements were made by both parties for Brell Ewart to go over to Bressingham and meet with Alan Bloom, agree the deal and for Brell to have a look over 6233. Brell travelled over by train to Thetford and was met there by David Ward and the two went by car to Bressingham.

Brell recalls:-

"After having a good look at 6233 and going inside the firebox I went to The Hall where Alan lives. We sat together at the kitchen table, had a cup of tea and agreed the deal, although Alan was very sad at letting 6233 go. I feel that had it been his decision alone it may not have been sold, but the board of Trustees had a duty to look after the long term interests and well-being of the Museum at Bressingham and 6233 could not generate cash to do that other than by its sale. We shook hands on the deal, and I paid a 10% deposit. I left with very mixed emotions, feeling elated with the deal and the prospects that 6233 gave, but also very sad knowing that we were taking away a locomotive that Alan had given so much to since 1971. At the end of it all I consoled this emotion by asking myself what was best for the locomotive? Clearly a move to us and with that the prospects of future running on the mainline".

Brell Ewart returned home and briefed the other Trustees of The Princess Royal Class Locomotive Trust.

On 15th November, 1995 a joint press statement by The Bressingham Steam Museum Trust and The Princess Royal Class

Locomotive Trust announced that agreement had been reached between the two parties for the locomotive to be sold to the latter. In the statement the Bressingham Trustees also gave their reasons for their decision to sell saying:- "the sale is in the best interests of the locomotive and the Museum."

The cost of the purchase of 6233 was initially met by Whitehouse Construction Co Ltd, Brell Ewart's construction firm at Ashbourne. It must be remembered that there was very little advanced notice of Bressingham's intentions, and therefore very little time for the P.R.C.L.T. to raise the purchase price. Brell Ewart's company were at the time looking hard for a promotional avenue to carry out civil engineering work on the newly privatised national railway network, and so owning 'DUCHESS OF SUTHERLAND' for a period was a tool to do this with. So it transpired that, whilst the P.R.C.L.T. was raising the necessary funding through the continued operation of 46203 'PRINCESS MARGARET ROSE' on main line excursions, etc., in the interim period Whitehouse Construction would have the use of the locomotive for those specific promotional commercial purposes.

THE MOVE TO THE WEST SHED AT THE MIDLAND RAILWAY CENTRE.

An order was placed with Messrs. Alleleys of Studley, Warwickshire, to transport 6233, and a date was set for the New Year on 1996. The Princess Royal Class Locomotive Trust already had the space inside the extensive new West Shed for 6233, and so no other arrangements were necessary.

On Thursday, 23rd January, 1996 6233 'DUCHESS OF SUTHERLAND' was slowly hauled out of her storage shed at Bressingham to ensure that she could be correctly positioned in good time for the loading onto a low loader the following weekend, should the weather later become unfavourable.

Trustees Brell Ewart and Howard Routledge travelled by road to Bressingham on Thursday afternoon, 1st February and joined up with David Ward for evening dinner. After a night at local lodgings and an early breakfast both were soon on site at Bressingham.

After what might be termed 'a few interesting moments' whilst positioning the tender, it was finally expertly loaded onto a low loader that had arrived at Bressingham on Friday, 2nd February. The engine then followed, being hauled up a long ramp and onto

a larger trailer, ready for the move the following day under police escort.

The tender set off by road on a route using the A17 and the M1 motorway, to the Buttterley Company's works yard close by the Midland Railway Centre's main site, and the following morning was unloaded onto the Butterley Company's private line and re-railed. It was then taken down their own branch from their works and onto the Midland Railway Trust's main line on the Saturday afternoon and, hauled by a diesel shunting locomotive, it was duly positioned in the centre road of the new West Shed to await the arrival of the engine.

Back at Bressingham, a split hydraulic hose on the tractor unit had caused some worrying moments on the Friday during the loading of 'DUCHESS OF SUTHERLAND' herself, but fortunately a replacement was secured and fitted early on the Saturday morning. 6233 therefore began the long road journey to her new home in Derbyshire a little late, the Norfolk County Constabulary escort having kindly agreed to a postponement of the departure time for half an hour or so to enable the new hose to be fitted and the repairs completed.

Departure from Bressingham was a sad moment as the locomotive had been a flagship of the collection for many years in the early days. Alan Bloom could not face seeing the final departure and so remained indoors. Brell Ewart recalls:-

"The moment the lorry started up and moved along the drive towards the gate at Bressingham I looked round and saw many sad faces. Having experienced two road moves out of Barry Scrapyard with 80080 and 80098 in the 1980s, elation was the order of the day. Here we now were taking delivery of one of the most prestigious locomotives one could name, only to be faced with emotional sadness at the moment of handover. Both Howard Routledge and I will never forget the feelings we had on that cold Saturday morning. It was almost akin to being at a funeral and the saying of final farewells to a great friend. Even now, several years later, I still recall the sadness of the moment."

The approved route involved a long detour of about 60 miles from the direct road route, and the convoy travelled via Thetford to Swaffham, where the gigantic load caused quite a stir as it negotiated the main town centre on busy market day ! Fakenham in North Norfolk was the next town, and then round the outskirts of Kings Lynn. This detour was necessary because of a maximum 30 ton axle load restriction placed upon the most direct route.

However, good progress was made once the cavalcade, consisting of police escort vehicle, the tractor unit towing the low loader with 6233 aboard, and either followed or preceded by Brell Ewart's Range Rover and David Ward's car got underway. The remainder of the route involved travelling through the outskirts of Peterbrorough along the ring road, and thence to Duddington where the Leicestershire police escort took over and David Ward took his leave.

The route continued along the A47, where Brian Radford then met the convoy as 6233 sailed majestically down a long sweeping curve of road led by the police escort and followed by Brell Ewart plus a quite lengthy motorcade tail-back. A special fuel stop had to be made at Houghton-on-the-Hill, where the tractor and low loader, that had been away

6233 having been propelled into position on the line to be used for loading onto the lorry, awaits for her final departure from Bressingham. (Howard Routledge)

The tender stands awaiting loading Friday, 2nd February 1996 (Howard Routledge)

the A563, where Brell and Howard made contact once more. The convoy continued on through Anstey to join the A50 and thus onto the M1 motorway at Junction 22.

Light was now fading, and there were dark clouds hovering overhead plus the occasional snow flurry, as the convoy made good speed at around 40 m.p.h. to where the Derbyshire police escort took over for the final leg of the run. They decided to complete the journey in the fading light, and leaving the motorway at Junction 28, the cavalcade turned off onto the A38 and thence via the old A61 to Swanwick, finally arriving in total darkness in the Butterley Company's secure works yard at 6.14 p.m.

Here 6233 was stabled overnight inside the security compound, and photographs and video footage were shot by means of an arc of car headlights illuminating the scene whilst a silvery, hazy moon, occasionally shone through the scudding clouds overhead. The tractor unit, with its extremely competent crew on board, left for its home base, by now having been away from home for no less than a total of ten days.

from home base for a number of days, pulled onto a filling station forecourt. The back end had to be steered independently to allow the tractor unit to pull alongside the diesel fuel pump. The garage owner was rather alarmed at such an outsized load being so manouvered, and quickly moved one of the new cars on display on the forecourt out of harms way!

The low loader driver said 'fill her up,' and for a moment a quizical look crossed the garage owner's face as he clearly thought to himself "Does he mean that huge locomotive or the tractor unit !" As it was the tractor unit took on £272 worth of fuel whilst a crowd of onlookers from the nearby housing estate lined the road to gaze at the impressive 'DUCHESS OF SUTHERLAND', a most unusual load it must be admitted. This was almost certainly the only time a Stanier Pacific has ever been in a petrol station forecourt, and probably the last!

At Bushby the police escort took an unexpected right hand turn off the main road and led the convoy up Humberstone Drive and through the outskirts to Scraptoft, thereby unfortunately temporarily loosing Brell Ewart and Howard Routledge who had gone on ahead to find a good photographic vantage point. This diversion involved climbing a climb of about 1 in 15 up a fairly narrow road between banks of overhanging trees, and the effort took every ounce of power that the tractor unit could develop in the very lowest reserve gear to keep it moving forward. Brian Radford had a heart stopping moment when the tractor stalled as he followed close behind. Had the unit run back it would have wiped out both his car and also the others now tailing the unit.

However, having breasted the summit, it was now a fairly easy route through the northern outskirts of Leicester via Glenfield, Field Head and onto

On the Sunday morning a new tractor and crew arrived at 10.35 a.m. and the unloading soon began. The full engine load was slowly backed across the road and the trailer carefully lined up with the Butterley Company's tracks leading into its works. Many volunteer hands made light work of erecting the temporary ramp. The tractor unit was then re-positioned at the rear of the trailer in order to provide the necessary winch control via a steel hawser hooked onto the drawhook of 6233. Slowly and carefully she was reeled out down the sloping ramp of rails aligned with the Butterley tracks, any additional control being provided from the cab end by a four-wheeled match truck attached to the drawbar pin with ex B.R. 350 h.p. 0-6-0 diesel shunting locomotive 08 590 at the other end.

Duchess of Sutherland sits on the low loader in the yard at Bressingham (Howard Routledge)

Once on the rails, and now sandwiched between two diesels, and with a matchtruck at its rear, 6233 was moved extremely slowly down the Butterley Company's line connecting their works towards the Midland Railway Centre's main line. At the turnout at which the spur serving the West Shed complex diverged to the left and onto its yard the trailing shunter and truck were dropped off and 6233 was eased into the headshunt by the Class 08 shunter and then propelled into the new West Shed to join her waiting tender. With the fall plates lifted clear, the two were re-united by coupling the drawbar to make 'DUCHESS OF SUTHERLAND' complete once more. She looked impressive inside this purpose built locomotive facility - a fitting location for a fine locomotive. For the remainder of the day she was the centre of attraction to the assembled gathering that had come to take a look at the Duchess in her new home.

The Princess Coronation passes through the village of East Rudham on Saturday 3rd February 1996 (Howard Routledge)

The River Nene is crossed on the outskirts of Peterborough (Howard Routledge)

The filling station at Houghton-on-the-Hill, in Leicestershire. Surely the strangest ever load on a road vehicle to require fuel in such a location. (J B Radford)

A tight fit as the lorry takes fuel. (J B Radford)

6233 is slowly winched off the low loader and back on to the rails in the Butterley Works unloading area. (J B Radford)

With the Class 08 shunter leading and the Class 03 at the rear with a match truck, Duchess of Sutherland is eased slowly down the Butterley Branch line. This half mile move was the longest distance she had travelled in one direction on her own wheels for many years. (J B Radford)

On the West Shed yard 6233 is hauled forward onto the arrival road before being propelled back into her new home. (J B Radford)

A NEW HOME FOR THE 'DUCHESS OF SUTHERLAND'

The locomotive works and shed of The Princess Royal Class Trust is situated on land owned by the Trust adjacent to the Midland Railway Centre's main site at Swanwick Junction, near Butterley in Derbyshire. Designated the 'West Shed' it was completed in January, 1996 and is a fine portal-framed building containing three roads of standard gauge track, each long enough to accommodate two Pacific locomotives. Other stock and locomotives can be housed in the shed thus enabling the whole P. R.C.L.T. stock to be housed under cover.

In the same building, on the North side, is a raised area with two lengths of 21 inch gauge track that provides accommodation for the two Hudswell Clarke 'Princess Royal' class outline diesel locomotives. These are important items in the collection since they were originally built to Billy Butlin's order in 1938 for use in his holiday camps and in fact quite accurate outline copies of the 'Princess Royal' class locomotives. The first, 'PRINCESS MARGARET ROSE' has already been restored to full working order, whilst her sister 'PRINCESS ELIZABETH' awaits the resources to cosmetically restore her. One of the original bogie coaches has also already been restored. At the end of this workshop area is a museum gallery given over to the display of paintings, photographs and artifacts associated with the history of the Stanier 'Princess Royal' and 'Princess Coronation' classes of locomotive.

Later that year visitors were able to admire the new shed and its facilities at the 'Stanier Pacific Spectacular' weekend of 28th and 29th September, 1996 when the new arrival was proudly exhibited alongside her older sister No 46203.

'DUCHESS OF SUTHERLAND' now had a new home and new owners in The Princess Royal Class Locomotive Trust. Buying the locomotive had been the relatively easy part. Raising the purchase price and financing the major overhaul had now to be achieved. This was to prove the hardest part, as will now be told.

On 15th June 1996, 6233 stands alongside 46203 inside the West Shed on display.
(Howard Routledge)

Standing on the West Shed yard Duchess of Sutherland poses for the last time before the asbestos removal necessitated the removal of boiler cladding sheets on 28th September 1996. (Howard Routledge)

Chapter Eight

Overhaul to Mainline Running Condition

It had always been the intention of The Princess Royal Class Locomotive Trust to return 'DUCHESS OF SUTHERLAND' to main line running condition. The first priority after arrival at West Shed however was to remove the asbestos lagging blankets from the boiler and firebox. This work should by law have been carried out at Bressingham prior to the sale: however dispensation was given and the work was done at the West Shed, where a better facility existed for access round the locomotive to do the work. A specialist was brought in to carry out the removal under controlled conditions with the public being excluded for the period. To remove the barrel sheeting the nameplates had to be removed. This task was exceptionally time consuming as each set screw had seized solid in the backing plate and so had to be drilled out. The name 'QUEEN MARY' seemed very appealing during this work, it being a very short name with fewer set screws holding it on!.

was that there was no money to buy 6233, let alone overhaul it. The Trustees' think tank started work by reviewing what had been achieved by the Trust thus far and how this had been done so successfully. The Trust, in its few short years of existence, had already achieved much: its own locomotives - three in all - its own coaches - two- , its own shed and most significantly it owned the whole lot outright. Furthermore these acquisitions had been achieved without having to resort to borrowing money. The shed alone was valued at over £100,000 and the Trust held the freehold to boot. The review highlighted the fact that all this had been done by frugal use of monies available, good planning, and by utilising what resources the Trust had in the best possible way.

However, pressure was now on the Trust to get things moving with 6233. Suggestions were made of bank loans; appeals to the public for funding; writing to well known benefactors with begging letters; and even seeing who won the lottery on a Saturday evening and writing to them. Needless to say most of these stood little chance of success !

At one of the regular meetings held between the Trust and Lesley Colsell, the museums' advisor from the East Midlands Museum Service, the Trustees set out the dilemma. She suggested consideration be given to a Heritage Lottery Application and duly sent a suite of guidelines to the Trustees. It was immediately clear that a considerable amount of work was needed in developing and writing an application if there was to be any possibility of success. Following due consideration all the Trustees agreed that this was a feasible option.

After some initial consideration being given for an application for funding to assist the purchase the locomotive, since its purchase was the most urgent consideration,

With boiler cladding and asbestos insulation removed 6233 stands outside West Shed on 21st July 1998 (Howard Routledge)

The initial plan to raise money for the purchase of the locomotive by the Trust ran into unexpected difficulties with the premature failure of the boiler tubes in 46203 'PRINCESS MARGARET ROSE' whilst at Carlisle. After a little delay she was returned to West Shed in May, 1997 where it was found that the small tubes had failed due to the thinning of wall thickness at the firebox end. With this terminal problem the fund raising potential from mainline tours with 46203 disappeared. Clearly a new initiative had to be taken to ensure funding was in place by 1998 when Whitehouse Construction, who had temporarily funded the purchase of 6233, wished to divest themselves of the ownership of the Duchess.

The planning for the Heavy General Overhaul on 'DUCHESS OF SUTHERLAND' began in early 1997, and although at this time The Princess Royal Class Locomotive Trust still did not own the locomotive there was clear intention to do so. The problem facing the Trust

and the fact that subsequently overhaul could start in five, ten or whatever number of years, Brell Ewart had the idea of applying for a combined grant for both purchase and overhaul. This idea was initially met with no more than a mild enthusiasm by the Museum Service (EMMS) advisors, for it had never been done before so far as they knew. However the Trust had nothing to lose other than time and effort in writing the application. Brell Ewart and Brian Radford set to work. Data was collected and collated on all matters relating to the Trust, the locomotive, and in fact anything remotely connect with both. Various trustees were set tasks of gathering information. Brian Radford took the lead with the engineering records and historical data, whilst Howard Routledge started trawling the photographers' network nationwide to increase the collection of photographs of the locomotive service days. Malcolm Baker produced some impressive figures from the railtours that had been run with

46203, most of which had been organised by the 46203 group starting in 1990, and subsequently by PMR Tours from 1991 onwards.

The Heritage Lottery Fund information pack contained very comprehensive guidelines on how to assemble an application, so this was a good starting point for writing the application. In the following weeks and months computers were used to assemble the scripts and data for the many sections in the complete application. The advancement of such technology was a great advantage when it came to shuffling the order of texts, titling sections in different fonts, and spell checking, not to mention all the other trappings that go with Microsoft. Twenty first century technology at its best working for the best of the twentieth century !

By the November of 1997 the application was complete and no less than six full copies of the suite of documents were required. This copying exercise alone took Brell Ewart and Chris Powell, the Trust Vice Chairman, over twelve hours to complete. The documents were then put in a large cardboard box and it was quickly despatched on its way to London addressed to the HQ of the Heritage Lottery Fund. All that could be done then was wait, plan, and keep fingers crossed.

At this time Standard Tank locomotive No. 80098 was well on the way to completion. The new West Shed was proving to be worth every penny spent on its construction and more as the volunteers and paid staff worked through the Winter of 1997/8, making excellent progress on this overhaul that had in fact started in 1990.

The self imposed deadline set by the Trust for any award from the H.L.F. to be made was 30th June 1998 as this was the date by which Brell Ewart's company, who owned 6233 as an interim measure, had said they would have to sell if not to The Princess Royal Class Locomotive Trust, to whom they had always given first option to buy, then to one of two American business men who had shown keen interest in taking her across the Atlantic to the U.S.A.

June 1998 was fast approaching and the Trust, had still heard nothing. No whispers, no tip-offs, no hearsay. Just a worrying silence. The only good thing was the project had not been rejected, so in an almost illogical way, spirits were kept up by thinking the longer nothing was heard, the better the chances were.

With only four weeks to the deadline, a phone call came from the H.L.F. asking for a meeting within two days and for an inspection of the locomotive to be made by a valuer appointed by the HLF. Two days later Brell Ewart and Brian Radford were showing Mr Gooderham, a Partner of Cheffins, Auctioneers from Cambridge, round the West Shed, and very impressed he was too. Cheffins had been selected by the Heritage Lottery Fund to value the locomotive as they regularly held auctions of steam traction engines and showmans' engines, and this really was the nearest that anyone could get to mainline steam locomotives for an independent valuer to assess.

One week later, following a quick positive reply to a telephone enquiry by Brian Radford asking how the awards committee meeting had gone (immediately passed on to Brell Ewart of course !) a formal letter was received from the H.L.F. advising the Trustees that the application had been successful. A grant was to be made of £324,508 representing 75% of the total project cost of £432,677, and stating that the project was to start in August 1998.

Massive relief all round. The future of 'DUCHESS OF SUTHERLAND' was secure and better still in all likelihood forever more.

The Heritage Lottery Fund placed a national news embargo for the announcement of the award on all the media, thus enabling themselves to set an announcement date. This suited the Trust well and enabled time to develop a launch date and 'event'.

The Trustees elected to announce the award with an 'unveiling' ceremony on Tuesday 21st July 1998 in the West Shed. For the event No 6233 was covered in an enormous red cloth totally concealing the locomotive and tender. With the press, representatives of E.M.M.S. (who had been so helpful), and many other local dignitaries present, Brell Ewart opened the proceedings and was followed by Brian Radford who gave a eulogy on the locomotive. The two then cut the ribbon and, by careful engineering, the cloth dropped to the floor thus exposing the locomotive and the announcement of the grant, all to the great applause and enjoyment of the admiring gathering.

In the HLF application submission documents, a fully detailed Project Team had been listed. For the Trust this was a simple exercise as the team already existed and in fact had done so for almost twenty years since the work on 80080 started in November 1980.

So the Project Team to overhaul 'DUCHESS OF SUTHERLAND' was assembled.

The principals were:

Project Leader :	Brell Ewart
Chief Engineer :	Eric Riley
Consulting Engineer :	Brian Radford
Steam Fitters :	Barrie Wheatley
	Mick Boothby (Fulltime)
Skilled fitters :	John Riley
	Graham Oulsnam

With the project attracting wide exposure in the local press a number of other people joined the project in the early days. In addition a good number of other volunteers who could carry out the hundreds of unskilled tasks were available. Before work could start on the Duchess, the Standard Tank No. 80098 had to be finished, as with such a small organisation it had been proven to be impractical to work on more than one locomotive at any one time. This meant that, although the Heritage Lottery Fund had given the Project Start date to be August 1998, in reality it was going to be October 1998 before work would commence.

Again, thanks to the text in the HLF application a `campaign plan `was already written. In very simplistic terms this was:-

LOCOMOTIVE
- Strip the locomotive down to bare frames.
- Strip the boiler, lift and send to specialist repair workshop.
- Overhaul wheelsets, axleboxes, motion.
- Rebuild bottom end
- Refit boiler and fittings

TENDER
- Strip
- Repair body and extend water tank
- Overhaul frames and wheelsets
- Rebuild

The official start date was August 1998 with completion set for March 2000; eighteen months in total. Some people had viewed this as very ambitious, but what they may not have been aware was that in 1989/90 the same team had overhauled 46203 in 16 months and this without the West Shed and all the facilities therein !

In 1998 many preserved locomotive groups with main line certification were contemplating whether to fit air brakes to their locomotives. If 6233 was to be so fitted clearly the best time was during this overhaul. By Autumn 1998 only two locomotives had been fitted and become operational, and both of these used a combination brake system where the brakes on the locomotives were kept the same i.e. steam or vacuum. These brakes were applied through a combination air valve so that the control of the locomotive brakes was through an air system that also controlled the train air brakes.

At this time Ex L.N.E.R. locomotive No. 4472 'FLYING SCOTSMAN' was undergoing overhaul at Southall in West London, and the system being fitted to this locomotive was a full air brake - that is to say the existing locomotive brake, vacuum cylinders in their case, were being removed and replaced with air cylinders on both engine and tender.

After debating the merits of each system within the team, Eric Riley advised that by far the best option was to fit a full air brake. Thus this was to be the chosen system for 6233, and although it was to be very costly both in time and money, it was finally proven to be worth both the effort and expense.

THE OVERHAUL COMMENCES

When 'Princess Coronation' and 'Princess Royal' class locomotives were overhauled during service at Crewe Works in L.M.S. and British Railways days, No. 3 Bay in the Erecting Shop at Crewe Works was dedicated to handle the 'Big Uns' or 'Lizzies', as the two classes were colloquially known. In these bays special tools and equipment was kept for these locomotives.

A Heavy General Overhaul could be done at Crewe Works by British Railways in two to three months. During the Second World War even this timescale was improved, although it is likely that the extent of the work during this period was always kept to an absolute minimum. Such timescales were achieved with the many supporting workshops within Crewe Works where the various specialities were carried out on component parts.

There was a dedicated boiler shop where the boiler was taken once removed from the frames and a refurbished boiler, usually from stock and previously taken off another locomotive, would by ready when required. Brass and iron foundries cast new parts and following a visit to the machine shop these were available to fit when called for. Trades such as coppersmiths, tinsmiths, welders, and fabricators were on hand from the massive numbers of skilled, semi-skilled and general labourers that were available on a shift basis in the works throughout the working service life of Stanier Pacific locomotives. Between 6000 and 7000 men worked in Crewe Works in the 1950s.

In 1997 when the planning for the overhaul of 6233 started, none of these massive resources were available to the Trust nor in fact were ever going to be. However in the Trust's favour was the fact that the team had already successfully overhauled one Stanier Pacific, namely 46203 'PRINCESS MARGARET ROSE', she being one of only two to have been fully overhauled since the end of their service life in mid 1960's, the other being 'DUCHESS OF HAMILTON'. This statement takes nothing away from the overhauls carried out at Bressingham by Alan Bloom's team on 6233, or the work on No 6201 'PRINCESS ELIZABETH' by the owning society, in the Mid 1970's. Neither of these would have fallen into a Heavy General Overhaul classification because the boilers were not lifted and the wheelsets were not removed.

The team had a list of necessary equipment to allow the overhaul to be carried out in the West Shed. A principal item on this list was a set of Matteson jacks, i.e. four electrically operated jacks, capable of lifting 25 tons each, that between them would be able to lift up a 100 ton locomotive. In the previous few years the trust team had often visited Crewe Heritage Centre when running on mainline duties. The foreman on site there was Tony Moseley who had good contacts within Crewe Works and it had almost become a standing joke about the desire of the Trust to acquire a set of jacks.

The story of need must have migrated to one of the Crewe Works managers, John Turnoc, for out of the blue Brell Ewart received a phone call from John advising that Adtranz were disposing of some scrap items that may be of interest to the Trust. Next day Brell Ewart and Eric Riley were in Crewe Works examining a set of Matteson jacks that were being disposed of. A deal was done and within two weeks a set of jacks arrived at the West Shed by courtesy of Peter Wood and his Scammell low-loader lorry. The jacks and control gear were cleaned off and over the next few months were overhauled and painted in a striking yellow livery. Following testing they were ready for work having had some bearings renewed and a

full electrical overhaul thanks to Bob Foster of the Midland Railway Trust. This now meant that the locomotive could be lifted to liberate wheel sets inside the West Shed, a task that otherwise would have been daunting, necessitating outside work during the winter months with two mobile cranes.

With the completion of Standard Tank 80098 in the late summer of 1998 the stage was now set for work to commence on 6233.

Several items of work had been on going before major stripping took place. On arrival at the West Shed in 1996, the Trust had employed specialists to remove the asbestos lagging on the boiler. This had already necessitated the removal of all of the boiler and firebox outer sheeting. As a result for some two years, from Autumn 1996 until Autumn 1998, 6233 had been shorn of her beautiful lines by the exposure of a rust coloured boiler barrel. Whilst the locomotive was in one piece with the boiler in situ, the opportunity was taken to manufacture new smoke deflectors. The originals had been removed at Crewe in 1964 and presumably cut up as scrap, and for all her preserved life she had been on display in the form as built in 1938, albeit with a double chimney.

The smoke deflectors had been added as a modification to the locomotive in 1946. Interestingly and helpfully, the tell-tale wear lines on the running plates where the originals had sat, were still there and so these were used to check the dimensional sketches the team drew up for manufacture. The original drawings for the deflectors had not survived and so visits were made by Howard Routledge to Carlisle Upperby Depot, where 46229 'DUCHESS OF HAMILTON' was residing at the time, in order to measure the ones fitted on her. Although 46229 had the de-streamlined front end, with the running plate gap in lieu of the curving fall plate, the main dimensions were the same.

The team had been joined at this time by Clive Fenn, from Derby, who had a great interest in the Princess Coronations and was actually building a five-inch gauge model of one in his spare time. Clive was very familiar with the fine detail of the class and it was he who led the group manufacturing these prominent features. The hand-hold cups in the deflectors were spherical on the inner face and several attempts were made before a technique was perfected for their manufacture. Great care was taken with the dimensioning and a number of trial fits were made before the completed deflectors were painted with primer and then placed in store until the overhaul was finished and final fitting could be done, some two years away at least.

Before stripping commenced, the new smoke deflectors were made and trial fitted. Duchess of Sutherland stands in the West Shed in September 1998 with deflectors fitted for the first time in over 35 years. The hand grab holes in the deflectors still await the fitting of the spherical protector cups and foot hole back plates on the inside face of the deflectors. (Brell Ewart)

Autumn 1998 and the boiler is lifted off and placed on accommodation bogies using the 75 tonne rail crane owned by Peter Wood. (Brell Ewart)

The boiler departs the West Shed for the Severn Valley Railway on the low loader lorry. The chimney and all tubes were removed prior to the move, but the smokebox was left on in order to make craning easier. (Brian Radford)

STRIPPING

The boiler was lifted off in Autumn 1998 using the 75 tonne rail crane owned by Peter Wood - a wonderful piece of British engineering in itself and available thanks to the generosity of Peter. In January 1999 the boiler was transported to the Severn Valley Railway Boiler Shop at Bridgnorth on a low-loader lorry, thanks to the generous assistance of Chris and Kevin Balls from J. C. Balls & Sons of Ambergate. This vehicle was too long to get onto the forecourt of the West Shed without some improvisation. In true civil engineering style Brell Ewart arranged for a temporary road to be built over the Butterley Branch adjacent to the West Shed entry ramp to allow the large lorry to enter the site and then, when loaded, move slowly out with the boiler.

Over the years since 1980 and through various locomotive projects, the restoration team had learned by experience that shot blasting is the only way to clean steel. It was therefore planned to shot blast the whole of the engine and tender frame structures and as many other parts as possible. However shot blasting is a dirty, slow, and labour intensive operation. It can only be carried out successfully in controlled conditions and certainly not inside a new workshop. The dirt and expended shot goes everywhere, as Alan Bloom had found years before. To be done outside needs good weather and of course the frames needed to be got outside. The question was how to get them there without the wheels under them. To add further complication, when a steel surface has been blasted it must be painted within two hours and preferably then be inside under cover.

Careful thought by the team developed a method of working. With the driving wheels out, the frames could be rolled in and out of the West Shed sitting on only the front and rear trucks, which, if left assembled could thus act as accommodation bogies. When the whole frames were completed then these trucks could be taken out from under the frames using the Matteson jacks and renovated in turn. The plan worked to perfection.

The driving wheelsets were liberated by lifting the frames clear of the wheelsets, rolling the front truck away, followed by the driving

The frames are scraped and pipework is removed prior to shotblasting in winter, 1998. (Brell Ewart)

Eric Riley keeps a close watch as the frames clear the leading driving wheels during the lift. (Brell Ewart)

The frames are lifted clear of the wheelsets using the set of 100 ton Matteson jacks Inside the West Shed in Winter 1998. The cranks pins have been protected with wood slats prior to transporting the wheelsets to the Severn Valley Railway for turning. (Brell Ewart)

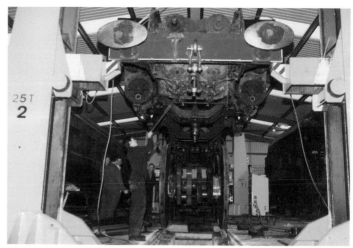

View from the front as the frames are clear of the wheelsets. The position of the outside cylinders in relation to the forward location of the inner cylinders can be clearly seen. The crank axle (leading driving wheelset) can be seen waiting to be wheeled forward. (Brell Ewart)

wheelsets. No one had ever seen a set of L.M.S Pacific locomotive main frames lifted clear of the wheelsets using Matteson jacks, for it had never been done before. From start to finish it took one hour. Over the next few weeks the driving wheel sets were themselves shot blasted and painted with primer before being sent to the Severn Valley Railway workshops at Bridgnorth for tyre and journal turning. Close inspection revealed that the tyres were new in 1960. The trailing driving axle had a stamping on the axle end '6250' indicating that it had been fitted at some time to No.6250 'CITY OF LICHFIELD'. It was almost certain therefore that the wheelset was replaced on 'DUCHESS IF SUTHERLAND' during the Heavy Intermediate repair in 1961. With the driving wheelsets away from West Shed more space was available for work to be done on the frames. Over a period of weeks, the frames were rolled out each Saturday to the forecourt of the West Shed where several hours of shotblasting was done, usually by Brell Ewart, before the straining forklift truck pushed them slowly back inside. All available hands were then mustered onto the priming painting. As the weeks went by the frames were transformed from a grimy black colour, to a pristine and clean brown primer colour.

Generally the frames were in excellent condition, and bearing in mind they had been made from the best high tensile steel, this is not surprising. Very few defects were found, these being limited to a handful of loose or broken rivets and fragmented running plates and the sub-frames under them. Running plate fractures were a regular occurrence on LMS engines, for whereas the main frames were designed to be flexible, the running plates were not, and one can only assume this item was considered consumable and could thus be renewed or repaired as required.

In the case of 6233, as renewal was now taking place the opportunity was therefore present to improve matters. With this in mind, and a degree of difficulty rivetting new items in place due to obstructions, the option was taken to bolt the structure together thus allowing some flexibility as bolts do not 'fill the hole' they are in as hot rivets do. Two problems solved in one move ! Thus domed head bolts today hold these running plates on to the sub frames.

The cylinders and steam chests bores were measured and a decision taken to re-bore the steam chests in order to remove some ovality. The Severn Valley Railway sent up their mobile equipment with operators Richard Kempton and Roy Mort, to carry out the precise cutting on all four chests. With this work complete Ian Crampton, from the Midland Railway Trust, machined new valve heads using new castings, and valve rings to the enlarged sizes. The oil passageways to the inside steam chests and cylinders were causing a major concern. They were blocked solid with congealed oil and carbon dirt that had lain there for at least 38 years and very likely longer than that. The question was how to get it out. Good lubri-

cation to valves is absolutely essential. The passageways were an integral groove in the cylinder block castings and tucked behind the steam chest liners. The last thing the team wanted to do was to have to remove the liners in order to clear these lines - this was the very last option. A contact was made with Dr.Roger Cox, an industrial chemist with his own business in Ashbourne. Roger is a railway enthusiast and his father a former footplate-man, so he understood the problem. Roger produced an acidic concoction, and every Wednesday night for many weeks Roger, often accompanied by his wife Pat, came to the West Shed and replenished, or if necessary renewed, the liquid cocktail that was slowly eating its way through the blocked lines. Small funnels pushed into the head of the oil lines were left topped up with the acid formula as it did its work by gravity. After many weeks the first line finally blew through with compressed air, to be followed in the coming weeks by the remaining lines. This was a triumph of ingenuity and a great relief to everyone in the team.

With the frames now showing a pristine gloss red on the internal face and gloss black on the outside, the newly repaired and refurbished lubrication pipework could be re-fitted. John Riley, the Trust's resident volunteer expert in this discipline, had been planning this work for some time. Jigs, together with many small contraptions used for forming the pipework through the tortuous routes from lubricator to delivery point, were dutifully brought out by John over the many weeks spent by him in individually forming the many hundreds of yards of small bore pipe. Each pipe was cleaned, straightened, annealed, blown through with compressed air and then

Now stripped bare the frames receive the coats of red for the inner faces and black for the outer surfaces on 18th May, 1998. New running plates have been fitted. (Brell Ewart)

The wheelsets, having been refurbished at The Severn Valley Railway, receive new coats of paint and the axleboxes have been lifted in position ready for being reunited with the main frames by May, 1998. (Brell Ewart)

finally pressure-tested before being refitted into its final position. Many were repaired with new sections of copper pipe in order to remove life expired portions where the friction of rubbing against another pipe or surface had reduced the wall thickness to zero.

Meanwhile the locomotive wheelsets were at the Severn Valley Railway workshops being refurbished by Dave Reynolds, their wheel lathe operator. The tyre profiles were reformed together with checks on the journals for true-ness on all the wheelsets from the locomotive and tender. It was on the crank axle that the first major problem encountered with the whole project arose. On the crank axle big end journals a pitted zone, highlighted by discolouration, was evident of both journals. This was a scar from the seven years of static display at Ayr where water had eventually displaced any oil on the surface and had then sat there through the various seasons over the seven year period, creating rust on the surface of the journal. With the wheelset back at Butterley, a specialist came to the West Shed and using a most ingenious home made device, cut a few thousandths of an inch off the journals. Even then, Dave Reynolds from the Severn Valley Railway had to come and hand true these up to achieve the standard required.

Over a period of weeks, several journeys were made to the Severn Valley to collect and deliver more wheelsets. This enabled work to continue at the West Shed as the sets were returned. Several coats of paint were applied to each wheel and axle. Meanwhile the axleboxes had been taken to the Midland Railway Trust's Machine Shop where Ian Crampton was white metalling and machining them. A plan was devised to re-fit the driving wheelsets, to be followed some weeks later by the trucks. With the trucks, the main springs and frames needed to be fully assembled before being fitted under the locomotive. Furthermore sited above the front truck was the locomotive's inside cylinders with all their drain cock gear and cylinder cladding, all of which needed to be in place before the truck was finally positioned. The underkeep pads on all wheelsets were examined and found to be life expired. A chat with Graham Nangreave, the Mechanical Foreman at the Severn Valley Railway, soon resulted in all the pads being sent to Bridgnorth for re-weaving with new Worsted wool. On return they were immersed in new oil to give a good soaking ready for re-fitting with the wheelsets.

The three driving wheelsets had been returned on 14th November, 1998, and work had gone ahead fitting the axleboxes etc. prior to re-wheeling the frames. Once the necessary work on the frames had been completed and the various fittings re-attached, the Matteson jacks performed their invaluable duty once again, and the main

frames of 6233 were lifted with ease to allow the driving wheelsets to be re-fitted. Although a simple job, many small items requiring many hands are needed with this operation and so on Saturday, 10th July, 1999 the volunteer team turned out in strength to carry out the lift. With the driving wheelsets in place and frames lowered back down onto them a new visual aspect was given to the project.

With work on-going on both front and rear trucks, several small teams were now at work on concurrent projects. The whole of the West Shed floor space was now taken up with small groups fully active on individual tasks. The Crewe Works Erecting Shop foremen would no doubt have been very impressed !

On any such project forward planing is the key to success, and during this period Eric Riley would often be seen in deep discussion with Brell Ewart as they analysed and planned the fine detail for the next stages of work. Some mistakes were however made. With the frames re-wheeled, the brake hangers and stretchers could be re-fitted. When stripped some months previously it was apparent that the hangers were twisted. In fact no two were the same. It had been wrongly assumed that wear and tear had taken its toll on these misshapen items and so they were duly straightened on the 50 ton press. When refitted it was immediately apparent that they were twisted to fit each location on the locomotive and so each one had to be bent back to its original shape by trial and error - a very long, tedious and extremely frustrating job! It all proves that in this business one never stops learning.

With frames lifted on the Matteson jacks, the wheesets are rolled into position ready for re-wheeling. The slidebars, radius rods and combination levers are now fitted along with new cylinder cladding. (J.B.Radford)

The frames are lowered and all eyes are on the axleboxes to ensure that they align with the horn guides. Brell Ewart stands at the control desk of the Matteson jacks controlling the slow descent of the frames. (J. B.Radford)

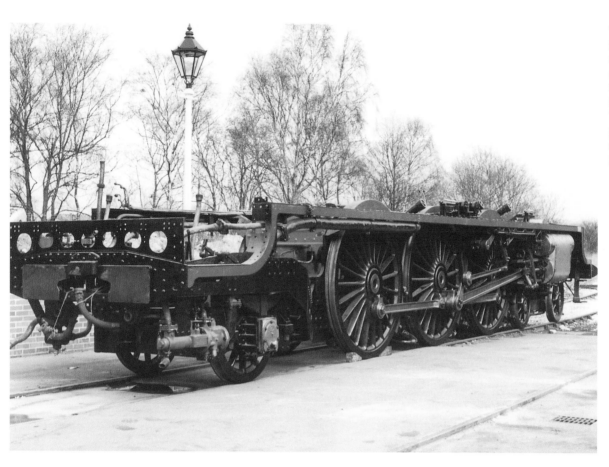

With motion now fitted and bottom end is on display outside the West Shed in the Spring of 2000. The injectors and pipework have also been fitted. (J.B.Radford)

THE TENDER

With the main frames from the locomotive re-wheeled attention turned to the tender. The tender was divided into two elements of work, the body and the frames. The tender body was lifted off for examination again using the 75 tonne rail crane. The team had already gained valuable experience with an L.M.S tender when 46203 was overhauled a decade earlier. Although minor differences existed between the tenders of the two locomotive classes, and furthermore there were build variations within the 'Princess Coronation' class tenders, they were of the same basic design. The frames were almost identical, and it was with the frames that work started. With wheelsets removed the structure was shotblasted and, as with the tender from 'PRINCESS MARGARET ROSE', the inner skirts were found to be 'life expired' and required renewal. With new rivetting where possible, and bolts where not, these new long steel plates were soon in place: the job being done with the whole chassis inverted on two accommodation bogies on No 4

road in the West Shed. Dragbox surgery was required at both ends and the redundant water scoop gear cut off. As with the locomotive, the main frames were in excellent condition due to the quality of steel used when built, and with new paint applied they looked as good as the day they were first assembled in Crewe Works. Re-wheeling again transformed the scene inside the shed, and with both tender and locomotive frames re-wheeled progress was becoming more visisble as each week passed.

The tender tank body was sent away to a sub-contractor in Ashbourne for major repairs and alterations to be made. Transported on the preserved low loader owned by Peter Wood it made a fine and unique sight travelling through Derby and along the A52 still resplendent with L.M.S. gold leaf letters and crimson lake livery. At the works of the Ashbourne firm of Hill and Webster Limited, the life expired rear platform of the body was immediately cut out to allow a design survey to be done. The work had to incorporate the extension to the tender water space, replacement of any life expired steel, renewal of the footplating and the

The tender body sits on stands inside the workshops of Messrs Hill and Webster in Ashbourne. The rear coal plate and tool tunnel have been removed in readiness for the additional water tank to be fitted. (Brell Ewart)

On completion at Ashbourne, the tender body leaves Hill and Webster's yard on Peter Wood's preserved Scammell low loader for the journey back to Butterley. (Brell Ewart)

The tender body is lifted off the low loader with the 75 ton crane. (Chris Powell)

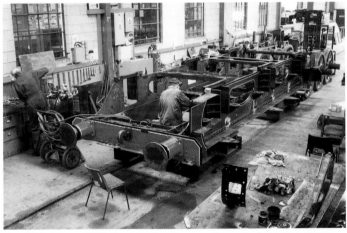

On 18th May, 1999 the tender frames, inverted on accommodation bogies, are being stripped inside the West Shed. The wheelsets stand beyond, awaiting their turn for refurbishment. (Brell Ewart)

removal of the scoop operating screw handle and recess. A new operating handle and rodding from tender front to the rear platform for the coal pusher was also required This was necessitated due to water tank being extended through the rear of the tool tunnel, thus conflicting with the existing route of this operating mechanism.

For a company with the on-site capacity of Hill and Webster Limited the whole job was easy, but for it to have been done in the West Shed without folding presses, guillotines and various welding sets, the work would have taken several months. Within weeks a refurbished body was returning to the West Shed for shotblasting and painting. Following a spell on accommodation bogies the

tender tank was positioned on the Matteson jacks to allow the luxury of several easy trial fittings onto the frames.

The tender tank now had the enhanced water capacity of 5,000 gallons, part of which being held in a 1,000 gallon capacity top tank. The ingenious, yet simple design of this allows water be released into the main tank as required either through a float valve or a direct valve. The tender frame also now had water pipe fittings accessible through the rear frame openings, enabling the tank to be filled from hydrants or road tankers at ground level. This change was achieved with the minimum practicable alteration to the rear platform of the tender, but the air vent 'mushrooms', so visible on rear view photographs from the past, had to be removed.

The coal-pusher, overhauled by the members of the regular Wednesday evening team, was lifted into the coal space with the Midland Railway's Trust's 'Iron Fairy' mobile crane, and was tested with compressed air. The force with which the pusher operated without a load on it was quite awesome, and in fact was moving the whole tender backwards and forwards with each stroke of the ram.

THE AIR BRAKES

At this time the air brake designs began to take hold of the whole project. Following a false start when the team originally elected to sub-contract the work, the decision was taken to bring the work 'in house'. An old friend of the Trust, Kim Malyon was engaged to work alongside Mick Boothby on the project.

Advice was taken from several experts. David Russell from Halcrow Transmark, Keith Nicholson from Interfleet Techology Ltd. as well as the Trust's Vehicle Acceptance Body RESCO.

Peter Hodgson, a former Derby Railway Technical Centre engineer and now the head of Hodgson Structures Ltd., his own firm, was engaged to carry out the design work on the modifications to the locomotive for the various items of equipment, and John Duncan, the MSLOL Engineer, produced the modified schematic layouts.

The 'FLYING SCOTSMAN' locomotive had by now re-entered traffic with the same system, and it was proving to be an exceptionally good one. The P. R.C.L.T. team was able to keep in regular contact with the '4472' team as a result of Kim Malyon having done much work on that locomotive, together with Keith Nicholson, John Duncan and David Russell, all of whom having been involved in what was in effect a prototype for the new system. The P. R.C.L.T. clearly had a good team assembled to cope with this difficult design area.

With initial designs approved, work had commenced on the air braking system for the tender, the first element of which was to design and manufacture a new main brakeshaft and cylinder mounting structure for the tender. The position of the cylinders necessitated a recess to be made in the bottom of the tender tank as the brake cylinders projected above the floor in the water tank. This involved some delicate overhead welding from underneath. The Matteson jacks were now in almost daily use lifting the tender body on and off the frames to allow easy access and trial fitting. An early decision had been taken to manufacture new air reservoirs for the systems using stainless steel, since, although these were initially very expensive, the lifetime benefit was viewed as worthwhile. After several weeks fitting by Kim Malyon and Simon Towell, the installation of the air brake system on the tender had almost reached completion. Coupled to a mobile compressor the brakes were operated for the first time by air and the system worked well.

With the tender complete, attention returned to the engine frames and the new air brake installation. In addition to design work on the tender as described above, Peter Hodgson was also engaged on the design of the structures required to hold the pump, cylinders, and air reservoirs on the engine frames, and had re-designed the brake lever arms and main shafts.

With the Railtrack Group Standards there seemed to be more restrictions and requirements than one could contemplate.

The two locomotive air brake cylinders mounted on the frames. The two primary arms can been seen running from the brake cylinder pistons back to the main brakeshaft. (Howard Routledge)

The steam driven air compressor sits in place mounted on the main frame cross stretcher support brackets. (Howard Routledge)

However Peter found his way through the many volumes and produced designs that were approved. Brian Radford, a P. R.C.L.T. Trustee who had worked for Inter-City as a Senior Project Engineer until his retirement, then stepped in to oversee and draw together the various engineering design process elements and ensure that the resultant package would meet not only the design criteria but also the requirements of the final design scrutiny stage, an essential part of the Vehicle Acceptance Body certification process. Blue Print Rail Ltd.of Belper, Derbyshire were contracted to produce, on computer, the suite of engineering drawings necessary to support the manufacturing process. These would eventually become part of the documentation necessary to meet the requirements of the design scrutiny process that would be applied to the design changes by the Vehicle Acceptance Body (VAB).

The new main brakeshaft and the very long primary arms were now fabricated and assembled. The length of the primary arms on the main brakeshaft dictated the cylinder positions, and the location only just fitted between two existing sandboxes. The design calculations of the braking system on both engine and tender started out from the necessity of having the same brake force output as that designed for the original steam cylinders. It would have been simple to increase the braking force, but this was neither desirable nor permissible since such an action would `pick the wheels up' when a brake application was made, or put in laymans terms, lock the wheels up and skid them along the rails.

With the known desired force, known new cylinder sizes, and known air cylinder pressure, the length of the primary arms and secondary arms were calculated. To make manufacture and fitting easier, and checking afterwards, the existing secondary arms were retained for reference.

The question may be asked as to why was all this work necessary if the brake force was the same as before ? The answer is simply the difference between air and steam. Air is constant, whereas steam is not. For example, early on in a steam locomotive's day/shift of duty, the locomotive is unlikely to be hot and therefore condensation takes place. The force delivered by the cylinder will therefore not be at full efficiency. Also the steam in the locomotive boiler might not be at full pressure, although it has to be said that the calculations for braking force were always calculated at 85% of boiler pressure. As a result of these factors a steam brake is always considered as not giving a constant output and thus is deemed 'not constant' as a brake system.

However with an air brake system, the brake pressure is always the same. Hot weather, cold weather, hot or cold locomotive, the pressure at the cylinder will be the same and so the brake force is

always the same and can thus be regarded as constant. This then allows testing of the braking efficiency of a locomotive to be measured accurately and also compared with other air braked diesel and electric locomotives.

The difficulties to be overcome with the locomotive were numerous. Being a prototype for the L.M.S. locomotives in preservation (only 'FLYING SCOTSMAN' had gone before with the same system albeit with minor differences) the team was treading new ground. The installation team made up of Hill and Webster staff who did the specialised welding, Ian Crampton from the Midland Railway who did the machining, Kim Malyon, Simon Towell, and Mick Boothby, from the P.R.C.L.T. who did the fitting, all ably supported by Eric Riley. The team elected to retain as much of the existing rigging and equipment as possible, which kept new areas of design and build to a minimum.

Making a new main brake shaft was unavoidable. This process started with obtaining the necessary metallurgical specification, then sizing the shaft dimensionally to fit the sizes of the existing main end bearings that were to remain. New primary brake levers were designed with the secondary levers remaining. The latter housing the trunion through which the adjustment screw, for the brake, fitted. This item was retained as existing, and to house this, the existing primary lever, when new, was forged at the leading end to form a fork. This was fastened to the single steam brake cylinder piston rod. For the new build it was simpler to make two double leafed arms, braced down the centre line between the two leaves.

The new primary arms on the main shaft were to be sweated on, and Eric Riley had the ingenious idea of cooling the main shaft to shrink it in size as well as heating the arm ends to expand them, thereby creating a differential in size sufficient to permit the two to be assembled. It worked perfectly and, with the arms in place, the precise dimensioning of the main cylinder structure could be assessed. The centre line of each cylinder had to be plotted to determine the positioning and thus fastening of each of the new cylinders. The brake cylinders had been acquired through Metcalfe Railway Products who in turn had obtained them from a manufacturer in Eastern Europe as none were available on the British market.

The mounting structure for the cylinders was another part of the design work undertaken by Peter Hodgson. With the cylinders fitted the brakes were tried for the first time using a mobile compressor through a temporary connection, and having proved that the mechanism worked, all of the ancillary items on the system could now be fitted. For some time however progress seemed to take two steps forward and one back - such is the life of prototype engineers!

Three second-hand, steam-driven air compressors had been

obtained some months earlier with the aim of making two operational ones and a supply of spare parts. One of these had been stripped, re-assembled and then mounted on a jig on the workshop floor. The practicalities of having a temporary steam supply to test this compressor were insurmountable, so an air supply was used to test it in lieu of steam. Following a satisfactory running and with all ancillary pipework fitted to the locomotive, the time had come for the air compressor to be positioned. With the mounting structure welded into place on a main frame stretcher bar, the overhauled steam driven compressor was lifted into position. This was an awkward job and lifting gear had to be slung under the belly of the boiler barrel. Clearances at the top were only inches between the top of the pump and the boiler barrel in order to achieve a ground clearance at the bottom.

At this time several operational troubles had emanated on other locomotive air brake installations with detritus material coming through the air-side of the pump delivery from the pump itself. To remove this, or at least minimise it, Kim Malyon and Keith Nicholson had the idea of introducing an additional reservoir tank, mounted vertically, close to the pump. By introducing the airflow at a tangent near the bottom of this tank, the centrifugal force would take the detritus material to the inside face of the tank and away from the supply outlet, which was close to the top. As a secondary advantage, the air was also being cooled and thus condensing some of the water vapour at the same time. An electrically operated drain valve was fitted to the lowest point on this tank to be operated by a push button from the cab. As dirt and water collected in the tank bottom it was smartly ejected in a two-second burst of air through the valve when in operation.

Many of the other valves and fittings of the air brake system had to be positioned under the removable wooden cab floor - not exactly the most desirable location - but inevitability ruled the day as there was no other option available to the team.

BOILER

As mentioned earlier, the boiler had been transported by road in Autumn 1998 to the Severn Valley Railway at Bridgnorth where it was unloaded from the lorry by the overhead crane in their boiler repair shop. The Severn Valley Railway staff, Graham Beddows and Alun Rees, had inspected the boiler at the West Shed almost two years earlier before it had been lifted off the locomotive, although at that time the tubes were still in situ. Before transportation the tubes had been removed at the West Shed so that on arrival at Bridgnorth the boilersmiths were able to start without delay on the firebox and tubeplate repairs.

The overall assessment on the boiler was that a lot of work was required in the firebox. Every copper lap on the inner box was

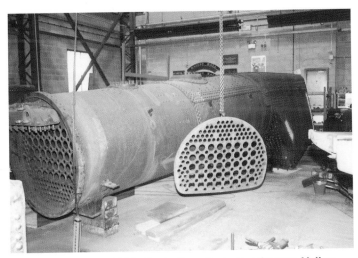

On 25th January, 1999, the boiler sits in the Severn Valley Railway boiler shop, the old firebox tube plate having just been removed. (Brell Ewart)

burned away. Furthermore it was clearly evident that heavy caulking had taken place over a number of service years on the inner firebox laps. This had resulted in gouging of the wrapper plate. The firebox tubeplate was well worn, bulging in places, and again laps were very poor. Due to the 'drumhead' shape of this plate a replacement was a very appealing option due to the comparative ease of fitting a new one, but this decision was left to the boilersmiths to make. From the experience the team had gained with the boiler from 46203 both during overhaul and the six years of service in preservation, it was known that detailed inspection would be required on the inner face of the firebox steel outer wrapper plate in the area around the top row of side stays to see if any cracks had started to develop.

The first few weeks at Bridgnorth were spent removing the tube-

View taken inside the boiler barrel looking back towards the firebox. The former location of the removed tubeplate can be clearly seen. The first rows of stays between inner and outer firebox are also clearly visible.
(SVR, PRCLT collection)

The new steel front tube plate awaits fitting.
(SVR, PRCLT collection)

plates, foundation ring and items such as the main steam pipe. This allowed a close and full inspection to be carried out. Cracking was discovered on the outer wrapper as had been feared. The repair for this was the introduction of four long patch plates, which in turn entailed the removal of some 256 stays.

Arrangements had been made in advance with the Severn Valley staff for the P. R.C.L.T team to make regular visits to inspect and discuss the work as it progressed. Eric Riley, Mick Boothby and Brell Ewart were to make a number of visits to Bridgnorth over the next year.

Decisions were quickly made to renew both tubeplates and to patch the outer wrapper in four places. The rest of the concerns were negated with the removal of the foundation ring that allowed inspection into the water space. The outer wrapper plate thickness was excellent much to the surprise of everyone.

On the inner firebox laps, the building back of the copper on the doorplate laps was so extensive that the boilersmiths opted to weld in strips of copper. These new pieces are known as inserts and this technique has been carried out by the Severn Valley boilersmiths

Mounted on two heavy steel trestles and bolted down, the during the hand-flanging copper tube plate process takes shape with Andy Tranter swinging the heavy mallet and Richard Watkins ready to apply further heat. (Duncan Ballard)

A new copper insert is positioned ready to be welded into place on the left-hand doorplate lap on the inner firebox. (Brell Ewart)

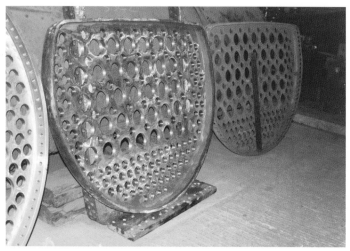

The completed copper tube plate, with tube holes etc. already drilled, awaits fitting. (Brell Ewart)

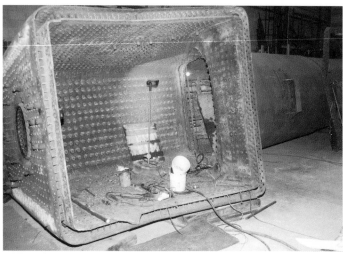

With the boiler laid on its side, the cavernous firebox is seen. The foundation ring has been removed together with the firebox tubeplate. (Brell Ewart)

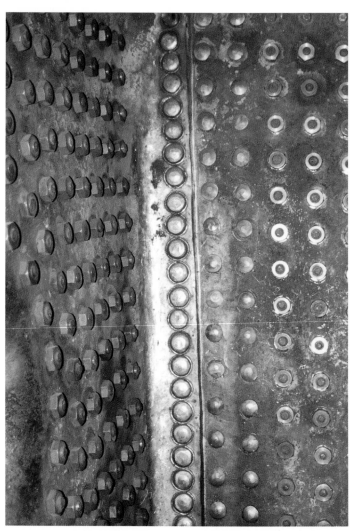

The same lap joint as above, now welded in and with lap studs fitted. New stay nuts have also been fitted to the stay ends and the first two rows of outer wrapper stays have been rivetted over. (Brell Ewart)

Turned back again in its correct position, the new patches have been fitted to the outside of the steel firebox. The foundation ring is back in position. The white coloured areas are from the crack detector spray, indicating that tests have been carried out to locate any further cracks in the boiler shell. New washout plugs are also now fitted. (Brell Ewart)

The boiler back at the West Shed in Spring, 2000. The new smokebox is fitted in place with temporary bolts and the whole boiler has had several coats of protective paint. The crinolines have also been re-fitted. (J.B.Radford)

over a number of years. To facilitate this procedure the boiler was rotated a number of times in the shop using their overhead crane so that the section being worked on was horizontal. With the boiler laying on its side a full appreciation could be made of the huge cavernous size of the firebox.

As the months went by progress soon turned from stripping to rebuilding. Once the necessary vital dimensional details had been determined from the original boiler engineering drawing, the front steel tubeplate was ordered by the S.V.R. from an outside supplier. In fact the new one contained one extra tube hole to the original, a single washout plug position having been removed.

The copper firebox tubeplate was manufactured on site at Bridgnorth by laboriously hand flanging the plate over a purpose made former, once more using dimensions this time gleaned from the original firebox drawing. A century earlier all tubeplates would have been made this way.

The small tubes were delivered to Bridgnorth from the West Shed in late summer after having made a detour en route to the West Midlands to have their ends swaged. These tubes had been acquired by the Trust some months earlier in order to gain a bulk purchase price with another batch. The large tubes were acquired by the Severn Valley Railway.

During this period two Pacific type locomotive boilers were under overhaul in the Bridgnorth Boiler Shop at the same time - the boiler from ex L.N.E.R. A4 class Pacific 60009 'UNION OF SOUTH AFRICA' and that from 6233. It was very interesting to see how very much smaller the A4 one was in comparison. It is probably the only time ever that these two types of boiler have been together in one shop under overhaul and repair.

Throughout the repair to the boiler, the Trust's own boiler inspector John Glaze had made many visits to Bridgnorth, and a very comprehensive record of the work done had been kept by him which eventually went forward into the locomotive's records on completion. The scale of the work carried out by the Severn Valley Railway under the leadership of Graham Beddowes was immense.

A few facts and figures:-

Replacement rivets 600
New sidestays 500 +
New Patch Screws 100+
40 lineal feet of copper welding.
2 New tubleplates

The team in the Bridgnorth boiler shop was foreman Graham Beddowes and Job foreman Richard Watkins, assisted by Andy Tranter, Duncan Ballard and David Howell.

The boiler was finally returned to Butterley on 25th March, 2000, thanks again to the generosity of Kevin and Chris Balls from J. C. Balls Contractors at Ambergate who very kindly sent their large low loader lorry to transport it. On arrival the boiler, now fully tubed and therefore several tons heavier than when it left, was lifted off the lorry on the main Swanwick Site and then moved up to the West Shed on the bogie bolster wagon that the Trust had acquired in the meantime.

The smokebox wrapper had been under manufacture in the West Shed for some weeks and was ready to lift into position immediately. This was another well-worked example of production line planning enabling a smooth flow of the project. After some deliberation Brell Ewart and Eric Riley took the decision to have the boiler lifted on to the locomotive for a trial fit. Several advantages accrued in doing this although there was the disadvantage of lifting it back off again before the final fit. However the really big gain was that a snug fit of the smokebox in the saddle was ensured and in view of the massive size of the smokebox it was `better safe than sorry'. Futhermore advantage was also accrued in ensuring all the new air pipes and other fittings were clear of the boiler when in position.

The smokebox wrapper had been rolled from a sheet of steel 22ft long, 9ft wide and weighing over 1 ton. It had been supplied rolled by Messrs Hill and Webster Limited of Ashbourne and, thanks to that company's generosity, two sets of wheel rollers were loaned to the Trust to enable the whole assembly to be rolled round when on the

The immensity of the fire box, boiler and smokebox can be seen to good effect in this photograph taken during the boiler's first steaming. A scaffold with platform was erected at the firebox end to facilitate the firing process. (Malcolm Baker)

On 28th July, 2000, the boiler, now complete with new cladding sheets and ashpan, is lowered on to the frames. (Peter Fitton)

The painting team sand down the cabside prior to application of the first of many coats of paint in December, 2000. (John Stiles)

workshop floor. This was a massive aid when rivetting the front door ring into the large cylinder, and allowed all of the rivets to be hammered from an 'on top' position as the whole smokebox was slowly rolled round as the rivetting progressed. This was the fourth locomotive smokebox the team had made from new, and the experience from previous ones was a great advantage with this massive one.

The smokebox was attached to the boiler with temporary bolts and the boiler, complete with new ashpan, was lifted into position on the locomotive for the trial fit on 8th April, 2000, the 75 tonne diesel rail crane belonging to Peter Wood again being used. With the boiler and smokebox sitting in the frames and saddle respectively, the smokebox was rivetted to the boiler front ring but not fastened to the saddle. This was to be done at the final fit.

Several problems were now highlighted. A number of air brake pipes positioned in the trailing truck zone were being fouled by the ashpan door linkages and so these had to be moved to the other side of the locomotive. Very tight clearances were evident between trailing frames and ashpan and this problem was overcome by mak-

ing a very small recess in the ashpan. With all checks made the boiler was removed and placed on accommodation bogies on No 4 Road and got ready for its formal initial steam test.

For this the boiler sat on the two accommodation bogies and was positioned outside the West Shed. The first part of the process was to submit the boiler to a hydraulic test up to a pressure of 375 lbs per sq.in., and this was achieved on 22nd June, 2000 with no problems. A fire was then lit, and a temporary blower from a mobile compressor was used to create the vacuum in the smokebox to draw the fire as it was gradually built up. Over a period of three days the boiler pressure was allowed to rise until for the first time, on 30th June, full boiler pressure was achieved and the safety valve lifted. The formal examination was witnessed by John Glaze, the boiler inspector, and then, following cooling over the next three days, the boiler was washed out before being rolled back inside on No 4 Road of the West Shed. The first few washouts after a major overhaul always flush out large volumes of detritus, and this washout was no exception.

The team of tinsmiths working on the cladding were now able to commence the manufacture of the new cladding sheets for the boiler barrel and firebox. The old ones had been retained as patterns with all but two of these being beyond re-use on the locomotive. The new sheets were made from galvanised steel treated on the inner surface with special primers and etching paints. Handling these large sheets was not easy and the whole process took several weeks. The insulation material used for lagging the boiler barrel and firebox had been tried some two years earlier on 80098, and this ceramic based material had proven to be exceptionally

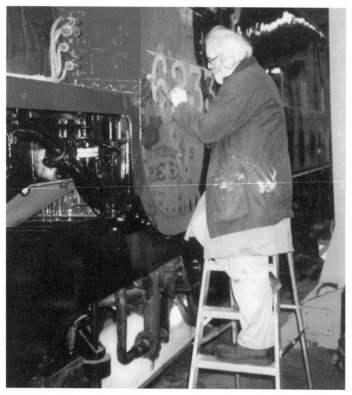

Bob Timmins sets out the numerals on the cabside in undercoat prior to applying the final gold leaf and shading. (Graham Poole)

The driving position of 6233 showing all air and vacuum gauges, AWS equipment and brake valves. (Chris Powell)

successful in service.

With all the cladding sheets fitted except for where the crane slings were to be positioned, the boiler, complete with new ashpan, was lifted onto the engine frames on 28th July, 2000.

The pace of work now moved up a gear. Controls and associated parts were fitted in the cab area and the cab structure itself lifted on. This cab structure had already been modified to lower the height from 13ft 3¼ins to 13ft 1in using the same principals and methodology used on 46203 over a decade earlier.

Once the cab was in place the locomotive began to be a recognisable item once more for the first time in several years, and was now attracting considerable public interest at a level not previously seen in the West Shed. New laminated safety glass was fitted to the cab front and side windows to meet the Railtrack Group Standards, replacing the ¼ inch thick plate glass from yesteryear.

The air brake apparatus now again took over the main element of the work with the main controls being positioned in the cab and the various runs of pipework connected between these and and the underfloor fittings.

Within two weeks the locomotive was paired with the tender and moved outside for a first steaming.

With the boiler cladding now in place this gave the first indication of the insulation performance, the boiler retaining heat for an amazing seven days from fire dropping.

The Automatic Warning System (AWS) now took centre stage on the installation programme. Although schematic drawings were available, no one had ever fitted the system for an air-braked locomotive to an LMS cab layout and so it really was a matter of trial and error to site the component parts in suitable locations. Two battery boxes housing the batteries were made and fitted to give a sustainable electrical supply, for the Railtrack Group Standard had now made an AWS failure into a locomotive failure, and several steam locomotives had failed on the mainline with this fault. The final result for 6233 was a large battery case mounted above the coal tunnel roof on the tender, with a supplementary reserve supply sited in the existing AWS battery box on the right hand (fireman's) side of the running plate in front of the cab. The latter also supplied power to the cab lighting, another mandatory Group Standard requirement.

With the air braking installation now almost complete, the full testing of the system commenced. Kim Malyon, who had masterminded the installation of the system, and Keith Nicholson, from Interfleet Technology Ltd. of Derby,

On 17th January, 2001 the first fire was lit as 6233 stood outside the West Shed. (John Stiles)

who was to test and sign off the system as being compliant with Group Standards, worked together over a period of several days as exhaustive system testing proceeded. Initially from an external compressed air supply, a static test proved the system and its functional integrity. This was followed by using air from the actual steam-driven air pump situated between the locomotive main frames, with the locomotive in steam. Setting up a braking system is a unique event to each locomotive and each one has to be 'tuned up' individually. After several day long visits by Keith, he finally gave the 'thumbs up' for running in tests to take place on the Midland Railway Centre line

Duchess of Sutherland stands in the yard raising steam on 17th January, 2001. Painting remains incomplete with no lining yet in place. (John Stiles)

With painting only partially completed 6233 moves for the first time on 18th January 2001 in the West Shed yard.
(J. B. Radford)

many of the steam powered systems were tried - the injectors and ejectors, the sanding equipment, and finally the coal pusher.

Then it was out onto the Midland Railway Centre's main line for a series of slow speed return trips between Swanwick Junction and Pye Bridge as the Duchess found her feet again, the runs being eventually extended back to Butterley station to give her a better trial trip. Inevitably a check of the air brake and lubrication systems as well as the rest of the locomotive revealed a number of joints that needed tightening and other small adjustments. These were quickly attended to. During February, 2001 6233 ventured out on many occasions onto the Midland Railway Centre running line at Butterley for day long running-in trials in order cover 1,000 miles. This figure was agreed between the overhaul team and the Trust's VAB as a suitable distance to run to enable the axlebox bearings to settle in and the various systems to bed down, and also to hopefully ensure that there were no hidden problems that might emerge once she returned to the main line for trials.

at Butterley. It is of course fundamental that any locomotive has to have a workable braking system that will bring it to a stand before any running can take place. So it was a natural progression for events that the system must be proven before 6233 could commence running in trials.

On Wednesday, 17th January, 2001 a fire was lit in the boiler, and the long process of warming the engine up and bringing her to life again finally began. Steam pressure was slowly built up, and the following day, and with Eric Riley at the controls, the regulator was eased open and closed twice and then opened once again, and at 1.38 p.m. 6233 'DUCHESS OF SUTHERLAND' moved slowly forward along the West Shed sidings under her own power for the first time since she had last run at Bressingham in 1976. During the afternoon

At this time the smoke deflectors were left off in order to gain access to the outside main steam pipe glands which, being of a rather crude design, were viewed by the team as a likely source of trouble during the running-in period. These particular glands are a simple 'spigot and socket' design with the gap between the two pipes sealed with a compressed gland packing. However because the packing is not wholly contained, and can be squeezed through the gap into the steam pipe, the design is somewhat flawed. It has to be said that on the same joint of the 'Princess Royal' class of locomotives the tapered washer design, under compression, seals the joint in a more satisfactory manner, and it is difficult to understand why this was not used in this later build of 'Princess Coronation' class locomotives. On the second day of trial running the left hand side gland blew out, but, wearing heat resistant gloves, the fitters performed the difficult task of

6233 in steam on the Midland Railway Trust's main site on 25th April, 2001 having a further steam test. The smoke deflectors have not yet been fitted and the temporary nameplate displaying the Trust's web-site address is affixed to the boiler side.
(John Stiles)

refitting the packing on a hot locomotive.

The final task of the overhaul was the repainting of 6233 in the original 'Midland Red' special livery used for the five original non-streamlined 'Princess Coronation' class locomotives when they were first turned out of Crewe Works way back in 1938. Fortunately the original detailed specification had survived, together with official drawings of the numerals and 'L.M.S.' letters, thus allowing a complete specification to be handed over to R.P. 'Bob' Timmins of Cleobury Mortimer, the signwriter and coach painting specialist who was contracted to carry out the work. Assisted by his son, Bob had a history of being able to deliver a superb final finish, and had worked on the coaching stock for the Orient Express Pullman coaches and on other high quality locomotive and coach painting projects.

Some preliminary surface preparation and undercoating had already been carried out, but Bob re-assessed this and did some remedial work before applying the final undercoat, coats of finishing colour and varnish necessary to give the finish required. A full specification of this livery is given in Appendix 6 along with details of subsequent liveries carried by the locomotive throughout its service life. A few minor departures were made from the original specification on a purely practical basis. The paintwork, including the cabside numbering and the tender lettering - the latter all applied by hand using pricked-out prints taken from the original full sized drawings and in gold leaf shaded vermilion - had been completed by the time the final running-in turns were undertaken along the M.R.T.'s main line. In this form, without smoke deflectors, she looked magnificent, and a photographic record was taken. This was how she had originally appeared when she first entered traffic in July, 1938 with of course the exception of the double chimney, the addition of the modern components for the air-braking equipment and the alterations to the tender.

With the locomotive now complete, and the actual Design Scrutiny process itself completed by a separate division of the Blue Print Rail organisation on behalf of the Vehicle Acceptance Body, it was time for a meeting with the engineers who were to sign off the locomotive to allow for main line running on Railtrack. This meeting took place in May, 2001 at the former British Railways' Technical Centre on London Road Derby. Chaired by David Russell from Halcrow Engineering, with Rob Redfern, Managing Director of Resco Railways Ltd, and Keith Nicholson, from Interfleet Technology Ltd., present. The meeting discussed the various elements of the Railtrack Group Standard requirements and agreed dates for the light engine test run and then the loaded test run on Railtrack. The dates were to be Wednesday 4th July, 2001 for the light run and Wednesday 18th July for the loaded run.

The 4th July day was to be the date for the air brake test runs combined with the statutory 50 miles light engine run. Data for the testing of the braking system performance had been developed by Keith Nicholson and a programme set out for the number of full brake applications to be made at a variety of speeds and at set locations on the route of the day. The location of each proposed stopping point was necessary in order to know the gradient of the track, which would of course have an effect on the stopping distance. In order to complete the required number of brake applications some 200 miles needed to be run in the day. This meant two circuits round the Derby - Chesterfield - Beighton - Sheffield - Erewash Valley route.

With further on-site testing continuing into late May and June, the test day of July 4th, 2001 soon came round, and at 10.00am on a very bright sunlit morning, 6233 stood at the colour light signal on the Ironville curve at Codnor Park Junction awaiting 'the road'. Two coaches made up the formation of the train - support coach 99041 and special saloon 6320. After over an hour's wait, the signal turned green and 6233 eased the short train out and over the crossover to the Up Slow line and then set back on the Down Slow line to Pye Bridge Junction. At Pye Bridge, with the sun now beating down on the train and its passengers, the Traction Inspector, Bill Andrew from West Coast Railway, was advised by Railtrack from Toton Signal Box that a points failure at the junction, due to train detection

Inspector Bill Andrews of Crewe testifies how dirty the coal was on the test run of 4th July, 2001! (John Stiles)

failure on the little used line, was preventing the movement across to the Up Slow line. After a further long delay the permanent way gang eventually arrived and within minutes 6233 and train had been re-routed back onto the 'up' main and the train finally left bound for Derby, now running over two hours late. No further time was to be lost on this day of testing and so it was with some speed that 6233 made her way with the short train down the Erewash Valley main line, round through Trent and on to Derby over the former Midland Counties Railway route. Following a brief stop at Derby station, the short train set off northwards and commenced the brake testing at Milford.

Following a brief stop at Chesterfield to pick up David Ward, the route of the day saw the first water stop at Whittington where a quick refill enabled some time to be recovered. The testing procedure was being supervised by Keith Nicholson from Interfleet Technology Ltd., supported by David Russell from Engineering Link, who had set up the decelerometer measuring instrument and recording sheets in the support coach. The communication link with the driver was provided on the footplate by Wayne Jones of Resco, relieved later in the day by Brian Penney from Engineering Link. Rob Redfern, the Managing Director of Resco was also present to witness the procedure on behalf of the Vehicle Acceptance Body. Contact between locomotive and test engineers in the coach was by two-way radio, and Kim Malyon, with his broad Norfolk accent, left a lasting memory of his two-way conversations with Wayne Jones on the footplate with all those present.

Although classed as 'light locomotive' tests 6233 had a formation of two coaches, No. 99041 the P.R.C.L.T.'s converted MK 1 BSK Support Coach and No.6320, the P.R.C.L.T.'s 1927 LMS Directors Saloon, both having air brakes. Brake applications were to be made at a number of pre-determined locations from a variety of speeds above 20mph. On the day, with one exception, all brake applications were at the Full Service rate using the automatic brake on the locomotive. Test No 21 was an Emergency brake application. Stopping distances and brake entry speeds were determined using a Simret 3000R Brake Test Meter.

TEST RESULTS

Test No.	Location	Gradient	Speed (mph)		Stopping Distance (m)	
			Required	Actual	Actual	GM/RT2042
1	MP134½ Milford Tunnel (North)	Level	55	55.1	515	900
2	MP140 Wingfield Tunnel (North)	1/417R	50	50.2	440	833
3	MP145 App. Chesterfield	1/323F	60	55.1	602	900
4	MP153 Eckington	1/544F	30	30.2	173	365
5	MP160 Woodhouse	1/137R	45	45.4	304	754
6	MP151 Dronfield	1/100F	50	50.1	609	833
7	MP146 Chesterfield	1/323R	35	36.2	225	483
8	MP141 Clay Cross - Doe Hill	1/160R	40	40.1	263	608
9	MP138¾ Doe Hill – Westhouses	1/230F	50	48.5	386	833
10	MP127 Ilkeston	1/471F	60	60.3	689	961
11	MP135 Duffield - Belper	1/435R	65	65.2	829	1015
12	MP140 Wingfield Tunnel (North)	1/417R	80	81.3	1211	1144
13	MP145 Stretton	1/342R	40	37.2	256	608
14	MP145 App. Chesterfield	1/323F	35	34.8	235	483
15	MP147¼ Tapton Jct. – Whittington	1/343F	40	42.7	309	608
16	MP148½ Whittington	1/349F	25	24.5	120	256
17	MP149½ Barrow Hill	1/406F	25	25.8	127	256
18	MP153 Eckington	1/544F	20	18.5	80	177
19	MP143¾ Stretton - Wingfield	1/343F	65	66.5	814	1015
20	MP135 Belper - Duffield	1/435F	55	57.2	567	900
21	MP124 Stanton Gate	1/471R	50	52.2	393	833

Stopping distance and brake entry speeds were determined using a simret 3000R Brake Test Meter. All stopping distance figures quoted are gradient corrected.

The table of brake test results from 4th July, 2001. (Courtesy Interfleet Technology Ltd.)

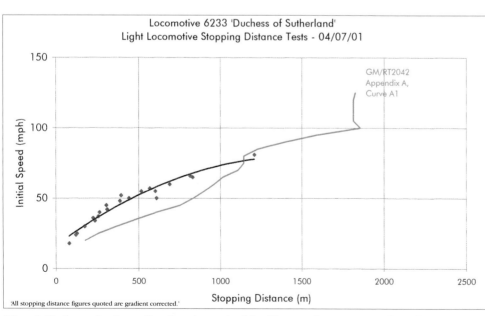

The plotted graph of results showing actual braking performance against the GM/RT2042 requirements. Only the high-speed test at 81.3mph failed to meet the standard as was predicted. Every other one fell well inside the minimum requirement. (Courtesy Interfleet Technology Ltd.)

TEST CONCLUSION

From the results of the tests it can be clearly seen that the locomotive was, with one exception, capable of stopping well within the requirements of Group Standard GM/RT2042, Appendix A, Curve A1 which is for locomotives required to operate over routes signalled in accordance with Appendix 1 of Signalling Group Standard GK/RT0034 (i.e. anywhere). The exception where the Group Standard stopping distance requirement was exceeded was from an initial speed of 81mph, considerably in excess of the normal light locomotive maximum speed of 60mph.

Very few enthusiasts knew the train was running, and as such the event was witnessed by only a few line-side photographers. The late start to the day caused by the points failure at Pye Bridge, inevitably meant a late finish to the day and so it was that the last brake test was carried out at milepost 124 at Stanton Gate on the final run back north along the Erewash Valley line before re-entry on to the Midland Railway Trust's line at Codnor Park Junction, some nine hours after the train had first departed. With the tests complete the Final Certificate for Vehicle Design was issued on September 10th, the previous, one allowing 6233 to run on Railtrack, being a temporary one valid for a period of only one month.

The job was complete. The overhaul had lasted some 900 working days and had consumed over 15,500 volunteer man-hours and a further 10,300 paid staff hours. Many specialist sub-contractors had contributed and played vital roles in the overall restoration project. Almost to a man the same team who had commenced the project in October, 1998 had seen the job through to completion.

'DUCHESS OF SUTHERLAND' was now able to take her place on the main line for the first time since 1963 in revenue earning capacity. Exciting times lay ahead. No one knew how exciting these would turn out to be and how events were to turn out with 6233 hauling the Royal Train the following year.

Duchess of Sutherland coasts past Tapton Junction , Chesterfield at 6 p.m. on the second circuit of brake test trials. 4th July, 2001. Support coach 99041 and saloon 6320 form her short train. (John Palmer)

6233 coasts into Sheffield Midland station at 7.15 p.m. on 4th July, 2001. (John Palmer)

THE LOADED TEST TRAIN

In order to comply with Railtrack Group Standards and meet the demanding scrutiny that forms part of the many volumed suite of engineering dictates, main line steam locomotives have to complete a test run with a load equal to that they would normally expect to haul when in service. Whereas it is one thing to see a locomotive run light engine, with all its many items of engineering working well, it is a very different test to require the locomotive to work hard, at maximum speed and then assess its performance. Furthermore all locomotives have to be fitted with spark arresting systems if they are to be certificated to work in the summer months. Part of this test and assessment can only be made when the locomotive is working hard and with a load behind her, so this test is carried out on the loaded test run.

With the successful light engine run completed on 4th July the day and date was already set for the loaded run two weeks later on Wednesday, 18th July. By a remarkable coincidence this was 63 years to the day since 6233 had left Crewe Works brand new to enter L.M.S. service.

The chosen route was again the Derby - Sheffield - Derby figure of eight, and the load was to be 14 bogies. As part of the assessment for the new Air Brake system, Mr Paul Russenberger of Her Majesty's Railway Inspectorate was on board the train and was to ride for part of the journey on the footplate of the locomotive to assess the air brake operation. Since the change to the braking system was a comprehensive one and also safety critical, new legislation meant that HMRI (Her Majesty's Railway Inspectorate) had to give a certificate to confirm they too were happy with the changes made, and Mr Russenberger's visit was part of that process.

The train left Derby with Inspector Bill Andrew in charge as driver. It was so long, and so carefully did he ease her out of Derby Station and round the curve to Trent, that it took a full two minutes to clear the station platform. Speed was steady as the route took the train to Trent and then northwards along the Erewash Valley, with the several speed restrictions in place. It was a fully loaded test since every seat was taken on the train, and a full compliment of 670 passengers were therefore enjoying haulage behind 6233 out on the mainline for the first time.

A water stop at Whittington was completed in swift time, and the train left early and following an efficient climb into Sheffield from Beighton and through Darnall, the train had several minutes to wait before a platform was available in Sheffield Midland station. In the growing darkness the fans gathered round the locomotive, and after the customary `whistle up' they re-boarded for what was to be the climax of the evening - the climb from Sheffield to Dore.

With a steady beat 6233 soon mastered the climb, but disaster lay ahead, for after passing through Bradwell Tunnel the brakes came on and the train pulled sharply to a halt just south of Dronfield Station.

A check with the footplate found that all air pressure in the main reservoirs had been lost. After a look underneath the locomotive at the pump, the fault was diagnosed as terminal and diesel assistance was summoned. After a long 90 minute delay the train was on the move again with Class 45 diesel 45112, summoned from Derby, now at the head of the train to provide air, and rapid speed was made to Chesterfield, where an additional stop was made before the train progressed to Derby. Here the Class 45 was replaced by two Class 31 diesels to take 6233 and coach back to Butterley.

Back in the workshop the following day the fault was found to be quite simply too tight a fit of the piston in the shuttle valve on the air compressor, and this was duly modified to give more clearance. Therefore, with the Certifying Engineer's blessing, the full certificates for the locomotive were finally issued. The engineers on board that night made little of the failure, explaining that this was just what a test run was for, but the failure bit very hard with the team who had worked for so long on the locomotive. They vowed to ensure that such an unforeseen mechanical failure would not happen again.

6233 'DUCHESS OF SUTHERLAND' was now fully certificated and took her registered number on the TOPS system as 98834, the first two digits 98 indicating that she was a private locomotive, the next 8 for a Class 8, and 34 being the nearest available two numbers to the last two of the locomotive, since there was already a class 8 with 33 at the end - the LMS class 8F 2-8-0 No. 8233 at the Severn Valley Railway.

Confidential meetings and discussions were now taking place between Brell Ewart and English Welsh and Scottish Railway about a very special event for 2002. Only a handful of people knew the subject. This was soon to take centre stage, but not until 6233 had become a reliable and proven locomotive on main line duty.

Duchess of Sutherland sets out from Derby with 'THE NIGHT OWL', her first revenue earning duty, on 18th July, 2001, exactly 63 years to the day since she left Crewe Locomotive Works brand new in 1938.
(John Whitehouse)

Chapter Nine

Return To Main Line Duties

After a gap of 38 years the return of 6233 'DUCHESS OF SUTHERLAND' to some of her old haunts and stamping grounds could now be contemplated.

Her first subsequent duty however was to appear at her re-naming ceremony on Tuesday, 6th September, 2001. At mid-day, on a sunny platform at Butterley station, a distinguished group of guests saw 6233 'DUCHESS OF SUTHERLAND' gently coast into the station with her train, her nameplate discreetly covered by a Union flag, and come to a halt before the assembled company.

Brian Radford then gave a brief resume of 6233's history, and Brell Ewart then thanked all of the invited guests who were present, representing as they did the various engineering specialities and other bodies, all of whom having made a significant contribution during the acquisition, restoration, and certification process of the locomotive. He paid a glowing tribute to the P.R.C.L.T volunteers who had devoted thousands of hours of unpaid effort towards the achievement of what had been a magnificent display of dedication and long term commitment, which would now enable the locomotive to be seen at its best working trains over the main line once more.

The guests were Mr Mike Stanier and his wife Ann; Councillor & Mrs. John Jeffrey (Mayor and Mayoress of Amber Valley Borough Council); Gill Gardiner, Chair of East Midlands Committee, and Jason Waddy (Heritage Lottery Fund); Rosemary Bower and Lesley Colsell (East Midlands Museums Service); Rick Edmundson (Managing Director) and Rob Redfern and Wayne Jones (R.E.S.C.O.); David Russell, Brian Penney and Tony Broughton (Engineering Link); James Rollin, Keith Nicholson and Frank Alcock (Interfleet Technology Ltd.); Peter Hodgson (Hodgson Structures Ltd.); Steve Chadwick and Don Webster (Blue Print Rail); James Shuttleworth (West Coast Railways); Matthew Golton (E.W.S.); Bernard Staite (Rail Charter Services); John Duncan (C.M.E., M.S.O.L.), Peter Sturley (National Railway Museum); Chris Milner (Railway Magazine) and John Stiles, Mick Boothby, Graham Poole and John Balls from the P.R.C.L.T.

Brell Ewart then introduced Mike Stanier, grandson of Sir William A. Stanier, the Chief Mechanical Engineer of the L.M.S. responsible for the design of the locomotive, as Guest of Honour who said how pleased he had been to be invited to perform the re-naming ceremony. After paying tribute to the team responsible for restoring the locomotive he pulled the Union flag away to reveal the sparkling chromium-plated nameplate 'DUCHESS OF SUTHERLAND' to a round of applause from the assembled company.

All then boarded the train for a special lunch as the train ran a shuttle service with Standard 2-6-4T No. 80098 at the other end, along the M.R.T. main line to Riddings and back, pausing on the Butterley reservoir causeway for the main part of the luncheon which consisted of 'Pacific Melon Hawaii,' 'Coronation Roast Topside of Beef and Yorkshire Pudding, with Duchess Potatoes and Vegetables' and 'Sutherland Apple Flan' followed by coffee and mints. The train crews were:- Eric Riley (driver) & Howard Routledge (fireman) of 6233 and Malcolm Butler (driver) & Ian Crampton (fireman) of 80098.

MAINLINE

The Trust had set a strategy for 6233 of running mainline tours, where ever possible, with the promotion of the tour by PMR Tours, the trust's own tour division. The view in support of this decision was that it gave the trust control of all matters relating such as routes, days of running and most important of all funding and hopefully profits. With the lead-time for any operation being 14-16 weeks, early planning was, and still remains, an essential ingredient.

The Trust wanted to make the first few runs over an easy route for the locomotive in order to give a 'running in' period, and so the North Wales Coast line was chosen. At the same time approaches had already been made by the Royal Train operators, this being covered in Chapter 10 of this book, so this route really selected itself. The Trust was also approached for the locomotive to attend various open days and Galas

CENTRAL RIVERS DEPOT OPEN DAY

Bombardier, the owners of Central Rivers Depot at Barton under Needwood near Burton-on-Trent, made contact with the Trust for 6233 to attend their open day, on Sunday 16th September. Several employees of Bombardier were volunteers who had worked on the locomotive overhaul and, along with that was the factor that their depot was in fairly close proximity to the West Shed at the Midland Railway Centre, so that 'DUCHESS OF SUTHERLAND' was the obvious choice if a steam locomotive was to be used as an attraction.

Owing to staff shortages for the footplate, 6233 was hauled to Central Rivers from Butterley by a Class 66 that was also to remain there on display for the open day. The train consist, comprising of Class 66, 6233, special saloon 6320 and support coach 99041, left Codnor Park Junction of Saturday 15th September with the route being through Trent, Sheets Stores Junction, the Castle Donnington Branch, and Burton before entering Central Rivers through the washing plant, much to the consternation of all concerned due to the heat from the locomotive chimney being unsuited to the plastic covering of the roof washing equipment !

Following the day-long static display at Central Rivers, the same train ran back home to Butterley late on Sunday 16th.

Mike Stanier, grandson of Sir William Stanier, pays tribute to the team who had restored Duchess of Sutherland to working order at the official re-dedication ceremony on September 6th 2001.
(John Stiles)

THE SEVERN VALLEY GALA 2001

During the time that the boiler from 6233 had been under heavy repair at the Severn Valley Railway's Boiler Shop at Bridgnorth, many discussions and informal chats had taken place with Severn Valley staff. A promise had been given by Brell Ewart at that time that the locomotive would return in steam one day to run on the line, and this prompted Alun Rees to contact Brell Ewart and arrange for the 'DUCHESS OF SUTHERLAND' together with the special saloon 6320 to visit the S.V.R. for their 2001 Autumn Gala.

Arrangements were made with West Coast Railways to move the locomotive with 99041 and 6320 on Thursday, 20th September from Butterley to Kidderminster via Derby, where 6233 ran round in order to run smokebox first to Kidderminster.

Over the three day gala 'DUCHESS OF SUTHERLAND' was the undoubted star of the show, hauling the Severn Valley's L.M.S set of vehicles, newly repainted in their original livery. This historic and magnificent spectacle was enjoyed by all those who attended the event. The Trust's saloon 6320 was marshalled at the back of the set, then in its striking 'aircraft blue' livery with gold lining, much to the annoyance of those taking colour photographs. The event was a huge success, with the second highest number of passengers ever carried during a Gala Weekend. The locomotive and coaches then ran back to Butterley on Monday, the 24th, the locomotive being turned on the Kidderminster turntable before departure.

6233 pauses outside Kidderminster Signal Box (SVR) on Sunday 23rd September 2001. (Martin Welch)

Arrival at Bridgnorth Station on the Severn Valley Railway, Sunday 23rd September 2001, with the 14.26 train ex Kidderminster. This was the first occasion for over half a century that the locomotive had hauled a set of LMS stock and possible one of the first ever on GWR territory!
(Martin Welch)

CREWE - HOLYHEAD - CREWE:- 'THE NORTH WALES COAST CORONATION' AND 'THE YNYS MON DUCHESS'.

The first main line runs proper were on Sundays, 14th October, 2001 with 'The North Wales Coronation' and on the 21st October 2001 with 'The Yns Mon Duchess'. 6233 left Butterley on Friday, 12th October, with support coach 99041 and the Trust's special 1927 saloon 6320, to travel over to Crewe Heritage Centre for stabling until the first Sunday run over the north Wales line to Holyhead.

The stock for these runs was the 'Riviera Trains' Mk1 set based in the Carriage Shed at Crewe South depot. It was a rare sight indeed therefore to see 'DUCHESS OF SUTHERLAND' reverse through Crewe station propelling support coach 99041 and make its way to the sidings adjacent to the Carriage Shed where the stock was shunted onto it using the in-house Class 08 0-6-0 diesel shunter. At right time, 6233 eased the empty stock forward and across the main lines south of Crewe Station and into Platform 12. The trust's LMS 1927 Saloon 6320 had been marshalled at the rear of the formation, and on both runs a number of patrons and special guests enjoyed a full day of excellent 'haute cuisine' catering in the superior ambience that this vehicle offers. Both proved excellent running in turns for 6233 and the performance of the locomotive showed great promise for what would be in store on future runs. Unknown to passengers was the fact that the runs were also being used as precursor trials for a very special event the following year as detailed in the next chapter.

Standing at Platform 12 Crewe Station on Sunday October 21st, with blower on, waiting for departure time. This was the second rehearsal day for the Royal Train that was to run nine months later. (A. Howard Thomas)

BRISTOL to PLYMOUTH. 'THE MAYFLOWER'.

As a result of the unavailability of LNER A4 Pacific No 60009 'UNION OF SOUTH AFRICA', it was 6233 'DUCHESS OF SUTHERLAND' that stepped at short notice into the breach for a run from Bristol to Plymouth over the Devon banks on Saturday, 27th October, 2001. Thus it was that on Friday 26th October, in pouring rain, 6233 left Crewe to run via Wolverhampton, Bescot, and Kidderminster to Bristol Barton Hill Depot that was to be her home for the next few days. Alun Rees joined the support crew at Kidderminster. The South Devon banks had last been visited by a Princess Coronation during the 1948 Locomotive Exchanges, and so

**Above.
Saturday 27th
October 2001,
6233 departs
from Bristol
Temple Meads
Station, with a
ten-coach train
bound for
Plymouth. This
was to be the
heaviest train
over the route
run in the
preservation
era hauled with
one steam
locomotive.**
(John Stiles)

**Left.
Beside the
coastline of
Devon 6233
hurries the train
along having
passed through
Parsons Tunnel.**
(John Stiles)

On Saturday 8th December, 2001 an immaculate Duchess of Sutherland departs from Derby with a train bound for St Pancras. (John Stiles)

The visit to St Pancras by 6233 was the first time ever that a Princess Coronation Class locomotive had graced this station. It is likely to have been the one and only visit. (John Stiles)

a return visit by another member of the class was eagerly awaited. 'DUCHESS OF SUTHERLAND' did not disappoint, and magnificent performances were achieved in both directions over this arduous route, with the locomotive hauling a train of ten vehicles when the maximum number for a single locomotive is usually restricted to nine. 6233 returned home with the two coaches from Bristol on a sunny Sunday afternoon, the 29th October.

DERBY- ST PANCRAS

With A4 60009 still unavailable, 'DUCHESS OF SUTHERLAND' was booked for a run up to the capital - London. Leaving Derby at lunchtime on Saturday 8th December, 6233 ran via Loughborough

and Corby to Kettering, crossing Harringworth Viaduct en route. Following a water stop at Kettering the train was soon crossed over to the Up Fast line and 'DUCHESS OF SUTHERLAND' showed what an LMS pacific can really do, with some high speed running. There was a stunning sight for spectators at St Albans as the pacific majesterially thundered at high speed through the station on the Up Fast line before being slowed for signals at Kentish Town. Here there was a sixteen minute delay awaiting a platform at St Pancras, which unfortunately caused a late arrival.

Standing at the buffer stops on Platform 8 at St Pancras, 'DUCHESS OF SUTHERLAND' made a fine sight, the first and only time, so far as anyone present could remember, that a 'Princess Coronation' class locomotive had graced or would grace this historic terminus, since St Pancras is now under intensive re-develop-

18.32 on Saturday 8th December, 2001 as 6233 stands in the St. Pancras trainshed. This was to be the last steam hauled train to run into St. Pancras before development started for the Channel Tunnel link, and possibly the last steam ever into the famous London terminus. (John Stiles)

6233 is turned on the turntable at Old Oak Common depot on 14th December, 2001. (Howard Routledge)

ment in order to create a second London terminus for the Eurostar train service to the Continent.

6233 was then hauled on the rear of the train to Old Oak Common depot where she was to stay for one week until her return north working a second special train seven days later.

EUSTON TO DERBY
'THE CAPITAL DUCHESS'

Prior to the 15th December, 2001 on only one occasion since steam ended in the 1960s had a 'Princess Coronation' Class locomotive graced the Euston terminus, and 6233 was to be the second to do so. On the Saturday morning, attached to the rear of the stock, she was hauled round to Euston by a Class 47 Diesel from the Old Oak Common depot sidings. 6233 set off in fine style, and her determined assault on Camden Bank was worth the train fare alone as she stormed up, accelerating all the way, running alongside a Class 91 electric locomotive on the Caledonian Sleeper empty stock working which kept pace with her throughout. Sadly it all ended too soon, for 6233 was eased to negotiate the North London line and then down to Acton on the G.W. main line. In wonderful late autumn sunshine 'DUCHESS OF SUTHERLAND', with Driver Davies

of Acton at the regulator, showed her paces along the Great Western main line to Reading and Didcot where the train turned north for Oxford. Following a very speedy water stop, the train then ran through the Cotswolds to enter Birmingham and, following a further water stop on the northern outskirts, arrived in Derby as the sun was going down.

LIVERPOOL TO YORK
'THE YORKSHIRE CORONATION'

In preparation for the following day 6233 ran to Crewe on Friday 8th March and was turned in order to leave her facing tender first for Liverpool at the rear of the empty coaching stock that was to come off Crewe Carriage Sidings. Following a water stop in Edge Hill Carriage Sidings the train was hauled into Lime Street Station where 'DUCHESS OF SUTHERLAND' stood proudly at the head of the train in a location she had once graced many times in the past. It was hard to believe that she was returning in steam to the city after a thirty-eight year absence from what had been her final home.

On time 6233 eased away, with the Driver taking time to allow the locomotive to get hold of the train. Manchester Victoria saw a large posse of photographers bearing witness to 6233 as she stopped for more passengers to board before the slog up Miles Platting Bank.

Across the Pennines the weather was mixed, and with a stop at Wakefield Kirkgate Station to take water from a road tanker, York was reached on time. In very wet weather 'DUCHESS OF SUTHERLAND' went on to the National Railway Museum site to replenish coal and water before rejoining the train and heading west for the climb up Standedge bank. Through Huddersfield the locomotive made a rousing noise to the obvious enjoyment of passengers waiting for service trains under the trainshed roof. Liverpool was reached in the dark and 6233 stood at the terminus buffer stops as the train awaited the move back to Crewe.

'DUCHESS OF SUTHERLAND' returned to Butterley on Monday, 11th March.

Saturday 15th December, 2001 and Duchess of Sutherland awaits departure time in Euston Station, her return being some thirty eight years after her last visit! (Howard Routledge)

DERBY TO CREWE AND RETURN:-
'THE CORONATION OWL'.

In keeping with Trust traditions set over recent years, the annual PMR Tours main line season has started with an evening run on Wednesday, 20th March, 2002, and with a new route via Lichfield giving access to the West Coast Main Line at Lichfield agreed, some high speed running was in prospect. However, with the late arrival of the empty stock at Derby, the evening was a little compromised, but nevertheless 'DUCHESS OF SUTHERLAND' rose to the occasion with some high speed running to Burton, down the curve to join the main line to the north, and made a fine sight as she emerged from the darkness to sweep at high speed through Stafford - a sight that rekindled happy memories of times past. With a water stop and turn at Crewe, the pace of the evening slowed on the return journey due to engineering work and a failed freight train just before Lichfield, making the final arrival in Derby an hour behind schedule.

6233 takes water on Platform 12 at Crewe on Saturday, 13th April 2002, as youngsters, like many thousands before them in years gone by, admire the Duchess of Sutherland. (J.B.Radford)

DERBY TO BLACKPOOL:-
'THE BLACKPOOL DUCHESS'.

Steam trains to seaside resorts for day trips have long been part of the railway traditions and services, and on today's railway they are almost non existent. It was therefore not surprising that a large number of passengers booked to travel on this train from Derby to Blackpool on Saturday, 13th April, 2002. With an interesting route through Stoke-on-Trent, Crewe was the designated essential water stop on Platform 12 before 6233 stretched her legs and put in a good turn of speed on the Down Fast line of the West Coast Main line to Preston station where the route to Blackpool diverges. Arrival in the West Lancashire resort was greeted with hundreds of well wishers who lined the route to welcome only the second Stanier pacific ever to reach the town. With Blackpool tower looming in the background 'DUCHESS OF SUTHERLAND' made a spirited start for the return journey, and picked up time until the train reached Crewe. Here she was detached with her support coach and special saloon for stabling at the Heritage Centre to await her next duty.

Saturday 13th April, and 6233 gathers pace past local factories at Derby on her way to Blackpool with a special excursion train. (John Palmer)

With the world famous tower overlooking Blackpool North Station, the second Princess Coronation locomotive to visit the town makes her early evening departure for Crewe. (Peter Fitton)

Saturday 20th April, 2002 Duchess of Sutherland makes her first ascent of Grayrigg Bank for thirty eight years. A few minutes later she was to climb Shap in the fastest time ever recorded. (John Stiles)

CREWE TO CARLISLE via SHAP:-
'THE CITADEL EXPRESS'.

One of the most eagerly awaited routes for 6233 to run was the West Coast main line over Shap, and two trains were arranged for 20th and 27th of April, 2002. With demand for seats being high, 'DUCHESS OF SUTHERLAND' set off from Crewe on 20th April in a spirited fashion and ran, with several good turns of speed, to Carnforth where a water stop was taken in the up and down loop thanks to the help of West Coast Railway Staff from their yard. From Carnforth 6233 now showed her true ability with a fine climb over Grayrigg followed by the climb of Shap with the best ever recorded ascent by a preserved steam locomotive in a time of 5mins 32secs for the stretch between mileposts 31½ and 37¼ at an average speed of 62.4 m.p.h. In fact there was one more coach in the formation compared to the second best performance by 60532 'Blue

Peter'. But for a mysterious brake application (caused by someone on the train) 6233 would have done even better. With the train now well ahead of time the proposed stop at Penrith was foregone, and the train arrived at Carlisle some 37 minutes early. With the locomotive turned and serviced, the return leg of the day was also made in fine style.

The run of the 27th April was not so good. Poor steaming after Carnforth necessitated a stop in Grayrigg loop where, following an examination, 'DUCHESS OF SUTHERLAND' continued, still putting up a magnificent show on the climb over Shap with the sixth best performance ever recorded. At Carlisle further examination revealed a blow from a leaking calked seam in the firebox and, to ensure that this fault did not compromise the return leg of the trip, assistance was summoned for a diesel to pilot 6233 back to Crewe. However a repair was quickly effected without difficulty the following day and the locomotive returned to Butterley on the 29th under her own steam. The fact that 6233 had again put up one of the best runs ever over Shap with such a defect indicates the massive capabilities the boiler of a 'Princess Coronation' engine. It would be fair to say that no other locomotive boiler design could have continued to produce steam to enable such a performance to be put in with such a defect.

6233 powers through Oxenholme on Saturday 27th April, 2002 bound for Carlisle. (Dougie Dunstan)

Duchess of Sutherland eases round the curve of York Station under the magnificent station canopy on 11th May, 2002 on her way to Scarborough. (John Stiles)

LEICESTER TO SCARBOROUGH:- 'THE SCARBOROUGH CORONATION'.

'DUCHESS OF SUTHERLAND' headed another day trip to the the seaside on Saturday, 11th May, 2002 with a train starting from Leicester and, after taking an unusual route to York, it continued steam hauled by 6233 throughout to Scarborough. With a total mileage of over 300 in the day 6233 gave another fine performance, the route covering new ground beyond York as she again broke into new territory. A sunny day enabled all passengers to enjoy the resort whilst the locomotive was being serviced and turned ready for the return run back to Leicester where she arrived six minutes late after a severe signal check in the Chesterfield area put paid to what could have been an early arrival.

Saturday 11th May, 2002 and 6233 sets the train back under the semaphore signal gantry at Scarborough on her way to being serviced and turned. (John Stiles)

With a heavy train, Duchess of Sutherland departs from Scarborough for Leicester on 11th May, 2002. (John Stiles)

THE ROYAL TRAIN:-

This historic, highly prestigious duty for 6233 'DUCHESS OF SUTHERLAND' on 11th June, 2002 is covered in full in the next chapter of this book.

CREWE to CARLISLE:- 'THE CUMBRIAN CORONATION'.

For 6233's first ever journey over the Settle to Carlisle since her return to the main line on Saturday, 29th June, 2002, the traditional route from Crewe was chosen, and there was some impressive high speed running up the West Coast main line as far as Farington Junction, where the train diverged, with water taken at Cherry Tree Station before the start of the climb through Blackburn and on to the Settle to Carlisle line at Hellifield. Here again 'DUCHESS OF SUTHERLAND' showed her true capabilities with a fine performance for, following a severe speed restriction at Settle Station, she accelerated the train back to speed on the 1 in 100 rising gradient. The summit was breasted in style, Carlisle being reached several minutes early.

Here 6233 left the train with her support coach and returned down the West Coast main line over Shap to Carnforth to lay over until her next duty.

CARLISLE TO GLASGOW :- 'THE CORONATION SCOT'.

Beattock bank has always been the other West Coast Main Line challenge for the evaluation of performance assessment of a locomotive, but, coming so soon after meeting the challenges of both the Settle and Carlisle line and Shap, everyone expressed full confidence in the locomotive's capabilities of fully meeting this old challenge with no less of a performance. The train had left Manchester Victoria as 06.22 and, despite the early start, passengers were not to be disappointed as, on Saturday, 13th July, 2002 'DUCHESS OF SUTHERLAND', after coming on to the special train with her support coach and special saloon 6320 at Carlisle, she set off in fine style reaching 70 before Gretna Junction and storming the stiff

6233 crosses Ribblehead Viaduct on her first journey in steam over the Settle and Carlisle line Saturday, 29th June, 2002. (Howard Routledge)

climb up Beattock bank which she topped at 37 m.p.h. running 22½ minutes early. With a water stop at Abington, 'DUCHESS OF SUTHERLAND' ran majestically into platform 11 at Glasgow Central station some 42 minutes early as a result of some very slack timings.

Headed by Fragonset Class 47 diesel-electric 'Dionysos' the complete train reversed round a triangle of lines to reverse it for the return trip, and duly arrived for servicing at Polmadie depot, a location that 6233 had graced on countless occasions some three decades and more back in the previous century whilst working such prestigious express trains as 'The Royal Scot' and 'The Mid-Day Scot'. History was being made again with this visit to Scotland's second city, and this particular aspect of the day was not lost on any of the passengers who were thrilled to re-live past times. The return journey to Carlisle was carried on in the same vein with Inspector Driver John McCabe in total mastery of the locomotive. The day was regarded as being one of the finest days out ever on a main line special train by many of the passengers, such was the performance of 'DUCHESS OF SUTHERLAND'. 6233 came off the train at Carlisle and then travelled south behind the special to Carnforth to await her next turn of duty.

Inspector John McCabe and Howard Routledge take a breather on arrival at Glasgow Central on 13th July, 2002. (J.B.Radford)

Two generations of West Coast trains stand alongside each other at Glasgow. The DVT No 82141 is bound for London Euston and 6233 for Carlisle. (J.B.Radford)

Climbing through Greskine on her way to Glasgow, majestically 6233 powers up Beattock Bank on Saturday, 13th July, 2002. (Maurice Burns)

Duchess of Sutherland stands in Platform 11 at Glasgow Central station on 13th July, 2002 resplendent in her rich LMS livery, after having arrived 42 minutes early with her 12 coach train after the run from the water stop at Abington where she had also arrived ahead of schedule by some 32 minutes. (J.B. Radford)

CARLISLE TO DERBY:- 'THE MIDLAND CORONATION'.

One week later, on Saturday, 20th July, 2002, and with the train starting from Derby in the early morning, 'DUCHESS OF SUTHERLAND' made a leisurely run over Shap with support coach from Carnforth to Carlisle to await the arrival of the special train.. On a wet Saturday afternoon, 6233 coupled on to the train in Citadel Station before setting off round Peteril Bridge Junction and on to the Settle to Carlisle line. Following a water stop from the column at Appleby 'DUCHESS OF SUTHERLAND' pounded up the 1 in 100 past Mallerstang to Ais Gill summit from where she ran down to Long Preston for water from a road tanker. A further stop to top up water was necessary at Hellifield, where time was lost, resulting in a late run through the suburbs of Leeds and Sheffield. With a diversion at Chesterfield onto the Goods line, a late arrival at Derby finished the day before 6233 headed back to her home base, the P.R.C.L.T.'s West Shed at Butterley, and a rest before the Autumn 2002 programme commenced.

With her Carlisle to Derby train 6233 reaches the summit at Ais Gill on Saturday 20th July, 2002. The support coach 99041 and the LMS Directors Saloon compliment the livery of the Princess Coronation as she heads south. (John Stiles)

So DUCHESS OF SUTHERLAND had already, in her first year of service back on the main line, run over the major and most arduous routes available to steam traction. Back in 1964 who would ever have considered that in 2001-2 she would again be heard working hard over Shap and Beattock, returning to her old haunts at Crewe, Glasgow, Liverpool, and Euston, not to mention breaking new ground at Bristol and Plymouth, York and St. Pancras plus the seaside resorts of Blackpool and Scarborough and also the Settle to Carlisle line, which she had visited only once before in her former life. Such a story would have been dismissed out of hand as sheer fantasy only a few years ago.

Now back to top class condition, and looking as good as when she was first turned out from Crewe Works in 1938, 6233 'DUCHESS OF SUTHERLAND' should continue to give pleasure, excitement, thrill and spectacle for many more years to come to all those who enjoy steam locomotive traction at its best where it belongs - on the mainline.

The team who look after her are to be congratulated on their dedication to this historic locomotive. Long may it continue.

The grandeur of the Settle and Carlisle line is shown at its magnificent best as 6233 runs through Selside on 20th July, 2002. (John Stiles)

Chapter Ten

The Royal Train

The Royal Train was last hauled by steam traction in service days during the 1960s. One of the last scheduled 'Princess Coronation' class workings was on 10th August, 1962 when locomotive No 46240 'CITY OF COVENTRY' worked the Royal Train from Euston on its way to Ballater, conveying Her Majesty The Queen, HRH Prince Charles, HRH Princess Anne, HRH Prince Andrew and Viscount Linley on their way to Balmoral Castle.

As far as is known (4)6233 'DUCHESS OF SUTHERLAND' never worked The Royal Train in service days, although she was standby for the above train and actually followed the Royal working away from Euston and presumably as far as Crewe with the down 'Merseyside Express'.

However, one later further special duty for two members of the class occurred in connection with Her Majesty The Queen's visit to Merseyside in 1962. On 13th December 46248 'CITY OF LEEDS' was called up at short notice in lieu of a Type 4 diesel electric and brought out of store at Crewe North to work the Royal Train from Euston to its overnight stabling point in south Lancashire. The honour of working the Royal Train into Liverpool Lime Street station the following day fell to 46220 'CORONATION' herself, she having worked light from Edge Hill depot to Lowton Junction to take on the task. Afterwards 46248 'CITY OF LEEDS' re-appeared to work the train from Lime Street to Watford Junction where the royal party de-trained for a road trip to Windsor. 46220 was then put into store again, but returned to traffic in January, 1963, being observed working between Crewe and Carlisle, and on 22nd January was seen on Warrington depot in steam and ready to work the 8.20a.m. fitted freight to Carlisle.

Royal Trains from Euston were, and still are, a regular working, and as such the arrangements and procedures were often already set up and repeated. In steam days, top quality coal would be brought onto Camden depot for the job, and the Motive Power Department would select the locomotive to be involved. This selection was carried out on the basis of her being a 'well run in' locomotive with probably 30,000 miles since its last Heavy General Overhaul. The locomotive would then be taken out of normal duties to allow preparation, a special mechanical examination, and of course special cleaning. Dick Hardy, former Shed Master at Stewarts Lane on the Southern, recalls that a Royal Engine took nine days to prepare for the Ascot races jobs that ran annually from Victoria to Ascot, with a 'Schools' Class 4-4-0 locomotive as motive power and usually Pullman coaches used for conveying the Royal party.

On the London Midland Region a set of burnished buffers, draw hook and shackle were kept for Royal use only, and would be made available at Camden for fitting to the chosen locomotive. Special headlamps were also kept for such duty.

As diesel traction became more reliable, and routes were electrified, the natural progression to the new motive power took place. By 1967 steam had apparently been permanently consigned to the history books so far as Royal Train traction was concerned.

However, in early Summer of 2001 Nigel Harris, the managing editor of EMAP Publications, the publishing house for Steam Railway Magazine, spoke with Brell Ewart by phone. Nigel explained that he had recently met with Chris Hillyard, the Royal Train Manager following an article being prepared for publication about the Royal Train. With the year 2002 being Her Majesty Queen Elizabeth ll's Golden Jubilee Year, this could be the ideal time to run a Royal Train with steam traction. The question put by Nigel was " Would the 6233 team be interested?" It was a simple, quick and positive answer!

Brell registered this interest in writing and within days Matthew Golton, the Rail Express Services General Manager was on the phone to discuss the fine detail. Matthew explained that, subject to a suitable response from the Royal Household, and with the ultimate agreement of Her Majesty, the job could proceed, although it was made abundantly clear that many obstacles would have to be overcome before the job was reality.

Matthew Golton (left) and David Brown (right). Both were instrumental in making the operation the success it was and either or both attended every meeting held during the planning stages. (Howard Routledge)

The Trust quickly made the decision to nominate a small group of P. R.C.L.T. Trustees to handle the development of operation. These were Brell Ewart, being Chairman, David Ward the former Intercity Special Trains Director, who had held the responsibility for the Royal Train whilst with InterCity; Brian Radford who had worked on designs for the Royal Train Stock, and Trustee Howard Routledge, a former Police Sergeant, who had worked on several Royal visits during his career in the police service .

The operational staff from the Royal Train insisted that a total embargo of information was to remain in place for the foreseeable future, in line with their normal procedures.

Matters moved rapidly and within a short space of time E.W. S., the Train Operating Company, had identified a date, the North Wales Coast line as the route, and an operation on which 6233 could haul the train. The proposal was put to the Royal Household and a positive response was received within days. It was made clear to the Trust from the outset that the security services may advise against it on security grounds. In fact like all Royal visits and events, a handful of reasons could always be found as to why the event should not happen.

The dreadful terrorist attacks on 11th September, 2001 in the U.S.A. cascaded impact into security matters, and although not directly involved in such considerations it was clear to the Trust that reviews were taking place following that date.

With 6233 now booked to make two runs along the North Wales Coast run on 14th and 21st October, 2001, an ideal opportunity presented itself for a 'rehearsal' run on the route and for all the parties involved to meet and consider the fine detail and issues raised. The support crew for the 14th October North Wales run was selected with the aim of using the same people on the day in 2002, although only those Trustees named previously knew it at the time.

The 'North Wales Coronation' steam tour on 14th October, 2001 using 'DUCHESS OF SUTHERLAND' ran with a number of representatives from Railtrack, First North Western, E.W.S, British Transport, Police and The Royal Train staff who were to be involved with the operation on board, and these formed a small, discreet group on the train. During the layover at Holyhead the group travelled by road to the proposed overnight stabling point at Valley, and there joined up with the locomotive and had a further private site meeting with Brell Ewart and David Ward on site. To counter questions from within the support crew, these 'enquiring visitors' were passed off as a 'Railtrack audit' using some elastication of the facts!

The event was now still on for 2002, and with a route, dates and even times in place, total secrecy and security were of the highest importance. Even the locomotive visit to Valley on the 14th October was overseen by security people, the location being a nuclear flask handling facility.

Christmas 2001 passed and as the weeks of the New Year slipped by, further detail was gradually added. A second meeting at Valley Sidings took place in late January 2002 when detailed measurements were taken on the site to position the Royal Train consist with 'DUCHESS OF SUTHERLAND' at the head, within the siding complex. At this meeting details for the light engine and support coach moves were also discussed and options evaluated.

In February 2002, a further meeting took place at Wolverton in the Royal Train Shed where checks were carried out to ensure that the air brake pipes and other connections on the end Royal Train coach and those on the P. R.C.L.T. support coach to which it would be coupled were fully compatible.

The mainline programme for 'DUCHESS OF SUTHERLAND' in 2002 was planned around the now fixed date of June 11th, leaving a comfortable period before the date to prepare the locomotive and turn it out in the very best condition achievable.

Brell Ewart had researched the Royal events at the time of Her Majesty's Coronation in 1953 and discovered that the London Midland Region had in fact produced a 'Royal Crown' headboard mounted on the smokebox door of locomotives hauling the principal express trains of the day, such as 'The Royal Scot', during Coronation week. Although no precise details of these headboards had survived, Brell was able to extract detail from photographs and proposed that one be made for this event. The idea was put forward to E.W.S who in turn passed it forward to the Royal Household, and it was readily agreed.

By Spring 2002, with the event only weeks away, Brell sought permission from EWS to release limited information to the volunteers at the West Shed who would have to know about the job in order to prepare the locomotive and coach. So it was at a Trustees meeting in April that Brell, chairing it, announced under AOB that the locomotive was to haul the Royal Train. With only three Trustees already knowing, there was a stunned silence. The decision immediately came to the fore about who would be in the support crew, and, as it would have been in railway service, the list was drawn up based upon seniority and experience.

A West Shed team lead by Eddie Dolby and John Riley started work in April making the headboard, initially a wooden template, followed by the real thing and, after several trial fits, the design and the details of the mounting arrangement were finalised and the headboard duly made. This was painted, in full colour, by Tim Baker of Ashbourne, who annually had painted the famous footballs used in the Ashbourne Royal Shrovetide Football game held in the town, a local custom in which play had been started by royalty in the past. Tim was also very knowledgeable on the fine detail of heraldic matters, and was therefore able to produce the detail and correct

Lamp maker, John Beesley of Berkhamsted, fabricates the special lamps for the Royal Train. At the time of manufacture he was unaware of the role destined for the lamps. (PRCLT Collection)

The lamp presented to Her Majesty The Queen. The front bezel and locking pin handles were all made from brass. The locomotive number is in the style of that on the cabside and Camden was the home depot of 6233 and that of many Royal Train locomotives in steam days. (Howard Routledge)

The side with the special plaque commemorating the event. The lamp is now mounted permanently on the wall of the Queens Saloon, just inside The Principal Door. (Howard Routledge)

colours, and thus the finished article was completed, an amazing piece of local craftsmanship.

Brian Radford had also established that British Railways London Midland Region had kept a special set of locomotive headlamps at Camden, and later at Willesden, for Royal Train duties. A new set of four was thus ordered from John Beesley, lamp manufacturer of Berkhamsted, but the order was for two pairs, thus disguising the number of four that easily could have let the secret out - four lamps being the Royal Train headcode, the only train to use such a combination.

It had been the provisional plan for The Royal Household to announce the event at the beginning of 2002 - The Golden Jubilee Year. However the events of 11th September, 2001 in the U.S.A. had changed any such thinking as Britain went on to high alert with planes being diverted round London on approaches into Heathrow airport and members of the Royal Family and Government being given additional security.

As the months of 2002 slipped by there seemed to be no sign of any announcement. Further complications in this matter came to light when the Trust was briefed that since the event was to be in Wales, it would be for the Assembly for Wales to handle all publicity.

The 'Steam Railway' magazine editorial staff were becoming very anxious as first March came and went and April arrived. It was becoming clear to all the railway parties involved that the 'secret' could not be held much longer as the nearer the date came, the more personnel had to be involved, and the ability to contain the information therefore diminished. A Press Release was finally made on April 23rd, but only after a number of discussions between Matthew Golton and the Royal Household.

The immediate response received by the Trust was overwhelming, and the Trust's Internet website went into overdrive as visitor numbers shot up from 3000 per month, eventually peaking at over 60,000 per month.

6233 carried out her last main line duty before the event on Saturday 11th May with a special from Leicester to Scarborough and back, the train covering some 310 miles in one day and hauled by 'DUCHESS OF SUTHERLAND' throughout. The locomotive returned to Butterley and the West Shed in the early hours of 12th May.

A comprehensive plan of cleaning, preparation and maintenance was in place to start on 13th May. Both full time staff and volunteers started the intensive programme in order to have the locomotive and its support coach resplendent for the day.

Support Coach No 99041 was re-painted in LMS Crimson Lake livery with black and yellow lining, and although not historically accurate, it was viewed by David Ward and Brell Ewart to be the best compromise, since the Royal Plum livery colour of the Royal Train was not permissible. Although not historically correct, the Crimson Lake livery was chosen since it matched the livery of the locomotive,

and certainly married much better with the Royal Train than the Carmine and Cream livery would ever have done.

As with all quality painting, it is the preparation that takes the time. This support coach had last been repainted in 1993, and for only four years of that time had it been stabled outside. The bodywork was therefore reasonable, but as with all restoration projects, the 'while we are at it' syndrome began to take over. All the internal finishes were cleaned or refurbished, all brass door handles were removed for burnishing, and the bogies were steam cleaned.

Bob Timmins, specialist coach painter and signwriter, and his son started work on Monday 19th May on 99041, with a further order also to paint the trust's L.M.S. Director's Saloon No. 6320 in the same livery at the same time. This vehicle was not needed for the Royal Train but was needed to go to Crewe for subsequent work following 11th June, and its then 'aircraft blue' livery needed to be changed anyway. The weeks from mid May saw intense activity on these coaches, with as many as 12 volunteers working on them at any one time.

On Sunday 26th May an evening meeting in a hotel at Crewe took place with the Royal Train's footplate crews rostered for the job from EWS, Traction Inspectors, Senior EWS staff and the 6233 support crew all gathering for a full briefing session on the whole event. Matthew Golton, General Manager Rail Express Systems, ran through the locomotive movements and times. Emphasis was placed on the need to control the locomotive fire, and everyone was advised so that they had a clear understanding that there was to be no blowing off and no black smoke! In fact smoke was a factor about which the Royal Train staff were particularly anxious, since the whole train was fitted with air conditioning, and any smoke in the air intakes of this system would set off the alarms in the train. A Special Royal Train Notice was to be posted in all parts of the train on the day to explain this. The shunting operations required at

The locomotive crews, support crew and EWS managers who managed the operation on June 11th.

Back Row left to right:-
Steve Wainright (EWS Traincrew Manager), Eddie Williamson (Fireman a.m.), Bob Hart (Fireman p.m.),
Graham Massey (Driver a.m.), Mick Boothby (PRCLT), John Riley (PRCLT), Bob Morrison (Driver p.m.),
Barrie Wheatley (PRCLT), Eric Riley (PRCLT), Howard Routledge (PRCLT).

Front Row left to right:-
Gareth Jones (Traction Inspector p.m.), Jim Smith (Traction Inspector a.m.), Matthew Golton (General Manager R.E.S.),
David Brown (Special Services Manager, R.E.S.), Peter Davies (Reserve Traction Inspector), Brell Ewart (Chairman, PRCLT).
(Howard Routledge)

The Trust's team of engineers, fitters and cleaners stand alongside the locomotive on Sunday 9th June. Every one of them played a part in the preparation and cleaning of the locomotive and coach during the weeks leading up to June. (Howard Routledge)

The EWS locomotive crew for the morning run:- Traction Inspector Jim Smith, Driver Graham Massey and Fireman Eddie Williamson. (Howard Routledge)

Valley for 6233 and the support coach were explained together with the coupling up to the Royal Train at Holyhead. After some 4 hours the meeting closed with every individual left in no doubt as to what was expected on the day. Again the need for confidentiality was emphasised.

In the West Shed, the preparations were now on-going on a 7 days per week and 12 hours plus per day, basis. The locomotive was given a full boiler examination out of steam and then in steam, and the mandatory annual mechanical two day exam was brought forward to 21st and 25th May. This was being done so that the authorities could be assured every possible opportunity was being taken to ensure that the locomotive was in the best mechanical, boiler condition and overall presentation possible for the day.

Monday 3rd June saw the coaches now painted in their new livery and lined out, and in the case of the saloon the LMS style armorial devices being applied. All wheel tyres were white-wall painted in order to match Royal Train Standards, and activity was intense on all fronts.

On Wednesday 5nd June, Keith Nicholson from Interfleet Technology carried out a full diagnostic check on the air brake system of the locomotive followed by an in-steam check of the system on Sunday 9th June.

Saturday 8th June brought a respite in what had been prolonged bad weather and for a few hours the sun shone. 6233 was pulled out by the Class 03 Shunter and posed on the West Shed frontage for photographs with the team of volunteers which had now spent hundreds of hours preparing and cleaning her, prior to the fire being lit at 5 pm.

Fire raisers Howard Routledge and Brell Ewart returned to the locomotive at 06.00 hours on Sunday the 9th June in order to raise steam in time for examinations starting at 11.00 hours. The weather, that had started fine and sunny, deteriorated in the afternoon to heavy, incessant rain and so the two coaches, both of which still had areas of wet paint and varnish, remained inside the shed, being shunted to different shed roads between the bursts of heavy rain. With

The official Royal Train timing sheets for the journey from Euston through to Crewe and beyond covering 10th June, 11th June and 12th June. Copies of these were distributed to everyone in the train. Note the Duchess of Sutherland logo on the bottom left.
(Royal Train, PRCLT Collection)

examinations complete, the support crew assembled in the evening with all preparations complete.

At 05.00 hours on Monday morning 9th June, 6233 moved forward propelling coaches 99041 and 6320 in order to top up the tender from the water crane located at Swanwick Junction. With the EWS Traction Inspector Gareth Jones, Driver Ray Poole, Fireman Tony Lewellyn and the P.R.C.L.T. support crew having boarded, the

short train eased out of Swanwick Junction and ran down to Ironville. Following the operation of the ground frame, 6233 moved round the curve and onto the Erewash Valley Down Fast line. With Signal TT97 showing green 6233 was reversed by Driver Ray Poole and the train set off towards Chesterfield and Barrow Hill tender first, where following running round, the formation was set for the journey to Crewe via Derby.

11th June 2002, 05.30 hours at Holyhead, and Duchess of Sutherland sets back on to the Royal Train.
(Mick Foster)

Through Chesterfield the two coach train ran on the Up Slow line and was passed by an early morning Virgin HST train bound for the West Country. Very few passengers, if any, would have realised they were passing the Royal Train engine of the morrow.

From Derby the train ran via North Staffs Junction, Stoke on Trent to Crewe station where David Ward boarded the train before it ran over to the Heritage Centre where coal was taken and coach 6320 was dropped from the formation. At 11.30 hours, with the sun shining 'DUCHESS OF SUTHERLAND', with 99041 behind, slipped out of the Heritage Centre and backed into Crewe Station to await the signal for the Chester line.

On leaving Crewe the next stop was the Holywell loop, where a ten minute stop was made to allow a local service to pass, before proceeding non-stop to Holyhead. Here the tender was replenished with water taken from the Sealink Hydrant on the Quayside, and 6233 then ran round 99041 and the short train set off, tender first, for Valley.

Security was evident for the first time as 6233 pulled into the Valley Nuclear Electric Sidings, where a small group of uniformed police witnessed the arrival. Three large bags of coal were loaded onto the tender by hiab from the waiting lorry to supplement that already in and to ensure that there was sufficient for the run the following day.

At Valley a complicated shunt was planned to turn both the locomotive and coach in order to have the formation of 6233 ready to leave tender first with 99041 attached to the front of the engine by its passenger end. After considerable debate and a reasonable amount of puzzled looks by un-informed members of the team, this move was completed promptly and efficiently by those with a clear understanding of what was required! The locomotive was then stabled by the fenced compound, and in bright sunlight the support crew then enjoyed tea and a birthday cake in celebration of Brell Ewart's birthday, it quite coincidentally being on the same day as the H.R.H. The Duke of Edinburgh's!

The RAF provided a spectacular flypast with planes regularly landing and taking off from nearby RAF Valley for the remaining hours of daylight whilst the support crew gave the final spit and polish to the locomotive and coach.

The fire raisers, Brell Ewart and Howard Routledge, again performed the early turn starting at 02.00 hours in readiness for a 03.18 hours. departure to Holyhead. As the early rays of dawn broke 'DUCHESS OF SUTHERLAND' slipped out of Valley Nuclear Electric Sidings and onto the Down Fast line to Holyhead where again, following a run round, the tender was topped up with water, this time from the coach watering pipes.

Meanwhile in London, Her Majesty The Queen and His Royal Highness, The Duke of Edinburgh, attended by The Countess of Airlie, Sir Robin Janvrin, Mrs Kay Brock, and Major James Duckworth-Chad had left Buckingham Palace by road at 22.45 hours on Monday 10th June. They had arrived at Euston and boarded the Royal Train at 23.00 hours with departure from Euston at 23.15 hours from where the train had run non-stop to Crewe where, after a three minutes stop, it ran on to Holyhead.

With the Royal train due into Holyhead at 05.00 hours 6233 eased up to a location adjacent to the signal box on the Up Fast line to await in silence the arrival of the Monarch. Two minutes early the Royal Train ran by and into Holyhead Station, and was then followed down the 1 in 75 falling gradient within minutes by 6233 and 99041.

With Her Majesty The Queen asleep in her Saloon, only two coaches away from where the coupling of the buckeye was taking place, the shunting move itself had been discussed many times by the individuals who now had to carry it out. As such everyone knew

The Royal Train Notice, copied to every one on The Royal Train on 11th June, explaining the difficulty that could arise with the on-train air conditioning. Both Her Majesty and His Royal Highness also had copies of this.
(Royal Train, PRCLT Collection)

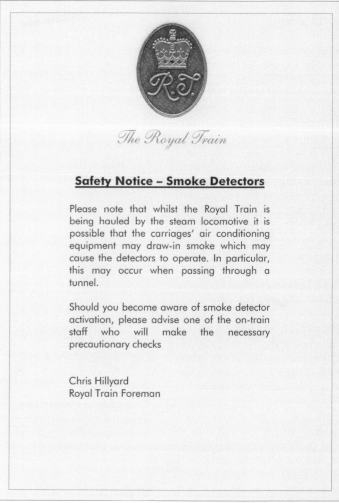

The Royal Train

Safety Notice – Smoke Detectors

Please note that whilst the Royal Train is being hauled by the steam locomotive it is possible that the carriages' air conditioning equipment may draw-in smoke which may cause the detectors to operate. In particular, this may occur when passing through a tunnel.

Should you become aware of smoke detector activation, please advise one of the on-train staff who will make the necessary precautionary checks

Chris Hillyard
Royal Train Foreman

what was required. Royal Train Officer, Norman Pattenden M.B.E., was in charge, resplendent in pinstriped suite, waistcoat with pocket watch with chain, English rose in his suit lapel, and bowler hat. After two very gentle attempts, with little momentum, to couple the buckeye ended in failure, the third and final kiss of the connections saw the buckeye couplings mate up and, following a brake test, the train then awaited departure. At 05.42 hours the starter signal arm was raised and Driver Graham Massey opened the regulator. The train inched slowly and quietly out of the station and under the road bridge at the end of Platform 1, the start being in fact so smooth that Royal Train staff commentated later that they did not realise that they were on the move. With slow beats 'DUCHESS OF SUTHERLAND' eased the train over the crossovers and started up the 1 in 75 gradient - so slowly in fact that a few anxious glances crossed the support coach as everyone sat in silence witnessing history being made as the Royal Train returned to steam traction again after a lapse of 35 years.

The anxiety was short lived however as, with regulator opened and sanders on, 6233 lifted the 501 ton train and accelerated, as only 'Princess Coronation' class locomotives can, up the incline. The speed went rapidly up to 50 mph before Driver Massey shut off to slow down for entry into Valley Nuclear Electric Siding. Speed slowed to walking pace as the train ran slowly in and then round the sharp curve before coming to a stop where a Railtrack flagman diligently stood to attention displaying a yellow flag fully unfurled. The train glided imperceptibly to a stand exactly in the position required.

The early morning sun was now bathing the whole of Anglesey and Holy Island as the electricity and water systems were re-connected to the support coach and tender in order for the train to leave some hours later with the locomotive batteries charged and the tender full.

The security presence was now very visible, and all foot traffic on the site was kept to an absolute minimum in order to not disturb either Her Majesty or His Royal Highness who were only two coach lengths from where activity was taking place around the locomotive.

The relief crew of Inspector Gareth Jones, Driver Bob Morrison, and Fireman Bob Hart along with Brian Radford and David Ward arrived at 08.15 hours and, after showing their passes, were allowed through the two security checks. The relief crew were to travel 'on the cushions' to Bangor where they would take over from Traction Inspector Jim Smith, Driver Graham Massey, and Fireman Eddie Williamson.

As the hours and minutes ticked by, police activity became very visible, and a few photographers could been seen peering through the perimeter gate some 50 yards away. That would be as near as they were to get to this stabling point!

With departure set for 09.18 the Class 47 diesel electric No. 45772 'WINDSOR CASTLE' started into life at 09.00 hours and the fire in 'DUCHESS OF SUTHERLAND' was 'brought round.' After the 09.19 hours Holyhead to Euston express had passed, running slightly late, it was 09.24 before the Class 47 slowly eased the train towards the Signal Box and then out on to the Up Fast Line. With 'DUCHESS OF SUTHERLAND' just behind the Valley Station starting signal the train came to a stand to await time. A small group of local residents, having become aware of this very special event, stood on the platform adorned with Union flags.

Several minutes late, at 09.32, the signal was at last raised and with a blast on the Stanier hooter, 6233 moved the train off. The need to arrive at Llanfairpwll Station at 10.00 hours precisely had been highlighted to everyone and the timings for the section between Valley and Llanfairpwll were not generous. Armed with this knowledge Driver Graham Massey, with Inspector Jim Smith

standing behind him, needed no further encouragement to get 6233 up to speed. The train set off, accelerating with every beat, and with 'DUCHESS OF SUTHERLAND' now in full cry, the train swept past RAF Valley and the adjacent golf course where early morning golfers on the links all raised their clubs in a Royal salute to the Royal Train and the passing monarch - a truly fine sight. Speed continued to increase as the train swept through Rhosneiger and Ty Croes on the rising gradient, the beat of the locomotive in perfect syncopation with the white steam and smoke being whipped off the chimney top by the moderate cross wind. Speed continued to rise as the train tore through Bodorgan Tunnels and then down the mile-long falling gradient of 1 in 98 before easing out in the valley and on to the rising gradient of 1 in 97. It was clear to all that the arrival time of 10.00 at Llanfairpwll Station was now going to be achieved as Gaerwen was passed in fine style, and with less than two miles to go before Llanfairpwll Station, the brakes came on and the train slowed at 09.50. An early arrival looked imminent, so speed slowed to almost walking pace as gently the station with the longest name in the world slipped slowly past. The thousand strong crowd on the station forecourt burst into a loud cheer and the band struck up with a resounding rendition of 'Men of Harlech'. Driver Massey brought the train to a gentle stand once more with the engine cab alongside a Railtrack Flagman, with his yellow flag unfurled, a minute and a half before time.

Mr Chris Hillyard, The Royal Train Manager, quickly had the Principal's door of the Queen's Saloon open and stood with head bowed as first Her Majesty The Queen and then His Royal Highness, The Duke of Edinburgh, alighted onto the platform. They were greeted by The Lord Lieutenant of Gwynedd, Professor Eric

06.30 hours, and following the arrival at the Valley Nuclear Electric Sidings 6233, still attached to the Royal Train is kept quiet, thus allowing Her Majesty and His Royal Highness to have breakfast before the departure for Llanfairpwll. (Mick Foster)

Driver Graham Massey accelerates Duchess of Sutherland hard to recover some of the lost minutes as the Royal Train passes RAF Valley. (John Stiles)

At Holyhead the Royal Train Manager Chris Hillyard (right) and Deputy Manager Peter Richardson, both resplendent in Royal Train blazers, pose alongside 6233. (Mick Foster)

Royal Train Officer, Norman Pattenden MBE. A career railwayman of note, Norman was later to say that June 11th was one of the most memorable days he had ever had with the Royal Train. (Howard Routledge)

The Royal Train running through Bangor Station. (E.N.Kneale)

Sunderland, who presented The Deputy Lord Lieutenant and other local dignitaries. The Royal Party then left the Station by car for the fifteen minute drive to Beaumaris Castle where a twenty one gun salute was fired to mark the occasion.

Meanwhile back at Llanfairpwll Station at 10.10 hours 'DUCHESS OF SUTHERLAND' whistled up and eased the train away. The B.B.C. Royal Corespondent, Jenny Bond, and her cameraman were now on the footplate filming a sequence for the B.B.C. One O'clock Lunchtime News Bulletin.

At 10.16, five minutes early, the train eased gently into the centre road at Bangor station where the B.B.C. staff were assisted down and escorted to the Up Platform. Now bathed in bright sunshine the train stood posed for photographers and public alike to enjoy the spectacle.

With a red flashing tail lamp having replaced the special set of

The train sweeps majestically through Bangor en route for Llandudno Junction. (Martin Welch)

Royal Train headlamps on 6233, the Class 47 diesel No 47787 'WINDSOR CASTLE' took the train back on the journey to Holyhead at 10.52 with 6233 now at the rear, and arrived five minutes early at 11.35 back into Platform 1 at Holyhead. The First North Western train company had extended the coach watering hoses in the sidings at Holyhead and two of these were fed into the tender of 6233 to replenish the 1800 gallons used since departure from Valley Nuclear Sidings. The ashpan on 6233 was also cleaned out and the firegrate cleaned.

The Royal Train headlamps were now put back on the locomotive ready for the third leg of the journey, and unusually many of the Royal Train's on-board staff posed for photographs with the loco-

Above.
Along the scenic coastline at Llanfairfechan, 6233 makes easy work of the empty coaching stock movement towards Llandudno Junction. (Peter Fitton)

The P.R.C.L.T. staff pose with Royal Train Staff at Llandudno Junction.
Back row left to right:-
Howard Routledge, Mick Boothby, David Ward, Eric Riley, Brian Radford, Barrie Wheatley, John Riley.
Front row left to right:-
Norman Pattenden MBE (Royal Train Officer), Brell Ewart, and Chris Hillyard (Royal Train Manager.)
(John Stiles)

motive in the bright sunshine.

Departure time was set for 13.04 hours, but at 12.51 the signals were pulled off and 6233 whistled up and the train set off. With an easy time schedule the train took a leisurely pace, this being appreciated by the many hundreds of people lining the stations to witness the spectacle. At 14.02 the train eased into Llandudno Junction Platform 1 where yet again the Railtrack Flagman was positioned to indicate the exact stopping position. The permanent way in the Platform 1 precincts at Llandudno Junction had already been

searched by a line of police with sniffer dogs a few minutes before the train was due in from Holyhead, but later in the afternoon they would carry out the same exercise forward from the locomotive front buffer beam out to where the platform loop line joins the Down Fast line by the overbridge east of the station. Crowd barriers were in place down the centre of the full length of the platform at Llandudno Junction, with a press pen adjacent to the locomotive. Several of the volunteers from the West Shed had made the journey by road to Llandudno Junction and along with about a hundred

Second group of those responsible for the performance of 6233 on the day. Back row left to right:- Driver Bob Morrison, Howard Routledge, Mick Boothby, Inspector Gareth Jones, Matthew Golton, Eric Riley, Barrie Wheatley, John Riley, Fireman Bob Hart. Front Row :- David Ward, Brell Ewart, Brian Radford. (John Stiles)

members of the public enjoyed the spectacle of the locomotive awaiting the arrival of their Monarch.

The two hour lay-over allowed for a final wipe down of the locomotive, and yet again many photographs were taken. The staff from the Royal Train took full advantage of this and group photographs were taken of the Royal Household staff, the Royal Train Staff, the Catering Staff as well as the support crew, together with The Royal Train Manager, Chris Hillyard, and the Royal Train Officer, Norman Pattenden, M.B.E. Members of the public who were on the platform at this early time were treated to this flurry of activity and clearly enjoyed the spectacle.

Her Majesty The Queen was due to arrive in the station forecourt at 16.15 hours, and as the clock moved ever closer to this time excitement grew as a police helicopter circled overhead indicating the imminent arrival of the Royal Party. The presentation line formed up and Norman Pattenden made a last minute check to ensure everyone was lined up and ready.

The Queen and Prince Philip now came into view walking down the platform, and as the Queen made her way across to the general public, where a number of school children were cheering and waving their union flags, The Duke started chatting to David Ward and Brian Radford. The Duke asked about the ownership of the locomotive and commented on the excitement of the run from Valley to Llanfairpwll that morning and his surprise at the speed the train had travelled. Her Majesty then walked across to join the Duke and shook hands with Brian and David, moving down the line to meet the other members of the support crew, Howard Routledge, Barrie Wheatley and John Riley lined up alongside the support coach. Moving down the platform to the line-up alongside 'DUCHESS OF

Her Majesty The Queen's dresser and assistant dresser from the Royal Household, enjoy a visit to the footplate during the lay-over at Llandudno Junction. (John Stiles)

Staff from a variety of organisations come together as a special team to operate the Royal Train when it is out on its journeys. Here catering staff and stewards from Virgin Railways and Rail Gourmet pose for a group photograph with Royal Household staff. (John Stiles)

Her Majesty The Queen walks down the platform at Llandudno Junction accompanied by The Lord Lieutenant of Gwynedd, Professor Eric Sunderland. (Graham Allen)

SUTHERLAND' herself, Mr Paul Ruston, representing First North Western Train Operating Company was then presented to Her Majesty, followed by the English Welsh and Scottish Railway staff comprising Mr Matthew Golton, General Manager, Rail Express Systems, E.W.S. Traction Inspector Gareth Jones, Driver Bob Morrison, and Fireman Bob Hart. Her Majesty again commented how fast the train seemed to go earlier in the day. His Royal Highness, The Duke of Edinburgh, followed the Queen with individuals being presented by the Deputy Lord-Lieutenant of Gwynedd, Mr Alun Evans. Eric Riley was then presented to the Queen by the Lord Lieutenant followed by Mick Boothby and finally Brell Ewart

Brell presented the Queen with the special commemorative headlamp, complete with its brass plaque and crowns, and explained that it was a fully operational working lamp that had been hand-

made for the day. Her Majesty said how very pleased she was with the gift and handed it to her Equerry, Major James Duckworth-Chad, who was standing behind Her Majesty. The Duke then shook hands

Brell Ewart presents Her Majesty with the special commemorative headlamp. (Gwyn Roberts)

Her Majesty chats with members of the 6233 support crew. (Gwyn Roberts)

After having viewed the front of locomotive with the Royal Train headboard and lamps, Brell Ewart accompanies Her Majesty back along the platform. The Queen was most impressed and interested about the story of the headboard and lamps. (Graham Allen)

with Brell Ewart following which Brell then invited Her Majesty and His Royal Highness to view the front of the locomotive. Brell explained to them that the headboard had been made from details of those used in 1953 at the time of Her Majesty's Coronation, and that it had been hand painted. The Duke was most impressed with the array of headlamps and Brell explained that they were all working lamps and were in the special formation used only as a Royal Train code, with one at the top of the smokebox and three along the top of the buffer beam. The Duke commented that a lot of work must have been done to get the locomotive so clean. The Royal party then walked back along the platform, again stopping adjacent to David Ward and Brian Radford, and the Duke asked about the support coach, what it was used for and also where the coal on the locomotive came from. The Royal Party then proceeded along the Platform and boarded the train.

Although an on-schedule 16.25 departure was possible it was decided by Railtrack Control in conjunction with The Royal Train Officer, Mr. Norman Pattenden, that departure would be delayed until 16.45, and so a few minutes was available to make up the fire. Fireman Bob Hart got to work with the shovel and filled the back of the firebox in readiness. A timetabled First North Western Train left in the Up direction at 16.35, and with only minutes now to go before departure, the blower was opened, much to the delight of the

assembled crowd as a cloud of black smoke gushed from the chimney as the steam draught from the blower cleared the soot build-up in the boiler tubes that had accumulated during the two hour lay over. Within seconds this had gone and the Driver awaited the signal.

At 16.42 the signal was green and with a long hoot on the whistle, the regulator was eased open and very slowly 6233 eased the train away. On a slight falling gradient 'DUCHESS OF SUTHERLAND' moved the train smoothly out down the loop and rejoined the Up Fast line. With the regulator now opened wide the four-cylindered Stanier pacific started her work.

Crowds of onlookers cheered as the train passed underneath the over-bridge lined with hundreds of well wishers, many waving union flags, and speed increased as the train accelerated away. With the regulator now fully open the cut-off was wound back and, with speed still increasing, the train tore through Colwyn Bay Station with whistle blowing to the excited crowd. Many railway enthusiasts had gathered on the Old Colwyn section to see the train attack the short 1 in 100 gradient, and they were not disappointed as 6233 tore past. Every bridge and vantage point was crowded with people watching the magnificent spectacle of the Sovereign's Train being hauled by a top class express steam locomotive.

At Llysfaen the regulator was eased for the run down through Abergele where crowds lined the route shoulder to shoulder on the station approaches. Colwyn Bay and Prestayn Stations were well filled with the public witnessing this extraordinary spectacle. None of them could have been in any doubt that this was the Monarch's Train adorned as it was with its magnificent headboard. Speed was reduced through Rhyl station, where crowds again thronged the station platforms, but was soon re-established through Mostyn and Holywell Junction, where there was now no need for the train to go into the loop as had been the original pathing plan. Connah's Quay and Mold were passed with many union flags in evidence before Chester Racecourse where speed was eased for the long sweeping curve into Chester as the train entered the city. Through the centre roads at Chester station at 17.41, now just one minute early, the locomotive, now at long cut off, eased the train away from the station to the salute of a passing multiple unit.

The locomotive was then given more steam to take the train on the rising gradient of the next ten miles to Beeston Castle before the coal shovelling ceased and the mini-skyscrapers of Crewe now came into sight as the Royal Train ran past the steelworks and then alongside Crewe Works where 'DUCHESS OF SUTHERLAND' had originally been built.

The Royal Party walks back along the platform before boarding the train. (Mick Foster)

With Traction Inspector Gareth Jones keeping his diligent eye on the watch, the train drew round the curve on the Chester line, past the Crewe Heritage Centre and rumbled across the many points and crossovers into Crewe Station. The train's arrival was into an almost deserted Platform 12 and was witnessed only by a few yellow vested British Transport Policemen together with several railway personnel, including David Brown, the E.W.S. Special Services Manager who had personally spent more time planning the event than any other person, and who had now come to witness the finale. Slowly the train ran down the platform and came, almost imperceptibly to a stand at 18.12 and 30 seconds against the booked time of 18.14.

During the layover at Crewe, Her Majesty came to the principal door in her saloon and expressed her delight at the steam haulage experience and the obvious pleasure it had given to the many spectators lining the route. Matthew Golton, General Manager Rail Express Systems, was personally thanked by Her Majesty.

As the support coach and locomotive were promptly uncoupled from the train, Chris Hillyard, The Royal Train Manager, came forward and passed on Her Majesty's thanks to the support crew and locomotive crew from EWS, and presented Brell Ewart with a commemorative Royal Train Plaque recording this most remarkable event.

Within minutes 6233 and support coach 99041 departed to turn via the Gresty Lane and Basford Hall triangle, where, after a number of phone calls from the footplate staff, the signalboxes responded with speed and 'DUCHESS OF SUTHERLAND' was soon re-entering Crewe Station on the adjacent road to the Royal Train that by now had the Class 47 47798 'PRINCE WILLIAM' diesel locomotive on the front, awaiting departure time.

With a salute on the whistle to announce her arrival, 6233 ran very slowly past the Queen's Saloon. Her Majesty came to the window and, with the saloon window curtains drawn back, gave private thanks to the footplate crew. She was joined by His Royal Highness, The Duke of Edinburgh, from the droplight window of his saloon standing adjacent, who leaned out and again, with a huge smile, clearly indicated his immense enjoyment. With a toot on the whistle 6233 then moved slowly off, being watched by the Duke from the open window until she had disappeared into the cathedralesque arches of Crewe Station. The locomotive then crossed over to Crewe Heritage Centre to be met by the jubilant staff from the centre.

The footplate crew climbed down, and the somewhat emotional and informal group stood together and revelled for few precious moments at the feat they had accomplished as a team. Matthew Golton and Brell Ewart thanked everyone, the EWS team departed and the support crew started the disposal of the locomotive and coach.

Thus ended a most remarkable and historic day - a day that most people with any morsal of railway interest would have regarded as near impossible or at best highly unlikely to happen. For those involved there was the pride of knowing that the job had been done in the very best traditions, and knowing that in the 160 years of Royal Train Travel, no locomotive could have run better or been turned out looking finer.

In the days following the 11th June The Princess Royal Class Locomotive Trust was advised by Chris Hillyard that Her Majesty had requested that the lamp she had been presented with be mounted in her Saloon, No 2903, close to the Principal Doors.

Later that week a letter was received by the Trust Chairman, Brell Ewart, from Mrs Kay Brock, the Assistant Private Secretary to Her Majesty, expressing the sincere thanks of Her Majesty, and His Royal Highness for a most enjoyable day, and thanking the Trust for all the hard work that had gone in to the preparation They both wished the Trust well for the future.

Duchess of Sutherland is eased out of Llandudno Junction by Driver Bob Morrison as a loud cheer went up from the crowd of well wishers on the platform. Her Majesty witnessed the departure from inside the Principal Door. (John Stiles)

Running down the loop at Llandudno Junction Duchess of Sutherland gathers speed before crossing onto the main line. Hundreds of spectators gathered on the overbridge and embankment at the eastern end of the station to witness the departure. (Martin Welch)

6233 hurries the Royal Train through Abergele. Crowds had waited for several hours to await its passing. All rose to their feet to cheer as the train Royal Train swept by and were acknowledged by Driver Bob Morrison and Inspector Gareth Jones from the footplate.
(Arnold Battson)

Extract from The Court Circular for 11th June 2002

"Buckingham Palace 11th June 2002."

" ...The Queen and The Duke of Edinburgh afterwards viewed the steam locomotive Duchess of Sutherland, at Llandudno Junction, were received by Mr Matthew Golton, (General Manager Rail Express Services, English Welsh and Scottish Railways) and Mr Paul Rushton (General Manager Merseyside and North Wales First North Western) and met the crew and volunteers of The Princess Royal Class Locomotive Trust."

Photographs of the Royal train headed by 'DUCHESS OF SUTHERLAND' were used in a number of national newspapers, with articles in all the enthusiast railway magazines over the following days and weeks.

This very special and highly prestigious event not only showed the very best that Britain's railways were still capable of achieving but also what the railway preservation movement at its finest could aspire to half a century after it took its first faltering steps.

The Princess Royal Class Locomotive Trust in conjunction with The Royal Train, EWS, and Alstom had arranged for a team of video cameramen, led by Mr. Jeremy English, to film the event. In the subsequent weeks this film was edited and a complete story of the day reproduced on video for sale to the public. Copies of these were sent to Buckingham Palace and to all those taking part.

The Royal Train stands at Euston 13th June 2002 on completion of the Golden Jubilee Tour of Wales having brought Her Majesty The Queen and His Royal Highness The Duke of Edinburgh non-stop from Cardiff. Royal Train Manager Chris Hillyard holds the presentation headlamp, having had instructions from Her Majesty to permanently affix the lamp in her personal Saloon No. 2903. (Mick Foster)

This appendix comprises reproductions of the complete L.M.S. and B.R. Service History Cards of 'Duchess of Sutherland', which were kept at C.M.E. Headquarters, plus the third Engine Record Card as an example of the records kept at the home depot, and which went with the locomotive whenever it was transferred to a new shed.

Repairs were divided into two categories, scheduled or casual, and under these headings were then further sub-divided into heavy or light. On the Engine History and Record Cards for 'Duchess of Sutherland' the following codes are used:-

L.C.	Light Casual.	N.C.	Not Classified.
E.O.	Engine Only.	L.S.	Light Service.
H.S.	Heavy Service.	T.R.O.	Tender Repair Only.
L.O.	Light Overhaul.	H.O.	Heavy Overhaul.
L.I.	Light Intermediate.	H.G.	Heavy General.

Heavy repairs depended on the condition of the boiler and tyres with general repairs being carried out at pre-determined intervals depending on the mileage run or days in traffic. For the 'Princess Coronation' class the average mileage between general repairs varied from about 191,000 in 1940-5 to 205,000 in the period 1946-50 and 192,500 in 1951-9, very much better than for the 'Princess Royal' class which in the 1946-50 period had gone down to around 139,000 miles run. A service repair would be carried out at some time between these general repairs, and there was on average about 1.5 of these service or intermediate repairs in that period, although the last five engines, with their manganese axleboxes, tended to average only 1.2 as a result.

Depending on the amount of work listed on the Shopping Proposal Form, which was sent in from the home depot, the Shopping Controller would categorise the level of repair in advance of the locomotive arriving on works. Mileage records were considered together with any previous repair work carried out, and this enabled the works to maintain a controlled workload and also ensure that not too many locomotives of the same class were out of traffic at any one time.

Service or casual repairs could fall into any category - light or heavy - with casual repairs being done on an 'ad hoc' basis to correct some defect or damage. Repairs fell into the heavy category if they involved any one of the following items of work:-

Re-boilering.
Boiler to be removed from the frames for whatever reason.
New tyres on four or more wheelsets.

or any two of the following items:-

New Cylinders.
New axles.
Re-tubing boiler.
Turning the tyres on wheelsets.
Re-fitting axleboxes.
Overhaul of motion or brakework.
Boiler repair whilst still in the frames involving not less than 15% of the stays.

At a general repair the boiler was always taken out of the frames. On all types of locomotive the maximum time between these was about five years in order to comply with Board of Trade regulations relating to steam locomotive boilers. At a heavy general repair the intention was to return the locomotive to as nearly 'as new' condition as possible. In the case of the 'Princess Coronation' class a generally repaired boiler from another member of the class, and already in stock, was always fitted to enable the locomotive to be out in traffic once again with the minimum of delay.

A light repair involved work undertaken in the following areas:-

New cylinders.
New axles.
Replacing more than 50% of the boiler tubes.
Turning the tyres on four or more wheels.
Refitting axleboxes.
Overhauling motion.
Fitting a patch to the boiler.
Re-lagging the boiler.
Fitting four or more axleboxes.
Welding, patching of straightening frames.
Re-boring cylinders and re-facing ports.
Removal and repair of tanks.

Apart from random running repairs, so far as daily maintenance was concerned depots carried out two groups of standard examinations as laid down in the MP11 booklet. The first was based upon the time in traffic and comprised:-

'X' day and 'Boiler Full' examination carried out every 6 to 8 days.
Washout and 'X' day examination every 12 to 16 days

And multiples of these intervals at 3 to 5 weeks, 7 to 9 weeks and 9-15 weeks. The 'X' day examination schedule for Stanier Pacifics listed about a dozen or so items to be tested and examined to try to ensure that unexpected failures did not occur whilst in traffic. The remaining timed exams related mainly to boilers and associated steam fittings.

It was policy to wash out boilers when cold, so they were allowed to cool slowly by controlled flushing with cold water. The boilersmith could then carry out his internal examination and any repairs or caulking of seams done before the boiler was re-filled with cold water and steam pressure raised slowly over time.

The second group of repairs was based on mileage run, were related mainly to components subject to wear and tear, and were done at 5-6,000 miles up to 15-18,000 miles without dismantling except in the case of the big-ends which were stripped down every 10-12,000 miles to check on their condition and for any signs of the white-metal cracking or lifting off the bearing surface. Piston rings were changed every 20-24,000 miles on the 'Princess Coronation' class, since they were unlikely to run up to the No. 6 examination, done at 30-36,000 miles, at which the cylinders were opened up and all rings renewed anyway.

In all of this the Mechanical Foreman at a depot had a heavy overall responsibility to keep an eye on all of his locomotives and ensure that the overall mechanical condition of them was good, so that when he submitted his shopping proposal, usually eight months after a classified repair for Pacifics, when scrutinised by the Shopping Bureau they could ensure that it was an accurate reflection of a locomotives condition, backed up if necessary by their Inspector if there was any doubt, before they acceded to the request.

LMS **ENGINE HISTORY CARD.**

DUCHESS OF SUTHERLAND   E.R.O. 3666
O.P. 4/7 20.1.58

PASSENGER TENDER ~~SHUNTING~~ SUPERHEATED
~~FREIGHT TANK NON-SUPERHEATED~~
NON-STREAMLINED.   CLASS M.P. 7₈ (1·51) WHEEL TYPE 4.6.2 NAME OF TYPE *PRINCESS (CORONATION)* C.M.E. COSTING GROUP No. 46

ENGINE NUMBER **6233** **46233**

EMPTY WEIGHT 98.7 WORKING WEIGHT 108.2
CRONE PISTO 16/11/38 95.10 105.5

DIAMETER OF DRIVING WHEELS 6.9' WHEEL BASE (E. & T.) 62'-11 C.M.E. GL3648 73-10½ 27/11/58

CYLINDERS—No. 4 DIAMETER 16¾ STROKE 28 OVERALL LENGTH OVER BUFFERS (E. & T.) 73.93

BOILER.—E.S. REF No. 100 A DIVNL. REFCE. 1 A NS BELPAIRE OR ~~ROUND TOP~~ TAPER TUBES 129 – 40 STEEL ~~COPPER~~ BOILER PRESSURE 250 LBS.
CME GL364(3) 57/11/18 FIREBOX GRATE AREA 50 SQ. FT. TRACTIVE POWER AT 85% B.P. 40,000 LBS.

C.A. COSTS REFCE. No. 1F

BRAKES { VACUUM (~~DUMP EJECTOR~~) ~~WESTINGHOUSE~~ STEAM } VALVES { PISTON ~~SLIDE~~ } MOTION WALSCHAERT ~~STEPHENSON JOY~~ CARRIAGE WARMING { WITH ~~WITHOUT~~ } STEAM SANDING 18. 7. 38.

ALLOCATION (DIVISION & DATE) W

BUILT BY C R E W E. DATE BUILT

TOTAL COST £. T. 1509 PATTERNS, ETC. INCLUDED £. T. 29 SUPTCE. INCLUDED £. T. 43 CHARGED TO M. & R.E. MIN. No. 1276 DATE 27/10/37.

MILEAGE AT .... – TOTAL (LIFE) .... SINCE LAST GENERAL REPAIR ....
DATE TAKEN OUT OF TRAFFIC FOR BREAKING UP .... DATE ACTUALLY BROKEN UP .... SCRAP VALUE. GROSS £ .... COST OF CUTTING UP £ .... NET £ .... DATE CREDITED COMPLETE RENEWALS ....

NOTES :— Previously 6233, re-numbered 46233, W.E. 2.10.48.

{ 805002 ^
{ 65'291·1950

IMPROVEMENTS, ETC.

DATE	ORDER No. (N.W. &c.)	PARTICULARS	ALLOCATION CAPITAL £ s. d.	REVENUE £ s. d.	SUPTCE. £ s. d.	TOTAL £ s. d.
22.3.41	6865	X6802. Double Blast Pipe & Chimney	31. 3. 3	35. 18. 0		67. 1. 3
4.9.43	5/18 6817 & 5495.	Steel in place of Monel Stays	11. 0. 0	2. 10. 0	—	8. 10. 0
15.11.44	X7769	Imp. Type Piston Head & Rod P.E.3/10/43)	20. 0. 0	80. 0. 0	—	100. 0. 0
P.E.3/11/45	5495	Steel in place of Monel Stays. (20/5/45)	70. 0. 0			70. 0. 0
P.E.23/3/46	Misc.	Add'l. Clothing on Inside Cylinders.	28. 0. 0	—		28. 0. 0
P.E. 5/10/46	X8326	Smoke deflector plates (24/8)	44. 0. 0	1. 0. 0		45. 0. 0

TECHNICAL ALTERATIONS ETC.

RENEWAL PROVISION   (Section No............)   **TENDER**

YEAR	GROSS REP. COST PER TON	ENGINE (INCLUDING BOILER) GROSS REP. COST	NET RESIDUAL VALUE	NET REP. COST	BOILER GROSS REP. COST	NET RESIDUAL VALUE	NET REP. COST	ENGINE (EXC. BOILER) NET REP. COST	LIFE ENGINE (EXCLDG BOILER) Yrs.	BOILER Yrs.	ANNUAL PROVISION ENGINE (EXCLDG BOILER) £	BOILER £	PREFIX	No.	DATE ATTACHED
1938	91.20	8,709	526	8,183	2,574	219	2,355	5,828	30	10	194	236	LMS	9751	18.7.38.
1939	97.37	9,299	584	8,715	2,759	250	2509	6,206	30	10	207	251			
1940	113.44	10,834	723	10,111	3,229	315	2,914	7,197	"	"	240	291			
1941	119.11	11,375	743	10,632	2,992	309	2,683	7,949	"	"	265	268			
1942	128.70	12,291	745	11546	3160	319	2841	8705	"	"	290	284			
1943	126.72	12,102	741	11,361	3,367	314	3,053	8,308	"	"	247	305			
1944	132.68	12,671	713	11,958	3,431	290	3,141	8,817	"	"	294	314			
1945	130.55	12,467	634	11,833	3,410	233	3,177	8,656	"	"	289	318			
1946	137.31	13,116	674	12,442	3,554	285	3,269	9,173	"	"	306	327			

ORIGINAL COST		YEAR OF DEPRECIATION	STANDARD LIFE
ENGINE £	9,181.	First. 19......	30. YEARS
TENDER £	1,478.	Final. 1968.	
TOTAL £	10,659.		

ABOVE INFORMATION USED FOR DEPRECIATION PURPOSES ON AND FROM 1/1/48.

HT 10/8/47 ⌀ 40233

20.1.58 Engine Number 0233

BOILERS

			FITTED						TAKEN OUT					
DATE FITTED	REG'D No.	ECON. STOCK REF'CE	SELF. OR R.T.	VALUE Shell / Firebox	FROM	DATE NEW Shell / Firebox	MILEAGE Shell / Firebox		DATE RECOVERED	DISPOSAL	VALUE Shell Firebox		MILEAGE Shell / Firebox	
8·3·41	10305	100/MS	B		6234									
4·8·43	10284	100AMS	B		6235									
19·5·45	10297	100A NS	B		6234				28·10·47	Stock	608	304	560,567	560,567
28·10·47	10646	100AM	B	1136 758	6250	Mar 1943	241,411 241,411		19·5·50	Stock	866	354	402,959	402,959
19·5·50	10645	100AMS/M	B	745 696	6229	Aug 1943	442,872 442,872							

HEAVY AND LIGHT REPAIRS

BOILER
1 – NEW. 2 – CHANGED.
3 – LIFTED AND PUT BACK.
4 – REPAIRED ON FRAMES.

DATE Taken out of Traffic	Returned to Traffic	No. of Weekdays out of Traffic	Class of Repair	Mileage since previous heavy repair Heavy	Light	Boiler *	Repch. to Cost A/c	COST OF REPAIRS Total (K.R.O.3578)	Revenue Portion N.W. included	Net Engine (Excludg N.W. Rev. & Boiler)	Recov'd Boiler (Excludg T. & M.)	Total (Engine and Boiler)
10·7·39	27·7·39	16	L.S.		97,250							
1·7·40	16·7·40	14	L.S.		183,347							
5·2·41	8·3·41	28	H.G.	225,944		2						
5·6·41	18·6·41	12	T.R.O.									
25·3·42	22·4·42	25	L.S.		63,258							
16·10·42	13·11·42	26	H.S.	103,145								
2·4·43	4·8·43	32	H.G.	49,602		2						
5·1·44	10·2·44	32	L.O.		39,002							
16·5·44	2·6·44	16	TRO									
12·10·44	3·11·44	20	L.S.		87,658							
18·4·45	19·5·45	27	H.G.	120,418		2						
15·2·46	7·3·46	18	L.O.		47,421							
3·8·46	24·8·46	19	H.S.	80,970								

MILEAGE
SINCE PREVIOUS REPAIR | JAN. 1ST TO DATE SHOPPED

26·7·47	28·10·47	81	H.G.	64,098	36,303 35,766	2C	73	3,132	–	2150	496	2646
3·11·47	14·11·47	11	No repair	–	–	80c						
19·8·48	29·9·48	36	L.S.	59,249	52,605	4C	262	1,460	..	..	..	1,460
30·9·48	20·10·48	18	N.C.(Rep)	72	52,677 SINCE PREVIOUS GEN. OR INT.	4C	274	56				56
18·7·49	12·8·49	23	L.I.	55,700	40,371	4C	515	1,400	..	..	–	1,400
12·4·50	19·5·50	38 32	H.G.	46,599	16,544	2C	767	2090	–	1869		
14·3·51	10·4·51	22	L.C.	62,130	13,383	(C) C	100	1,028	–	–	–	1,028

DISTRICT ALLOCATION

SHED	DATE
Camden	13·7·38
Crewe N	20·5·44

STORED

SERVICEABLE or UNSERV.	DATE In	Out

SUMMARY

YEAR	REPAIRS EXPENDITURE Heavy	Light	Running Repairs & Shed Exams.	Total	COAL ISSUED Mileage	Tons	Lbs. per Mile	WEEKDAYS OUT OF SERVICE Heavy & Light Repairs	Running Repairs & Exams.	Other Purposes	Not Required	Stored Serviceable	Unserviceable	Total
1938	(36 wks)	–	33	–	13,108									
	(13 wks)				46,599	1063	51	2	20	–	1	–	–	23
1939					89,436			16	70	–	1	–	–	87
1940					82,750			14	71	–	1	–	–	85
1941					74,992			40	43	–	1	–	–	84
1942					54,163			50	63	–	1	–	–	114
1943					89,591			32	30	–	1	–	–	63
1944					60,844			68	41	–	1	–	–	110
1945					58,840			27	70	–	1	–	–	98
1946					68,680			37	38	–	–	–	–	75
1947					40,947			81	54	–	–	–	–	135
1948					67,934			54	36	–	1	–	–	91
1949					70,426			23	53	–	11	–	–	87
1950					65,291			32	38	–	12	–	–	82

805002A6 (JM12·47)

B.R.   ENGINE HISTORY CARD   ~~Selected List~~ 20.1.58   E.R.O. 3666.

PASSENGER ~~FREIGHT MIXED TRAFFIC~~   "DUCHESS OF SUTHERLAND."   ENGINE NUMBER
TENDER ~~TANK~~ SUPERHEATED ~~NON-SUPERHEATED~~   46233
~~DIESEL ELECTRIC MECHANICAL~~

| | | CLASS M.P. | 8 | WHEEL TYPE | 4-6-2 | NAME OF TYPE | CORONATION TAPER | |
| EMPTY WEIGHT | T. 95 - C. 10 | WORKING WEIGHT | T. 105 - C. 5 | DIAMETER OF DRIVING WHEELS | 6' 9" | WHEEL BASE (E. & T.) | 62' 11' | |

| | CYLINDERS.—No. 4 | DIAMETER 16½" | STROKE 28 | OVERALL LENGTH OVER BUFFERS (E. & T.) 73' 10½' | C.A. COSTS REFCE. No. 1F |

BOILER.—E.S. REF. No. 100 ANS   DIVN'L REFCE. 1A   BELPAIRE OR ROUND TOP 3   TUBES. No. 129 & 40   STEEL ~~COPPER~~   BOILER PRESSURE 250 lbs.   BR 3
              100 ANS/M
BEARINGS, ROLLER—(Make) —   FIREBOX GRATE AREA 50 SQ. FT.   TRACTIVE POWER AT 85% B.P. 40,000 lbs.

BRAKES   VACUUM (~~ADT~~ EJECTOR) ~~XXXXXXXXX~~ STEAM   VALVES {PISTON SLIDE}   MOTION {~~GARRATT~~ WALSCHAERT ~~XXXXXX~~ ~~JOY LENTZ~~}   CARRIAGE WARMING ~~WITH XXXX~~

SPECIAL FEATURES :— ~~Electric lights, Self-Cleaning Smokebox, Rocking Firegrate, Self-Emptying Ashpan, Manganese Steel Axlebox Liners."~~   **STEAM SANDING**   DATE BUILT July 18th 1938

BUILT BY CREWE   LOT No.   REN'L PROG.   AUTHORITY :—Min. No. 1276   DATE 27/10/37

MILEAGE AT 31.12.50 870,293 TOTAL (LIFE)   SINCE LAST GENERAL REPAIR

DATE TAKEN OUT OF TRAFFIC FOR BREAKING UP, ETC.   DATE ACTUALLY BROKEN UP

NOTES :—   W.W.E. 8.2.64
             LM 1963 Prog.

IMPROVEMENTS, ETC.

DATE	ORDER No. (N.W. &c.)	PARTICULARS	ALLOCATION CAPITAL £ s. d.	REVENUE £ s. d.		TOTAL £ s. d.
24.1.52	R.1013	3Kg. of tell-tale device to give warning of excessive heating on big ends	1-19-6	–	–	1-19-6
29.11.52	E.2194	Removal of Sandguns & equipt	12.7.10	11.0.10		1.4.0
PE2x1.53	E2212	Prov. of cast steel inside cyls. (Add. to PE 29.11.52) (Add. to PE.21.55)	351.6.4	345.13.8		703.0.0
PE.5.11.55	E.3329	Modified Piston for Cont. Blowdown valves	4.0	13.6		17.6
PE29.12.56	E3869	Fitting strengthened axlebox guides	36.8.6	134.18.9		171.7.3
PE2.11.57	R7x61	Prov. of Speed Indicators	126.16.10	24.15.2		151.12.0
PE.3.10.59	E.4983	A.T.C.	302.9.0			302.9.0

DISTRICT ALLOCATION

M.P. DEPOT	DATE	M.P. DEPOT	DATE
Crewe North	20.5.44		
CARLISLE U.	14.6.58		
CREWE N.	20.9.58		
~~Carlisle~~ U	24.60		
Crewe N.	23.4.60		
Camden	30.4.60		
Edge Hill	17.9.60		

ORIGINAL COST		YEAR OF DEPRECIATION		STANDARD LIFE
ENGINE £ 9,181	FIRST :—	19		30 Years
TENDER £ 1,478				
TOTAL £10,659	FINAL :—	1968		

Above information used for Depreciation purposes on and from 1/1/48.

TENDER

Prefix	No.	Date attached
LMS	9751 28.10	18.7.38

*= Includes Dep'tl. Admin   20.1.58   E.R.O. 3666 Back

CLASSIFIED REPAIRS (WORKSHOP AND M.P. DEPOT)
(✱ BOILER:—A=Changed, B=Lifted out and put back, C=Repaired on frames)

ENGINE NUMBER 46233

DATE		WEEKDAYS OUT OF SERVICE				Class of Repair	Where repaired	MILEAGE		✱ Boiler	Cost Form Serial No.	COST OF REPAIR (Excludes barrel and firebox where boiler repaired to Stores Order)	
Taken out of traffic	Returned to traffic	Waiting Repair Decision	Waiting Works	On Works	Total			Since previous General or Intermediate repair.	Jan. 1st to date shopped			TOTAL as per cost form £	Revenue Portion of New Works Included £
	19.5.50				32	H.G.	Crewe			A			
14.3.51	10.4.51	-	-	22	22	L.C.	"	62.130	13.383	C	100	1.028	-
19.12.51	24.1.52	-	5	24	29	H I	"	115,835	67,088	C	20	1,841	
15.10.52	29.11.52	4	3	32	39	H.G.	"	68,576 = 68,778		A	317	2,764	3.57
16.1.54	10.2.54	-	1	20	21	L.I.	"			C	47	*2,771	
14.3.55	7.5.55	8	5	33	46	H I	"			C	471	*2,791	-
31.8.55	3.10.55	-	6	22	28	L.C.(EO)	"		32,143	C	571	*1,540	1
25.12.55	30.1.56	2	3	23	28	L.C.(EO)	"		Nil	C	123	*1,140	-
25.10.56	8.12.56	1	8	29	38	H.G.	"	101,032	57,407	A	260	*3,954	135
10.10.57	23.10.57		9	2	11	N.C.(EO)	"	62,823	58,740				
24.2.58	12.4.58	-	2	38	40	H I	"	92,569	12,589				
1.8.59	26.9.59		4	44	48	H.G.	"	101,590	50,441				
18.1.61	21.2.61	-	5	24	29	H.I.	"	98,848	1,929				
10.7.61	24.8.61	8	6	25	39	L.C.(E.O)	"	22,364	23,997				

ANNUAL STATISTICS

Year	Mileage	Fuel Oil Issued (Gallons)	WEEKDAYS OUT OF SERVICE									
			CLASSIFIED REPAIRS				Running Repairs & Exams.	Not Required	STORED		Total
			Waiting Repair Decision	Waiting Works	On Works	Total			Serviceable	Unserviceable	
	870,593										
1951	67,088		-	5	25	30	61	-	-	-	91
1952	74,461		4	3	53	60	41	-	-	-	101
1953	90,220		-	-	-	-	61	-	-	-	61
1954	76,890		-	1	20	21	39	2	-	-	62
1955	51,530		10	13	55	78	26	4	-	-	104
1956	61,490		1	9	52	62	46	2	-	-	110
1957	75,897		-	-	-	-	66	1	-	-	67
1958	63,439			2	38	40	39	1	-	-	80
1959	70,858										
1960	77,402										
1961	38,464										
1962	26,839										
	1,644,271	Advised to Mr Wenlock 29-10-63									

BOILER CHANGES

Date fitted	Registered No.	New or Repaired	Economic Stock Reference	Belpaire or Round Top
19.5.50	10645	R	100 ANS/M	B
29.11.52	10304	R	100 ANS/M	B.
8.12.56	9934	R	100 ANS	B
26.9.59	10641	R	100 ANS/M	B.

STORED (SERVICEABLE OR UNSERVICEABLE)

S. or U.S.	DATE		S. or U.S.	DATE	
	In	Out		In	Out
S	6/10/62	W5 2/63			
S	14/10/63	32.64			

THIRD ENGINE HISTORY CARD (FRONT AND BACK)

C.M.E. DERBY 25 MAR 1950 2 JUL 1949 FITTED WITH INTERNAL GAUGE FRAME PIPE

METAFLEX JOINTS FITTED

ENGINE RECORD CARD (3) E.R.O. 19002

Region or Division: Western Name: Duchess of Sutherland Number: 46233

Class (M.P.): 8 P Type: - Built by: Crewe Date: 23 July 1938

PASSENGER TENDER SUPERHEATER * Wheel arrgt.: 4-6-2 Wheel base (E. & T.): 62 ft. 11 ins.

~~FREIGHT TANK NON-SUPERHEATER~~ * Diameter of driving wheels: 6 ft. 9 ins.

Engine & Tender—Weight in working order: 161 T. 12 C. Overall height from rail level: 13 ft. 3 ins. Cab.

No. of cylinders: 4 Dia.: 16½ ins. Stroke: 28 ins. Overall length over buffers (E. & T.): 73 ft. 10¼ ins.

Class of boiler: No. ~~10645~~ ~~10645~~ ~~10304~~ ~~9937~~ 10641 No. of tubes: 40 Large Dia. 5.1/8 ins.

Heating Surface: 2807 sq. ft. Sup = 830 sq. ft. 129 Small Dia. 2.3/8 ins.

Boiler pressure: 250 lbs. per sq. inch BR (std) Plugs Firebox grate area: 50 sq. feet

Tractive effort at 85% B.P.: 40,000 lbs. Type of motion: Walschaert

Radius of minimum curve: 6 chains (or 4½ chains dead slow) None Feed pump † Left H. Drive

Brakes †: Stm. Eng. Vac. Train Valves †: Piston Tablet Catching Apparatus †: None

Injectors (Type & Size): D.& M. Exh. 12 mm/G.& C. 13 mm.

Axle boxes (Coupled wheels) †: Steel. Mechanical Lubrication* {Cylinders, Axle boxes} Atomiser Lubrication ~~Fountain Lubrication~~

CARRIAGE WARMING APPARATUS*: ~~Front end~~ Tender end ~~Both ends~~ ~~Without~~

SANDING *: Steam ~~Mechanical~~ Back - FRONT ~~De-sanding~~

WATER PICK-UP APPARATUS *: Forward direction ~~Both directions~~ ~~Internal fittings only~~ ~~Without~~

~~Roller Bearings~~ - ~~Bogie.~~ ~~Bissel~~ ~~Coupled.~~ ~~Tender~~ SPECIAL FITTINGS:— * ~~Manganese Liners~~ - ~~Bogie.~~ ~~Bissel~~ ~~Coupled.~~ ~~Tender~~

~~Rocking grate~~ ~~Hopper ashpan~~ ~~Self-cleaning Smokebox~~ Smokebox deflector plates ~~Spark arrester~~ ~~V.C.R.~~

Revg. Gear: Screw ~~Lever~~ ~~Power~~ ~~SPEED INDICATOR~~ ~~Speed indicator~~ ~~Roller Bearings~~ ~~Vacuum pump~~ CONTINUOUS ~~Continuous~~ blowdown ~~Blow-off cock~~ ~~A.T.C.~~ ATC

Speed Indicator.

~~Trip cocks~~ ~~Condenser~~ ~~Sand gun~~ Gangway doors ~~Storm Sheets~~ ~~Back Cab~~ ~~Limousine Cab~~

~~Tender weather boards~~ Coal bunker access doors ~~Coal rails~~ Coal pusher ~~Fitted for Snow plough~~

Electric Light Double Chimney ~~Smokebox Regulator~~ Stm. Operated Cyl. Cocks

*—Delete items not applicable. †—State type. [P.T.O.

~~Steel Fireboxes~~ Brake Valves Combination Disc Valve for Engine and/or Train

B.R. No. 2.10.48.

TENDER				ALLOCATION		SHOPS			
Prefix	No.	Capacity Water (gals.)	Capacity Coal (tons)	Depot	Date	In	Out	Repair	Where
	9751	4000	10			14. 8. 47	28. 10. 47	Gen	Crewe
						4. 11. 47	14. 11. 47	Hot Box	" NC
						30. 8. 48	29. 9. 48	Gen	" L.S.
						2. 10. 48	20. 10. 48	Hot Box	" NC
						18. 7. 49	12. 8. 49	LI	"
						13-4-50	19-5-50	HG	"
						14. 2. 51	10. 4. 51	LC	
						27. 12. 51	24. 1. 52	HI	"
						23 10 52	29 11 52	Gen	"
						18. 1. 54	10. 2. 54	LI	"
						29. 3. 55	7. 5. 55	HI	"
						7. 9. 55	3. 10. 55	LC	"
						3 1 56	30 1 56	LC	"
						5.11.56	8.12.56	HG.	"
						26-2-58	12-4-58	HI	Crewe
						6-8-59	26-3-59	HG	Crewe
						24-1-61	21-2-61	HI	"
						26-7-61	18-8-61	LC	"

Experiment Nos. (if fitted)

~~C/LD/1307 (TEN 9751)~~
~~C/LD/1344~~
C/LD/1372
C/LD/1381.
~~C/LD/1381~~

Appendix 2
6233 Service History

Out of traffic	Returned to traffic	Wait'g decis.	Wait'g works	On works	Total days	Class of rep.	Mileage since previous repair heavy	light
10/7/39	27/7/39				16	L.S.		97,450
1/7/40	16/7/40				14	L.S.		183,347
5/2/41	8/3/41				28	H.G.	223,944	
(boiler no.10305 and double blast pipe and chimney fitted)								
5/6/41	18/6/41				12	T.R.O.		
25/3/42	22/4/42				25	L.S.		63,258
16/10/42	13/11/42				25	H.S.	103,145	
2/7/43	7/8/43				32	H.G.	49,602	
(boiler no. 10287 fitted)								
5/1/44	10/2/44				32	L.O.(E.O.)		39,002
16/5/44	2/6/44				16	T.R.O.		
12/10/44	3/11/44				20	L.S.		87,658
18/4/45	19/5/45				27	H.G.	120,418	
(boiler no. 10297 fitted)								
15/2/46	7/3/46				18	L.O.(E.O.)		47,421
3/8/46	24/8/46				19	H.S.	80,970	
(smoke deflectors fitted)								
26/7/47	28/10/47				81	H.G.	64,098	34,303
(boiler no. 10646 fitted)								
3/11/47	14/11/47				11	No repair done		
19/8/48	29/9/48				36	L.S.	59,249	52,605
30/9/48	20/10/48				18	N.C.(E.O.)	72	52,677
18/7/49	12/8/49				23	L.I.	55,700	40,371
12/4/50	19/5/50				32	H.G.	46,599	16,544
(boiler no. 10645 fitted)								
14/3/51	10/4/51				22	L.C.(E.O.)	62,130	13,383
19/12/51	24/1/52	-	5	24	29	H.I.	115,835	67,088
15/10/52	29/11/52	4	3	32	39	H.G.	68,576	68,576
(boiler no. 10304 fitted)								
16/1/54	10/2/54	-	1	20	21	L.I.	98,616 ?	2,568
14/3/55	7/5/55	8	5	33	46	H.I.	82,227	7,905
31/8/55	3/10/55	-	6	22	28	L.C.(E.O.)	24,238	32,143
25/12/55	30/1/56	2	3	23	28	L.C.(E.O.)	43,625	Nil
25/10/56	8/12/56	1	8	29	38	H.G.	101,032	57,407
(boiler no. 9937 fitted)								
10/10/57	23/10/57	-	9	2	11	N.C.(E.O.)	62,823	58,740
24/2/58	12/4/58	-	2	38	40	H.I.	92,569	12,589
1/8/59	26/9/59	-	4	44	48	H.G.	101,590	50,741
(boiler no.10641 fitted - last heavy general repair)								
18/1/61	12/2/61	-	5	24	29	H.I.	98,848	1,929
10/7/61	24/8/61	8	6	25	39	L.C.(E.O.)	22,364	23,997

End of recorded engine repair history.

NOTES ON REPAIR CLASSIFICATIONS:-

H.G.=Heavy General;	H.I.=Heavy Intermediate;	H.S.=Heavy Special;
L.I.=Light Intermediate;	L.C.=Light casual;	L.O.=Light Overhaul;
E.O. =Engine Only;	T.R.O.=Tender Repair Only;	N.C.=Not Classified.

BOILER CHANGES FROM ENGINE RECORD CARDS.

Date fitted	Registered number	Ex engine number	Date new shell/f'box	Mileage shell/f'box
18/7/38	10304	New	1938 build prog.	Order B408
8/3/41	10305	6234	1938 build prog.	Order B408
7/8/43	10287	6235	1939 build prog.	Order B414
19/4/45	10297	6234	1938 build prog.	Order B408
28/10/47	10646	6250	March, 1943	241,411 Order B415
19/5/50	10645	6229	August, 1943	442,872 Order B415
29/11/52	10304	6240	1938 build prog.	Order B408
8/12/56	9937	6247	1937 build prog.	Order B402
26/9/59	10641	6242	1939 build prog.	Order B415.

Appendix 3
Technical Modifications

PART ONE:- TECHNICAL MODIFICATIONS TO 6233/46233 FROM THE RECORD CARDS.

Date	Order No.	Job No.	Modification	Cost
22/3/41	6865	5205	Double blast pipe and chimney fitted.	£67.1s.3d
4/9/43	5/18681	5495	Steel in place of Monel metal stays.	£8.10s
15/4/44	X7769	5329	Improved type piston head and rod. (p.e. 3/10/43).	£100.0s.0d
p.e. 3/11/45		5495	Steel in place of Monel metal stays. (20/5/45).	£70.0s.0d.
p.e. 23/3/46	Misc.	(5389)	Additional clothing on inside cylinders	£28.0s.0d
p.e.5/10/46	X8826		Smoke deflector plates. (24/8/46).	£45.0s.0d
2/10/48	7071	5472	Fitting of feed water strainers to tender.	£53.4s.0d
24/1/52	R1013	5555	Fitting of tell-tale device to give warning of excessive heating of inside big ends.	£1.19s.6d.
29/11/52	E2194		Removal of sand guns and equipment.	£1. 7s.0d
p.e. 24/1/43	E2212	5665	Provision of cast steel inside cylinders. (add. to p.e. 29/11/52).	£703.0s.0d
p.e. 5/11/55	E3329		Modified piston for continuous blowdown valves. (add. to p.e. 8/10/55).	17s.6d
p.e. 29/12/56	E3689	5755	Fitting strengthened axlebox guides.	£171.7s.3d
p.e. 2/11/57	R7461	5794	Fitting of Speed indicators (Smith-Stone speed indicating equipment.	£151.12s.0d
p.e. 3/10/59	E4983		Fitting of Automatic Train Control equipment.	£302.9s.0d

46233 in Crewe Locomotive Works for a light intermediate repair in 1954. (J.F. Clay)

PART TWO:- JOB NUMBERS ISSUED FOR 'PRINCESS CORONATION' CLASS LOCOMOTIVES.

*(The work was done when engine or tender was shopped for normal repairs unless
specified as requiring special shopping for the work to be done more urgently.)*

Job No.	Date issued	Description of work to be carried out
4968	14/5/38	N.V. lock nuts to be replaced by nut and cotter on axlebox hornclips.
4990	26/1/39	Mod. to regulator rod pin - pin with flats replaced by round one *(Job cancelled - see Job No. 5282)*
4983	28/6/39	Fitting of gland to outside cylinder steam pipes to overcome steam leakage due to relative movement.
4991	26/1/39	New bronze link coupling in horizontal dome type regulator.
5043	5/7/40	Removal of Stone-Deuta speed indicating equipment from 6220-6224 and replacing it with British Thompson-Houston Co. Ltd. equipment.
5156	17/8/39	Increased side play in wheels to permit easier traversing of six chain curves.
5205	6/4/40	Double blast pipe and chimney, 6220-6233. To be fitted as engines pass through the shops for general repairs "in similar manner to 6234 which has proved satisfactory in service."
5208	8/4/40	Fitting drain cocks to Class H exhaust injectors to prevent freezing up.
5256	1/8/41	Air Raid Precautions - modified catches for loco. cab windows to allow ventilation.
5257	25/6/41	Damper door gear modification - holes in platform plates to prevent dirt accumulation.
5274	27/2/42	New standard firebricks for brick arches.
5290	27/2/42	Strengthening of spring brackets to prevent fractures.
5294	19/3/42	Provision of stops & strengthening reversing screw levers.
5319	16/10/42	Fitting spring catch on coal pusher operating lever to prevent it falling down.
5329	16/2/43	Improved type piston head and rod (requires provision of new front cylinder covers. Engines to be called on works specially when material is available.)
5340	15/4/43	Alterations to tender shrouding to increase coal capacity, following trials with the tender of engine No. 6224 (streamlined tenders only.) *(Job cancelled on 24/5/43 in favour of job no. 5347.)*
5347	4/6/43	Removal of tender shrouding altogether on streamlined versions.
5368	26/1/44	Modifications to coal pusher piston valves and pusher steps.
5389	23/11/43	Additional clothing on inside cylinders *(to be fitted when engines are next in shops.)*
5391	3/4/46	Provision of two additional washout plugs at the front end of the boiler barrel.
5403	15/2/45	Deflector plate for exhaust injector overflow on R.H. side of tender to prevent exhaust injector overflow blow-back fouling the underkeep oil.
5413	3/5/45	Provision of stronger bogie control springs & lubricator pads to improve riding.
5429	4/12/45	Fitting smoke deflector plates on nine non-streamlined engines, Nos. 6230-6234 and 6249-52, following experimental fitting of those to engines 6232 and 6252, "which are also to be included in this instruction."
5434	29/12/45	Removal of streamlined casing from 24 engines to give greater accessibility and reduce maintenance costs plus fitting of smoke deflectors to same.
5472	16/12/46	Fitting of feed water strainers to tenders to prevent foreign matter causing injector failure.
5491	8/1/48	Provision of new bogie bottom frame bars, spring details and safety clips 'due to recent failures.'
5495	25/9/47	Larger diameter spring links on certain 4,000 gallon tenders to prevent failure *(applied to 'Princess Coronation' class tenders Nos. 9816-7 and 10622.)*
5517	15/9/48	Fitting larger cab windows to 24 de-streamlined engines.
5537	8/8/49	Fitting speed indicating equipment to 25 engines including 19 4-6-2 class engines as follows:- 46257 to have Smith/Stone drive and mounting. 18 others to have B.T.H. equipment and modified drive and mounting. *(Numbers of engines not specified)*
5539	9/11/49	Fitting of top feed deflector plates in lieu of top feed trays in earlier taper boilers including 'Princess Coronation' type.
5555	9/5/50	Fitting of 'tell-tale' devices to give warning of excessive heating of inside big ends to 364 engines including nos. 46220-57.
5582	1/9/50	Mods to intermediate axleboxes and guides on 4,000 gallon tenders with Timken roller bearings including 46256 and 46257. *(Cancelled 23/4/52)*
5588	24/10/50	Mods. to centre carrier bar on engines 46253-46257 fitted with rocking grates as built.
5622	10/10/51	Discharge of continuous blowdown pipe into ashpan *(4,291 tender engines including 46220-6257.)*
5625	4/10/51	Fitting of rubber washer to bottom bearings of brake hangers of tenders with compensated brake gear.
5665	6/6/52	Conversion to cast steel inside cylinders. *(To be caried out if cyls. require renewing)* All engines involved completed by 4/1/57 including 46200-1, 46203-12 and 46220-57.
5667	13/6/52	Mods. to tender feed water gear on tenders 9816-7 and 10622-4 attached to engines 46253-7.
5745	20/5/55	Provision of footholds in smokeshields of nine ex. L.M. Class 8 engines nos. 46230-4 and 46249-52 not so fitted, due to narrowing of foot framing.
5755	6/2/56	Fitting strengthened axlebox guides *(as engines pass through the shops for general repairs.)*
5768	23/8/56	Removal of redundant feed water valves on 140 4,000 gallon tenders including nos. 9816-7 and 10622-4.
5794	20/8/57	Provision of Smith/Stone speed indicating equipment to engines 46200-1, 46203-12 and 46220-46255, to be fitted at Crewe- special shopping. *(Completed 10/9/58)*.
5827	14/3/60	Fitting of Automatic Warning System on L.M.R. steam locomotives, 1960 programme *(no details available)*
5828	14/3/60	Fitting of Automatic Warning System on N.E.R. steam locomotives, 1960 programme *(Locomotive numbers not given, but additions on 10/8/60 included 46222, 46233, 46224, 46227, 46230, 46231 and 46232 operating on the Scottish Region.)*
5847	2/1/61	Fitting of Automatic Warning System on steam locomotives 1961 programme *(no details)*.

Appendix 4
6233 Annual Mileages

At year end	Mileage in year	Total mileage run
1938	46,599	46,599
1939	89,436	136,035
1940	82,750	218,785
1941	74,992	293,777
1942	54,163	347,940
1943	89,591	437,531
1944	60,844	498,375
1945	58,840	557,215
1946	68,480	625,695
1947	40,947	666,642
1948	67,934	734,576
1949	70,426	805,002
1950	65,291	870,293
1951	67,088	937,381
1952	74,461	1,011,842
1953	90,220	1,102,062
1954	76,890	1,178,952
1955	51,530	1,230,482
1956	61,490	1,291,972
1957	75,897	1,367,869
1958	63,439	1,431,308
1959	70,258	1,501,566
1960	77,402	1,578,968
1961	38,464	1,617,432
1962	26,839	1,644,271

1963 Not recorded.

NOTE:- The official Engine Record Card bears a note:- "1,644,271 advised to Mr. Wenlock 29-10-63." The locomotive was placed in store on 6th October, 1962, but was returned to traffic on 2nd February and was then used fairly frequently between until 14th October, 1963, when it was put into store for a second time. During 1963, from known workings, a calculated further mileage of around 13,000 was covered, making a final total of approximately 1,657,270 in service with the L.M.& S.R. and B.R. 46233 was taken out of storage again on 3rd February, 1964, but the authors do not believe that she was actually used again before being officially withdrawn during that week ending 8th February, 1964.

Appendix 5
6233 Depot Allocations

IN SERVICE MOVEMENTS:

Date from	Code	Depot
18th July, 1938		New, first trip to Euston.
23rd July, 1938	1B	Camden
20th May, 1944	5A	Crewe North
14th June, 1958	12B	Carlisle Upperby
20th September, 1958	5A	Crewe North
2nd April, 1960	12B	Carlisle Upperby
23rd April, 1960	5A	Crewe North
30th April, 1960	1B	Camden
17th September, 1960	8A	Edge Hill
6th October, 1962		Stored in serviceable condition
2nd February, 1963		Taken out of store
14th October, 1963		Stored in serviceable condition
3rd February, 1964		Taken out of store
w.e. 8th February, 1964		Withdrawn from service.

LATER MOVEMENTS:

14th June, 1964	On Crewe South depot awaiting works Then moved into Crewe Works for restoration.
15th September, 1964	Moved to Ayr diesel depot.
19th October, 1964	Tender moved to Butlin's Heads of Ayr holiday camp.
21st October, 1964	Engine moved to Butlin's Heads of Ayr holiday camp.
1st March, 1971	Locomotive moved by rail from Ayr to Norwich.
21st March, 1971	Locomotive arrived at Bressingham Steam Museum.
2nd August, 1993	Locomotive moved by road to the East Lancashire Railway for 25th Anniversary Steam Railway Festival.
18th July, 1994	Locomotive returned by road to Bressingham Steam Museum.
2nd –4th February, 1996	Locomotive moved to West Shed of the P.R.C.L.T.

FIRST LIVERY - 18th July, 1938 (as new):-

Full Official Specification:-

ENGINE:

Platform angle, boiler, splashers, footsteps, engine panel, cab - Midland Red lined out as follows:-

Cylinder casing: 1¹/₂ " wide black line at each edge with ³/₈" gold line inside black. Each edge of gold lined with 1¹/₁₆ " vermilion.

Platform angle: 1" wide black line at lower edge with ³/₈" gold line above black. Each edge of gold lined with 1¹/₁₆" vermilion.

Front end of boiler immediately behind smokebox: 1¹/₄" wide black line adjoining smokebox, followed by ¹/₂" gold line. Each edge of gold lined with ¹/₈" vermilion.

Firebox in front of cab angle: Cab angle all black, ¹/₂" gold line on firebox, *immediately in front of cab angle. Each edge of gold line with ¹/₈" vermilion line.

(*Author's note:- In order that the lining out did not disappear inside the cab when the boiler was at normal working temperature an allowance of 2" was made by painting a Midland Red strip of that width on the firebox cladding band before positioning the gold lining.)

Splashers: ³/₄" black line all round edge, ¹/₂" gold line inside black. Each edge of gold lined with ¹/₈" vermilion line.

Footsteps: 1" black line at edge, ³/₈" gold inside black. Each edge of gold lined with ¹/₈" vermilion line. Treads black.

Engine panel and cab sides: 2¹/₄" black line at edge, ¹/₂" gold inside black. Each edge of gold lined with ¹/₈" vermilion line.

Buffer beam: Vermilion with 1¹/₈" black line all round the extreme edge and ³/₈" gold line all round the inner edge of black line.

Buffer casings: Vermilion with 1¹/₂" black line all round the outside edge and a ³/₈" gold line separated from the black by a vermilion line.

Motion, tyres, buffer heads, cylinder and steam chest covers - bright metal.

Remainder of engine black.

TENDER:-

Frames and tank sides: - Midland Red lined out as follows:

Frames: 1" black line at edges, ³/₈" gold line inside black, each edge of gold lined ¹/₁₆" vermilion.

Sides: 2¹/₄" black line at edge, ¹/₂" gold line inside black, each edge of gold line ¹/₈" vermilion (Author's note: The tender back was also Midland Red and lined out as above.)

Remainder of tender black:

Numbers on engine: 12" deep

'LMS' on tender 15 " deep.

Power classification insignia: 2³/₈" deep.

ADDITIONAL INFORMATION FROM OFFICIAL DRAWINGS AND OTHER OFFICIAL SOURCES:-

ENGINE:-

Front numberplate:-6233 painted silver with black background.
Shedplate also painted silver with black background.

Nameplate:- 'DUCHESS OF SUTHERLAND' - cast brass but chromium plated with black painted background.

Builders plate:- Cast brass with polished letters, figures and rim with background painted black.

Boiler, smokebox door and cab handrails:- bright metal

Cabside 12 inch numerals:-

'6' as shown on L.M.S. drawing No. DS-4342

'2' and '3' as shown on L.M.S. drawing No. DS-4340

These were centred vertically equidistant between the bottom of the cab-side windows and the bottom of the cab side panel and horizontally equidistant from each edge of the cab side sheet. The numbers were equally spaced with an overall width of 44 inches.

Colour:- Gold leaf shaded vermilion. (per L.M.S. letters dated 25th June, 1936 from Stanier refering to the "standard vermilion shading" and 11th October, 1937 from S.J. Symes)

The power classification figures and letters '7 P' were centred below the two cab windows 2¹/₈ inch deep letters in gold shaded vermilion (per L.M.S. letters dated 25th June, 1936 from Stanier and 11th October, 1937 from S.J. Symes.)

Figure '7' to Derby Sketch S.4079, and letter 'P' to Derby Sketch S.4344.

Cab interior:- White roof, grained upper sides, drop black bottom half, then two coats finishing varnish

TENDER:-

14 inch lettering:- 'L' as shown on L.M.S. drawing No. DS-4295.
'M' as shown on L.M.S. drawing No. DS-4296.
'S' as shown on L.M.S. drawing No. DS-4297.

Colour:- Gold leaf shaded vermilion. (Per L.M.S. letters dated 25th June, 1936 from Stanier and 11th October, 1937 from S.J. Symes.)

Location:-

The 'M' was centred exactly above the centre of the middle axle of the tender, and the 'L' and 'S' were centred 4 feet - 10¹/₂ inches either side of the 'M'. The height from the bottom of the tank (i.e. measured from the top of the fixing flange to the bottom of the gilt (NOT the shading) was 2 feet - 6 inches (Per Derby Sketch D-2540/2.)

Builders plate:- Polished brass letters, numbers and rim with black background.

Tender capacity and numberplates:- Polished brass letters and figures and outer rim with black background.

SPECIAL ADDITIONAL NOTES:-

1. The smokebox door hinges and pin were painted black and not polished.
2. Smokebox door dart handles and mounting boss were polished.
3. The front face of the engine front numberplate numbers and the shed plate code and its front facing rim were finished in silver to match the chromium plated brass nameplate lettering.
4. The makers' plate lettering and its rim were polished brass.
5. The top surface of the splashers was painted black.
6. The sandbox filler caps and the outer surface of the surrounding support plates were finished in Midland Red, but the filler pipes behind were painted black.
7. The centre portion of the cab roof was painted black between the rain strips and only the outer portions on each side between the rain strips and the cab side sheets were finished in Midland Red.

A letter sent out on 26th May, 1941 stated the necessity of reducing the amount of painting as much as possible, and continued "All lining should be discontinued." This policy was clearly applied to 6233, as the official photographs of her with a double chimney and taken on 20th April, 1942 show. She remained in this livery throughout the 1939-45 war, even when fitted with smoke deflectors (painted black) during her repairs at Crewe Works from 3rd to 24th August, 1946, after which she was patch-painted until the application of the second livery.

SECOND LIVERY - when out-shopped 28th October, 1947 (Ivatt intermediate black livery):-

ENGINE:-

Painted black - glossy finish.

Running platform angle: 2¹/₂" wide maroon band edged with ³/₈" straw line with ³/₈" black line at top and bottom of running angle.

Boiler barrel - first lagging band (smokebox end) and last lagging band (front of firebox): Maroon edge with ³/₈" straw line each side.

Firebox lagging band: Maroon edged with ³/₈" straw line each side but with 2" black band adjacent to cab front plate framing angle to allow for boiler expansion.

Cab sides: 2¹/₂" wide maroon band around edges of sides and bottom only with ³/₈"straw line at inside edge.

Numerals: 12 inch Gill Sans Serif unshaded,straw coloured lined maroon with straw margin outside placed centrally on cab side 30" from the bottom. Total width 50 inches.

Power classification: Placed centrally below running number and same style (approx. 2¹/₂")

Cylinders casing bands: ½" black at front of leading band and at rear of trailing band, then vertical band 1 ¼" wide maroon band with ⅜" straw either side.
Buffer beams and buffer stocks: Vermilion
Footsteps: Black with no lining.
Wheels: Black, but all tyre rims bright as machined.
Motion and cylinder/steam chest covers: Bright finish.
Nameplate: Straw borders and letters, maroon background.

TENDER:-
Painted black - glossy finish
Tender tank sides and end: Black beading strip, then lined all round with 2½" wide maroon band edged with ⅜" straw at inside edge.
Tender frames: Black - no lining.
Lettering: 14 inch Gill Sans Serif unshaded,straw colour lined maroon all round, with straw margin outside, centred on middle axle.

> Centre of 'M' to centre of 'L' 5'-3".
> Centre of 'M' to centre of 'S' 5'-0"
> Bottom of letters 2'-6" from top of fixing flange.

THIRD LIVERY:- when out-shopped 19th May, 1950 ('Caledonian Blue' livery)

(Information taken from Derby drawings nos. D49-18750 (engine) and D49-18749 (tender).

ENGINE:-
Blue livery with exception of smokebox, smokebox saddle and outside steam pipes.
Running platform angle: Blue with a ½" black line along the bottom edge, a ½" blue line above that and a ⅛" white line above the blue (i.e. next to the main blue of the angle.) Lining to follow the actual edge of the running platform angle throughout and not to disregard the fillet at each end.
All boiler clothing bands: Blue with central 1" wide black band and outer edges painted with ⅛" white band.
Firebox clothing bands: Blue, unlined.
Smoke deflectors: Plain black.
Smokebox, saddle, outside steam pipes, etc.: Black
Handrails: Black
All parts below the platform angle: Black and unlined, except for motion which is to remain bright.
Cylinder clothing: Black with ⅛" white band at each edge.
Splashers: Blue lined out at top edge only with ½" black band, ½" blue band and ⅛" white band except when a splasher is extensively screened by external fittings, when it should not be lined.
Cab side: Blue with inset lining panel 5" from bottom and sides and 4" below cab side windows. Lining as follows:- top corners and bottom back corner: from outer edge ⅛' white, ½' blue, 1" black with outer corner radius of 4", plus ½" blue edged with ⅛" white on inside with a corner radius (outer edge of blue) of 2⅝" struck from a different centre ⅜" in at an angle of 45 degrees. Bottom front corner adjacent to running angle: From outer edge:- ⅛" white, ½" blue, 1" black, with outer corner radius of 7" (to match 1" radius of edge of cabside plate) plus:- ½" blue edged ⅛" white on inside with a corner radius of 5½" (struck from a different centre as above).
Cabside numerals:- 8" Gil Sans Medium set with tops 10½" below bottom of cab side windows, and centred in lining panel.
Power classification: 2" numerals and letter set equidistant between top of cabside numerals and inner edge of lining panel. (To be painted in cream lining colour if transfers not available.)
Cab roof: Black
Buffer beam and buffer stocks: Signal Red to B.S. colour No. 537.
Frame extensions: Black

TENDER:-
Blue livery with inset lining panel 5" from bottom edge of tender side plate, 1'-5" from the outer edge of the front beading., 1'-4" from the back edge and 3" below the start of the curve at the tank top. At the top corner of the lining panel the front corner follows the inside edge of the beading and is set 9" away. At the rear top corner a curve of radius 1'-11" is set 7" below the horizontal beading at the rear of the tender tank side and runs out to 9"at the corner radius of the lining panel. The corner radii are 4" from the outside of the outer ⅛" white band with a ½" blue and ½" black band inside. Two further bands of ½" blue with a 2⅝" radius (on a different centre) set in by ⅜" on a 45 degree angle plus a ⅛" inner white band complete the lining panel.
Tender tank backplate: Blue, unlined.
Handrails: Black
Exposed parts of tender top: Black
Buffer beam and buffer stocks: Signal Red to B.S. colour No. 537.

B.R. 'Lion & Wheel' crest: One left hand and one right hand required (Lion must face forward)
2'-4" high transfer to be placed centrally on the panel between the horizontal rows of rivets and between the third and fourth vertical rows of rivets. Bottom of the square block lettered 'BRITISH RAILWAYS' to be 2'-6 ½" from bottom of tender tank side plate (10'-8¼" from the leading edge of the front beading and 11'-2" from the back edge of the tender side.

Note:- Black and white lining colours are items 8 & 10, R.F.U. R.E. Paint Specification No. 8

FOURTH LIVERY - when out-shopped on 29th November, 1952. (Green livery.)

(First B.R. 'Brunswick Green' livery officially the old Great Western Railway colour)

ENGINE:- Green applied to the boiler, cab sides and front, running angle, tender sides and back.
Running platform angle: Green lined out at the lower edge with a black line and an orange line above next to the green.
Boiler clothing bands: Black lined at the edges in orange.
Cylinder clothing: Glossy black lined out at edges in orange.
Cab side: Oblong panel of black edged each side with orange.
Cab side numerals: Gill Sans Serif
Power classification:- Numerals and letters set midway between the top of the numerals and the inner edge of the lining panel.
Smokebox, frames, wheels, etc.: Glossy black
Buffer beams: Vermilion.
Nameplates: Black background.
Below running platform, wheels, etc.: Black

TENDER:-
Green tank sides and rear lined out in black edged with orange.
B.R. early 'Lion & Wheel' crest. One left hand and one right hand required (Lion must face forward.) 2'-4" transfer placed centrally in the lining panel.
Frames, wheels, etc: Black.

FIFTH LIVERY - When out-shopped on 26th September, 1959. ('Brunswick Green' livery)

As fourth livery but with later B.R. emblem having 'BRITISH' and 'RAILWAYS' either side of a central crest. The locomotive remained in this livery until withdrawn from service by British Railways during the week ending 8th February, 1964.

LIVERIES APPLIED DURING PRESERVATION.

SIXTH LIVERY:-

When out-shopped from Crewe Works in August, 1964.
Following purchase by Butlins for display at their Heads of Ayr holiday camp in Scotland, the locomotive was re-numbered 6233 again, and repainted in a representative pre-war Midland Red L.M.S. livery with gold insignia, incorrectly shaded, the cabside numerals being located in post-war positions and not in the middle of the cab sides as pre-war.

SEVENTH LIVERY:-

When overhauled and returned to working order after being loaned to the Bressingham Steam Museum in Norfolk the locomotive was repainted in her correct L.M.S. Midland Red livery as built. She was steamed again on 30th May, 1974 and ran for about two years.

EIGHTH LIVERY:-

When outshopped at the West Shed of the P. R.C.L.T. on 18th January, 2001. Following purchase by the Princess Royal Class Locomotive Trust and a full general overhaul, the locomotive was repainted once more in the full special Midland Red livery that she had carried when first built at Crewe in 1938. The few minor departures from this were for purely practical reasons.

Appendix 7

London, Midland & Scottish Railway

6233 Dynamometer Car Tests

Report No. 83, 1945

TABLE No.1

DYNAMOMETER CAR TESTS.

1.34p.m. Crewe - Carlisle. Engine No.6233.

Load 530 tons. October 30th, 1945.

Location	Booked Time.	Actual Time.	Blr. Press.	Reg.	Cut off	Wtr.	Steam Chest Temp. °F.	Exhaust Steam Temp. °F	
Crewe	1.34	1.40	230						
		43	207	½	20	Full	496	226	
Coppenhall Jc.	1.39	1.45	225	.4	20	½	536	221	
		47	230	½	20	½	566	"	
Winsford Jc.	1.46	1.51¼	235	½	20	½	612	229	
Hartford			232	"	17	"	617	241	
Acton			235	"	"	"	586	246	
Weaver Jc.	1.54	1.57½	225	.4	17	⅞	573	249	
Moore Troughs			218	⅓	17	Full	567	261	
Warrington	2.4	2.8½					Slow line Warrington to Winwick.		
Winwick Jc.	2.9	2.36	240	Full	30	"	556	228	
		39	230	"	25	¾	586	221	
Golborne Jc.			217	"	"	⅞	589	218	
Golborne			212	.8	17	½	588	"	
Wigan	2.19	48	195	Full	"	⅞	576	218	P.W. check Boars Head
Standish Jc.	2.27	54	230	"	17	¾	581	217	
		56	220	"	"	⅞	586	217	
			210	.4	"	½	576	214	
Euxton Jc.	2.35	3.2½	202	¼	26	⅞	556	276	
Leyland			Coast		26		546	349	P.W. check Farington Jc.
Preston	2.42	3.11	"	¼			526	296	
Oxheys Jc.	2.45	3.11	227	Full	17	⅞	576	223	
Barton		18	222	.6	17	"	597	218	
Brook Troughs			220	½	17	¾	587	218	
Garstang	2.54	3.24	240	½	17	Full	581	218	Sigs. Garstang
		26½	"	"	"	"	607	"	
		29	220	.4	"	"	602	"	
Bay Horse			215	"	"	"	604	"	Sigs. Bay Horse.
Lancaster	3.7	40½	232	.6	"	"	576	218	
		43	222	.4	"	"	589	"	
Bolton-le-Sands			215	¼	"	"	597	"	
Carnforth	3.14	3.47	"	Full	"	"	607	216	
		50	206	"	"	"	613	218	
Burton & H.			200	"	"	"	610	"	
Milnthorpe			"	"	"	"	617	"	
		57	203	"	"	"	612	"	
Oxenholme	3.31	4.1	225	"	24	"	610	224	Sigs. Oxenholme S.
		5	224	"	"	"	617	223	
		8½	218	"	"	"	"	222	
		11	"	"	25	"	617	221	
Grayrigg			"	"	"	"	"	221	
Low Gill			212	½	17	⅞	609	218	
Troughs			235	F	"	"	632	218	
Tebay	3.51	4.19	"	"	"	"	"	"	
		4.22	240	"	"	¾	637	218	
		25	230	"	30	F	620	226	
		27	240	½	30	"	607	231	Sig. check.
Shap S.	4.3	28½	"						

P.T.O.

TABLE No.2

DYNAMOMETER CAR TESTS.

12.42p.m. Carlisle - Crewe. Engine No. 6233.

Load 524 tons. October 31st 1945.

Location	Booked Time	Actual Time	Blr. Press.	Reg.	Cut off	Wtr.	Steam Chest Temp. °F	Exhaust Steam Temp. °F	
Carlisle	12.42	12.52½	230						
		58	225	Full	35	¾	536	226	
		1.1	212	"	27	½	576	220	
Wreay			207	"	25	"	586	216	
		6½	205	"	30	"	591	221	
			208	"	24	"	607	220	
Southwaite			208	"	"	"	"	"	
			210	"	20	"	"	218	
		13	212	"	"	⅝	609	"	
Calthwaite			215	"	"	¾	612	"	
		18	212	"	16	½	614	216	
		22	218	"	"	"	612	"	
Penrith	1.11	1.24¼	218	"	"	"	617	217	
		28	205	"	19	¾	"	218	
		33	207	"	25	Full	603	219	
		36	213	"	"	⅞	609	218	
		40½	216	"	20	"	607	214	
Shap			218	"	"	"	"	216	
Shap S.	1.34	1.45½	218	"	"	"	"	218	
			200	1st	55	"	591	380	
Tebay	1.40	1.51	"	¼	"		586	389	
Low Gill			"	Full	13	Full	576	226	
Grayrigg			208	¼	55	"	526	312	
Oxenholme	1.54	2.3	202	"	"	"	571	364	
Milnthorpe			215	Full	10	"	586	216	
Burton & Holme			"	"	"	"	597	216	
Carnforth	2.8	2.14½					Signal check Carnforth.		
			220	"	22	"	586	220	
			212	"	15	⅞	"	216	
Hest Bank			200	"	17	¾	576	218	
Lancaster	2.15	2.23	198	"	"	"	584	218	
		28	188	"	17	½	579	219	
Bay Horse			213	"	20-16	⅞	586	219	
			208	"	14	¾	597	216	Sigs. Brock.
Barton & B.			200	"	17	Full	605	218	
Preston	2.41	2.50	240	"	30				
			235	"	15	"	571	216	
Farington			230	"	"	"	586	216	Sigs. Farington
Leyland			"	"	"	"	591	"	
Euxton Jc.	2.50	3.2¾	230	Coast					
Balshaw Lane			233	"	15	Full	597	218	
			225	"	"	"	"	216	
Coppull			220	"	"	"	"	"	
Standish Jc.	2.59	3.13	210	Coast					Signal check.

P.T.O.

TABLE No.1 cont'd.

Location	Booked Time	Actual Time	Blr. Press.	Reg.	Cut off.	Wtr.	Steam Chest Temp °F	Exhaust Steam Temp °F	
Shap			225	.4	17	Full	602	241	
Penrith	4.18	4.47½	210	"	"				
			220	"	"	"	607	248	
			220	"	"	"	"	218	
Plumpton	4.23	4.53	225	"	"	"	"	"	C.W. shut off at Southwaite.
Wreay			205	"	"	"	566	246	
Carlisle	4.38	5.6							

Dampers — 3-4 notches back damper

Pressure Gauge — Steam blowing off at 240 lbs/sq.in.on gauge.

Smokebox Ash — Approx. 2 barrow loads of fine ash.

Steaming has not been entirely satisfactory but was better on the banks than on the level. Management of the engine and firing were quite satisfactory.

The blowdown on this engine is operated by steam taken from the steam chest.

TABLE No.2. Cont'd.

Location.	Booked Time	Actual Time	Blr. Press.	Reg.	Cut off	Wtr.	Steam Chest Temp. °F	Exhaust Steam Temp. °F.	
Wigan	3.7	3.19	185	Full	10	Full	P.W. check Boars Head.		
			188	"	"	"	546	214	
Golborne			190	"	"	"	"	"	
Winwick Jc.	3.18	3.28	"	"	"	"	"	"	
Warrington	3.22	3.33¾	200	"	15	"	571	217	
Moore Troughs			185	"	16	"	581	217	Pricker used.
Preston Brook			180	"	16	⅞	"	216	
Weaver Jc.	3.32	3.43½	175	"	10	"	586	214	
Acton Bridge			"	"	15	"	583	"	C.W. off at Winsford
Winsford			180	"	"	¾	566	"	
Crewe	3.53	4.7							

Dampers — 3-4 nicks back damper

Smokebox Ash — 2 barrow loads - fine

Pressure Gauge — Blow of steam from safety valves at 210 lbs/sq.in. increasing in intensity up to pressure of 240 lbs/sq.in.

Steaming again unsatisfactory. Hard clinker formed on the bars.

TABLE No. 3

DYNAMOMETER CAR TESTS.

1.34p.m. Crewe - Carlisle. Engine No.6233

Load 535 tons. November 1st 1945.

Location	Booked Time	Actual Time	Blr. Press.	Reg.	Cut off	Wtr.	Steam Chest Temp. °F.	Exhaust Steam Temp. °F	
Crewe	1.34	2.35							
Coppenhall Jc.	1.39	2.41½	220	.6	10	Full	536	214	
Minshull Vernon			210	"	"	"	544	213	
Winsford			207	⅓	"	"	547	214	
Hartford			205	Coasting					Sig. check
			208	½	10	Full	550	"	
Acton Bridge			205	"	"	"	566	"	
Weaver Jc.	1.54	2.55¾	202	Coasting					Sig. check
			208	.6	10	"	556	213	
Preston Brook			207	½	"	"	556	213	
Warrington	2.4	3.4	235	Coasting					
			240	Full	14	Full			
Winwick Jc.	2.9	3.8	225	"	"	"	586	216	
Golborne Jc.			220	"	"	"	"	"	
Golborne			205	"	10	¾	571	213	
		3.14	200	½	15	"	"	216	
Wigan	2.19	3.17¾	210	.7	14	Full	576	215	
			"	"	17	"	"	218	P.W. Slack.Boars Hed
Standish Jc.	2.27	3.25	225	½	28	"	564	216	
			220	"	"	"	"	"	
			212	Full	17	"	"	"	
Euxton Jc.	2.35	3.35	240	Coasting					Sigs. Farington
Preston	2.42	3.44½	"	"					
Oxheys Jc.	2.45	3.48	223	Full	17	Full	571	218	
		52	212	½	15	"			
Barton & Broughton		"	"	"	12	"	581	212	
Brook Troughs				.7	12	⅞	581	212	
Garstang	2.54	3.57½	207	½	12	"	576	211	
Bay Horse			205	¾	18	Full	681	216	
		4.11	200	Full	18	"			
Lancaster	3.7	4.15	200	¾	18	"	576	218	
Hest Bank			208	¼	15	"	"	216	
Bolton-le-Sands			200	½	18	"	581	218	
Carnforth	3.14	4.22½	"	"	"	"	591	218	
		25	"	"	"	⅞	591	218	
Burton & Holme			196	"	"	Full	593	218	
Milnthorpe		4.30	208	"	"	"	606	218	
			200	Full	"	"	596	218	
Oxenholme	3.31	4.36	200	"	20	"	602	218	
		39	195	"	"	"	594	216	
		41½	200	"	28	⅞	586	218	Pricker used.
		44	205	"	"	Full	596	"	
		46	209	"	"	"	602	221	

P.T.O.

TABLE No. 4

DYNAMOMETER CAR TESTS.

12.42p.m. Carlilse - Crewe. Engine No.6233.

Load 525 tons (17) November 2nd 1945.

Location	Booked Time.	Actual Time.	Blr. Press.	Reg.	Cut off	Wtr.	Steam Chest Temp. °F	Exhaust Steam Temp. °F	
Carlisle	12.42	12.50							
		56	210	Full	35-40	Full	456	226	
		58	205	"	40-35	"	556	231	
		1.1	210	"	25	"	571	222	
Wreay			205	"	"	¾	576	224	
Southwaite			20C	"	"	⅞	591	224	
		8½	"	"	20	¾	596	219	
Calthwaite			206	"	"	⅞	598	219	
Plumpton	1.4	1.15	212	"	18	"	605	218	
		18½	215	"	16	¾	611	218	
Penrith	1.11	20½	217	"	"	"	610	218	
		23½	219	"	18	⅞	616	220	
Clifton & L.			218	"	"	"	"	218	
		29	222	"	25	Full	609	221	
		31	225	"	"	"	616	222	
			227	"	"	"	621	223	
Shap		33½	230	"	20	⅞	621	219	
			225	"	"	"	614	219	
Shap S.	1.34	1.39	220	"	"	"	596	219	
		47	195	.6	18	Full	546	216	
Low Gill			205	"	"	"	"	"	
Grayrigg				Coasting					
Oxenholme	1.54	56½	212	"					
Milnthorpe				"					
			225	.8	15	Full	486		
Carnforth	2.8	2.9	217	Full	"	"	518	214	
Bolton-le-Sands			222	"	"	"	556	218	
Hest Bank			212	"	"	"	"	"	
Lancaster	2.15	2.17	220	"	"	"	568	"	
		21	210	"	"	"	576	"	
Bay Horse			200	"	"	"	579	"	
		2.27½	"	"	"	"	586	"	
Brook Troughs			"	¼	"	"	576	"	
		2.33	"	Full	"	"	576	217	
Preston	2.41	2.40		Coasting					Stop for signals.
			225	Full	18	Full	220		
Farington			"	"	15	"	218		Signal check.
Euxton Jc.	2.50	2.52¼	227	"	18	"	571	220	
Balshaw Lane			"	"	15	"	581	218	
			218	"	"	"	576	215	
Coppull			200	Full	15	Full	576	216	
Standish Jc.	2.59	3.1		C asting					P.W. slack.

P.T.O.

TABLE No 3
Cont'd.

Location	Booked Time	Actual Time.	Blr. Press.	Reg.	Cut off	Wtr.	Steam Chest Temp. °F	Exhaust Steam Temp. °F	
Grayrigg		4.49	215	Full	28	Full	608	221	
			212	"	17	¾	616	217	
Low Gill			218	"	"	"	621	218	Signal Check.
Tebay	3.51	4.59	222	"	3.5	⅞	631	236	
			225	"	45	Full	640	263	Signal Check.
		5.4¾	"	"	35	"	628	236	
		5.6	222	"	30	"	616	234	
		5.12	223	Full to half.	45	"	602	231	
		5.15	227	½	45	"	611	241	
Shap Summit	4.3	5.16	"	"	"	"	"	"	

TABLE No. 4
Cont'd.

Location	Booked Time	Actual Time	Blr. Press.	Reg-ulator	Cut. off.	Wtr.	Steam Chest Temp. °F	Exhaust Steam Temp. °F	
Wigan	3.7	3.7½	212	⅓	15	Full	566	218	
Bamfurlong			223	"	"	"	566	214	
Golborne			204	Full	"	"	566	218	
			220	½	"	"	"	"	
Winwick Jc.	3.18			Coasting					Signal
Warrington	3.22	3.30	225	½	30	Full			
			200	Full	30-18	"	546	228	
Moore Troughs			210	"	18	"	558	218	Signal check.
Preston Brook			200	"	22	"	"	"	do.
Weaver Jc.	3.32	3.44	220	"	18	"	546	"	do.
Acton Bridge			218	"	"	"	564	"	
Hartford			202	"	18	¾	571	"	Signal check.
Winsford			204	"	15	½	576	216	
Crewe	3.53	4.7							

Top-left panel

TABLE NO.5

LONDON MIDLAND AND SCOTTISH RAILWAY COMPANY.

DYNAMOMETER CAR TEST DATA.   CAR NO.1

ENGINE.   6233, 4-6-2, Non streamlined.

TRAIN.   1.34p.m. Crewe – Carlisle, and 12.42p.m. Carlisle – Crewe.

DATE.   30th October, and 31st October 1945.

WEIGHT OF ENGINE & TENDER. TONS.   152.3 tons.
(2/3 COAL & WATER)

WEIGHT OF TRAIN BEHIND DRAWBAR.   550 tons Crewe – Carlisle 30th Oct.
(INCLUDING DYNAMOMETER CAR)   524 tons Carlisle – Crewe 31st Oct.

TRAIN MILES.   141.21 30th Oct.   141.19 31st Oct.

TON MILES. EXCLUDING WEIGHT OF ENGINE   148,535
            INCLUDING WEIGHT OF ENGINE   191,554

TIME.   ACTUAL RUNNING (MINUTES)   391.7
        "   INCLUDING STOPS (MINUTES)   403.5

SPEED M.P.H. AVERAGE   43.2 m.p.h. 30th Oct. 43.4 m.p.h. 31st Oct.
              MAXIMUM   74.0 "   "   80.0 "   "

WORK DONE. HORSE POWER MINUTES.   275063.9
            "   "   HOURS   4584.39

            HORSE POWER MINUTES PER
            TON MILE (EXCLUDING ENGINE)   1.85

COAL. (EXCLUDING SHED DUTIES) Barnboro' No.5 (Manvers Main)
       TOTAL WEIGHT, LBS.   17,408
       LBS. PER MILE 62.5
       LBS. PER TON MILE (EXCLUDING ENGINE) 12
       "   "   "   (INCLUDING ENGINE) 092
       "   " DRAWBAR HORSE POWER HOUR   ...   3.85
       "   " SQ.FT. OF GRATE AREA PER HOUR ...   54.2
            (ACTUAL RUNNING TIME)

GRATE AREA. ...SQ.FT. 50.0

WATER. TOTAL GALLONS   15,290
        GALLONS PER MILE 47.0
        LBS. PER TON MILE 69
        (INCLUDING ENGINE)
        LBS. PER DRAWBAR HORSE POWER HOUR ...   29.0

EVAPORATION. LBS. OF WATER PER LB. OF COAL   7.52

Top-right panel

REPORT NO. 83 DYNAMOMETER CAR TESTS 1945.
SUMMARY OF RESULTS -
COAL AND WATER CONSUMPTION TESTS OF 4-6-2 'CORONATION'
AND 4-6-0 'ROYAL SCOT' TAPER BOILERED ENGINES.

DATE	SECTION	WATER LB/D.B.H.P. HOUR.	WATER AVER- AGE	AVER. B.P. LB. /SQ. IN.	STEAM CHEST DEG. F.	REMARKS
ENGINE NO. 6233:-						
Run No. 829						
Oct. 30th	Crewe-Carlisle	29.9 }	} 29.0	220	572	Lot of sigs. But clear
					615	run on bank.
Oct. 31st	Carlisle-Crewe	28.1 }		212	-do-	Clear run on bank
						Some sig. checks.
Run No. 830						
Nov 1st	Crewe-Carlisle	29.65	-	205	565	Sigs. on bank
					593	
Nov 2nd	Carlisle-Crewe	25.1	-	218	575	Very good run. Time
					610	saved on banks etc.
						(9 min early Winwick)
Run No. 829						
Oct 31st	Carlisle-Shap Sum.	23.8	-	210	602	Clear run
			-	212	608	
Run No. 830						
Nov 2	-do-	22.9	- C.-Pen	208	590	-do-
			P.-Sum	225	615	
ENGINE NO. 6252:-						
Run No. 831						
Dec 4th	Crewe-Carlisle	30.7 }	} 30.5	225	570	Load 462. Serious sigs.
					605	on bank & Lancaster.
Dec 5th	Carlisle-Crewe	30.5 }		225	570	Serious sigs. on bank.
					608	
Run No. 832						
Dec 6th	Crewe-Carlisle	29.8 }	} 29.9	212	565	Clear run on bank. Few
			}		610	sigs. level. Poorish
						steaming
Dec 7th	Carlisle-Crewe	30.0 }		220	570	Clear run on bank.
				200 BK	605	Some sigs on level.
Run No. 831						
Dec 5th	Carlisle-Shap Sum.	27.4				Serious sigs.
Run No. 832						
Dec 7th	-do-	25.6				Clear run.

Bottom-left panel

TABLE No.6

LONDON MIDLAND AND SCOTTISH RAILWAY COMPANY.

DYNAMOMETER CAR TEST DATA.   CAR NO.1

ENGINE.   6233 4-6-2, Non streamlined.

TRAIN.   1.34p.m. Crewe – Carlisle, & 12.42p.m. Carlisle – Crewe.

DATE.   1st November, and 2nd November 1945.

WEIGHT OF ENGINE & TENDER. TONS.   152.3
(2/3 COAL & WATER)

WEIGHT OF TRAIN BEHIND DRAWBAR   535 tons Crewe – Carlisle
(INCLUDING DYNAMOMETER CAR)   525 "   Carlisle – Crewe

TRAIN MILES.   141.19 Crewe – Carlisle. 141.21 Carlisle – Crewe.

TON MILES. EXCLUDING WEIGHT OF ENGINE   149671.9
            INCLUDING WEIGHT OF ENGINE   192681.4

TIME.   ACTUAL RUNNING (MINUTES)   398.0
        "   INCLUDING STOPS (MINUTES)   404.0

SPEED M.P.H. AVERAGE. 41.5 Crewe – Carlisle. 42.6 Carlisle – Crewe
              MAXIMUM. 74.0 "   "   75.0 "   "

WORK DONE. HORSE POWER MINUTES   266604.05
            "   "   HOURS   4443.067

            HORSE POWER MINUTES PER
            TON MILE (EXCLUDING ENGINE)   1.78

COAL. (EXCLUDING SHED DUTIES) Barnboro' No.5 (Manvers Main)
       TOTAL WEIGHT LBS.   17388
       LBS. PER MILE 61.6
       LBS. PER TON MILE (EXCLUDING ENGINE)   .116
       2"   "   "   "   (INCLUDING ENGINE)   .09
       "   " DRAWBAR HORSE POWER HOUR   3.92
       "   " SQ.FT. OF GRATE AREA PER HOUR   54.2
            (ACTUAL RUNNING TIME)

GRATE AREA. ...SQ.FT... ...   .   50.0

WATER. TOTAL GALLONS   12095
        GALLONS PER MILE 42.8
        LBS. PER TON MILE 63
        (INCLUDING ENGINE)
        LBS. PER DRAWBAR HORSE POWER HOUR   27.2

EVAPORATION. LBS. OF WATER PER LB. OF COAL   6.96

Bottom-right panel

DATE	SECTION	WATER LB/D.B.H.P. HOUR.	WATER AVER- AGE	AVER. B.P. LB. /SQ. IN.	STEAM CHEST DEG. F.	REMARKS
FROM REPORT NO. 82. ENGINE NO. 6131 ('Royal Scot' T.B.)						
Run No. 823						
March 6th	Crewe-Carlisle	30.6 }	29.45	250	-	No C.W. Good run
March 7th	Carlisle-Crewe	28.3 }		250	-	-do- Few sigs after
						summit.
Run No. 824						
March 8th	Crewe-Carlisle	29.8 }	29.65	250	-	No C.W. Good run.
March 9th	Carlisle-Crewe	29.5 }		240	-	-do- Few sigs after
						summit.
						Clinker on bars.
Run No. 823						
March 7th	Carlisle-Shap Sum.	25.4				
Run No. 824						
March 9th	-do-	24.3				
REPORT NO. 83 ENGINE NO. 6131 ('Royal Scot' T.B.)						
Run No. 833						
Dec 11th	Crewe-Carlisle	35.0X				Serious check on bank
Dec 12th	Carlisle-Crewe	30.3				Sigs. Clifton
Run No. 834						
Dec 13th	Crewe-Carlisle	29.5 }	29.3			
Dec 14th	Carlisle-Crewe	29.1 }				
Run No. 833						
Dec 12th	Carlisle-Shap Sum.	27.6				Sigs. Clifton
Run No. 834						
Dec 14th	-do-	25.2				3 _ mins. late Summit.
						Average b.p. 218.

NOTE:- The test runs with 'Jubilee' class 6P 4-6-0 No. 5736 with larger boiler, i.e.:-
Run No. 825 on 1st May from Crewe to Carlisle and the return trip on 2nd May, 1945 and
Run No. 826 on 3rd May from Crewe to Carlisle and the return trip on 4th May, 1945,
were not listed in the summary of results.

Appendix 8
Accidents and Incidents Involving
'Princess Coronation' Class Locomotives

Date	Engine No.	Location	Details	Lives lost
8/4/39	6234	Watford Junction	Engine slipped on starting. Driver unable to close regulator. Rail head damaged and one piston valve spindle broken.	None
31/10/39	6228	Headstone Lane	Engine slipped on starting. Driver unable to close regulator. Rail head damaged.	None
10/9/40	6224	Cleghorn, Craigenhall, nr. Carstairs.	Boiler explosion due to uncovered firebox crown and an inexperienced crew.	1 *(fireman)*
16/11/40	6232	Berkhamsted, Herts.	Train ran into falled girders of bomb damaged bridge.	None
15/5/44	6225	Mossband Signalbox near Gretna.	Derailment due to poor condition of track. Signalbox demolished.	3
6/10/44	6230	Hartford	Over-run of signals and collision with rear of freight train.	None
21/7/45	6231	Ecclefechan	Over-run signals and collision with freight train setting back.	2 *(engine crew)*
17/11/45	6224	Between Rugby & Nuneaton	Struck lineside equipment.	None
18/5/47	6235	Lambrigg Crossing, Grayrigg Bank.	Collision with light engine: 4-4-0 No. 565	None
21/7/47	6244	Grendon nr. Polesworth.	Derailment due to track failure on curve.	5
7/3/48	46224	Lamington	Boiler explosion due to defective water level gauges.	1 *(driver)*
17/4/48	46251	Winsford	Collision with rear of preceeding train. - signalman's error.	24
26/5/49	46230	Douglas Park nr. Uddingston.	Signals and points set incorrectly and train derailed.	None
19/11/51	46252	Polesworth station	Train derailed on fast to slow crossover: - driver missed signal.	None
16/8/52	46224	Etterby Junction	Light engine over-ran starting signal and ran tender first into a passenger train standing at signals.	None
8/10/52	46242	Harrow and Wealdstone Station	Multiple collision due to signals passed at danger. Other engines were rebuilt 4-6-2 No. 46202 "Princess Anne" and 4-6-0 No. 45637 "Windward Islands."	112 *(total in incident including crew of 46242)*
8/8/53	46231	Abington	Track buckled in heat derailing last seven coaches of the "Royal Scot."	None
3/2/54	46250	Watford Tunnel	Coaches derailed by broken rail.	None
13/1/60	46231	Carlisle Station	Collision with rear of express already in the platform.	None
?/1961	46222	Kilmarnock	Engine slipped and driver could not close the regulator. Railhead worn away to the web. (Incident witnessed by the late Derek Cross.)	None

Appendix 9
Allocation of Boilers to
'Princess Coronation' Class Locomotives

Numbers quoted are the actual registered boiler numbers. The actual dates that boilers were fitted to engines are taken from Crewe Boiler Allocation notebooks which have survived for the period from 25/10/44 to 28/2/56. Dates with an 'x' suffix are dates that the engines left works.

PART ONE - BY ENGINE NUMBER.
(Repaired boilers except where otherwise stated)

Engine No	Boiler changes.
6220	9937 new 5/6/37x, 10637 new 5/1/40x, 9939 14/5/43x, 10292 30/9/46, 10640 19/12/49, 10302 4/8/52, 10295 15/6/55, 10296 13/8/60x.
6221	9938 new 19/6/37x, 10303 6/11/40x, 10637 17/7/43x, 10294 3/6/46, 10694 22/2/50, 10292 10/11/52, 10694 5/10/55, 10298 7/9/61x.
6222	9939 new 26/6/37x, 10638 new 14/1/40, 10298 28/7/43x, 10287 12/7/45, 10296 26/6/47, 12471 25/9/50, 10295 24/6/53, 12472 11/3/55, 10289 27/1/59x.
6223	9940 new 3/7/37x, 9939 17/4/40x, 9938 1/11/41x, 10642 new 30/5/42x, 10301 18/6/45, 10297 14/11/47, 10292 10/3/50, 10297 8/9/52, 9940 22/7/55, 10299 2/7/60x.
6224	9941 new 17/7/37x, 9937 25/5/40x, 10300 5/11/40x, 10289 16/11/43x, 10290 8/3/45, 10305 16/5/46, 10301 2/4/48, 10303 26/7/50, 10643 21/4/52, 10293 28/9/54, 9941 24/9/57x, 10288 27/1/62x.
6225	10297 new 14/5/38x, 10302 27/8/40x, 10290 22/8/42x, 10291 22/7/44x, 10638 20/2/47, 10642 15/2/50, 12472 25/2/53, 10645 17/12/54, 10301 7/8/58x, 10693 7/10/61x.
6226	10298 new 28/5/38x, 9941 14/9/40x, 9940 3/1/42x, 10304 25/7/42x, 10302 1/10/45, 9939 2/8/48, 10306 30/4/51, 10296 2/4/54, 10638 10/5/57x, 10640 18/6/60x.
6227	10299 new 11/6/38x, 10298 31/12/40x, 10288 17/12/42x, 10642 1/8/45, 10299 7/3/47, 10638 21/7/50, 10637 16/3/53, 10298 11/8/56x, 9938 18/5/61x.
6228	10300 new 18/6/38x, 9940 31/8/40x, 9937 2/8/41x, 10295 16/5/44x, 9941 8/9/47, 10693 1/9/50, 10694 6/2/53, 10288 9/5/55, 10291 2/9/59x.
6229	10306 new 7/9/38x, 10305 25/9/43x, 10298 5/1/46, 10645 24/11/47, 9938 23/1/50, 10639 21/3/52, 9939 4/3/54, 10302 6/1/56, 10297 8/10/59x.
6230	10301 new 2/7/38x, 10299 1/11/41x, 10302 9/2/43x, 10641 11/6/45, 9940 14/1/48, 10305 28/3/52, 10644 1/6/55, 10302 8/4/60x, 10694 27/1/62x.
6231	10302 new 2/7/38x, 10639 new 1/6/40x, 10300 27/11/43x, 10643 9/8/45, 10644 21/11/47, 9941 15/12/50, 10301 9/11/53, 10287 23/5/58x, 10646 5/4/61x.
6232	10303 new 2/7/38x, 10640 4/9/40x, 10301 21/1/43x, 9937 1/2/45, 10298 24/3/48, 10644 17/10/51, 12470 7/1/55, 10290 22/2/57x, 10303 28/10/60x.
6233	10304 new 23/7/38x, 10305 8/3/41x, 10287 7/8/43x, 10297 2/5/45, 10646 22/9/47, 10645 19/4/50, 10304 29/10/52, 9937 8/12/56x, 10641 26/9/59x.
6234	10305 new 6/8/38x, 10297 3/1/41x, 10294 2/9/44x, 10300 10/1/46, 10305 15/9/48, 10293 1/2/52, 9941 26/3/54, 12470 5/7/57x.
6235	10287 new 1/7/39x, 10299 22/6/43x, 9939 23/12/46, 10641 5/5/47, 10299 20/10/50, 10693 (with Hulson grate) 21/4/53, 10291 9/3/55, 10646 26/2/58x, 9940 17/1/61x.
6236	10288 new 29/7/39x, 10643 new 11/10/41x, 10289 22/6/45, 10643 21/1/48, 12470 5/11/51, 10306 27/10/54, 10637 11/7/58x, 10301 17/2/62x.
6237	10289 new 12/8/39x, 10293 17/9/43x, 9938 30/1/47, 10290 8/8/49, 9940 27/8/52, 10643 21/2/55, 10639 19/10/57x, 10645 18/2/59x.

Engine No	Boiler changes.
6238	10290 new 16/9/39x, 10641 new 24/7/41x, 9938 8/1/45, 10637 2/12/46, 10302 21/1/49, 10298 3/3/52, 10693 (Hulson grate off) 29/8/55, 10287 4/7/61x.
6239	10291 new 2/9/39x, 9941 22/4/44x, 10693 13/8/47, 10297 14/6/50, 10300 7/5/52, 10640 26/7/54, 10294 15/3/57x, 10306 13/3/59x.
6240	10292 new 30/3/40x, 10306 6/11/43x, 10291 6/6/47, 10304 9/12/49, 9938 9/6/52, 10289 30/9/54, 9939 17/7/58x, 9941 13/4/62x.
6241	10293 new 6/4/40x, 10640 29/5/43x, 10694 3/1/47, 10295 26/8/49, 10294 23/4/53, 10637 3/11/56x, 10643 11/2/58x.
6242	10294 new 18/5/40x, 10296 6/6/44x, 10640 28/3/47, 13043 8/6/49, 10299 4/8/53, 10641 17/4/57x, 10639 19/6/59x.
6243	10295 new 1/6/40x, 10292 24/12/43x, 10304 4/2/46, 10637 16/5/49, 10640 2/9/52, 10287 13/1/54, 10293 16/11/57x, 10288 18/12/59x, 10290 14/8/61x.
6244	10296 new 13/7/40x, 10639 8/1/44x, 10288 4/3/46, 9937 25/6/48, 10301 20/9/50, 10642 (with Hulson grate) 25/5/53, 10299 11/7/57x, 10644 11/6/60x.
6245	9940 repaired 26/6/43x, 10306 17/9/47, 10287 17/11/50, 10290 13/3/53, 10292 3/11/56x.
6246	10645 new 11/8/43x, 10639 16/9/46, 10289 6/10/48, 9937 27/11/50, 10646 20/5/53, 10640 2/5/57x, 9937 5/4/60x.
6247	10303 repaired 13/9/43x, 10293 19/5/47, 10289 25/5/51, 9937 25/1/54, 10297 26/9/56x, 12472 25/7/59x.
6248	10638 repaired 2/10/43x, 10290 28/10/46, 10288 11/2/49, 10641 5/3/51, 10638 31/8/53, 10304 19/2/57x, 10294 22/8/59x.
6249	10644 new 19/4/44x, 10287 30/9/47, 12472 30/8/50, 10645 9/1/53, 10639 27/8/54, 10296 31/8/57x, 10293 27/4/60x, 9939 ? (*See note below)
6250	10646 new 20/5/44x, 10303 25/8/47, 10291 27/3/50, 10303 1/10/52, 9939 24/8/56x, 9938 30/11/57x, 10300 27/1/61x.
6251	10693 new 3/6/44x, 10642 23/6/47, 10300 8/4/49, 10288 29/10/51, 9938 28/1/55, 10642 21/9/57x, 10295 4/11/60x.
6252	10694 new 24/6/44x, 10645 25/11/46, 10295 15/10/47, 10639 9/3/49, 9939 7/12/51, 10641 22/1/54, 10303 26/1/57x, 10304 5/2/60x.
6253	12470 new 14/9/46x, 10296 15/1/51, 12471 2/11/53, 13043 4/11/55, 10300 25/1/58x, 13043 2/6/60x.
6254	12471 new 17/9/46x, 10646 9/8/50, 13043 28/1/53, 10305 (converted to rocking grate) 19/9/55, 12471 17/4/57x, 10642 25/4/61x.
6255	12472 new 16/10/46x, 10294 26/6/50, 10291 11/12/52, 10300 8/12/54, 10305 2/11/57x.
6256	12473 new 13/12/47x, 13044 (new) 16/3/51, 12474 7/5/54, 12473 15/12/56x, 13044 15/8/59x.
6257	12474 new 19/5/48x, 12473 3/10/52, 13044 19/10/55, 12474 13/3/59x.
Spare boilers:-	BS1/39 10693/4 fitted to 6251 and 6252 when new. BS1/78 13043/4 first fitted to 6242 and 6256.

PART TWO - BY BOILER NUMBER.

Boiler No.	Fitted to engines nos.

Order No. B402 (1937):-

9937   6220 5/6/37x, 6224 25/5/40x, 6228 2/8/41x, 6232 1/2/45, 6244 25/6/58, 6246 27/11/50, 6247 25/1/54, 6233 8/12/56x, 6246 5/4/60x.

9938   6221 19/6/37x, 6223 1/11/41x, 6238 8/1/45, 6237 30/1/47, 6229 23/1/50, 6240 9/6/52, 6251 28/1/55, 6250 30/11/57x, 6227 18/5/61x.

9939   6222 26/6/37x, 6223 17/4/40x, 6220 14/5/43x, 6235 23/12/46, 6226 2/8/48, 6252 7/12/51, 6229 4/3/54, 6250 24/8/56x, 6240 17/7/58x, 6249 ? (*See note)

9940   6223 3/7/37x, 6228 31/8/40x, 6226 3/1/42x, 6245 26/6/43x, 6230 14/1/48, 6237 27/8/52, 6223 22/7/55, 6235 17/1/61x.

9941   6224 17/7/37x, 6226 14/9/40x, 6239 22/4/44x, 6228 8/9/47, 6231 15/12/50, 6234 26/3/54, 6224 24/9/57x, 6240 13/4/62x.

Order No. B414 (1939)

10287   6235 1/7/39x, 6233 7/8/43x, 6222 12/7/45, 6249 30/9/47, 6245 17/11/50, 6243 13/1/54, 6231 23/5/58x, 6238 4/7/61x.

10288   6236 29/7/39x, 6227 17/12/42x, 6244 4/3/46, 6248 11/2/49, 6251 29/10/51, 6228 9/5/55, 6243 18/12/59x, 6224 27/1/62x.

10289   6237 12/8/39x, 6224 16/11/43x, 6236 22/6/45, 6246 6/10/48, 6247 25/5/51, 6240 30/9/54, 6222 27/1/59x.

10290   6238 16/9/39x, 6225 22/8/42x, 6224 8/3/45, 6248 28/10/46, 6237 8/8/49, 6245 13/3/53, 6232 22/2/57x, 6243 14/8/61x.

10291   6239 2/9/39x, 6225 22/7/44x, 6240 6/6/47, 6250 27/3/50, 6255 11/12/55, 6235 9/3/55, 6228 2/9/59x.

10292   6240 30/3/40x, 6243 24/12/43x, 6220 30/6/49, 6223 10/3/50, 6221 10/11/52, 6245 3/11/56x.

10293   6241 6/4/40x, 6237 17/9/43x, 6247 19/5/47, 6234 1/2/52, 6224 28/9/54, 6243 16/11/57x, 6249 27/4/60x.

10294   6242 18/5/40x, 6234 2/9/44x, 6221 3/6/46, 6255 26/6/50, 6241 23/4/53, 6239 15/3/57x, 6248 22/8/59x.

10295   6243 1/6/40x, 6228 16/5/44x, 6252 15/10/47, 6241 26/8/49, 6222 24/6/53, 6220 15/6/55, 6251 4/11/60x.

10296   6244 13/7/40x, 6242 6/6/44x, 6222 26/6/47, 6253 15/1/51, 6226 2/4/54, 6249 31/8/57x, 6220 13/8/60x.

Order B408 (1938)

10297   6225 14/5/38x, 6234 3/1/41x, 6233 2/5/45, 6223 14/11/47, 6239 14/6/50, 6223 8/9/52, 6247 26/9/56x, 6229 8/10/59x.

10298   6226 28/5/38x, 6227 31/12/40x, 6222 28/7/43x, 6229 5/1/46, 6232 24/3/48, 6238 3/3/52, 6227 11/8/56x, 6221 7/9/61x.

10299   6227 11/6/38x, 6230 1/11/41x, 6235 22/6/43x, 6227 7/3/47, 6235 20/10/50, 6242 4/8/53, 6244 11/7/57x, 6223 2/7/60x.

10300   6228 18/6/38x, 6224 5/11/40x, 6231 27/11/43x, 6234 10/1/46, 6251 8/4/49, 6239 7/5/52, 6255 8/12/54, 6253 25/1/58x, 6250 27/1/61x.

10301   6230 2/7/38x, 6232 21/1/43x, 6223 18/6/45, 6224 2/4/48, 6244 20/9/50, 6231 9/11/53, 6225 7/8/58x, 6236 17/2/62x.

10302   6231 2/7/38x, 6225 27/8/40x, 6230 9/2/43x, 6226 1/10/45, 6238 21/1/49, 6220 4/8/52, 6229 6/1/56, 6230 8/4/60x.

10303   6232 2/7/38x, 6221 6/11/40x, 6247 13/9/43x, 6250 25/8/47, 6224 26/7/50, 6250 1/10/52, 6252 26/1/57x, 6232 28/10/60x.

10304   6233 23/7/38x, 6226 25/7/42x, 6243 4/2/46, 6240 9/12/49, 6233 29/10/52, 6248 19/2/57x, 6252 5/2/60x.

10305   6234 6/8/38x, 6233 8/3/41x, 6229 25/9/43x, 6224 16/5/46, 6234 15/9/48, 6230 28/3/52, 6254 (converted to rocking grate) 19/9/55, 6255 2/11/57x.

10306   6229 7/9/38x, 6240 6/11/43x, 6245 17/9/47, 6226 30/4/51, 6236 27/10/54, 6239 13/3/59x.

Order B415 (1939-40)

10637   6220 new 5/1/40x, 6221 17/7/43x, 6238 2/12/46, 6243 16/5/49, 6227 16/3/53, 6241 3/11/56x, 6236 11/7/58x.

10638   6222 new 24/1/40x, 6248 2/10/43x, 6225 20/2/47, 6227 21/7/50, 6248 31/8/53, 6226 10/5/57x.

10639   6231 new 1/6/40x, 6244 8/1/44x, 6246 16/9/46, 6252 9/3/49, 6229 21/3/52, 6249 27/8/54, 6237 19/10/57x, 6242 19/6/59x.

10640   6232 new 4/9/40x, 6241 29/5/43x, 6242 28/3/47, 6220 19/12/49, 6243 2/9/52, 6239 26/7/54, 6246 2/5/57x, 6226 18/6/60x.

10641   6238 new 14/7/41x, 6230 11/6/45, 6235 5/5/47, 6248 5/3/51, 6252 22/1/54, 6242 17/4/57x, 6233 26/9/59x.

10642   6223 new 30/5/42x, 6227 1/8/45, 6251 23/6/47, 6225 15/2/50, 6244 (with Hulson grate) 25/5/53, 6251 21/9/57x, 6254 25/4/61x.

10643   6236 new 11/10/41x, 6231 9/8/45, 6236 21/1/48, 6224 21/4/52, 6237 21/2/55, 6241 11/2/58x.

10644   6249 new 19/4/44x, 6231 21/11/47, 6232 17/10/51, 6230 1/6/55, 6244 11/6/60x.

10645   6246 new 11/8/43x, 6252 25/11/46, 6229 24/11/47, 6233 19/4/50, 6249 9/1/53, 6225 20/1/55x, 6237 18/2/59x.

10646   6250 new 20/5/44x, 6233 22/9/47, 6254 9/8/50, 6246 20/5/53, 6235 22/6/58x, 6231 5/4/61x.

Order BS1/39 (spares) (1944):-

10693   6251 new 3/6/44x, 6239 13/8/47, 6228 1/9/50, 6235 (Hulson grate) 21/4/53, 6238 (Hulson grate off) 29/8/55, 6225 7/10/61x.

10694   6252 new 24/6/44x, 6241 3/1/47, 6221 22/2/50, 6228 6/2/53, 6221 5/10/55, 6230 27/1/62x.

Order B464 (1946-7)

12470   6253 new 14/9/46x, 6236 5/11/51, 6232 7/1/55, 6234 5/7/57x.

12471   6254 new 17/9/46x, 6222 25/9/50, 6253 2/11/53, 6254 17/4/57x.

12472   6255 new 16/10/46x, 6249 30/8/50, 6225 25/2/53, 6222 11/3/55, 6247 25/7/59x.

12473   6256 new 13/2/47x, 6257 3/10/52, 6256 15/12/56x.

12474   6257 new 19/5/48x, 6256 7/5/54, 6257 13/3/59x.

Order BS1/78 (spares) (1949)

13043   6242 new 8/6/49, 6254 28/1/53, 6253 4/11/55, 6253 2/6/60x.

13044   6256 new 16/3/51, 6257 19/10/55, 6256 15/8/59x.

NOTE:-

*Note 1:- In his book "The Duchess - Stanier's Masterpiece" Roger J. Mannion records the last boiler fitted to No. 6249 as being 9939. This is not shown on the engine record card, and the last recorded repair was a heavy intermediate before she was out-shopped on 9th February, 1962. Boiler changes were normally made only at heavy general repairs, but records of later repairs are often incomplete. Boiler 9939 was taken off No. 6240 and replaced by 9941 on 13/4/62. Since 6249 was not withdrawn until w.e. 9th November, 1963 it could have been repaired and put on the engine around that time, but that seems unlikely in the circumstances.

However, there must have been other changes, e.g 6234 had boiler no. 12470 fitted on 5/7/57 but was not scrapped until w.e. 26/1/63; and 6245 had boiler no. 10292 fitted on 3/11/56 but was not scrapped until w.e. 12/9/64. It seems that after early 1962 the engine record cards were not kept up to date with the shoppings and the various boiler changes that occurred, which is also true of mileages and other data.

Allocation of Tenders to
'Princess Coronation' Class Locomotives

'PRINCESS CORONATION' CLASS TENDERS.
4,000 GALLONS OF WATER, 10 TONS OF COAL
Weights:- 28 tons 10 cwt light, 56 tons 7 cwt loaded except for
Nos. 10623 & 10624:- 28 tons 13 cwt light, 56 tons 10 cwt loaded.

FIRST ALLOCATION OF TENDERS.

Tender No.	Build date	Attached to eng.	Date Attached	Remarks
				Order No. T402.
9703	1937	6220	1/6/37	Type IV. Fabricated construction (per letter dated 28/8/36 ref. TK7675). Fitted with coal pusher. Streamlined.
9704	1937	6221	19/6/37	-do-
9705	1937	6222	22/6/37	-do-
9706	1937	6223	28/6/37	-do-
9707	1937	6224	13/7/37	Order N. T408.
9743	1938	6225	11/5/38	Type IV. Fabricated construction Fitted with coal pusher. Streamlined
9744	1938	6226	23/5/38	-do-
9745	1938	6227	7/6/38	-do-
9746	1938	6228	17/6/38	-do-
9747	1938	6229	7/9/38	Order No. T408.
9748	1938	6230	27/6/38	Type V. Fabricated construction Fitted with coal pusher. Non-streamlined.
9749	1938	6231	28/6/38	-do-
9750	1938	6232	1/7/38	-do-
9751	1938	6233	18/7/38	-do-
9752	1938	6234	4/8/38	Order No. T414.
9798	1939	6235	27/6/39	Type IV. Fabricated construction Fitted with coal pusher. Streamlined.
9799	1939	6236	27/6/39	-do-
9800	1939	6237	9/8/39	-do-
9801	1939	6238	14/9/39	-do-
9802	1939	6239	29/8/39	-do-
9803	1940	6240	27/3/40	-do-
9804	1940	6241	3/4/40	-do-
9805	1940	6242	15/5/40	-do-
9806	1940	6243	29/5/40	-do-
9807	1940	6244	12/7/40	Order No. T415.
9808	1943	6245	26/6/43	Type IV. Fabricated construction Fitted with coal pusher. Streamlined.
9809	1943	6246	11/8/43	-do-
9810	1943	6247	13/9/43	-do-
9811	1943	6248	2/10/43	Order No. T415.
9812	1944	6249	19/4/44	Type IV. Fabricated construction Fitted with coal pusher. Streamlined but fitted to a non-streamlined engine.
9813	1944	6250	20/5/44	-do-
9814	1944	6251	3/6/44	-do-
9815	1944	6252	24/6/44	

Note:- The remaining two tenders for order no. T415 and the engines to which they were to have been attached were not built until after the end of the war.

				Order no. T464. Type II. Partly rivetted.
9816	1946	6253	14/9/46	Fitted with coal pusher. Non-streamlined.
9817	1946	6254	17/9/46	-do-
10622	1946	6255	16/10/46	Order No. T464. Type II modified.
10623	1947	6256	13/12/47	Fitted with coal pusher. Non-streamlined. Roller bearing axleboxes.
10624	1948	6257	19/5/48	-do-

SUBSEQUENT TENDER CHANGES BETWEEN ENGINES.

The following had tender changes. All other tenders remained attached to the engine as first out-shopped as shown.

Eng. No.	Tender changes
6220	9803 (29/6/44), 9703 (6/8/44), 9804 (9/1/46), 9705 (3/8/49).
6221	9816 (17/11/61), 9359 (ex 'Princess Royal' 46206 and already fitted with a coal pusher) (18/10/62).
6222	9804 (3/8/49)
6223	9748 (6/5/46 - see Note 1 below)
6224	9748 (14/8/45), 9706 (6/5/46 - see Note 1 below)
6225	9749 (9/8/45), 9799 (11/3/49)
6226	No changes
6227	No changes
6228	No changes
6229	9802 (22/11/45)
6230	9707 (14/8/45)
6231	9812 (23/1/45)
6232	No changes
6233	No changes
6234	No changes
6235	No changes
6236	A79294 (10/6/48 - see Note 2 below), 9799 (21/6/48), 9749 (21/1/49), 9807 (24/12/52)
6237	9804 (17/4/44), 9800 (6/5/44)
6238	9801 (14/9/39)
6239	9747 (22/11/45)
6240	9703 (29/6/44), 9803 (6/8/44)
6241	9805 (13/3/44), 9811 (1/8/53), 9703 (21/9/56), 9811 (3/11/56)
6242	9804 (13/3/44), 9800 (17/4/44), 9804 (6/5/44), 9703 (9/1/46), 9816 (26/7/51), 9703 (1/9/51), 9811 (21/9/56), 9703 (24/10/56)
6243	No changes
6244	9809 (26/6/45)
6245	9807 (26/6/45), 9811 (3/6/52), 9805 (4/8/53)
6246	9749 (16/5/61)
6247	9811 (13/10/44), 9807 (3/6/52), 9749 (24/12/52), 9809 (16/5/61)
6248	9810 (13/10/44)
6249	9749 (23/1/45), 9743 (9/8/45)
6250	No changes
6251	No changes
6252	No changes
6253	9703 (28/6/51), 9816 (1/9/51), 9750 (24/12/54), 9816 (19/1/55) *Query:- 9704 attached in 1961 ?*
6254	No changes
6255	No changes
6256	No changes
6257	No changes

Notes:-

1. 6224 fitted with non-streamlined tender 9748 (ex 6230) on 14/8/45, then with streamlined tender 9706 (ex 6223) on 6/5/46.
6223 was then fitted with non-streamlined tender 9748 on 6/5/46.

2. A 5,000 gallon capacity Ministry of Supply type eight-wheeled tender No. A79294, from a War Department 2-8-0 and temporarily lettered 'L.M.S.', was fitted to 46236 during the 'Locomotive Exchange' trials between London Waterloo and Exeter from 10th to 21st June, 1948 due to the lack of water troughs on the Southern Region.

Appendix 11
Disposal of
'Princess Coronation' Class Locomotives

LOCO. NO.	DATE WITHDRAWN *(week ending)*	DISPOSAL
46220	20/4/63	On scrap road at Crewe Works 12/5/63. Cut up at Crewe.
46221	18/5/63	On scrap road at Crewe Works 22/6/63. Cut up at Crewe
46222	on 24/10/63	Cut up at Crewe Works w.e. 2/11/63.
46223	4/10/63	Cut up at Crewe Works w.e. 19/10/63
46224	on 17/10/63	Cut up at Crewe Works w.e. 26/10/63
46225	12/9/64	In sidings at Carlisle Upperby shed by 19/9/64. Sold to Arnott Young, West of Scotland Shipbreaking Co. Troon Harbour, Ayrshire 11/64 and arrived 2/12/64.
46226	12/9/64	In sidings at Carlise Upperby shed by 19/9/64. Sold with others of the class to Slag Reduction Co., Barrow but movement order dated 15/12/64 and sale cancelled due to route restriction problems. Resold to Arnott Young, West of Scotland Shipbreaking Co. Troon Harbour, Ayrshire 12/64. Arrived 25/1/65.
46227	on 29/12/62	Stored out of use at Eastfield shed then at Carstairs until hauled to Crewe on 8/11/63. Cut up at Crewe.
46228	12/9/64	Stored at Crewe on 15/11/64. Sold to J. Cashmore, Great Bridge, Tipton, Staffs. 11/64. Cut up w.e. 9/1/65.
46229	15/2/64	Stored at Edge Hill from 12/63. Purchased by Butlins for display at Minehead Holiday Camp. Outside Crewe Works paint shop 15/2/64. Restored to L.M.S. crimson lake livery as 6229. On Crewe North shed 18/4/64. Moved to Minehead 4/64. Later purchased by the Friends of the National Railway Museum at York where it is currently on static display.
46230	on 6/11/63	In Crewe Works yard on 10/11/63 and cut up at there during w.e. 15/11/63.
46231	on 29/12/62	Stored out of use until hauled from Carstairs to Crewe on 8/11/63. Waiting works 10/11/63. Cut up at Crewe Works.
46232	on 29/12/62	Stored out of use until hauled from Carstairs to Crewe on 8/11/63. On Crewe South shed waiting works 10/11/63. Cut up at Crewe Works.
46233	8/2/64	Stored at Edge Hill from 10/63. Purchased by Butlins for display at Heads of Ayr Holiday Camp. Arrived Crewe Works on 14/6/64. Restored to L.M.S. crimson lake livery as 6233. Moved to Ayr 15/9/64. Moved to Bressingham Steam Museum 1/3/71 and then to the West Shed of the Princess Royal Class Locomotive Trust on 2-4/2/96. Restored to main line running order. Hauled the Royal Train between Holyhead and Crewe on 11/6/02. Currently hauling steam specials over Network Rail.
46234	26/1/63	In Crewe Works on 12/5/63. Cut up at Crewe.
46235	12/9/64	Stored at Crewe on 15/11/64. Preserved as part of the National Collection. Repainted in B.R. green livery lined out in orange and black and preserved initially in the Birmingham Museum of Science & Industry. Now in the new Museum of Science and Discovery at Millennium Point, Birmingham.
46236	14/3/64	Cut up at Crewe Works.
46237	12/9/64	In store at Carlisle Upperby shed on 1/2/64. Sold to Arnott Young, West of Scotland Shipbreaking Co., Troon Harbour, Ayrshire, 11/64 and arrived 2/12/64.
46238	12/9/64	In sidings at Carlisle Upperby shed by 19/9/64. Sold to Arnott Young, West of Scotland Shipbreaking Co. Ltd., Troon Harbour, Ayrshire, 12/64.
46239	12/9/64	Stored at Crewe on 15/11/64. Sold to J. Cashmore, Great Bridge, Tipton, Staffs. 11/64. Cut up w.e. 9/1/65.
46240	12/9/64	Stored at Crewe on 15/11/64. Sold to J. Cashmore, Great Bridge, Tipton, Staffs. 11/64. Seen at Crewe North shed on 20/12/64 and at Oxley on 17/1/65. Delivered to Cashmore's. Tender being cut up on 27/3/65 and engine cut up shortly afterwards.
46241	5/9/64	Sold to J. Cashmore, Great Bridge, Tipton, Staffs. 11/64. Waiting cutting up on 23/1/65.
46242	on 18/10/63	Cut up at Crewe w.e. 2/11/63.
46243	12/9/64	Sold to Central Wagon Co., Ince, Wigan 1/65. Arrived by 15/3/65. Cut up 17/8/65.
46244	12/9/64	In sidings at Carlisle Upperby shed by 27/9/64. Sold to Arnott Young, West of Scotland Shipbreaking Co., Troon Harbour, Ayrshire, 12/64.

LOCO. NO.	DATE WITHDRAWN *(week ending)*	DISPOSAL
46245	12/9/64	Stored at Crewe on 15/11/64. Sold to J. Cashmore, Great Bridge, Tipton, Staffs. 11/64. Dispatched from Crewe 8/12/64. Cut up by 19/12/64.
46246	26/1/63	On scrap road at Crewe Works on 12/5/63. Cut up at Crewe.
46247	25/5/63	On scrap road at Crewe Works on 22/6/63. Cut up at Crewe.
46248	5/9/64	Stored at Crewe on 15/11/64. Sold to J. Cashmore, Great Bridge, Tipton, Staffs., 11/64. Arrived on 17/11/64. Cut up by 21/11/64.
46249	on 5/11/63	Cut up at Crewe Works w.e. 15/11/63.
46250	12/9/64	In sidings at Carlisle Upperby shed by 19/9/64. Sold to Arnott Young, West of Scotland Shipbreaking Co., Troon Harbour, Ayrshire, 11/64 and arrived on 2/12/64.
46251	12/9/64	Stored at Crewe on 15/11/64. Sold to J. Cashmore, Great Bridge, Tipton, Staffs. 11/64. Dispatched from Crewe 8/12/64. Cut up w.e. 12/12/64.
46252	1/6/63	Stored at Camden shed, London. Sent to Crewe Works w.e. 9/9/63. Cut up at Crewe.
46253	26/1/63	In Crewe Works on 21/4/63. Cut up at Crewe.
46254	12/9/64	Stored at Crewe on 15/11/64. Sold to J. Cashmore, Great Bridge, Tipton, Staffs. 11/64. Dispatched from Crewe 8/12/64. Cut up by 19/12/64.
46255	12/9/64	In sidings at Carlisle Upperby shed by 27/9/64. Sold to Arnott Young, West of Scotland Shipbreaking Co., Troon Harbour, Ayrshire 12/64.
46256	12/9/64	Although already taken out of traffic, worked the R.C.T.S. "Scottish Lowlander" railtour on 26/9/64. Stored at Crewe 15/11/64. Sold to J. Cashmore, Great Bridge, Tipton, Staffs. 11/64. Cut up w.e. 9/1/65.
46257	12/9/64	In sidings at Carlisle Upperby shed 2/64. Stored at Preston 9/64. Sold to Arnott Young, West of Scotland Shipbreaking Co., Troon Harbour, Ayrshire 11/64. Arrived 2/12/64 and cut up.

After the mass withdrawal of the remaining 'Princess Coronation' class pacifics in September, 1964 arrangements were soon made for their disposal for scrap. A total of eight members of the class formerly allocated to Carlisle were dispatched to the West of Scotland Shipbreaking Company at Troon Harbour. 46238 'City of Carlisle' can be identified as the last in the line in this sadly evocative photograph of four of them being hauled past Gretna to their fate by Class 8 2-8-0 No. 48104. The other three sold to the scrapyard on the same date were 46226, 46244 and 46255, and the first of these three is known to have arrived in the yard on 25th January, 1965. (Peter Brock)

Appendix 12
Others of the Class Preserved

There are two other members of the "Princess Coronation" class of locomotives preserved as follows:-

46229 'DUCHESS OF HAMILTON'

This locomotive was withdrawn from service by British Railways during the week ending 15th February, 1964 from Edge Hill motive power depot. Like 46233, she was purchased by Butlins and moved to Crewe Locomotive Works and restored for static display, being given back her old 6229 number again and on 25th March 1964 she was in the Paint Shop being repainted in a representation of the original L.M.S. crimson lake livery. She was on Crewe North motive power depot on 18th April, and was subsequently moved southwards, and on 24th April she was seen travelling through Birmingham Snow Hill station hauled by W.R. 4-6-0 6825 'Llanvair Grange' on her way south. Shortly afterwards, having been moved over the Minehead branch, she was put on static display on a short length of track in Butlin's Minehead Holiday Camp.

After being on display there for over eleven years, she left the camp on Sunter Brothers low loaders on 10th March, 1975, and was transported to Minehead station where she was placed on the branch line tracks the following day. On 13th March she was moved along the branch hauled by Class 25 Bo-Bo diesel electric locomotive No. 25059 to Taunton where she was placed inside the old lifting shop.

She continued her journey by rail on 17th March, and arrived at Swindon Locomotive Works where she was to have some mechanical attention, her smoke deflectors replaced and repainting again in the B.R. L.M.R. maroon livery. Still at that time on loan by Butlins to the National Railway Museum at York, she was moved there in May, 1976, and eventually purchased by the Friends of the N.R.M. for that museum.

Restoration to first class running order then began in the National Railway Museum workshop in York, and in this the N.R.M. were greatly assisted by Alan Bloom, who loaned several key items such as cylinder relief valves and bogie springs as well as patterns for the various firebars and brake blocks from 6233. When the tyre on the right leading coupled wheel of 6229 was found to be worn beyond re-turning limits, Alan Bloom offered to do an exchange with a wheelset from 6233, but in the event the N.R.M. decided to have new tyres made - undoubtedly the right decision.

'Duchess of Hamilton' returned to main line duties on steam-hauled special excursions on 10th May, 1980 and subsequently worked over a number of main lines, including the Midland's Settle-Carlisle line, putting up some splendid performances. She also appeared at the 150th Anniversary celebrations of the Liverpool and Manchester Railway at Rainhill. She is currently on static display in the National Railway Museum in York.

46235 'CITY OF BIRMINGHAM'

One of the last batch of the class to be withdraw, 46235 was taken out of service during the week ending 12th September, 1964 and subsequently set aside for preservation as the class representative in the National Collection. At first stored at Crewe North motive power depot, she was then hauled dead from Crewe to Nuneaton on 5th January, 1965 and again put into storage. Moved back to Crewe Works on 4th October, 1965, she was prepared for static display and repainted in the B.R. Brunswick green livery lined out in orange and black.

Still in Crewe paint shop on 24th April, 1966, she was eventually hauled dead to Saltley (Birmingham) motive power depot on 20th May, 1966, travelling via Wellington, Snow Hill, Bordesley and Camp Hill, and the following day was moved to Lawley Street goods yard. Here the engine and tender were separated and put onto low loaders for the short journey to the then Birmingham Museum of Science and Industry in Newhall Street. Here she was placed on a short length of track covered by plastic sheeting over a light steel framing, whilst the new exhibition hall was built around her.

Once commissioned, she was capable of being moved by hydraulic rams a short distance over the track upon which she was displayed, and by the use of clever lighting and mirrors, it was thus possible to see all of the motion in operation. Together with the associated interpretive material, she made an impressive exhibit.

She is currently on display in the new Museum of Science and Discovery at Millennium Point, Birmingham.

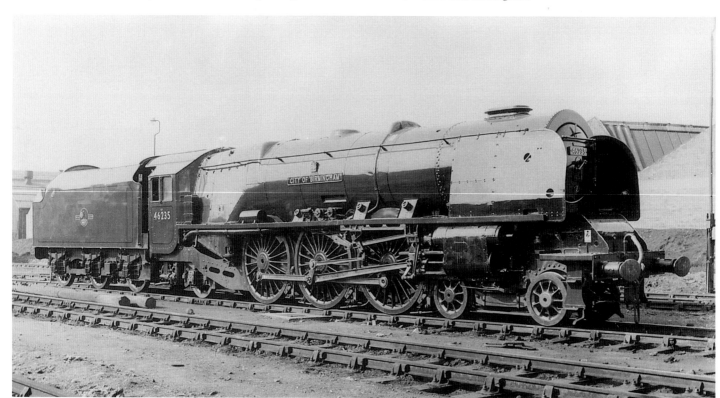

46235 'City of Birmingham' as currently displayed as a static exhibit in the new Museum of Science and Discovery, Birmingham in her final B.R. brunswick green livery. (Museum of Science and Industry, Birmingham)

6233 - Known Service Workings to 2002

Key: -
R = Record card   O = Observation
P = Photograph   S = Sighting
Pcs = Colour Slide   Pcp = Colour Print
RI = Restoration at Bressingham

Date	Location	Train	Information	Key
1938				
Jul	Crewe Works		Official Photo in Shop Grey	P
Jul	Shrewsbury	Running in turn		P
Sat 23Jul	Allocated Camden			R
Wed 24Aug		10.00am Glasgow-Euston		S
Sep	Lime Street	Merseyside Express	Up Train dep 10.10	P
Sep	Camden	Down Royal Scot		P
1938	South of Crewe?	Royal Scot		P
1938	Unknown	Royal Scot		P
1938	Acton Bridge	Glasgow-Birmingham		P
1938/39	Calthwaite	Up Mid-Day Scot	E E Smith	P
1938/39	Shap Wells	Down Royal Scot	Eric Treacy/NRM	P
1938/41	Crewe North MPD	On Shed	W Whitworth/NRM	P
			Miles in year 46,599	
1939				
Sat 15Apr	Euston Station		K T Primett	O
Mon 10Jul	Entered Crewe Works			R
Thu 27Jul	Left Crewe Works			R
1939	Polmadie	On shed	J L Stevenson	P
1939	Rugby	XP	R Humm	P
1939	Crewe North MPD		R M Tomkins	P
			Miles in year 89,436	
1940				
Mon 01Jul	Entered Crewe Works			R
Tue 16Jul	Left Crewe Works			R
			Miles in year 82,750	
1941				
Wed 05Feb	Entered Crewe Works			R
Sat 08Mar	Left Crewe Works			R
	Crewe Works		Official Photos	P
Thu 5Jun	Entered Crewe Works			R
Wed 18Jun	Left Crewe Works			R
Sat 09Aug	Blisworth	Unidentified XP		O
			Miles in year 74,992	
1942				
Wed 25Mar	Entered Crewe Works			R
Wed 22Apr	Left Crewe Works			R
Fri 21Aug		9.38pm Glasgow – Carlisle		O
Sat 29Aug		4.55am Carlisle – Glasgow		O
Sat 29Aug		7.29pm Carlisle – Glasgow		O
Mon 31Aug		7.29pm Carlisle – Glasgow		O
Tue 06Oct	Entered Crewe Works			R
Fri 13Nov	Left Crewe Works			R
			Miles in year 54,163	
1943				
Fri 02Jul	Entered Crewe Works			R
Sat 07Aug	Left Crewe Works			R
			Miles in year 89,591	
1944				
Wed 05Jan	Entered Crewe Works			R
Thu 10Feb	Left Crewe Works			R
Tue 16May	Entered Crewe Works			R
Fri 02Jun	Left Crewe Works			R
Mon 12Jun	Berkhamsted	06.50 Euston -Windermere	H C Casserley	P
Thu 12Oct	Entered Crewe Works			R
Fri 03Nov	Left Crewe Works			R
			Miles in year 60,844	
1945				
Wed 18Apr	Entered Crewe Works			R
Sat 19May	Left Crewe Works			R
1941-46	Unknown	XP		P
			Miles in year 50,840	
1946				
Fri 15Feb	Entered Crewe Works			R
Thu 07Mar	Left Crewe Works			R
Mon 29Jul	Arriving Euston 6pm		James Graham	O
Sat 03Aug	Entered Crewe Works			R
Sat 24Aug	Left Crewe Works			R
Mon 04Nov	Shrewsbury		R K Blencowe	P
			Miles in year 68,480	
1947				
1946/47	Crewe		W Whitworth/NRM	P
1946/47	Unknown MPD		W Whitworth/NRM	P
1946/47	Berkhamsted	Up XP	H C Casserley	P
Sat 26Jul	Entered Crewe Works			R
Tue 28Oct	Left Crewe Works			R
Tue 04Nov	Entered Crewe Works	Non Classified Repair (Tender Hot Box)		R
Fri 14Nov	Left Crewe Works			R
			Miles in year 40,947	
1948				
1947/48	Crewe North MPD		A G Ellis collection	P
1947/48	Thrimby	Train	E. Treacy / NRM	P
1947/48	Carlisle	Up XP W48	H G Tidey / NRM	P
1947/48	Near Shap Quarry	Up XP	R Humm collection	P
Sat 24Apr	Lichfield T V	11.37 ex Euston	HMRS/E S Russell collection	P
Sun 25Apr	Roe Green Jnc	Down Royal Scot	J H Tonge	P
Sun 25Apr	Sanderson Sidings	Down Royal Scot	W D Cooper collection	P
Mon 30Aug	Entered Crewe Works	Light Special Repair		R
Wed 29Sep	Left Crewe Works			R
Sat 02Oct	Entered Crewe Works	for non-classified repair		R
Wed 20Oct	Left Crewe Works			R
Tue 28Dec	Perth-Euston/Carlisle			O
			Miles in year 67,934	
1949				
1948/50	Crewe North MPD		P R Weathersett / NRM	P
1948/50	Scout Green	Down XP	E Treacy / NRM	P
Tue 04Jan	Euston - Carlisle			O
Wed 13Jul	Entered Crewe Works	Light Intermediate		R
Fri 12Aug	Left Crewe Works			
Sun 11Dec	Crewe North MPD		British Locomotive Society	O
			Miles in year 70,426	
1950				
Thu 13Apr	Entered Crewe Works	Heavy General		R
Fri 19May	Left Crewe Works			
May	Crewe North MPD		W Whitworth/NRM	P
Sat 03Jun	Wilmslow	Manchester-West of England XP	G Coltas	P
Sun 26Nov	From Crewe North	5.02am Crewe- Euston	Ted Padfield (fireman)	O
			Miles in year 65,291	
1951				
Wed 14Mar	Entered Crewe Works	Light Casual		R
Tue 10Apr	Left Crewe Works			
Sun 01Jul	Glasgow Central 9pm		James Graham	O
Wed 19Dec	Awaiting Works			R
Thu 27Dec	Entered Crewe Works	Heavy Intermediate		
			Miles in year 67,088	
1952				
Sun 20Jan	Crewe Works		British Locomotive Society	O
Thu 24Jan	Left Crewe Works			R
Wed 20Feb	Watford	Down Mid Day Scot W97	Harry Halls Logs	O
Sun 27Apr	Calthwaite	Glasgow-Birmingham	F Alcock	P
Thu 15May	Tebay	Down Mid-Day Scot	J Wilkinson	P
Mon 26Jul	Beattock	up train	J Roberston	P
May-Jul	Euston		E Treacy/NRM	P
May-Jul	Crewe		R K Blencowe	P
May-Jul	Beattock Summit	Down XP	A C Cawston / NRM	P
Sat 16Aug	Northchurch	Down Mid-Day Scot	E D Bruton	P
Tue 23Sep	Watford	Down Postal	Harry Halls Logs	O
Wed 01Oct	Shrewsbury		Stephenson Loco Society	P
Sun 05Oct	Crewe North MPD	On Shed	W Potter	P
Wed 15Oct	Awaiting Works			
Thu 23Oct	Entered Crewe Works	Heavy General		R
Sun 09Nov	Crewe Works		British Locomotive Society	O
Sat 29Nov	Left Crewe Works			
			Miles in year 74,461	
1953				
Sat 31Jan	Polmadie	Up Mid-Day Scot (h/b)	J l Stevenson	P
Sat 31Jan	Carlisle	Up Mid-Day Scot	F Alcock	P
Sun 15Mar	Calthwaite	Glasgow-Birmingham	F Alcock	P
Thu 28May	Scout Green	11.15 Birmingham-Glasgow	J E Wilkinson	P
Mon 1Jun	Camden mpd	On Shed	Ray Manning	O
Sat 13Jun	Approaching Tebay	Up Mid-Day Scot	J E Wilkinson	P
Thu 16Jul	Carlisle Kingmoor	11.10 Birmingham-Glasgow	Harry Halls Logs	O
Mon 03Aug	Tebay No2 Box	Up Mid-Day Scot (load 15)	J E Wilkinson	P
Mon 03Aug	Tebay No2 Box	Up Mid-Day Scot (load 15)	A G Ellis	P
Sat 08Aug	Tebay	Down Mid-Day Scot	J E Wilkinson	P
Sun 13Sep	Camden MPD		British Locomotive Society	P
Fri 02Oct	Polmadie MPD		J Robertson	P
Fri 02Oct	Polmadie MPD	On Shed	R K Blencowe	P
Fri 02Oct	Polmadie MPD	On Shed	A G Ellis Collection	P
Sun 04Oct	Crewe North	On Shed	Ray Manning	O
Fri 23Oct	Watford	Down XP W131	Harry Halls Logs	O
Tue 03Nov	Polmadie MPD		British Locomotive Society	O
Sat 05Dec	Watford	Down Mid-Day Scot W97	Harry Halls Logs	O
			Miles in year 90,220	
1954				
Sat 16Jan	Awaiting works			R
Mon 18Jan	Entered Crewe Works	Light Intermediate		R
Wed 10Feb	Left Crewe Works			R
Mon 19Apr	Clifton & Lowther	Up Mid-Day Scot	Railway Magazine	P
Sat 01May	Victoria Colliery Sidings Box	XP	R Hinton	P
Fri 11Jun	Perth		British Locomotive Society	O
Sat 03Jul	Low Moor, Shap	Down Mid-Day Scot	J E Wilkinson	P
Thu 05Aug	Perth		British Locomotive Society	O
Sat 14Aug	Perth		British Locomotive Society	O
Thu 26Aug	Perth		British Locomotive Society	O
Fri 27Aug	Preston	Down XP W131	Harry Halls Logs	O
Sat 04Sep	Preston	Up Mid-Day Scot	Ray Manning	O
1954	Crewe North MPD		J F Clay	P
			Miles in year 76,890	
1955				
Sat 22Jan	Watford	Down XP W91	Harry Halls Logs	O
Tue 25Jan		5.40pm Glasgow-Euston	C C Graham	O
Wed 02Feb		5.40pm Glasgow-Euston	C C Graham	O
Mon 14Mar	Awaiting works			R
Tue 29Mar	Entered Crewe Works	Heavy Intermediate		R
Sat 07May	Left Crewe Works			R
Sun 08May	Crewe Works		Harry Halls Logs	O
Sat 14May	Crewe North MPD		J E Wilkinson	P
Tue 24May		5.40pm Glasgow-Euston	C C Graham	O
Wed 15Jun	Edinburgh Princess St		W S Sellar	P
Sat 18Jun	Shap Wells	Up Mid-Day Scot	J E Wilkinson	P
Sat 09Jul	St Rollox MPD		J Robertson	P
Sat 16Jul	Nr Beattock Summit	10.05 Glasgow-Birmingham (W98)	J L Stevenson	P
Fri 12Aug		5.40pm Glasgow-Euston	C C Graham	O
Wed 31Aug	Awaiting works			R
Wed 07Sep	Entered Crewe Works	Light Casual Repair		R
Mon 03Oct	Left Crewe Works			
Wed 22Dec	Watford	9.51 Up XP W126	Harry Halls Logs	O
Sat 25Dec	Awaiting Works			
			Miles in year 51,530	

1956

Tue 03Jan	Entered Crewe Works	Light Casual Repair		R
Mon 30Jan	Left Crewe Works			
Tue 01May	Euston	Down Mid-Day Scot	Martin Welch	O
Mon 21May	Departing Euston	Down Mid-Day Scot	P H Groom	P
Tue 29 May	Euston	Down Ulster Express	Martin Welch	O
Tue 10Jul	Carnforth	Up Express passing Carnforth	John Hobbs	P
Thu 25Oct	Awaiting Works			
Mon 05Nov	Entered Crewe Works	Heavy General		R
Sun 02Dec	Crewe Works		British Locomotive Society	O
Sat 08Dec	Left Crewe Works			
1954/57	Rugby	XP	TEW / NRM	P
1954/57	Crewe North MPD		G W Sharpe collection	P
1954/57	Beattock Bank	XP	W J V Anderson	P
1954/57	Near Shrewsbury	Local stopping train	G Coltas	P
1954/57	Lichfield	Mid-Day Scot	G W Sharpe collection	P

Miles in year 61,490

1957

Thu 25Apr	Lichfield	XP	David Williams	O
May	Between Abingdon & Crawford	Up XP	W J V Anderson	P
Sat13Jul	Lichfield	Euston-Carlisle XP at 2.21	David Williams	O
Sun 11Aug	Camden		British Locomotive Society	O
Sun 25Aug	Polmadie mpd		Bob Burchall	O
Sat 31Aug	Mid-Day Scot	1.15pm Euston-Crewe	Steam days Dec97	S
Thu 05Sep	Lancaster	Down Mid-day Scot	Dennis Postlethwaite	P
Sat 14Sep	Lancaster	Glasgow-Birmingham	N A Machell	P
Sat 12Oct	Awaiting works			R
Mon 21Oct	Entered Crewe Works	Non classified repair		R
Wed 2Oct	Left Crewe Works			R
1957	Shap Summit	Up XP	P Conolly	P

Miles in year 75,897

1958

Sun 09Feb	Camden		British Locomotive Society	O
Mon 24Feb	Awaiting works			R
Wed 26Feb	Entered Crewe Works	Heavy Intermediate		R
Fri 28Feb	Watford	08.08 on W153 dh+45345	Harry Halls Logs	O
Sun 02Mar	Crewe Works	Erecting Shop	British Locomotive Society	O
Sun 30Mar	Crewe Works	Erecting Shop	British Locomotive Society	O
Sat 12Apr	Left Crewe Works			R
Sun 13Apr	Crewe Works	On Works	Ray Manning	O
Sun 27Apr	Liverpool Lime Street		Ray Manning	O
Sat 10May	Lichfield	XP	David Williams	O
Wed 21May	Euston	Down Mid-Day Scot	Martin Welch	O
Summer	South of Preston	08.40 Carlisle-Euston	W Ashcroft	P
Thu 19Jun	Watford	09.52 Dn XP W171	Harry Halls Logs	O
Sun 29Jun	Upperby MPD	On Shed 06.00hrs	Martin Welch	P
Sat 12Jul	Carlisle Station	between 2am and 4am	Ray Manning	O
Thu 17Jul	Rugby	Perth-London	Denys Worth	S
Wed 30Jul		Down Royal Scot	C C Graham	O
Sat 02Aug	Preston Station	Unknown	Peter Fitton	S
Sat 02Aug	Watford	Up W74 4.13	Harry Halls Logs	O
Fri 08Aug	Lancaster	Unknown	Peter Fitton	S
Mon 11Aug	Tebay	Euston-Carlisle XP	G Morrison	P
Thu 21Aug	Carlisle Upperby 12B		Harry Halls Logs	O
Sat 13Sep	Watford	Dn XP W63 10.49	Harry Halls Logs	O
Tue 16 Sep	Rugby (PM) ?		Denys Worth	S
Sat 11Nov	Crewe	Crewe-Euston	John Low	O

Miles in year 63,439

1959

Thu 01Jan	Watford	Up XP W126 9.07	Harry Halls Logs	O
Sun 15Feb	Arriving Euston 9.30am		James Graham	O
Thu 19Feb	Watford	Dn W157 9.02	Harry Halls Logs	O
Fri 17Apr	Stockport Station	Running LE tender first	Douglas Doherty	P
Fri 17Apr	Watford	Up XP W130 9.37	Harry Halls Logs	O
Sat 18Apr	Watford	Down XP W91	Harry Halls Logs	O
Sun 17May	Grayrigg	10.05 Glasgow-Birmingham (W98)	E R Morten	P
Tue 26May	Watford	Dn Xp W157	Harry Halls Logs	O
Sat 13Jun	Watford	Dn Xp W91 12.09	Harry Halls Logs	O
Thu 23Jul	Rugby	1.20pm Euston-Glasgow	M J Jackson	P
Sat 01Aug	Awaiting works			R
Thu 06Aug	Entered Crewe Works	Heavy General		R
Mon 17Aug	Crewe Works		C C Graham	O
Sat 26Sep	Left Crewe Works			R
Sep	Shrewsbury		G W Sharpe collection	P
Sep	Shrewsbury		G W Sharpe collection	P
Thu 22Oct	Watford	Dn W171 09.33	Harry Halls Logs	O
Pre10/59	Passing Edge Hill	Merseyside Express	J Corkhill	P
Pre10/59	Shrewsbury	Local stopping train	G W Sharpe collection	P
Pre10/59	Shrewsbury	Awaiting departure	G W Sharpe collection	P
Pre10/59	Greenholme	Down Royal Scot	E Treacy/NRM	P
Pre10/59	Unknown	Royal Scot	G W Sharpe collection	P
Pre10/59	Carlisle	Up XP	G Coltas	P
Summer	App. Cheddington	Crewe-Euston	M Welch	P
1959	Unknown MPD		A Macbeath collection	P
Tue 06Oct	Shap-Strickland Wood	Up XP	D M C Hepburne-Scott	P
Fri 30Oct	Crewe North MPD		Peter Fitton	S
PostOct59	Carlisle	Named train	T J Edgington	P

Miles in year 70,258

1960

Tue 05Apr	Passing Carlisle SB	Up Royal Scot	K Runton	P
Fri 08Apr	Watford	Dn XP W171 09.45 16 Vehicles	Harry Halls Logs	O
Tue 12Apr	Norton Bridge	XP	David Williams	O
Mon 18Apr	Stafford	down Royal Scot	British Locomotive Society	O
Apr	Upperby MPD	On Shed	R K Blencowe	P
Apr	Unknown location	On train	E Treacy/NRM	P
Mon 18Apr	Carlisle		D Forsyth	P
Sat 23Apr	Transferred to Crewe North			R
Sat 30Apr	Transferred to Camden MPD			R
Wed 04May	Watford	Up XP W126 08.26	Harry Halls Logs	O
Sat 07May	Departing Euston	Royal Scot	G Rixon	Pcs
Sat 07May	Departing Euston	Royal Scot	G Rixon	Pcs
Sat 07May	Departing Euston	Royal Scot	G Rixon	Pcs
Tue 10May	Watford	Up XP W484	Harry Halls Logs	O
Sat 10Jun	Watford	Up XP W126 08.03	Harry Halls Logs	O
Mon 13Jun	Lichfield TV	Up Royal Scot	E R Morten	P
Fri 24Jun	Watford	Up White Rose	Harry Halls Logs	O
Sat 25Jun	Watford	not noted stopped 12.24/28	Harry Halls Logs	O
Sat 09Jul	Rugeley TV	XP	David Williams	O
Tue 12Jul	Rugby	Down Midday Scot	D Smith	P
Sat 23Jul	Tamworth	XP	David Williams	O
Fri 29Jul		Up Royal Scot	Log from Paul Joring	Log
Sat 30Jul	Passing Tamworth	Down Royal Scot	N E Preedy	O
Sat 30Jul	Greskine Sig.Box	Down Royal Scot	W A C Smith	P
Mon 01Aug	Clifton & Lowther	Up Mid-Day Scot	J E Wilkinson	P
Mon 01Aug		Up Mid-day Scot	Log from Paul Joring	Log
Fri 05Aug	Watford	Up XP W56 3.36 9 vehicles	Harry Halls Logs	O
Fri 05Aug	Watford	Dn W71	Harry Halls Logs	O
Sat 20Aug	Crewe Station	Awaiting down express	A S Price	O
Apr-Sep	Beattock bank	Down Royal Scot	W J V Anderson	P
Apr-Sep	Hartford	Glasgow-Euston	E Oldham	P
Apr-Sep	Outside Upperby	Up Royal Scot	E Treacy/NRM	P
Apr-Sep	Outside Upperby	Up Royal Scot	E Treacy/NRM	P
Apr-Sep	Crawford	Up Royal Scot	E Treacy/NRM	P
Apr-Sep	Wreay	Up Royal Scot	Unknown	P
Apr-Sep	Crawford	Up Royal Scot	E Treacy/NRM	P
Fri 02Sep		Up Mid-Day Scot	Peter Fitton	S
Fri 02Sep	Watford	Up XP W126 08.03	Harry Halls Logs	O
Sat 17Sep				R
Sat 17Sep	Carlisle-Perth 1am	Down XP	James Graham	O
1960	Passing Camden	Up Royal Scot	Gordon Coltas	P

Miles in year 77,402

1961

Wed 18Jan	Awaiting works			R
Tue 24Jan	Entered Crewe Works	Heavy Intermediate		R
Sun 05Feb	Crewe Works	Erecting Shop	British Locomotive Society	O
Tue 21Feb	Left Crewe Works			R
Sun 26Feb	Crewe North MPD	Roundhouse	S D Wainwright	P
Sat 25Mar	Edge Hill MPD		Andrew Mellor	P
Mon 10Jul	Awaiting Works			R
Wed 26Jul	Entered Crewe Works	Light Casual		R
Thu 03Aug	Crewe Works		Hoper Collection	P
Mon 13Aug	Crewe Works	Erecting Shop	British Locomotive Society	O
Fri 18Aug	Left Crewe Works			
Sun 20Aug	Crewe Works		Ray Manning	O
Thu 24Aug	Leaving Crewe Works	In steam in convoy	Peter Fitton	S
Sat 02Sep	Rugby at 16.45	Liverpool -Euston	John Forman	S
Sun 24Sep	Rugby (1.30-2.00am)	12.30am Euston -Liverpool	James Graham	O
Wed 04Oct		8.25 Euston-Liverpool	Alan Macbeath	S
Tue 17Oct	Euston	1.55 ex Liverpool	R K Blencowe collection	P
Fri 20Oct	Euston	2.05 Euston-Liverpool	M Welch	P
Wed 25Oct	Euston	8.25 Euston-Liverpool	Alan Macbeath	S
1960s	Crewe	Freight	G W Sharpe collection	P
1961	Edge Hill		J Carter	P

Miles in year 38,464

1962

Wed 03Jan	Stafford	Down Red Rose	British Locomotive Society	O
Mon 15Jan	Nuneaton 14.19	08.40 Carlisle -Euston	John Foreman	O
Thu 18Jan	Birmingham New St.	08.45 Euston-Wolverhampton	British Locomotive Society	O
Sat 17Feb	Birmingham New St.	08.45 Wolverhampton-Euston	T J Edgington	P
Sat 17Feb	Hampton in Arden	16.02 Wolverhampton-Euston	John Forman	O
Sat 24Feb	Rugby	Down Red Rose	Peter Fitton	P
Sat 03Mar	Carlisle	Glasgow-Birmingham	A R Thompson	P
Sat 03Mar	Morecambe Sth Jcn	Glasgow-Birmingham	N A Machel	P
Mon 05Mar		14.05 Liverpool-Euston	Alan Macbeath	O
Tue 06Mar		14.05 Liverpool-Euston	Alan Macbeath	O
Tue 06Mar	Tamworth 15.58	14.05 Liverpool -Euston		O
Tue 06Mar	Euston	Liverpool Euston	Martin Welch	O
Thu 08Mar		14.05 Liverpool-Euston	Alan Macbeath	O
Fri 23Mar	The Comet	17.05 Manchester-Euston	J Corkhill	O
Sat 24Mar	Birmingham New St.	5pm Dep to Euston	S Creer	P
Tue 27Mar	Euston	up Emerald Isle Express	Martin Welch	O
Thu 29Mar	Birmingham New St.	16.15 Wolverhampton-Euston	British Locomotive Society	O
Fri 30Mar	Birmingham New St.	16.15 Wolverhampton-Euston	British Locomotive Society	O
Fri 30Mar	Watford	Up XP W108	Harry Halls Logs	O
Sun 01Apr	Carlisle	Euston-Glasgow sleeper	N E Preedy	O
Fri 06Apr	Hampton in Arden	16.15 Wolverhampton-Euston	John Forman	O
Fri 06Apr		23.45 Euston-Wolverhampton	John Forman	R
Sat 07Apr	Rugby	09.35 Wolverhampton-Euston	John Forman	O
Sat 07Apr	Rugby	09.35 Wolverhampton-Euston	Peter Fitton	Pcp
Sat 07Apr	Watford	Up W108	Harry Halls Logs	O
Thu 19Apr	Ashton	Down Euston-Perth	K Fairey	P
Sat 28Apr	Chester No 6 SB	09.20 Crewe-Holyhead	J Carter	P
Thu 31May	Camden MPD		R M Tomkin	P
Sun 03Jun	Edge Hill MPD		D.Williams	O
Fri 30Jun	1mile south of Preston	Glasgow-Euston	P Claxton	P
Sat 07Jul	Rugby	10.00 Liverpool-Euston relief	John Forman	O
Sat 07Jul	Tring	10.00 Liverpool-Euston	Peter Fitton	P
Tue 10Jul		12.20 Perth-Euston	Alan Macbeath	S
Fri 20Jul		13.30 Relief Liv-Euston	Alan Macbeath	S
Sat 21Jul	Rugby	XP	G Coltas	P
Sun 29Jul	Edge Hill Depot			O
Wed 08Aug	Watford	Down Irish Mail 09.11	Harry Halls Logs	O
Fri 10Aug	Rugby	The Emerald Isle Holyhead-Euston	John Forman	O
Fri 10Aug	Rugby	The Merseyside Express	John Forman	O
Mon 27Aug	Ashton Nr Roade	XP	L.Hanson	O
Tue 28Aug	Hunsbury Tunnel	Euston-Liverpool Relief	R.A.F Puyer	P
Mon 03Sep	Passing Ormskirk	14.00 Glasgow-Liverpool	British Locomotive Society	O
Tue 04Sep	Passing Ormskirk	09.50 Liverpool-Glasgow	British Locomotive Society	O
Wed 05Sep		09.15 Perth-Euston	Alan Macbeath	S
Thu 13Sep	Speke	Up Merseyside Express	Alan Macbeath	P
1962	Stafford	Merseyside Express	N Preedy	P
1962	Stafford	Merseyside Express	R Hinton	P
Sat 06Oct		Into Store		
Sun 18Nov	Edge Hill mpd		R Williams	O
Sat 08Dec	Edge Hill	In Store	Ray Manning	O

Miles in year 26,839

1963

Wed 30Jan	Merseyside Express	10.10 Liverpool-Euston	Alan Macbeath	S
Sun 10Feb	Camden MPD		British Locomotive Society	O
Wed 27Feb	Edge Hill Depot	In Steam	Alan Macbeath	S
Sat 13Apr	Brisco	Up freight	S C Crook	P
Sat 13Apr	Clifton & Lowther	Up freight	J S Whiteley	P
Sat 13Apr	Thrimby Grange	Up freight	J S Whiteley	P
Sat 23Mar	Edge Hill Depot		J Corkhill	P
Tue 28Apr	Edge Hill Depot			O
Sat 18May	Edge Hill Depot	Inside shed	Brian Rose	P
Fri 31May	Farringdon Jnc	Edge Hill-Carlisle Freight	W Ashcroft	P
Sat 01Jun	Carlisle	1M25 Relief up Royal Scot	H R Davies	P
Sat 01Jun	Bessie Ghyll	Relief up Royal Scot	P J Robinson	P
Sat 01Jun	Lancaster	Relief up Royal Scot	N A Machell	P
Sat 01Jun	Rugby	1M25 Glasgow-Euston relief	A J Forman	O
Tue 04Jun	Willesden MPD		P Groom	P
Thu 06Jun	Preston	06.15 Carlisle-Preston	J Clarke	P
Mon 30Jun	Willesden Jnc	Up Merseyside Express		S
Tue 16Jul		06.00 Warrington-Carlisle	J Corkhill	O
Tue 16Jul		19.11 Carlisle - Warrington	Alan Macbeath	S
Tue 16Jul	Lancaster Station	at 10.10 for Carlisle	Peter Rowlands	P
Tue 16Jul	Lancaster	Waiting to depart down Exp	P Rowlands	P
Fri 19Jul		06.00 Warrington-Carlisle	J Corkhill	O
Fri 19Jul		19.11Carlisle-Warrington	Alan Macbeath	S
Sat 20Jul		06.00 Warrington-Carlisle	J Corkhill	O
Sat 20Jul		19.11 Carlisle-Warrington	Alan Macbeath	S
Aug	Leaving Carlisle	Freight Train	Stephen Crook	P
Tue 06Aug	Between Colwich & Rugeley	1X85 Up relief	R Stokes	P
Tue 06Aug	Berkhamsted	1X85 up relief	K Fairey	P
Fri 09Aug	Kilburn High Road	Down Merseyside Exp	M Welch	P
Fri 09Aug	Berkhamsted	Down Merseyside Exp	H C Casserley	P
Mon 12Aug	Willesden Junction	Up Merseyside Express	N Whitwell	O
Fri 30Aug	Nuneaton	Liverpool -Euston relief 1A37	A J Forman	O
Sat 31Aug	Rugby	Euston-Liverpool 1Z10	A J Forman	O
Sat 31Aug	Aston Heath	1Z10 Empress Voyager	P Claxton	P
Sat 31Aug	Aston Heath	1Z10 Empress Voyager	Peter Fitton	P
Fri 06Sep	Blisworth	Down XP	Norman Preedy	O
Mon 30Sep	Carlisle Kingmoor	1X37 on Smokebox	Colin C Graham	P
1960s	Bushey Troughs	Down XP	P Riley	Pcs
Sun 20Oct	In Store 8A			
PostOct59	Tebay	7.11pm Carlisle-Warrington	P. Conolly	P

Miles in year estimated 13,000

1964

Fri 14Feb	Edge Hill MPD	In Store	Alan Macbeath	S
Thu 20Feb	Edge Hill MPD	In Store	N E Preedy	O
Sat 07Mar	Edge Hill MPD		British Locomotive Society	O
Sun 14Jun	Crewe Arrival Sidings		N E Preedy	P
Sun 21Jun	Paint Shop	Awaiting painting	Ray Manning	O
Aug	Crewe Works	Outside paintshop	D C Rogers	P
Sat 15Aug	Crewe Works		J W Ellison	P
Sat 30Aug	Crewe Paint Shop	Stood outside paintshop	Douglas Doherty	P
Sun 13Sep	Crewe Paint Shop	Awaiting move to Ayr	F G Butler	P
Tue 15Sep	Greenbank		W Ashcroft	S
Oct	Ayr mpd	Inside shed	David C Smith	P
Oct	Ayr mpd	Inside shed	David C Smith	P
Wed 21Oct	Ayr Station		D Cross (Railway Magazine)	S
Wed 21Oct	Alloway		D Cross	S
	Greenan-H of A Branch			P
Wed 21Oct	Greenan Siding		D Cross (Railway Magazine)	P
Sun 25Oct	Greenan to Butlins		W Hamilton	P
Sun 25Oct	Greenan Siding		Unknown	P
Sun 25Oct	Butlins, Heads of Ayr		D Cross	P
Mon 26Oct	Butlins, Heads of Ayr		D Cross	P

Miles in year : Nil

1965

Sat 31Jul	Butlins, Heads of Ayr		M L Inman	P

1967

Sun 28May	Butlins, Heads of Ayr		M Welch	P

1968

Wed 15May	Butlins, Heads of Ayr		A Beck	P
Sun 01Sep	Butlins, Heads of Ayr		W S Sellar	S

1971

Tue 09Feb	Butlins confirm 6233 will go to Bressingham			
Wed 24Feb	Butlins, Heads of Ayr With Banner		D Cross	P
Thu 25Feb	Townhead Coal sidings			P
Thu 25Feb	Ayr mpd		D Cross	P
Thu 25Feb	Ayr Station	En route to Bressingham	Derek Cross	P
Mon 01Mar	Carlisle Station	En route to Norwich	P W Robinson	P
Mon 01Mar	Carlisle Station	En route to Norwich	G J Jackson	P
Mon 01Mar	Lincoln	En route to Norwich	B Rose	P
Sat 06Mar	Norwich mpd	Inside depot	G R Mortimer	P
Sat 06Mar	Norwich Stn	Cabside showing "the writ"	G R Mortimer	P
Fri 19Mar	Norwich to Thetford by rail			
Sun 21Mar	Euston (Suffolk village)		G R Mortimer	P
Sun 21Mar	South Lopham		G R Mortimer	P
Sun 21Mar	Bressingham	At museum	G R Mortimer	P

1972

Mon 27Mar	Bressingham	Flue tubes removed		RI
Fri 30Jun	Bressingham	Locomotive boiler stripped		

1973

Wed 03Jan	Bressingham	Tender platework repair		RI
1973	Bressingham	Unknown		P

1974

Tue 28May	Bressingham	Loco steamed		RI
Tue 09Jul	Bressingham	Boiler Washout		
Sun 21Jul	Bressingham	In Steam	Profile of the Duchess Pl70	P
Thu 01Aug	Bressingham	Loco steamed safety valve adjusted		RI
Mon 14Oct	Bressingham	Boiler Washout		RI

1975

1975	Bressingham	In steam	J H Cooper-Smith	P
1975	Bressingham	In steam	Unknown	P
Sun 24Aug	Bressingham	In steam, demo. line	A C Gilbert	P
Sun 24Aug	Bressingham		N Knight	P

From 1976 until 1993, 6233 remained on static exhibition at Bressingham

1989

May	Purchased from Rank by Bressingham Steam Museum

1993

Mon 02Aug	The locomotive was moved by road to Bury for display at The East Lancashire Railway

1994

Mon 18Jul	The locomotive was moved by road back to Bressingham

1996

Fri 02Feb - Sun 04Feb	The locomotive was moved by road to The Princess Royal Class Locomotive Trust headquarters at The Midland Railway Centre

1998

Thu 04Jun	The Heritage Lottery Fund Grant for acquisition and restoration was awarded by The Heritage Lottery Fund
Tue 21Jul	The Heritage Lottery Fund Grant was announced by The Princess Royal Class Locomotive Trust for the acquisition and restoration of 6233

From October 1998 until March 2001 the locomotive was under overhaul at West Shed

2001

Wed 17Jan	West Shed	First steaming
Thu 18Jan	West Shed	First move under own steam
Fri 19Jan	West Shed	Test steaming
Mon 20Mar	West Shed	Loco coaled & fire lit
Tue 21Mar	West Shed	Running in
23-26Apr	MRC	Running in
19-24May	MRC	Running in
Wed 04Jul		Codnor Pk-Beighton Jcn-Sheffield-Trent-Derby-Beighton-Sheffield-Derby-Codnor Park Jcn + 99041 + 6320
Wed 18Jul		Derby-Sheffield-Derby THE DUCHESS NIGHT OWL
Tue 04Sep	MRC	EWS Driver training
Thu 06Sep	MRC	Re-dedication train
Sat 08Sep	MRC	Service trains
Sun 09Sep	MRC	Service trains
Sat 15Sep		Swanwick-Central Rivers - Diesel hauled +99041 + 6320
Sun 16Sep		Central Rivers Open Day then -Swanwick - Diesel hauled + 99041 + 6320
Thu 20Sep		Swanwick-Kidderminster-Bridgnorth + 99041 + 6320
Fri 21Sep		SVR Gala
Sat 22Sep		SVR Gala
Sun 23Sep		SVR Gala
Mon 24Sep		Kidderminster- Butterley + 99041 + 6320
Fri 12Oct		Swanwick-Crewe + 99041 + 6320
Sun 14Oct		Crewe-Holyhead & ret THE NORTH WALES COAST CORONATION
Sun 21Oct		Crewe-Holyhead & ret THE YNYS MON DUCHESS
Fri 26Oct		Crewe-Bristol Barton Hill + 99041 + 6320
Sat 27Oct		Bristol-Plymouth & ret THE MAYFLOWER
Sun 28Oct		Bristol-Swanwick + 99041 +6320
Sat 08Dec		Codnor Pk-Derby-Kettering-St Pancras-Old Oak Common
Sat 15Dec		Old Oak Common-Euston -Oxford -Derby-Swanwick THE CAPITAL DUCHESS

Miles in year 3,389

2002

Fri 08Mar	Butterley via Lichfield T.V. - Crewe + 99041
Sat 09Mar	Crewe-Liverpool-York-Liverpool-Crewe THE YORKSHIRE CORONATION
Mon 11Mar	Crewe-Lichfield-Derby-Butterley
Wed 20Mar	Butterley-Derby-Lichfield TV-Crewe & return THE CORONATION OWL
Sat 13Apr	Butterley-Derby-Blackpool-Crewe THE BLACKPOOL DUCHESS
Sat 20Apr	Crewe-Carlisle-Crewe THE CITADEL EXPRESS
Sat 27Apr	Crewe-Carlisle-Crewe THE CITADEL EXPRESS RELIEF
Mon 29Apr	Crewe-Butterley + 99041
Sat 04May	Midland Railway Centre on Service trains
Sun 05May	Midland Railway Centre on Service trains
Mon 06May	Midland Railway Centre on Service trains
Sat 11May	Butterley-Leicester-Scrbro and return THE SCARBOROUGH CORONATION
Mon 10Jun	Butterley-Crewe-Holyhead-Valley
Tue 11Jun	Valley-Holyhead-Bangor-Holyhead-Crewe THE ROYAL TRAIN
Sat 29Jun	Crewe via Blackburn-Carlisle-Carnforth THE CUMBRIAN CORONATION
Sat 13Jul	Carnforth-Carlisle-Glasgow & ret THE CORONATION SCOT
Sat 20Jul	Carnforth-Carlisle-Derby THE MIDLAND CORONATION
Sat 07Sep	Midland Railway Centre on Service trains
Sun 08Sep	Midland Railway Centre on Service trains
Sat 14Sep	Leicester-Blackpool THE BLACKPOOL DUCHESS
Mon 16Sep	Crewe- Kidderminster + 99040 + 6320
Fri 20Sep	SVR Gala - Kidderminster-Bridgnorth 3 trips
Sat 21Sep	SVR Gala - Kidderminster-Bridgnorth 4 trips
Sun 22Sep	SVR Gala - Kidderminster-Bridgnorth 2 Trips
Mon 30Sep	SVR LE + GWR saloon 4 round trips
Sat 05Oct	SVR Luncheon Train
Sun 06Oct	SVR Luncheon Train
Thu 10Oct	Bewdley-Highley special, then LE Bridgnorth
Fri 11Oct	Kidderminster-Bristol + 99040 + 6320
Sat 12Oct	Bristol to Plymouth and return THE DEVONIAN DUCHESS
Mon 14Oct	Bristol-Butterley LE + 99040 +6320
Fri 18Oct	Butterley-Crewe + 99040
Sat 19Oct	Crewe-Holyhead & return THE YNYS MON EXPRESS
Mon 21Oct	Crewe-Butterley + 99040

Miles in year 5,178

B.R. Special Notices for the movement from Ayr to Bressingham

Trainmen Footplate Personal Copy

BRITISH RAILWAYS : SCOTTISH REGION

SPECIAL NOTICE

REF: MPT/N/173/71

MONDAY 1ST MARCH. 1971

EXCEPTIONAL LOAD : PRIVATE TRADERS LOCOMOTIVE DUCHESS OF SUTHERLAND: AYR TO NORWICH.

DESCRIPTION: Ex BR Locomotive "Duchess of Sutherland" No. 6233 and tender, "dead" on own wheels.

Service Headcode		9 x 51	Headcode		9 x 51
Ayr	dep	12 58	Auldgirth		(16 01)
Annbank		(13 28)	Dumfries Yard	arr	16 E21
Mauchline	arr	14E10		dep	17*E34
	dep	14E15	Ruthwell		(17 58)
Auchinleck		(14 26)	Annan		(18 15)
New Cumnock		(14 44)	Eastriggs		(18 25)
Sanquhar	arr	15E11	Gretna Jct.		(18 37)
	dep	15E16	Mossland		(18X41)
Thornhill		(15 46)	Carlisle Yard		18 55

SIGNALLING: To be belled 2-6-1 throughout.

MARSHALLING: Hauling engine, brakevan for accompanying personnel, Locomotive No. 6233 with chimney first, brakevan for guard.

SPEED: Speed not to exceed 10 m.p.h. between Ayr and Mauchline, and 25 m.p.h. between Mauchline and Carlisle. Speed not to exceed 10 m.p.h. through following :-

Overbridge 224 between Sanquhar/Carronbridge (65m 57c)
Overbridge 265 between Thornhill/Closeburn (79m 60c).
All lower speed restrictions in operation must be observed.

Restrictions to be Observed during Journey, in Scottish Region to Gretna.

1. Stop and extreme caution through Overbridge No. 33 between Tarbolton and Mauchline.

2. Stop and extreme caution through Overbridge 141 between Mauchline and Auchinleck (43m 63c).

3. Stop and extreme caution through Overbridge No. 150 between Mauchline and Auchinleck (47m 18c).

4. Stop and extreme caution through Overbridge No.238 between Sanquhar and Carronbridge (69m 62c).

5. Not to travel more than 25 miles without stopping for examination.

RESTRICTIONS IN THE L.M. REGION FROM GRETNA

1. Side windscreen to be kept closed throughout.

2. Caution to be exercised when using crossover roads and connections between platforms and adjacent structures.

3. Speed not to exceed 25 m.p.h. throughout.

4. Not to travel over the Through Goods Lines at Carlisle.

MISCELLANEOUS INSTRUCTIONS/

Cont'd....

REF: MP?U/N/173/71

MONDAY 1ST MARCH, 1971

MISCELLANEOUS INSTRUCTIONS.

1. Special care must be taken when starting, stopping, shunting into sidings, going round sharp curves or through crossover roads.

2. The person in charge at starting point must see that the Goods Guard and Enginemen working the train are supplied with a copy of this Notice and they must be instructed to keep a sharp lookout throughout the journey, also to observe carefully the instructions contained herein.

ADVICE TO MEN WORKING ON THE LINE

Area/Station Managers must advise the Signalmen of the passage of the load and other responsible officials must similarly advise Lengthmen and others working on the line. Permanent Way Gangers must keep in touch with the Area/Station Manager and Signalmen, so that they may be advised of the Exceptional Load.

LOCO & LOCOMEN'S WORKINGS

A.M. Ayr   9X51   12 58 Ayr to Dumfries relieved and home passenger

A.M. Dumfries 9X51   17 34 Dumfries to Carlisle Yd. LD to Ayr, and
                             home passenger.

GUARD WORKINGS

A.M. Ayr   9X51   12 58 Ayr/Dumfries Yd. and HP.

A.M. Dumfries 9X51   17 34 Dumfries Yd/Carlisle Yd. and HP.

ACKNOWLEDGMENT OF RECEIPT OF CIRCULAR.

The following must acknowledge receipt of this circular by telephone IMMEDIATELY (Saturday excepted) to "MOVEMENTS MANAGER, TELEPHONE (041) 332-9811, EXTN. 2700/2655", using code word "BOLT" :-

    Control Glasgow   Carlisle.

    A.M.   Carlisle, Beattock, Dumfries, Kilmarnock, Ayr.

    P.W.I. Lockerbie, Dumfries, New Cumnock, Ayr, Irvine, Dalry.

                                              C.L. ROWBURY
GLASGOW : 24 FEBRUARY, 1971   MOVEMENTS MANAGER

BRITISH RAILWAYS
LONDON MIDLAND REGION

SPECIAL NOTICE   O.G. 3912

EXCEPTIONAL LOAD - AYR TOWNHILL DEPOT TO NORWICH VIA GRETNA JN., CARLISLE PASSENGER LINES,
APPLEBY, HELLIFIELD AND SKIPTON TO EASTERN REGION

DESCRIPTION AND DIMENSIONS
Ex. L.M.S. Class 8P 4.6.2. No. 6233 and tender."Duchess of Sutherland."

DEAD ON OWN WHEELS

Freight brake van to be marshalled between hauling locomotive and private steam
locomotive No. 6233, which must travel chimney first throughout.
Freight brake van also to be provided extreme rear for Guard.

SERVICE
SPECIAL TRAIN 9X51 MONDAY 1 MARCH 1971 AS UNDER :-
Times shown in brackets are passing times.

Gretna Jn.		(18 37)	Appleby		(21 37)
Mossband		(18X41)	Kirkby Stephen		(22 07)
		GL	Ais Gill	arr	22E37
Carlisle Yard	arr	18L55		dep	22E52
	dep	19E50	Blea Moor	arr	23E22
Carlisle No. 3		(19X53)		TUES	
		ML		dep	00*15
Carlisle Stn.		(19 57)	Settle Jn.		(00 50)
Carlisle No. 7		(20 00)	Hellifield	arr	01EL00
Pettril Bridge Jn.		(20 01)		dep	01EL15
Long Meg		(20 45)	Skipton Stn. Nth Jn.		(01 39)
New Biggin	arr	21E04	Skipton Stn. Sth Jn.	arr	01E42
	dep	21E20		dep	01E57

SCOTTISH REGION DIESEL & TC to Carlisle
CARLISLE DD 370 (CLASS 25) work 9 x 51 Carlisle to Hellifield LD to Carlisle
and as programmed.
EASTERN REGION (CLASS   ) work LD to Hellifield 9 x 51 to Leeds
CARLISLE TC   work 9 x 51 to Hellifield Return LD/AR.
EASTERN REGION (HOLBECK) TC work LD to Hellifield & 9x51 to Leeds.

RESTRICTIONS TO BE OBSERVED DURING THE JOURNEY (L.M.REGION)

1. NOT to travel over the Through Goods lines at Carlisle

2. Caution to be exercised when using crossover roads and connections between
   platforms and adjacent structures.

3. Side windscreens to be kept closed throughout or removed.

4. No long layovers owing to security risk.
5. FABRIC :- NOT to exceed a speed of 25 miles per hour throughout.

6. NOTRAMO:- NOT to travel more than 25 miles without stopping for examination.

SIGNALLING OF TRAIN
Block signalling as per Telegraph Code OGLO will apply.

RESTRICTIONS TO BE OBSERVED DURING THE JOURNEY (E.REGION)

1. OPPOS:- Running lines and/or sidings on right hand side of load looking in
   direction of travel must be clear, and nothing out-of-gauge must be
   allowed on the running lines and/or sidings on the LEFT HAND SIDE OF THE LOAD :-
   (a) March Whitemoor Jn. to March East Jn. if via No. 1 Platform line.

2. To stop and pass with extreme caution Footbridge No. 1861 at 44m. 1ch. between
   Spalding No. 1 and Welland Bridge.

Continued overleaf ....

RESTRICTIONS TO BE OBSERVED DURING THE JOURNEY (E.REGION)   Continued

3. NOT to go through No. 5 Platform at March station.

4. To stop and pass with extreme caution No. 1 Platform at March station.

5. LACER :- Must not use crossovers between platforms.

6. Windscreens to be turned back or removed.

7. To travel chimney first throughout.

8. FABRIC :- Must not exceed speed of 25 mph throughout.

9. NOTRAMO:- Not to travel more than 25 miles without stopping for examination

10. NO long layovers owing to security risk.

     ACCOMPANIMENT

     Private Caretaker to accompany throughout.

MISCELLANEOUS INSTRUCTIONS

Area Managers must arrange to advise all concerned in connection with the passage
of this load, including Signalmen and P.Way Staff.

ACKNOWLEDGEMENT

The following to acknowledge receipt by wire IMMEDIATELY TO GENMAN (04/7) CREWE
using the code
               "ARNO   O.G. 3912"

DIVISIONAL MANAGERS   -   Preston

CONTROL   -   Carlisle

D.C.E.   -   Preston

A.M./A.A.M.   -   Carlisle, Appleby, Skipton

CREWE
DATE   25.2.74
EXTN   2975
REF   04/7/72   CHIEF OPERATING MANAGER

6233 Duchess of Sutherland

Ayr	dep.	12 58	
Annbank	pass	13 28	
Mauchline	arr.	14 10	} Examination
	dep.	14 15	
Auchinleck	pass	14 26	
Newcumnock	pass	14 44	
Sanquhar	arr.	15 11	} Examination
	dep.	15 16	
Thornhill	pass	15 46	
Auldgirth	pass	16 01	
Dumfries	arr.	16 21	(Examination and change men
	dep.	17 34	
Ruthwell	pass	17 58	
Annan	pass	18 15	
East Rigg	pass	18 25	
Gretna	pass	18 37	

Maximum speed – 10 m.p.h. Ayr to Mauchline
25 m.p.h. Mauchline to Gretna

6233 DUCHESS OF SUTHERLAND

Keighley	pass.	02 23	
Shipley	pass	02 43	
Wortley Jct.	pass	03 13	
Whitehall Jct.	pass	03 15	
Engine Shed Jct.	pass	03 17	
Hunslet Sidings	arr.	03 27	
	dep.	04 07	
Calder Bridge	pass	04 57 *	
Doncaster Carr Box	arr.	06 13	
	dep.	06 32	
Boultham Jct.	arr.	08 53	} Examination and loco.
	dep.	09 32	
Sleaford S. Jct.	arr.	10 33	} Examination
	dep.	10 38	
Spalding	arr.	11 23	} Examination
	dep.	11 33	
Whitemoor	arr.	12 26	
	dep.	13 15	
Ely North	arr.	14 07	
	dep.	14 19	
Thetford	arr.	15 18	
	dep.	15 26	
Wymondham	arr.	16 20	
	dep.	16 27	
Norwich	arr.	16 58	